Graham Wootton

PRESSURE GROUPS
IN BRITAIN
1720–1970

An essay in interpretation with
original documents

ARCHON BOOKS
1975

Copyright © 1975 by Graham Wootton
First published 1975 by Allen Lane,
Penguin Books, Ltd, London
and in the United States of America as an Archon Book,
an imprint of The Shoe String Press, Inc.,
Hamden, Connecticut 06514

Printed in Great Britain by
Butler & Tanner Ltd,
Frome and London

Library of Congress Cataloging in Publication Data

Wootton, Graham.
    Pressure groups in Britain, 1720–1970.

    Includes bibliographical references and index.
    1. Pressure groups – Great Britain – History. I. Title.
JN329.P7W66 1975   322.4'3'0942   74-23832
ISBN 0-208-01500-0

Contents

To Mary

Preface

This book may be read as an introduction to the development and activities over 250 years of those private groups (other than parties) that have influenced or attempted to influence the course of government policy. It is not restricted to campaign groups (the Quakers' Meeting for Sufferings, Catholic Association, Anti-Concorde Project, Abortion Law Reform Association) but includes the more deeply rooted West India Committee, National Union of Teachers and T.U.C., National Farmers' Union and Confederation of British Industry, British Medical Association and British Legion, among others. This 'sketch for a portrait' is supplemented by about a hundred documents, largely drawn from original or inaccessible sources, covering the aims and objects, charters and constitutions, policy statements and appeals, etc., of the groups. Complementing the standard collections, these documents constitute a permanent storehouse of information for others to draw on for different purposes, not only professional scholars (sociologists and political scientists as well as historians) but also students and members of the general public.

The book may also be read as a contribution to the literature on political modernization, one of the most important and universal themes of contemporary inquiry. For the significance of the groups has not been limited to their immediate impact on public policy. Unintentionally they helped to secularize British politics (except in Ulster), contributed something to the trend towards equality and much to the growing 'capability', or effectiveness, of modern government, three of the facets of political modernization.

I wish first to thank Professor Bernard Crick, of Birkbeck

College, London, for his encouragement and support. Dame Lucy Sutherland, about to retire from the principalship of Lady Margaret Hall, Oxford, spared time to discuss the place of the East India Company and City of London in eighteenth-century politics. Lord Crowther-Hunt (Dr Norman Hunt), of Exeter College, Oxford, also spared time to discuss the corresponding role of the Russia Company, the Quakers and other Protestant Dissenters. I should like to thank them without committing them to what appears here. I am also grateful to Professor Bruce Graham, of the University of Sussex, for drawing attention to a source that I should have otherwise missed. For access and facilities I particularly thank Lord Feather and Mr Len Murray of the T.U.C.; Mrs Patricia Gill and staff at the West Sussex Record Office; the Reverend Peter G. Hayman and the Governors of Dunford House (Cobden Papers); Mr A. C. F. Hey and Mr J. A. Raven, Association of British Chambers of Commerce; Mr Michael King, Confederation of British Industry, Mr Gordon Kingham, National Farmers' Union; Mr W. Redmond, West India Committee; His Grace the Duke of Richmond and Gordon and Mr D. Legg-Willis (Goodwood MSS); Mrs H. A. Rosser, National Union of Teachers; Mr A. Thistlethwaite, British Medical Association; Mr Webb and staff at the Bishopsgate Institute; and Mr Martin Wright, Howard League for Penal Reform. I also acknowledge the ready assistance of the Brighton Reference Library, London Library, Boston Athenaeum and the Houghton Library, Harvard University.

As to personal debts, I am particularly grateful to Professor and Mrs D. M. Pryce, of 'Little Venice', London, also to Mr and Mrs J. E. P. Davies, Walton-on-Thames. As usual, however, my main debt is to my wife, Mary. I thank her for those summer hours of searching and copying that could have been more agreeably spent, for the preparation of the typescript and the reading of unusually demanding proofs.

The work, started in England, could not have been completed without generous subventions from the Tufts University Faculty Awards Committee.

Winchester,   GRAHAM WOOTTON
Massachusetts

Acknowledgements

Documents 2 and 9 from the Goodwood MSS are reproduced by courtesy of the Goodwood Estate Company Limited with acknowledgements to the West Sussex Record Office and the County Archivist; the Caribbean Universities Press, Barbados, for document 10; the British Medical Association for documents 18 and 32; documents 23, 24, 31, 32, 37, 39 and 42 from the Cobden Papers are reproduced by courtesy of the Governors of Dunford House with acknowledgements to the West Sussex Record Office and the County Archivist; the Association of British Chambers of Commerce for documents 38 and 72; the National Union of Teachers for documents 44 and 83; the Trades Union Congress for documents 45, 46 and 81; Columbia University Press, New York for documents 49 and 52; the National Farmers' Union for documents 56 and 77; document 57 (from Marvin Swartz, *The Union of Democratic Control in British Politics during the First World War*, © 1971 Oxford University Press) is reproduced by permission of the Clarendon Press, Oxford; *Home and Country* for document 58; the Engineering Employers' Federation for document 65; document 66 is reproduced with the permission of the Controller of Her Majesty's Stationery Office; the Confederation of British Industry for documents 59, 67, 68, 69 and 70; The Times Newspapers Limited for documents 71, 88(a), 93(b), 95, 96, 97, 99 and 101; the National Chamber of Trade for document 73; the National Economic Development Office for document 74; Aims of Industry Limited for document 75; The Economic League Limited for document 76; The Observer Limited for document 78; the Country Landowners' Association for document 79; the National Association of Schoolmasters for document 84; the Howard League for Penal Reform for document 85; Mr Anthony Moncrieff for document 87; IPC Newspapers for document 88(b); Guardian Newspapers Limited for document 90; *Shelter* for document 91; the Abortion Law Reform Association for document 93(a); The Anti-Concorde Project for documents 94(a) and (b); the Daily Telegraph Limited for document 98; the Council for the Advancement of Arab-British Understanding for document 100.

I

General Introduction

Pressure group is far from being an immaculate conception. A sample of the variations and inconsistencies, as well as of the overlap with such kindred notions as lobby and interest group, has already been published[1] but is only too easily enlarged. One of the most elaborate formulations in English was produced in the United States in 1942 by Dr Mary Dillon: 'a non-partisan organization of the people formed to exert influence upon the legislature, the executive, or other governmental agency through public opinion for the enactment or the rejection of certain legislation, or for the adoption, modification or discontinuance of a public policy'.[2] In England, however, where the systematic study of pressure groups was taken up in the mid-1950s, the concept suffered a sea-change: 'organized groups [wrote Professor W. J. M. Mackenzie] possessing both formal structure and real common interests, in so far as they influence the decisions of public bodies'.[3] Distinctions with a difference, evidently. Indeed, one element alone, 'real common interests' – as embodied particularly in trade associations, trade unions and professional bodies – cut the earlier concept to the quick.

By contrast, one element in Dr Dillon's definition – 'through public opinion' – seemed to gain support in the early 1960s from Professor J. W. Grove: the term 'pressure group' 'defines a class of activity rather than a species of association';[4] it is symbolic of the state of the art that he was then a colleague of Professor Mackenzie's at the University of Manchester. Certainly Dr Dillon had tended to make method, or mode of activity, a defining attribute, seeing 'the direct effort to influence legislators by personal contact' as the hallmark of a lobby, in contradistinction to the indirect effort – via public opinion – of a pressure group. That in turn was congruent with the definition of lobbying advanced by the scholar–diplomat, James (Lord) Bryce in 1921: 'besetting and worrying members of legislatures with persuasions to vote for or against a bill', and with his earlier (1888) definition of a lobby: 'persons, not being members of a legislature, who undertake to influence its members and thereby to secure the passing of bills'.[5] But some scholars have long been using 'pressure group' and 'lobby' interchangeably; one of them even coined the phrase 'The Indirect Lobby' for that opinion-making effort with which Dr Dillon had tried to characterize pressure groups.[6] Other writers combine one or other of those terms to make a pair for alternative use as the mood takes them. Many more cling doggedly to 'interest group' in the innocent belief that it is more neutral, or less emotive, than any of the usual rivals.

Such inconsistencies are disconcerting even to contemporary analysts; for historians they are disabling. How is one to know where to begin, what to select? To put one's faith in a particular definition now on offer would be to cut a particular swath through the fields of the past, tending to lead one away from the main path of understanding. Similarly, a stipulative definition of one's very own would inevitably pre-empt the historical experience within which the notion was actually embedded, and so inhibit reconstitution of both its emergence and development. How, then, may the spell of this particular 'bewitchment of language' be broken? The historical reconstruction of the terms used in the current definitions should enable us to cast it off. For, of course, the stretching of old words and the putting together of new ones, the time of their first appearance, coming into general circulation and cultural diffusion, as well as their sociological implications, constitute in themselves one kind of evidence. Like any other piece of evidence, it has to be checked against other sources, but within such limits many words incapsulate historical events and relationships. If most words for the common live animals of the fields are Anglo-Saxon and the corresponding words for such animals prepared for the table are Norman-French, that suggests the nature of the relationship between the natives and the invaders. In the high proportion of English words of French origin to be found in the realms of government, law and military affairs we have a hint of the nature of the French gift to civilization. When 'class' is stretched, as it was in the eighteenth century from a naval division and an educational unit to symbolize a broad social ordering, in partial substitution for 'degree', 'rank' and 'order', that points to a changing social structure. Turning this idea into a method of inquiry, one begins by tracking down the terms most relevant to the discussion to their first recorded appearance in more or less politicized forms or contexts.

Before the fear of a Catholic duke's succeeding to the throne had precipitated the Exclusion Crisis of 1679–80, 'the Protestant interest' had been spoken of (1674). By 1735 Bolingbroke was remarking upon 'a new, that is, moneyed interest, in opposition to the landed interest', referring, in whole or in part, to the Bank of England, the East India Company, the South Sea Company and possibly the Royal Exchange Assurance Corporation and the London Assurance Corporation. If to Bolingbroke's contrasted pair is added the commercial interest and the labouring interest, one has in hand the four sets of interests later identified by Arthur Young in his celebrated survey of England. Analytically distinct, although in social reality overlapping both the financial and commercial domains, lay that sober Dissenting Interest of which the core was judged in this period to consist of the Three Denominations, Presbyterian, Independent and Baptist. With the Quakers, also dissenters but commonly spoken of separately, they all suffered from civil and political disabilities that as Protestants they shared with Roman Catholics.

To the language of Interest, the nineteenth century added 'lobby' and its cognates. These were not British inventions but imports, like 'caucus' later, from the United States where 'lobby', 'lobby-agent', 'lobby-member' and perhaps 'lobbyist' appeared in the period 1819–32, quickly followed by the gerund 'lobbying'.[7] None of these was picked up by Noah Webster, who had completed in about 1825 the revised version of his original dictionary of 1806. He died in 1843

without ever giving the older term 'lobby' a political connotation or reproducing the new terms. It was the edition
produced in 1847 by his successor, Chauncey Goodrich,
that first recorded one of the new mintings. This was 'lobby-
member': 'a person who frequents the lobby of a house of
legislation'. If we pause to reflect upon the new nouns, we
gain a first impression of individual rather than group
activity. But of course the emergence of such a new role
implies the existence of a hirer or retainer, which did indeed
often take a collective form, such as a bank, firm, or muni-
cipality. A collective element was officially acknowledged
when, in the year following the Goodrich edition of Webster,
John Russell Bartlett produced his *Dictionary of Americanisms*
and cited the example of a committee that had gone to Al-
bany (the New York State capital) to lobby for a new bank
charter.[8] Strictly, that was in illustration of the verb 'to
lobby', now perhaps appearing for the first time. The noun
embodying or implying a collective reference was not recorded until 1864, when Noah Porter produced another
edition of Webster: 'That part of a hall of legislation not
appropriated to the official use of the assembly; hence, the
men who frequent such a place for the sake of business with
the legislators.'

Between Bartlett in 1848 and Webster-Porter in 1864, the
verb had been developing in a way that offers hints of a
changing political practice. For Bartlett in 1848, 'to lobby'
had been 'to attempt to exert an influence on the members
of a legislative body, by persons not members of such a
body', but within the confines of the lobby in the physical
or architectural sense. But for Webster-Porter sixteen years
later, it meant 'to address or solicit members of a legislative
body in the lobby or elsewhere away from the House, with
a view to influence [*sic*] their votes. This is practised by
persons not belonging to the legislature.' The phrase 'or
elsewhere away from the House' suggests that the activity
was beginning to gain another dimension.

Exactly when such words were imported into Britain would
require further research to determine. Charles Richardson
gave no place to them in his *Dictionary* published in London
in the 1830s and again in the 1860s. In 1849 and 1852 John

Craig of Glasgow University put 'lobby member' (minus the American hyphen) into his *Dictionary of the English Language*.[9] His formulation of it reads like a more colloquial version of Chauncey Goodrich in 1847; 'a man who loiters or hangs about the lobby of a house of legislation'. When, in 1862, *The Times*[10] gave currency to 'lobbying' (that 'well known institution at Washington'), it was thought sufficiently exotic to warrant quotation marks. Similarly, in 1873, the *Spectator*, referring to a recent scandal in the United States, wrote that Americans 'will not knowingly choose the agents of the "lobbying" Rings'. In England, the writer added, the check against such behaviour is 'caste pride': 'there are lobbyers among us, too, but they refrain from putting temptation into that crude form, and they are powerless against caste'.[11] As late as 1894 the *Yorkshire Post* walked delicately: delegates were sent to London (it recorded) 'to "lobby" members for their respective constituencies with a view to obtaining the largest possible majorities'.[12]

Even without the aid of quotation marks, however, the usage had been gathering momentum. In 1883 the *Pall Mall Gazette* put it all in a nutshell of distaste: 'American manners, American lobbyism, and American corruption'.[13] By the 1890s terms of the lobby family were evidently becoming domesticated, being used in the Press without the half-apology of quotation marks,[14] as also in the 1898 Report of the T.U.C. Parliamentary Committee.[15]

During the last quarter of the nineteenth century, then, 'lobby' and its cognates were tending to become part of the accepted political vocabulary. But the new terms did not drive out the native stock. Already a railway interest had been identified, and in the very decade – the 1890s – when 'lobby' and its variants seem to be gaining ground, the *Leeds Mercury* singled out a banking interest, and Mr Gladstone warned 'that interests were always awake, while the country too often slumbered and slept'.[16]

So, in England towards the end of the nineteenth century, both 'interest' and 'lobby' (etc.) were becoming common coin. Their present-day analogue, 'pressure group', however, had still not been minted. But the mould for it was (in effect) being prepared by the politicization of the 'pressure', which dates, if not from 1829 (document 12), then no later than 1844, when the Anti-Corn Law League was characterized by a Brighton newspaper in terms of 'pressure from without'.[17] (See also document 25 and *cf.* document 27.) By the 1870s and 1880s (at the latest) pressure from without was being recommended in so many words as a mode of political action: 'effective pressure upon the representatives of large constituencies' (1871);[18] 'the only pressure M.P.s could understand, was, if you will not vote for the measure we are supporting, we will not vote for you' (1879, from a delegate to the annual meeting of the Associated British Chambers of Commerce);[19] if the divided counsels at Westminster are to be overcome, 'it must be by means of pressure from outside' (1884).[20] In 1892 a contemporary writer, discussing the rise of organized public opinion 'as a great controlling power over the representatives' (in Parliament), singled out two modes of exercising it: 'first by publicly exacting pledges from them previous to their election, and next by putting pressure on them whilst Parliament is sitting, should the occasion arise'.[21] By 1905 the Postmaster General would be grumbling at the 'amount of pressure' inflicted on M.P.s by the postal workers (document 53).

On the face of it, most of that 'pressure' was directed at M.P.s as such, but awareness of the Government and government departments as increasingly *the* policy-making bodies can also be discerned. In 1877 the National Union of Elementary Teachers was said by the *School Guardian* (its official journal) to enjoy 'a very powerful share in that external pressure which regulates the administration of the [Board of Education] department'.[22] Twenty years later the Webbs reported:

No member for a cotton constituency, to whichever party he may belong, escapes the pressure. Meanwhile, in order to smooth the way for legislation, the employers will have been approached with a view to arriving at some common policy which the trade, as a whole, can press on the Government.[23]

Among commercial men two years later, Sir Stafford North-cote (son of the statesman and president of the Associated Chambers) commented upon their intense disappointment at having failed to get a certain measure through Parliament: 'this difficulty of legislating only shows the necessity of members of the Associated Chambers working double time to put pressure on their members [of Parliament] and Government Departments'.[24] In that same year frustration provoked the London Chamber into proposing the formation of 'a commercial department within the House of Commons' to obviate delays and bring 'the necessary pressure to bear upon the Government of the day'.[25] By 1920 even ex-servicemen's leaders would be speaking the language of 'pressure' and correctly identifying the 'proper' political recipient of it (document 62). Four years later the Workers' Birth Control Group was organized precisely 'to bring pressure to bear, through Parliament and otherwise, on the Ministry of Health . . .'[26] In 1926 the Central Landowners' Association took pride in having exercised 'a good deal of pressure when proposed legislation had been inimical to rural landowning', and in particular for having carried an amendment against the Government.[27] By 1930 Professor Ramsay Muir was observing with alarm that, for a generation past, 'sundry forces had organized themselves to resist the Government or to bring pressure to bear on it': such 'organized special interests outside of the regular machinery of the Constitution are, of course, exceedingly dangerous, whether they are made privately and behind the scenes, or openly and publicly'.[28] Three years later the Oxford historian, C. S. Emden, produced 'pressure group',[29] not with a flourish, however, but tentatively placing it within quotation marks,[30] just as words of the lobby family had been handled in the last quarter of the nineteenth century.

So 'interest' (in the relevant political sense) derives from the late seventeenth and eighteenth centuries. It is supplemented in the late 1840s by 'lobby-member' as, at least, a term in a dictionary, and in the 1870s and 1880s by several extensions of that as terms in known political use. 'Interest', however, is not displaced but takes on new forms (e.g. 'banking' for 'moneyed') at the very time when words of the lobby family are gaining ground and becoming increasingly accepted in political discussion. Meanwhile, in the mid-1840s, 'pressure' (in the relevant political sense) had emerged; like 'lobby' (etc.), it came more and more into circulation in the 1870s and 1880s. Now in this one may detect some convergence: 'lobby-member' and 'pressure' in the 1840s, followed in the 1870s and 1880s by greater 'velocity of circulation' on the part of both families of words, and then by additions to the 'interest' family in the 1890s. As against that, the appearance of 'lobby member' in this country in the 1840s may merely represent cultural diffusion, or, less grandly, the private enterprise of a Scotsman out to make an honest penny by compiling a dictionary partly from an American model. Moreover, there may well be examples of usage that have escaped one's own very small net. On the face of it, however, it looks as if the term 'pressure' can be used to uncover the evolving nature of the *thing*, meaning either the group or their increasingly institutionalized activities.

On that basis five circumscribing generalizations may be tentatively advanced. The recipients of pressure have been variously conceived: M.P.s individually and collectively, Parliament as a whole, the Government, departments and ministries. These are, of course, the central authorities, and it would be rash to assume that 'pressure' was not invoked *vis-à-vis* the local authorities, but at least it seems safe to conclude that historically the milieu has been that demarcated by the public authorities. Accordingly, if a journalist reports in the twentieth century that the General Secretary of the World Council of Churches has a thankless task, there being rival claims to settle, committees to flatter and 'pressure groups resisted', that is his affair. So, too, when a contemporary novelist reports that a 'small pressure group' went to work to abolish the rule that the Professor of Poetry at Oxford was required to be an Oxford M.A.

By the same token, the 'mobilized' influence has always been conceived as arising or occurring outside the domain of the public authorities. That is explicit in 'pressure from without' (Anti-Corn Law League) and in the perception of the National Union of Elementary Teachers as exerting 'external' pressure, and so on, but it is also implied throughout. It follows that, for historical study at least, neither M.P.s nor civil servants should be thought of as forming pressure groups. That these may influence policy is not at issue: no one doubts that the sources of public policy are multiple, not single. M.P.s in particular, too, may speak for pressure groups but are then to be regarded as instruments of pressure groups, not pressure groups themselves.

On the other hand, not all external sources of influence on government have been characterized as 'pressure'. The more inchoate or amorphous groupings or movements have been virtually excluded (unless that is an artefact of the examples one has happened to come across). In any case the exclusion has been sustained here in order to keep the book within reasonable compass. The Press also falls outside our purview. If *The Times*, under Delane in the last century or Dawson in this, the *Daily Mail* under Northcliffe, the *Manchester Guardian* under Scott and Wadsworth, had influence on public policy, it would not, on the evidence of the words, have entitled them to be ranked as pressure groups. So, too, with the covertly crusading television programmes today.

The exclusion of those other private bodies, the political parties, will occasion no dispute. Their history has been as chequered as their historiography, but the common thread has for long been the seeking of public office. If, to begin with, they can hardly be said to have *furnished* candidates for public office, they at least furnished familiar or convenient labels for them, and in that simple sense they structured electoral choice. Taken by itself, of course, the label may mislead: the Silver Badge Party which put up ex-servicemen's candidates for the General Election of 1918 with only one success never looked like anything other than a pressure group.[31] At one stage, in the 1960s, *Plaid Cymru* seemed, like the Scottish National Party, to be outgrowing their virtual pressure-group status, but the English Party (document 86) clearly belonged to the pressure-group end of the continuum. On the whole, although parties also eventually became, like pressure groups, sources of public policy, the distinction between them has been reasonably clear.

So gaining leverage from the historical use of 'pressure' (in the political sense), we exclude much from the field. As for what remains, it is crucial to observe that the referent of 'pressure' has never been exclusively either a campaign (or cause) group or an occupational (or professional) body, distinctions between types that many a present-day definition prescribes. Nor, historically, can it be identified by the method it employs. Even after the exclusions have been made, the historical variety bursts the bonds of contemporary convenience, and has to receive its due recognition.

So far the tide of 'pressure' has carried us back to the 1840s, tracing a certain pattern on the way. Ought we to rest our oars there? It would be inadvisable to do so. One cannot yet be confident of the date when the term was first used in the relevant sense. Besides, is there not in 'pressure from without' an echo of the common eighteenth-century reference to political influence from 'without doors' or 'out of doors'? One is also uncomfortably aware from general knowledge that the Anti-Corn Law League was preceded by the Catholic Association and the Anti-Slavery Society, which, *prima facie*, appear to have resembled it in at least one respect, *viz.*, in exerting 'pressure from without' even if the phrase was not used. There is also the appearance in the late eighteenth century of what the eminent historian, Richard Pares, in his Ford Lectures called 'a new and indispensable adjunct to our political life – the voluntary association for political objects by means of public pressure upon parliament'.[32] *His* use of 'pressure' serves as an electric shock to emphasize the limitations of the method here initially adopted. Useful as it may be, it is still geared to the words, i.e., to an implied nominal definition. This leaves open the possibility that the *thing* (the group, or the group acting in a certain way) appeared not merely before the *word* (naturally) but considerably earlier.[33] Since one should not let oneself be a prisoner of any single method of inquiry, one should concede in principle the possibility of a much earlier start. It could even be argued that the inquiry should begin with the influence of the City of London on the Elizabethan House of Commons.

The prospect is dismaying. In some Camford college, in a dusty room off a spiral staircase entered from a quiet quad, an obscure scholar may exist who could rise to the challenge, distilling from a lifetime's learning the (needed) essence of four productive centuries, but lesser men had better confine themselves to narrower tasks. Grasping at that straw, I confine myself to an attempt to sketch the rise and development of pressure groups in terms of the modernization of the British political system. That choice distinctly suggests an eighteenth-century starting-point, and aptly so in the light of Richard Pares's observation. Within that century, the starting date can be conventional: about 1720, say, with Walpole's star in the ascendant. What remains to be scaled is still a giant rock of 250 years: to overcome it, we have to proceed by stages, or periods. But which ones? The established footholds would be better than nothing, yet not secure enough. Periods of time ought to carve at the joints (as Plato said of concepts), i.e., ought to slice up reality in meaningful ways. Now what is meaningful here is taken to be the role of groups in the modernization of the British polity, and central to modernization generally is structural differentiation, which, precisely because it is divisive, contains the seeds of integration. But this – the celebrated paradox – requires still more differentiation. Thus, the spread of chambers of commerce (an aspect of structural differentiation) eventually requires something like the Associated British Chambers of Commerce (1860) by way of integration; of trade unions, the Trades Union Congress (1868), and so on.

Taking differentiation and integration as our guides, we alight upon this division: 1720–61; 1762–1822; 1823–59; 1860–1970. In the first, 'units' of political modernization (i.e., specialized structures) peep tentatively out, like snowdrops fearful of a cold reception. The second period is luxuriant, but the growths are frowned upon by those in high places, who have convinced themselves that they alone have a legitimate place in the garden. The years 1823–59 are marked by increasing political differentiation on a national scale, including political parties as 'machines', but also by understandably clumsy attempts at integration. From 1860 onwards political differentiation was both extensive and rapid, not merely 'on the ground' but 'up above', i.e., integration – by way of further differentiation into 'peaks' – was now being successfully arranged. As the new differentiated structures evolved into pyramids of private power, the relationship of 'society' to politics and Government began to change. Foolish as such phrases as 'the new feudalism' and 'the new Mercantilism' must always be (since they resurrect little at the expense of much), they may have heuristic value, i.e., point to *some* significant developments and so prompt further investigation. A preliminary indication along those lines will be presented in due course, but the main burden assumed here has rather been to set the scene by invoking the history, together with some documents for illustration but also for permanent reference. Since only a limited number of these can be reproduced in a volume of reasonable compass, original material has been given pride of place. So what is printed here can be no more than supplementary to the standard collections.

Like a suit bought 'off the peg', such a period-framework as this one 'fits where it touches', so that it may not match the other dimensions of political modernization, such as the strain towards equality, or the fitful but apparently inexorable expansion of the area on which the sun of government never sets. That cannot be helped: history as event is as careless of symmetry as history as art necessarily but vainly seeks it.

2

Introduction to the Rise and Development of Pressure Groups

1720–61

Structurally, 'modernization' means not merely a separating out, an amoeba-like dividing and re-dividing and so the continuous emergence of organizational forms, but also their differentiation and diversity, the better to concentrate and achieve. In so far as it concerned the influence of private groups on public policy, the development was not far advanced in this period. The relevant groups included the City of London, conceived both as a civic unit and as 'the moneyed interest', which was further analysable into the Bank o England, the East India Company and the South Sea Company, with, in some contexts, the Royal Exchange Assurance and the London Assurance Corporations; the Muscovy, the Levant and the Royal African Companies; the West India Interest, some employers and workers; the Quaker Meeting for Sufferings; the Protestant Dissenting Deputies and the Catholic Association. In varying degrees and with varying effectiveness, all these entities engaged in pressure-group activity. This made use of or evoked some specialization within the existing structures but not a separate entity *vis-à-vis* the outside world. Politically, such groups were diffuse, implying 'exclusiveness' (or ascription) in their recruitment. The (politically) more specialized organizations dedicated to a specific political objective (or closely related set of such objectives) and open to all 'believers' did not emerge until almost the end of the 1760s and did not obtain a permanent footing (by some tests of that phrase) until the 1820s or 1830s.

As à conurbation, London at mid-century fell little short

13

of 700,000 persons,[1] towering over Bristol, Norwich and the still smaller centres of Liverpool, Manchester, Birmingham and Sheffield. Electorally and administratively, it was composed of several distinct elements, including Southwark, a borough, Westminster and (another) London, both of which had been dignified as cities. As a unit of local government encompassing about 150,000 people, the City of London had certainly undergone much differentiation. At the base lay the twenty-six wards, each yielding a Court of Wardmote responsible for ward 'housekeeping' (scavenging, law and order, etc.) but also for electing (for life) the Court of Aldermen (twenty-six, including the mayor) and the Court of Common Council (the twenty-six just indicated together with some 200 citizens returned annually). Which of these two principal Courts constituted the 'real' government of the City we need not consider except to remark that the locus of authority varied over time according to custom but also, in this period, according to statute (1725 and 1746).[2] Standing a little apart, as it were, was the Court of Common Hall, made up by the mayor and some eight thousand liverymen, ornaments of the City guilds and companies. It elected various City officials, including the sheriff, nominated from aldermen who had been sheriff, two men for Lord Mayor, whose fate was then determined by the Court of Aldermen; it also returned the four Members of Parliament.[3] As such, this Court had become the natural focus for much political influence of the relevant kind. Yet it itself had other work to do and policy initiatives might also well up from the wards of Common Council, while some results of those initiatives were determined by the Court of Aldermen.[4] Although designed for internal purposes, both Common Council and the Court of Aldermen were or had been highly politicized, the latter hand-in-glove with some members of that other Court at St James's as well as with the Government of the day; the former tending towards the Opposition whatever its colour.

The Aldermen also performed another bridging function – to 'the City in its other capacity as "the moneyed interest", that small but growing number of persons closely and habitually concerned with that machinery for creating and

mobilizing credit which had been taking shape since the late
seventeenth century'.[5] Its central component was the Bank
of England, which, founded in 1694, had gradually replaced
the City in its other, corporate self as the pre-eminent lender
of funds to the Government. Granted a monopoly of *joint-
stock* banking in London, it was by no means the only
London bank even though known to some contemporaries
as 'the Bank of London'. Private bankers flourished too
(twenty-five in 1725), both 'West End' (e.g., Childs, Coutts,
Hoares, Drummonds), distinguished in part by their aristocratic and even royal clienteles, which their survivors enjoy
today, and 'City proper', the banks serving commerce.[6]
But their limitation to six partners circumscribed not only
their note-issuing power but their power to mobilize funds
for the Government, which became more and more dependent upon the Bank of England. In that way, the 'Bank
brought government borrowing under the direct control'
of the men of property, which tended to reconcile them to the
new (post-1688) political regime as the dissolution of the
monasteries and the sharing of the spoils had reconciled their
predecessors to the Tudors a century and a half earlier.[7]

If the Bank was the central pillar, it was buttressed by
the remaining two of the 'three great moneyed companies'
commonly identified at the time: the East India (a trading
concern originally chartered in 1600 but also a provider of
short-term credit) and the South Sea Company, also
launched for trading (1710) but confining itself almost
entirely to financial operations once it had recovered from
the bursting of its bubble in 1720. As these two were among
the largest stockholders in the Bank of England,[8] the line of
demarcation was not entirely distinct. With the Royal
Exchange and the London Assurance Corporations (both
1720), these three constituted 'the five Companies' whose
support Samson Gideon, the Jewish financier, advised the
Treasury to secure when a loan was required in 1757.[9]
Together they made up the solid centre of an already swirling
world of brokers, dealers, operators and go-betweens. In
combination or separately, this new 'moneyed interest' was
to play 'a decisive role in politics; no political group could
hope for success without support in the City'.[10] But the

exercise of such influence did not call for (or, at least, pro-duce) further differentiation; the matrix for it was formed by the companies and corporations themselves, which, accordingly, like the City as a civic body, may also be regarded as dual-purpose.

Almost as Aldermen linked City government to the Court of St James's and high politics generally, so the East India Company linked the moneyed interest to the universe of overseas trade. Permanent organizations for carrying on overseas trade had been developing from the mid-sixteenth century when, following in the steps of the old Merchant Adventurers and Merchant Staplers, came that exotic line of chartered companies: the Muscovy (or Russia), the Levant, Spanish, Eastland (for the Baltic) and several for the African trade. Typically, the earlier of these had been 'regulated', i.e., they followed the tradition of the Merchant Guilds in providing a normative framework within which trade was carried on individually. This arrangement was appropriate so long as the range of operations was not only not very extensive (as these forays are judged) but confined to countries where law and order more or less prevailed. Once beyond that range and outside that pale, joint ownership of the stock became essential, meaning (originally) stock-in-trade and not as in 'stocks and shares'. As 'regulation' had been replaced by the joint-stock principle, so free entry tended, in view of the risks and the outlays, to be replaced by Crown monopolies.

Of the resulting aggregates, the greatest was clearly the East India Company. Chartered in 1600, it first sent its ships to Indonesia for spices, but eight years later arranged to call at Indian ports. Soon, trade between India and England was being opened up from a foothold on the west coast, which was later expanded to take in Madras, Bombay and Calcutta. Fortified and garrisoned by the Company, these provided a framework for the import into England of cotton cloth, indigo and saltpetre that tended, as the century advanced, to oust the spices of the further East. But as the century advanced difficulties also accumulated. Inter-lopers sought a share of the harvest, among them 'Diamond Pitt', grandfather of Chatham. The principle of Crown

monopoly itself came under fire and was gradually abandoned, the European trades suffering the first inroads, then
the extra-European. The East India Company retained its
monopoly but despite the skill of Josiah Child, the ex-brewer
and victualler who became director, then governor, it was
forced into something like a shotgun marriage that produced,
by 1709, the United Company of Merchants Trading to the
East Indies.

Despite all the difficulties with which it had had to
contend (not forgetting the competition of the Dutch East
India Company), this East India Company stood out in the
eighteenth century as a major institution. When Charles II
returned from his travels in 1660, the paid-up capital of the
original company had been of the order of £400,000, and
£100 of stock could have been bought for £90. By 1703
what was known by then as the Old Company had a
nominal capital of £1,600,000, and for £100 of stock one
would have had to pay £120. The New Company could
boast of a capital of £2,300,000 and to acquire £100 of its
stock one would have had to pay out £186. By contrast the
capital of the Hudson's Bay Company was only £32,000.
Even the Royal African Company could not hold a candle
to the East India companies, its capital amounting to less
than one third of theirs.[11]

Such an accession of capital resources, with its implications for earning-power, provided the basis for the United
Company's role as provider of short-term credit for the
Government. This role illustrates again one facet of the
theme of differentiation: banking institutions had been
separating out not only from trading but also goldsmithing,
pawnbroking and even printing and bookselling, but the
process was far from complete, especially in the country,
where (e.g.) Lloyds (at Birmingham) and Gurney (at Norwich) combined banking with button-manufacturing or
wool-merchanting, i.e., they were dual-purpose within the
economic sphere. So, if with different 'weights' for each
function, was the United Company. Of more immediate
relevance, however, is structural 'duality' in the pressure-
group context, which the Russia, Levant and Royal African
Companies shared in this period not only with the United

Company but also the hat-makers, or Company of Felt-makers, the Company of Barber-Surgeons and the weavers and other early workers' combinations.

Yet even among economic groups and especially among religious ones, differentiation of the relevant kind was slowly developing. This was the period in which the West Indies glittered as the brightest jewel in the crown of the old British Empire. Marshalling provisions from England and slaves from Africa, the West Indians converted this 'input' into an output of low-cost sugar. Like the American but unlike the East Indian (and other exotic) trades, which were or had been organized as monopolies, the West Indian trade was 'free and individual'.[12] Lacking corporate form, the West Indian Interest was at first a diffuse one, but is analysable into four elements: (a) the resident planters; (b) those planters who preferred to live in England 'as absentee landlords, at least for a large part of their lives'; (c) the merchants, also based on the scepter'd isle rather than the Islands; as were (d) the colonial agents.[13] Of the three elements found in England, the colonial agents, as representative of the resident planters, had been busy since the 1670s, but worked informally. Living in England more or less permanently on wealth derived from the Islands, the absentee planters (or landlords) acquired the patina of country gentlemen. So equipped and endowed, they naturally entered Parliament. Thus of the Harewood (Yorkshire) family of Lascelles, which enjoyed large estates in Barbados and sold sugar in the City (Lascelles & Maxwell), three (who had apparently never travelled as far afield as Barbados) found their way into the House of Commons. Differentiation appeared in the period 1730–40, when a 'trade rate' was levied on imports into England.[14] Towards the end of that period, apparently, 'The sugar planters that Reside in England being Desirous to promote the Interest of the Sugar Colony's in every Branch of it . . . did . . . form themselves into a Society in London, which takes the Name of the Planters' Club.' But when, in 1743, the Government proposed to increase the duty on all imported sugar, the opposition of 'Agents, Planters and Factors' was apparently still only *ad hoc*. Their 'printed case' was circulated to 'every

Member of Parliament in Town', some of whom were also waited upon by deputations. The 'case' was published and little indeed was left wanting 'to make the clamour popular, and if possible get this d—d Bill as much abhored [*sic*] as the Excise Scheme'. Defeated it certainly was, the motion being carried against the Ministry.[15] The organization of the merchants (the West India Merchants) may also date from the 1740s (specifically, from about 1746) but if so it seems not to have become politicized until the 1760s.[16]

Among religious groups the tendency towards differentiation is even more marked. In the course of practising or protecting their faith, Quakers had slowly built up a national organization: at the base, the congregations in their 'Preparative Meetings' leading up to Districts (meeting monthly) which were arranged by counties (where meetings were quarterly), the whole being capped (from 1668) by a yearly meeting in London. In 1675 a specialized structure had been created: the Meeting for Sufferings, originally composed of twelve Friends all resident in London, and charged with securing relief from 'the cruelty and opressions [*sic*]' which they suffered 'under pretence of Law'.[17] As our period opens, the Meeting was gathering itself for an attempt to amend the Affirmation Act of 1696. The 1730s would see a campaign to abolish tithes.

Meanwhile other Protestant Dissenters had taken a leaf out of the Quaker book. The Three Denominations, (Presbyterians, Independents, Baptists) had long had organizations with 'latent political possibilities',[18] including, at the beginning of our period, Boards of Ministers in London that for some two decades at least (1702) had been working together to a certain extent, as in presenting joint addresses to the Crown and consulting each other on particular occasions. In 1716 lay Dissenters had formed a club and discussed a general correspondence on the Quaker model. In the early years of our period, this general tendency towards what is here called vertical differentiation led to the setting up of a local 'parliament' (the Dissenting Ministers in and about the Cities of London and Westminster) and a joint committee of nineteen (the Presbyterians enjoying the odd vote). Differentiation was carried further in October

1732, when a general meeting of the Dissenting Ministers created a new organization of laymen – the Dissenting Deputies – to campaign against the Acts from which their civil disabilities were derived. Out of this came, early in the following month, a campaign committee of twenty-one under the chairmanship of Samuel Holden, who had been governor of the Bank of England and remained its principal director.

Evidently, despite the Quaker inspiration, the Three Denominations had created a 'taller' and so a more complex structure than the Quakers, proceeding single-handed, had found necessary. In Ireland the Catholic Association of 1760 (document 1) took after the Quakers in that respect, and for the same reason. Yet it too represents a degree of differentiation (in this instance, horizontal), a separating-out from the given 'unit' (comprising the adherents of the faith, or the Church) for the prosecution of a political objective. The founding fathers were Thomas Wyse, of the Anglo-Norman family long settled in Waterford, John Curry (a Dublin doctor) and Charles O'Conor.[19]

If these, partly differentiated as well as undifferentiated, were the structures, to what political ends were they bent? As a list would be long, tending to be useful only for those limited purposes satisfied by a catalogue, it may be more profitable to answer the question obliquely by first recalling to mind the politico-economic environment within which the groups were obliged to act. For economic groups generally the backcloth is an economy regulated and supervised, in principle, by the State. Those who ventured to trade across the seas did so originally on terms royally determined. The wool trade and the corn trade, imports and exports generally and the flow of bullion and coin, the shipping industry – all had fallen within the ambit of the royal prerogative and then, during the Interregnum, of Parliament. In general that remarkable structure of legal control had weathered well. In addition, governments strove to protect home industry, fundamentally woollen manufacture as its central component and the principal occupation outside agriculture. Throughout the eighteenth century, neither sheep nor rams nor raw wool could be legally exported, nor (between 1719

and 1825) could artisans or artificers emigrate. The pro-
hibition on the export of textile machines and some other
equipment lasted until 1843.[20]

Apart from this 'canalization' of commercial and early
industrial activity, economic groups in their other guises as
employers (and employees) operated within the crumbling
but still discernible framework of the Tudor labour legislation. Its centrepiece had been the Statute of Artificers (1563),
which furnished not only the rules of apprenticeship but
also of the distribution of labour and so, in some measure,
of the distribution of industry. It also empowered the
Justices of the Peace to fix wages in relation to the supply of
labour (subject to the approval of the Privy Council). In
some districts the Justices had never acted; elsewhere, they
had formulated general rules, occasionally descending into
fine detail (as for the digging of ditches in varying kinds of
soil).

Such was, in faint outline, that sector of the politico-
economic environment which the commercial groups in
our opening period were obliged, in the short run, to accept
and which, accordingly, shaped in part their political objectives. What its existence meant generally was that the pursuit
of economic advantage necessarily entailed political engagement: to have and to hold economically, one had to think
and act politically. The experience of the original (London)
East India Company is instructive. Having paid hand-
somely for the original royal charter of 1600 granting it a
monopoly, it soon found itself in competition with a courtier
whom it had expelled from its ranks but who still retained
the ear of James I. As a Scotsman, James proceeded later
to charter a Scottish East India Company which the London
Company had to buy out. His son Charles carried on the
family tradition in permitting a new East India Company
to enter the fray (1635), although it only lasted four years.[21]
In 1657 Cromwell furnished a new charter permitting the
Company a permanent joint stock and strengthening its
position against interlopers. With an eye to a future renewal of its charter it then set a course keeping close to the
government of the day. That, in the 1680s, had meant the
Tories, for which the Company paid the price of having

the Whigs authorize a new, or English, East India Company (1698). After the amalgamation of 1709 had given rise to the United Company, it had to approach Parliament on several occasions in order to stay in profitable business. In 1711, after having been threatened by the new South Sea Company, it had its trading privileges extended to 1733, but even before that period had elapsed, these were drawing fire, the effect of which, however, was their confirmation for as far ahead as 1769. Challenged again long before that date, the Company secured another Act (1744) maintaining its special position until 1780, with three years' grace if that position were then undermined.[22]

Meanwhile the United Company had been trading under the royal charter that had followed on the heels of the Act of 1698 establishing the New, or English, Company. From the outset a close connection with government had been made probable by the loan of £2,000,000, interest on which was to be paid weekly by the Exchequer. By our period the loan was £4,200,000, absorbing the whole of the Company's nominal capital plus another million (in 1744). For trading capital, the Company had itself to borrow from the public by way of annuities and short-term bonds, and the amount of bonds issued was governed by Act of Parliament. Within the original (1600) geographical limits (east of the Cape of Good Hope and west of Cape Horn), the (by now, United) Company would have no British competitor but was expected each year to export British goods to the tune of one tenth of its total trade and on such terms as would not run away with too much bullion calculated by a specified formula. The export of bullion (which was bimetallic, i.e., gold and silver) had been prohibited by law until 1663 in accordance with the orthodox economics theory of the day, and was still frowned upon now. But India was not the most promising market for the sale of heavy woollen cloth from England, and so the East Indian trade did entail a large annual outflow of bullion, which evoked a continuous stream of criticism and so contingent political action.

That commerce entailed politics was made evident, too, in the measures passed by Parliament for the protection of home industry. By the eighteenth century Indian cotton (or piece) goods, superior to anything of the kind produced in Europe, 'had become the basic item of the Company's imports',[23] which also included (in this context) some silk cloth from India, and some raw silk from Bengal and China. Perturbed at the popularity in England of Indian cottons (for underclothes and bedclothes as well as stockings and dresses), the woollen and silk industries clamoured for protection. For long the Company held them off but in 1700 an Act of Parliament, distinguishing between white calicoes (or cloth) and printed, forbade the import of the latter (and muslins too) except for re-export. The import of Eastern silks was altogether forbidden.

In London, the calico-dyers and printers breathed a sigh of relief, especially when it appeared that the increased duty on white calico had not reduced effective demand. By 1719 the Company was importing two million pieces of white calico and the rival interests were furious. Woollen-weavers rioted and chased weavers of white calicoes from the streets, beating up the less fleet of foot and on some occasions even throwing acid on their clothes,[24] their turbulence providing one reason for the passing of the early Combination Acts. As for printed calicoes, the increase in the excise tax seems also to have failed to reduce effective demand. In 1721, at all events, Parliament was prevailed upon to pass the Calico Act prohibiting the use and wearing of printed calicoes for clothing or household purposes. Through all these pull-devil, pull-baker permutations, the woollen industry was ranged politically against the East India Company. Even Canon Law, still unrepealed today, was supportive, requiring Anglican clergymen to wear 'night-gowns of woollen cloth'.[25] But one 'latent', or unintended, beneficiary was the calico-printing industry which kept on willy-nilly and gained ground in 1735 when the Manchester Act specifically permitted printed fustians, i.e., fabrics with a linen warp and cotton woof, the most popular domestic fabrics of the day. By the same token the infant cotton industry appears to have been a beneficiary, as the infant silk industry may have been too, and even the Levant Company, which had long ago protested that 'if silk be brought from India where it is bought cheap with bullion,

B

it will ruin our trade with Turkey, whither we send cloth for their silk'.[26]

A late-sixteenth-century creation, the Levant Company was no infant. It had often found itself at odds with the East India Company. In this period it was also up against the oldest joint-stock company of them all, the Muscovy, or Russia, dating from the mid-sixteenth century. By now transformed (against the trend) into a regulated company, it had for its Josiah Child, Samuel Holden, governor of the company for twelve years as well as a power at the Bank of England. An opportunity to exercise his influence occurred after 1724 when the Prussians succeeded in replacing the English as the sole suppliers of cloth to the Tsarist forces. In succeeding years English cloth-exports declined, severely damaging the company. Early in 1730 Holden propounded a remedy to the Secretary of State: an Anglo-Russian trade agreement. But this had to run the gauntlet not only of other business interests in England, existing legislation and the prevailing economic philosophy but also of Russian indifference and even hostility. The treaty took almost five years to negotiate but it was achieved in December 1743. No doubt the wool producers and the cloth-manufacturers wanted it too, and in government circles diplomatic reasons (the wish for a *rapprochement*) were crucial. All the same Holden had helped to convince Walpole and to work out technical details with the Board of Trade Commissioners. In any event the company had achieved its objective, the treaty being basically what it had originally proposed.[27] Seven years later (Holden was now recently dead), the company managed to modify that part of the existing legislation which obstructed the full exploitation of the treaty by preventing the import, through Prussian territory, of raw silk from Persia (in return for exports of cloth). As the law stood, the silk had to be brought to England direct from Persia. That was the preserve of the Levant Company, but the Russia Company overcame its opposition. Time was running out for the Levant Company: in 1754 Parliament broke its monopoly.

By contrast, the star of the British West Indies was still rising. The English penetration of the essentially Spanish world of the Caribbean had started with the occupation of Barbados in 1625, and then of St Kitts and her sister islands, Antigua, Nevis and Montserrat. Like their French counterparts on Guadeloupe and Martinique (1635), the English settlers grew food for themselves and tobacco for the European market. But England also wanted sugar, especially for sweetening the new beverages (tea shipped on the East Indiamen but also coffee). Until the early sixteenth century the commonest sweetening agent for beverages and food had been honey but then sugar cane, long grown in southern Spain and Sicily, had been carried in stages through Madeira and the Canaries to Brazil, whence the Dutch took it to the West Indies in the 1630s when tobacco production was depressed in the wake of falling market prices. It caught on immediately in every sense and became the main cash crop, Barbados switching production in the 1640s followed by Antigua and the French islands. Jamaica, wrested from the Spaniards in 1655, turned to sugar-production later in the century but developed a speciality – the conversion of the molasses (a byproduct also serviceable as an inferior sweetener) into rum which fortified not only the Navy especially before battle, but many an English gentleman in the security of his own home, which tended, however, to be draughty.

Tobacco and sugar; coffee and sugar; sugar, molasses and rum (document 2) – their varying fortunes were so interrelated as almost to suggest a 'system' of relationships except that we know it was not really so neat and symmetrical. But in so far as it constituted a system, humans from distant Africa came to form part of it. Already, from the end of the previous century, Englishmen had been shipping some Negro slaves from Africa to the West Indies. Now the requirements of sugar-cultivation suddenly increased effective demand: for planting, manuring, weeding, cutting, milling and the conversion of the juice (by boiling) into crude sugar and molasses, all under a tropical sun. Mad dogs might do such work willingly but not Englishmen, so the solution was sought in an increase in the supply of African slaves. When, in 1640, Barbados made itself a sugar island, it had 1,000 slaves; five years later it had 5,000; forty years later, 46,000. Within our period of inquiry, Barbados alone imported (between 1712 and 1768) no fewer than 200,000 slaves. Between 1680 and 1783, over 2,000,000 African slaves were imported into the British colonies.[28]

This, obviously, was a substantial 'operation'. The chosen instrument was the Royal African Company. Descendant of many other African enterprises, it had originally concentrated on exporting textiles, metal goods and arms in return for gold, ivory, hides and wax. But it rode on a new wave, and by the beginning of the eighteenth century it had sent 500 ships to Africa, where it had constructed an 'infrastructure' of eight forts, carried 100,000 slaves to the plantations, imported 30,000 tons of sugar, all against a backcloth of exports worth £1,5000,000.[29] Exchanged for such goods, a slave worth an imputed £12 sold for about £20 in the colonies (1700). The selling price reached £30 in 1728 and £37 in the 1740s, although the buying price never exceeded £25.[30] The export values themselves should, of course, have embodied a profit element; indeed, each side of the triangle (England–Africa—West Indies and North American colonies) was meant to yield a profit, although it was not always secured in practice.

Together the sides of this triangle constituted 'the three great and closely connected trades in western waters'[31] in our period. But the composition of the African side had changed. Not having emulated the Dutch in the creation of a West India Company, we had left trade in the West Indies and the American colonies to individual enterprise. The Royal African Company had been a monopoly, but tending to confer a monopoly on London too. The monopoly broken, the trade was thrown open (subject to a charge), which boosted Bristol (the second port and city) and prepared the ground for Liverpool's extraordinary transformation into 'one of the wonders of the world' (as Defoe remarked), and soon (in mid-century) into the greatest of the slaving ports. By this time the Royal African Company was experiencing great difficulties. It had already received some parliamentary subventions for the upkeep of its West African forts. Now it appealed to Parliament again, gaining allies in the London merchants trading to Africa and the West

Indies, who also petitioned Parliament. Despite this assistance the Company lost its charter in 1752.

So the tide was increasingly a tide of 'individual commercial expansion' and it was running swiftly to the west; its three components between them made up 'a formidable political force',[32] in which the West Indians stood head and shoulders above the rest. In 1731 they drew attention in a Parliamentary petition to the 'considerable trade' between the northern American colonists and the French sugar islands, notably Martinique, which sent molasses and rum to Boston in return for horses, lumber and other commodities, and asked for relief. Encountering opposition, they were not relieved quickly, but in 1733 Parliament passed the Molasses Act. As it turned out, the Act 'was never effectively enforced',[33] and had to be strengthened later in the century, but the securing of it represented a signal victory for the West Indian Interest, essentially the planters. In the same decade the Sugar Act, in allowing sugar from the British West Indies to be shipped direct to Europe, allowed a breach of the Navigation Laws that increased the price of sugar in this country.[34] These two Acts constituted 'great triumphs'.[35] In 1743–4, led by two colonial agents, the planters and merchants vetoed the First Lord of the Treasury's proposal to increase the duties on all imports of sugar, the motion in the House being carried against the Ministry.[36] During the Seven Years' War, led by Alderman William Beckford of the well-known Jamaica family, the West Indians 'largely defeated a proposed tax on sugar'.[37] Even the settlement of that war (by the Peace of Paris, 1763) reflected their wishes, for the sugar-producing islands captured from the French were handed back to them at the expense of British gains in Canada. The alternative feared was a flooding of the sugar market.

William Beckford was an alderman of the City of London. To such a degree was the commercial light, especially coming from the export trades, refracted through the City of London as a civic institution that it cannot be easy even for experts to distinguish the one from the other. Noting the blurred line, one may simply recall some of the illuminating episodes. Walpole's Excise Scheme of 1733 constitutes one of these.

Partly for the purpose of undermining the national game of smuggling, but mainly as a corollary of his related reform of the traditional system of taxation in which excise taxes would replace the land-tax (the main direct tax), Walpole had been trying out (from 1723) the bonded-warehouse procedure for tea, coffee and similar commodities. This meant not a customs duty but an excise tax recoverable from the retailer,[38] and in time it yielded so much more revenue that Walpole proposed to give wine and tobacco the same bonded treatment. In this he had the support of the Virginians, who had their own grievances against the English tobacco factors, but at home he had to face a hurricane of criticism and abuse. Many persons and institutions were caught up in it, including the parliamentary Opposition and their Press, but the City of London was to be found in the eye of the storm. It moved the sheriff to present a petition to Parliament but also the London crowd to besiege Parliament and mob Ministers with cries of 'No slavery – no excise – no wooden shoes!'[39] And when 'the Bill was before Parliament the Lord Mayor and Corporation created a formidable and well-organized opposition to it and threatened unconstitutional action if it were passed'.[40] Walpole prudently retreated and withdrew his Bill. Three years later an attempt was made to cope with the new social evil of gin-drinking by a sharp increase in the tax and in the cost of a retailer's licence (Jekyll's Bill). Again the hand of the City (meaning the Common Council) has been discerned[41] in the threat of rioting. The Bill passed but did not work, and it was not until the early 1750s that a flood of petitions from the four corners of the land, partly produced by the power of Hogarth's cartoons, brought about effective measures. Still in the 1730s, our commercial rivalry with Spain precipitated the conflict usually personalized as the War of Jenkins' Ear (1739) to commemorate that gallant captain whom the Spaniards, seven years earlier, had unjustly deprived of an ear in an incident at sea. The City wanted war, and Pitt spoke for them in the famous words – 'When Trade is at stake it is your last Retrenchment; you must defend it, or perish.' Traders entirely agreed, but so did the nation, since the sound of church bells reverberated throughout the land. Walpole did not approve, but some of his colleagues, more responsive to the mercantile interests, were eager, and it was to one of them that Walpole, giving way, said: 'It is your war and I wish you joy of it.' The City was prominent again, although allied with other forces, in the overturning of the 1753 Bill permitting Jews to be naturalized, which the Ministry itself had introduced as an acknowledgement of the services rendered to Britain by the Jewish financier, Samson Gideon. The campaign to repeal was nationwide but in London the City's threat of force was once more evident.

In these and other agitations it is difficult to separate out the role of the City and of the parliamentary Opposition from the general clamour, but it seems clear that the Common Council of the City 'often' gave a lead, and, particularly between 1730 and 1780, tended to set its face against political authority.[42] In an earlier formulation, in the sixty-two years between Walpole's advance to power (1720) and Lord North's fall from it (1782) as punishment for the American disaster, the City in its public statements and the speeches of its M.P.s set itself against the government of the day with the exception, at most, of eleven years.[43] So there was a half century or so of 'suspicion and antagonism flaring from time to time, in the excitements of political life, into violent hostility'. How is that fairly consistent political orientation to be explained? The existence of a sociological line of cleavage following the government-inclined moneyed interest into the Court of Aldermen and tending to make the less moneyed cling to the Opposition was a factor. Here, again, lines tend to be blurred for, to some extent, the functional line of cleavage could be discerned within the corporate structure. The 'middling men' controlled the Court of Common Council, by now the general governing body. Their inner core, the liverymen, controlled the Court of Common Hall, which elected the four M.P.s. Accordingly, political initiatives usually welled up from one or other of these two institutions, if not from their ultimate source, the twenty-six wards. But if they proposed, the Court of Aldermen, at times, disposed. Common Hall nominated for the mayoralty (from aldermen who had served as sheriffs), but the Court of Aldermen made the selection. Elected for life, they comprised a smaller and more flexible body than any of the other institutions, apart from the Court of Wardmote, which was politically unimportant. As individuals at least, the aldermen outranked the others in financial resources as in social esteem and, combining political with financial support for the government of the day, were comforted by having the ear of those men in authority.

That factor, however, seems to have been no more than contributory; rather the City should be seen as one of the two great potential sources of support *for* the Opposition in its discouraging battle against almost impregnable Governments. In this light the City appears as a resource (the other main one being the country gentry) made use of by successive Oppositions. All the same the City was never merely a stick for beating governments but 'a force which approached politics in a manner from outside. It was, indeed, this sense of separation, of standing outside the dominant social and political system of the time, that gave the City in Opposition its peculiar flavour, and it was this sentiment . . . which really explains the persistency of the City's tendency to political opposition.'[44]

As a blurred line separated the mercantile from the civic, so the interstices between the civic and 'the moneyed' lay in shadow. But some of the objectives sought by 'the moneyed interest' stand out as clearly as in early morning sunshine. Its earnings came from financing not only private enterprise (as for overseas trade) but also governments, from the humdrum arts of peace as well as the wilder ventures of war. So one objective was to keep up the rate of interest on the National Debt. In 1737, for example, the united front of the moneyed interest prevented the reduction of the rate of interest on the National Debt from 4 per cent to 3 per cent and the transfer of £1,000,000 from the Sinking Fund to reduce the amount of the National Debt held by the Bank of England. Reduction in the rate of interest was achieved in 1749–50 but only at the cost of generous compensation to the principal City institutions. Individually, the components of the moneyed interest had their own fish to fry. Thus, the Bank of England, like the East India Company, sought to preserve its monopoly: as a result, 'banking legislation, extracted under pressure of the Bank of England, restricted the size of individual banks in England and Wales'.[45] The South Sea Company had to fight for its existence in another sense. Chartered for 'trading to the South Seas and other Parts of America', it seems not to have ventured into those distant Pacific waters or indeed to have done much trading at all. On the other hand, by 1720 it was fighting 'with every weapon at its disposal to secure a monopoly hold on the National Debt'.[46] But in the autumn its stock fell more briskly than the leaves (to 180 from a peak of 1050 the previous June); collapse ensued. Rescued by Walpole (who had got out in time before the crash), the Company survived as a financial institution, a holding agency for government stock.

In manufacture as well as commerce and high finance, the toast was (or might have been) 'to survival, prosperity and the confusion of our business enemies'. The clothiers set out (as Adam Smith remarked) to persuade the nation to identify their prosperity with its safety and, according to him, they succeeded. Certainly they had gained protection, directly and indirectly. Colonial cloth manufacturers in general had been prohibited and the particular rivals, the Americans, eventually defeated, while the ban on the export from this country of raw wool, rams and sheep was maintained. The related 'art and mystery' of hat-making (an Elizabethan development) also came to suffer the cold winds of American competition. In a petition to Parliament, the Company of Feltmakers in London complained that the Americans, in a position to get beaver skins at lower cost, had 'set up a manufacture of hats' competing not only in the foreign but also in the home market. Made aware of this heinous crime, Parliament passed the Hat Act, 1732, designed to circumscribe production in the colonies and cripple the export trade. In the same vein, the production of pig-iron in the colonies was acceptable, encouraged even, but not its further refinement and transformation into finished goods, nor steel-making, all of which were held back (1750) in favour of the Sheffield and Birmingham masters.

In their other role as employers, manufacturers sometimes joined hands with their workers in search of 'security': in 1720, the two sides in the silk and woollen industries collaborated in the successful petitioning of Parliament against the use and wearing of printed calicoes and linens. At other times, their interests manifestly diverged. In 1726 combinations of workers in the West Country woollen industry were reported upon and promptly proceeded against by Act of Parliament. Thirty years later the weavers of Gloucester successfully petitioned *for* the fixing of wages by the local magistrates, that remnant of the Tudor labour legislation. Meanwhile (in 1721) the tailors had by the same method obtained explicit authority to have their wages and hours of work regulated by the magistrates.[47]

It was not only the weavers and tailors (and others) who felt impelled to resort from time to time to pressure-group activity. Professional men were also drawn towards the same light. After the monks had been forbidden by the highest councils of the Church to practice surgery, the medieval barbers were left in command of the field until challenged by Renaissance rivals. In 1540 the two sides were joined in surgery by an Act of Parliament, giving rise to the Company of Barber–Surgeons. By the eighteenth century the very much smaller surgeon component decided to escape from this embrace (as the apothecaries had sought and gained their independence early in the previous century from the Grocers' Society in which they had been enclosed for some three centuries). In 1744 the surgeons suddenly petitioned Parliament for independence. With their leader's son-in-law strategically placed as chairman of the Commons committee investigating the petition, this was not likely to fail. The following year saw an Act establishing the Company of Surgeons, from which the Royal College (of London, then England) eventually emerged.[48]

The objectives for which the religious organizations were mobilized varied in part according to the position these occupied under the Toleration Act, 1689. In recognizing any right at all to public worship outside the Established Church, this Act is, of course, a great landmark, but its provisions really belied its name and subsequent reputation.

It excluded not only Unitarians but also Roman Catholics, whose position even deteriorated at the turn of the century. Paris might be worth a Mass to a king, but saying Mass here could now cost a priest £200 in fines and life imprisonment for high treason (while rewarding an informer with £100). Even in an age when property rights were deemed sacrosanct, Roman Catholic heirs could be ousted from the enjoyment of their land in favour of the next Protestant kin. Nor did the limited religious freedom extend to the civic or political. Dissenters of all kinds were barred from Oxford University and even at Cambridge they could matriculate and take the examination but not the degree. Above all, as a class they were all excluded from active participation in political life, in consonance with the cultural value that religious and political membership of the society ought to be identical. To be outside the State church was to be outside the State system.

For Quakers, nursing an objection to the swearing of oaths, the Act permitted a declaration of fidelity in substitution for the oaths of allegiance and supremacy. But they still had to face many situations in which oath-taking was required as part of the stereotyped transactions of collective living. So one of their major goals was to secure the right to affirm; by the 1720s they had launched three considerable campaigns to that end. They also objected to supporting the State Church by the payment of tithes, hence their Tithe Bill of the 1730s. The Three Denominations did not enjoy paying tithes either but their root objection was to their exclusion from holding public office, so what they wanted was the repeal of the Test and Corporation Acts. With Roman Catholics, such discrimination had a territorial and even 'racial' dimension, since the Reformation had failed in Ireland but not the force of English arms. There the Anglican Church had been imposed. Rights of conquest, ultimately, had given over three quarters of the acreage of Ireland to Englishmen or Anglo-Irish Protestants, many of whom, like the West Indians, were absentee landlords. By mid-century some £750,000 a year in rental remittals was being dropped at their presumably grateful feet on English soil. Like the West Indian economy, the Irish economy was subordinated to England's. Preferment in the Irish Church did not go to the Irish but to slake the thirst of the English patronage system, itself a buttress of the overall political system. The country was governed by a Lord Lieutenant who did not have to put up with the inconvenience of spending much time in Ireland; some of his officials were even less inconvenienced, with the leisure to make carefree use in England of salaries ranging from £2,000 to £9,000 a year.[49] Since the Irish Parliament had been deliberately made powerless, one half-anticipates the irony of its having been made representative at the same time. But even that consolation was denied it since most Irish people, as Catholics, could not take a seat in the Irish Parliament. It is no surprise that the first Catholic Association (document 1) should have appeared in Ireland as early as 1760. Its aims were to right these wrongs.[50]

From the point of view of differentiation for political purposes, all these groups rank in varying degrees as diffuse, implying 'ascription' as the basis for their recruitment. But some significant movements of public opinion (or feeling) in this period presaged the later specialized associations whose doors would be open to all. In 1733 Walpole, hoping to reduce in one fell swoop both the land-tax and the widespread smuggling, proposed (as already noted) to convert customs into excise, i.e., to raise revenue by a tax on home consumption (tobacco initially) rather than by duties on imports. This proposal was furiously attacked by the parliamentary Opposition and in the Opposition Press; a pamphlet war broke out; the municipalities dispatched representatives 'to sollicite [sic] against any new Excise'; the sheriffs of the City of London presented a petition to Parliament anticipating 'the most fatal Blow' ever given to the Trade and Navigation of Great Britain; angry crowds gathered outside the Commons and in the lobby and the court of requests.[51] Walpole, grabbed by the collar physically as well as metaphorically, retreated, dropping the Bill as he went. Now this movement apparently lacked a steering committee (i.e., that degree of specialization), and evidently 'latched' on to, and may have largely derived from, certain 'closed' structures, the cities and boroughs and especially the City of London.

It nevertheless encompassed the public at large; the exuberant 'Rejoycings' – bell-ringing, burnings-in-effigy, drinking-of-toasts – were too widespread to have been stage-managed as distinct from more or less genuine expressions of public feeling. In that sense the episode anticipates (along one dimension, openendedness) the specialized political associations of the later period. The same may be said in some degree of the agitation for war against Spain in 1739 (dignified by the memory of Captain Jenkins' ear), the campaigns before and just after mid-century to tax and regulate the sale of gin (whose consumption within a decade had increased *by* two million gallons a year), and the movement to reverse the Government decision (1753) making possible the naturalization of the Jewish-born. Significantly, the Government succumbed as the 1754 Election approached.

1762–1822

In this period the (politically) diffuse organizations were still prominent. Groups of workers, trade unions in embryo, were already experimenting with what have become common methods of industrial action, e.g., the miners' strike in the north-east in 1765, which by its impact on exports affected 100,000 colliers and seamen; also 'the first great strike of factory hands', which took place at Manchester in 1810, when the cotton-spinners brought out 'several thousand men' and provided strike pay at the rate of £1,500 a week.[1] But the continuance on the statute book of the Tudor labour legislation still constituted a standing invitation to take political action as well. In 1764 the journeymen tailors of London petitioned the Middlesex Justices for an increase in wages, and gained some ground; four years later, 2,000 of them took the high road to Parliament to present a petition for higher wages still. Glass-grinders and coopers trod the same path. Sailors, too, foregathered in their thousands to present a petition to the Commons, while some, colours flying and drums beating, bore down on St James's Palace in order to invite the attention of the King. In 1773 the silk-weavers, watermen, porters, carmen and others proposed to carry their several petitions to the same destination, but were prevented from doing so. Four years later the woollen-weavers carried their grievances to Parliament, while the framework knitters of Nottingham, being burgesses with a vote, were able to go one better in electing a Member of Parliament pledged to a bill for regulating wages in the stocking industry.[2] In the 1790s the cloth-workers in the main woollen towns kept up the petitioning; towards the end of the decade the weavers of Bolton were in association for the purpose, according to a local vicar writing to the Home Secretary, of 'petitioning Parliament and playing politics'.[3] Certainly they were playing politics at the time of the Weavers' Bill of 1808. In 1816 the journeymen paper-makers petitioned Parliament to suppress the new machinery just introduced. That phase was ending however with the ending of the Tudor labour legislation; indeed had already ended in 1813. But application to Parliament in that sense had scarcely been set aside before it was taken up again: in 1819 the first moves were made to reduce by statutory means the length of the working day. In the same period localized bodies of workers were attempting to form general unions (e.g., the Philanthropic Society and the oddly named Philanthropic Hercules). In 1821 the Co-operative and Economical Society was established. This was infused with the spirit of Robert Owen and, if it is not anachronistic to say so, lower-middle-class in composition. But Co-operation proved later to be an instrument of the manual worker in the North.

On occasion employers (or masters) joined hands with the 'workers' (or journeymen). In 1765 a bill before Parliament would have excluded French silks from the English market, greatly to the advantage of the silk industry of East London. The Duke of Bedford blocked it, however, and the whole trade turned out in protest; great numbers bearing black flags marched to Parliament and descended on Bedford House. Joint demonstrations of the same kind recurred in 1768 and 1773, resulting in the Spitalfields Act, which was intended to prop up the Tudor legislation governing the fixing of wages. It even brought about a 'negotiating body', the 'Union', enabling masters and journeymen *jointly* to state a case to the magistrates for the determination of piecework rates.

In their other role as merchants as distinct from employers, business enterprises naturally ploughed their own furrows, again using structures that were specialized to the task but, from the political standpoint, still diffuse. Thus the East India Company sought relief from the heavy burden of the duties on tea, one of its principal imports. With 15,000,000 pounds of tea unsold in 1767, the Company negotiated a reduction in the rate of duty, but only by agreeing to indemnify the Exchequer against an overall loss of revenue. Price elasticity was such as to bring about an increase in demand but not to the extent of obviating payment of the indemnity. Accordingly, in 1773, the Company obtained permission to ship tea direct to Boston, which undermined the local smuggling and prepared the way for the Boston Tea Party. In 1784 the Company secured a spectacular reduction in the rate of duty from 119 per cent to 12½ per cent, which produced a spectacular increase in sales and a marked decrease in the need to export bullion to China to cover purchases.[4]

Meanwhile, the Company's great accession of wealth and territory following the defeat of French arms in the Seven Years' War (1756–63) had raised far more fundamental issues than the duty on tea. The Company now acquired some of the attributes of a State: ought Westminster to accept that, and if so on what terms? The issue came to a head in Parliament in 1766, the outcome of which was that the Company kept its position in India in return for a handsome payment (£400,000 a year) to the British Treasury. Handsome but evidently not crippling, for the Company, having raised its dividend in 1766 from 6 per cent to 10 per cent, promptly increased this to 12½ per cent the very next year. The Government's response was the Dividend Bill limiting the dividend to 10 per cent, which the Company petitioned against, proposing a temporary agreement for three years.

Parliament endorsed the arrangement and legislated accordingly. But the equilibrium, like the agreement, was only temporary. By 1772 the Company was in financial difficulties and under criticism. In the East India Loan Act of the following year, the Government had to lend *it* money, the payment of £400,000 a year having been suspended. In the sister (regulating) Act, London took a hand in Indian administration, establishing in Calcutta a Governor-General and Council nominated in part by the British Government and supervised by the Secretary of State and the Treasury. But the problem of how any British Government could really manage India still weighed on official minds, as the Secretary of State's 1778 reflections and recommendations reveal, while others in public life expressed concern about its propriety, which the City of London had denied when the first step was taken. From the Company side, pressure on the Government was not inconsiderable since whatever official influence could be exercised had to be exerted through groups within its management, which gave them some leverage. At the same time the returning nabobs were not only building their Palladian houses but entering the House, where their numbers increased from six at the beginning of our period to twenty-two in 1774 and thirty-six in 1784.[5]

In the India Act passed ten years later the constitutional relationship of Government to Company was settled for as far ahead, as it turned out, as 1858. Under this Act the Company's administration of India was to be subject to the supervision of a Board of Control. But the Company's patronage and trade was retained in its own hands. Eventually, however, the trade itself was seriously challenged, as it had been sporadically throughout the century. The pressure emanated from the houses of agency in India, i.e., the private European businesses whose operations within the area bounded by the Indian Ocean, technically in breach of the Company's monopoly, enjoyed a *de facto* acceptance but which were still shut out from the direct trade with Britain. What they and their London connections began in the 1790s, the outports and the manufacturers in England sustained and completed in 1812–13. Led by the Liverpool merchants, the outports and provincial towns organized an *ad hoc* committee (or Deputation), which opened an office in Pall Mall with a full-time secretary, arranged the publication of more than thirty pamphlets, lobbied Ministers, and stimulated 135 petitions.[6] Many London merchants, now recognizing the danger to London's position as a whole, changed sides, persuaded the Common Council to back the Company and themselves aided the Company in the war of words. But it was too late, not so much in the day as in the epoch. The Company's monopoly of the Indian trade was broken, although that with China was still retained.

None of this pressure-group activity required, or at least produced, a degree of differentiation for political ends beyond that already attained for the discharge of basic functions. In other domains, however, the tendency towards organizational 'specificity' for pressure-group purposes is unmistakable. In the commercial sphere the evolving organization of the merchants trading to North America is one of the two outstanding instances. Rockingham's Administration of 1765–6 was, according to Burke, 'the first which proposed and encouraged public meetings and free consultations of merchants from all parts of the kingdom'. Certainly such consultations took place, which may have stimulated a closer working relationship among the merchants themselves. At all events, in order to reduce the rigour of the recently tightened rules against smuggling, the merchants were believed at the time to have made 'some effort at organized agitation' in the period August–September 1765. A more distinctive mode of organization was reached early in December when reverberations of the Stamp Act rioting in Boston precipitated a committee of twenty-eight leading London merchants trading to North America. Under the chairmanship of the American-born Barlow Trecothick, the Committee's formal task was to 'Consider the best Method of Application for Procuring the Relief and Encouragement of the North American trade, and to apply to the Outports and to the Manufacturing Citys and Towns for their Concurrence and Assistance', but in context this meant the launching and co-ordinating of a nation-wide agitation for the repeal of the Stamp Act. The outports (Bristol, Liverpool, Glasgow, etc.) responded by setting up local bodies and later supplying expert witnesses to the Parliamentary committee of inquiry. Thirty circular letters sent by the London Committee to the trading and manufacturing towns produced (in January 1766) twenty-three petitions to the House of Commons, 'all expressed in terms of concerted similarity'.[7] Repeal was, in the event, secured.

A distinctive organizational advance also occurred among one of the other great Interests, the West Indian. Already a Planters' Club (in London) and a Society of West India Merchants had been brought to life. On 1 January 1775, a letter signed by twenty-three West India planters was dispatched to Beeston Long, chairman of the Society of West India Merchants, requesting a joint meeting. Such a meeting took place at the London Tavern on 18 January. It was followed by others of the kind, but these do not seem to have been infused with an overwhelming sense of urgency, since the standing body, the Committee of West India Planters and Merchants, was not established until 29 April 1778.[8]

It was this body that bore the burden of pressure. In opposing such proposals as the one to introduce East India sugar into England (1792), it tried to maintain the Islands' grip on the supply of sugar. It also addressed itself to issues of foreign policy touching the West Indies, just as its *ad hoc* predecessors had emphasized to governments the defence needs of the region, not merely against the King's enemies in the conventional sense but rebels from within, since by comparison with Virginia, Maryland and the Carolinas the disproportion between slave and free was not only initially greater but aggravated by white absenteeism. Above all, perhaps, the new Standing Committee took responsibility for the defence of the 'system' against the attack on the slave trade which was under way in 1788 (documents 6 and 7). This challenge was important enough to warrant the setting-up of a special sub-committee of the Standing Committee, which kept in touch with Members of Parliament. If representation of the West Indians in the House was 'never as large as contemporaries seemed to have imagined',[9] the average was about a dozen (with a range of between nine and fifteen). Some of them worked in with the Committee; in 1788, for example, the two M.P.s for Liverpool (**Pennant** and **Gascoigne**) fought against an early abolitionist move.

As with the West Indians, so with the industrialists. Some political influence would continue to be carried by (politically) unspecialized bodies, as when the Company of Cutlers entered the fray against the East India Company. But the appearance of the Midland Association of Iron-masters (1762) showed which way the wind was blowing. It was soon followed (1764) by a 'policing' committee of employers in the Lancashire worsted industry created to deal with irregularities on the part of workers in the domestic (or putting-out) system, and by the Worsted Committee of twenty-seven founded in Halifax (1777) but covering Lancashire and Cheshire as well as the West Riding. Deriving its authority from the Worsted Acts, this Committee was a quasi-official body charged with 'policing' the Acts themselves, for which purpose it was 'empowered to nominate proper persons to be licensed by the Justices of the West Riding as Inspectors'. But its quasi-official status was not so inhibiting as to prevent the articulation of private interests. Meanwhile, another committee of manufacturers had been established to counter theft and embezzlement, and was advertising its role, offering the hope of tangible, earthly reward, in the *Manchester Mercury* (1772).

Two years later Lancashire manufacturers gained a victory in terms of the Navigation Laws. In 1766 these had been relaxed to permit some 'free ports' in the British West Indies, which enabled French colonial cotton to be purchased some 30 per cent below its price when obtained from metropolitan France.[10] The privilege was to have been withdrawn in 1774 but was renewed by the Government acting under some pressure. This episode may have been the catalyst for the formation that year of the Manchester Committee for the Protection and Encouragement of Trade, also known as the Manchester Commercial Committee (not to be confused with the Manchester Commercial Society of twenty years later). In 1780 it petitioned the Commons to permit the import of cotton in neutral, as distinct from British, ships, and it was granted temporary relief despite the Navigation Acts and over the head of other business interests.

In that decade Birmingham, too, developed an *ad hoc* committee (1783) that would later turn into a standing General Commercial Committee. In its case the catalyst was a proposal to repeal the law against the export of brass. The following year saw another Government move that had the effect of linking Birmingham to Manchester organizationally. What happened was that Pitt caught some cottons but especially fustians in the net of his new fiscal policy. A new excise tax on these was levied and excisemen empowered to enter a factory day or night. Led by the fustian-manufacturers, the cotton-men rose up in anger, the dyers and bleachers even deciding to close down until the Government changed its mind. The fustian-manufacturers preferred to rely upon propaganda (efforts 'to inflame the minds of the public') and constitutional methods. An appeal for funds quickly yielded 350 subscriptions. Glasgow followed Lancashire's lead, then other English interests, fearing the same fate, were mobilized: the ironmasters of the Midlands (January 1785) and Birmingham's General Commercial Committee, which circulated other centres calling on them to resist what they believed to be a dangerous drift towards applying the excise laws to all private households. Thus supported, the fustian-manufacturers presented their case to various officials in London, only to be met by coolness and condescension. Their grievances were compounded when, in February, Pitt introduced his 'Irish Resolutions', which would have made the British Isles a single fiscal unit, to the possible detriment of cotton-manufacturers in England. At least, as Lord Lansdowne remarked, the 'Manchester people' 'contrived artfully enough to confound the taxes lately imposed on manufactures with the Irish propositions'.

These, in any event, were the circumstances which precipitated the General Chamber of Manufacturers in 1785. It had been thought of the previous year by Josiah Wedgwood, the potter (as a device for preventing the emigration of workers); now he took the initiative in forming a 'Committee of Delegates' from England and Scotland, immediately to 'meet and sit in London' during the debate on the Irish Resolutions but ultimately to bring about a permanent association. Several meetings were held in London during March, the outcome of which was a decision that their work together 'do not cease with the present business' but be placed on a permanent footing there and then. As designed by a Manchester man, the Chamber was to recruit manufacturers only, as distinct from merchants, and to be normally based upon local groups or chambers. It would be financed by fees and subscriptions and run by a standing committee served by a permanent secretary from a City of London office.

Such longer-term plans did not inhibit the immediate tactics. From this putting together of the heads of the cotton and other manufacturers, ironmasters and potters, flowed some sixty petitions to the House of Commons, although the immediate source was deliberately local. The Government gave way to the extent of repealing the parts of the 'fustian tax' to which the cotton interests had most strongly objected. The General Chamber as such then took up the running against the Irish Resolutions. Pitt made some concessions, but the General Chamber continued to ask for more. Once again the petitions flooded in, engulfing the policy, which was abandoned to its fate.

As visualized in the first flush of this success, the longer-term objectives of the General Chamber were to amend still further the existing excise laws as well as to prevent their spreading, to obtain tariff adjustments as part of reciprocal trading agreements and to enforce the laws prohibiting the emigration of workers. Altogether, therefore, the General Chamber represents not only a measure of differentiation for political purposes but also a raising of its level. Even so, the objectives were not all of that order but also embraced such technical services as an exchange of information and a giving of legal advice. Moreover, the General Chamber remained rooted in its industrial or manufacturing soil, so to the extent that it constituted a *political* specialization it rested on, and was inextricably bound to, a 'functional' one, and in that sense was closed or 'exclusive' in its membership.

Membership soon became a problem, the General Chamber becoming divided over the attitude it was to adopt towards the Government policy of freer trade with France. These dissensions reflected the different competitive strengths of the older and the newer industries, which was also to some extent a territorial division between London on the one hand and the Midlands and the North on the other. In 1787, under the leadership of James Watt and Matthew Boulton, Birmingham set about forming a General Chamber that would 'have nothing to do with the Londoners except on particular occasions'. All they accomplished was to weaken the General Chamber still further: it lost face, access and influence over public policy. The centre of gravity returned to the localities. Scotland and Ulster were already astir (Chambers of Commerce were established in Glasgow, Belfast and Edinburgh in the period 1783–5). In Leeds the first body in England to be called 'Chamber of Commerce' had been established in 1785. In Manchester in 1793, under the impact of the war with France, a Committee for Commercial Affairs appeared, followed a year later by a Commercial Society. Modelled on the Leeds Chamber, it had 'to co-operate jointly in all applications to Government' as one of its principal objects. Exeter followed suit in the same year, and later took the initiative in proposing a general organization, the United Commercial Societies of England, which, however, did not get under way. Even the Manchester Commercial Society then went into a decline and revived only when specially stimulated, such as during the peace negotiations in 1801 and two years later in opposition to the weavers who had sought and obtained Parliamentary assistance by way of petition. Otherwise collective action remained *ad hoc* until the Manchester Chamber of Commerce was set up in 1820 following the City of London's lead in petitioning the Commons in favour of Free Trade. This organization covered manufacturers as well as merchants and, although abjuring 'party objects and party feelings', was essentially political in its orientation towards Parliament and in the 'removal of existing regulations injurious to the freedom of trade, and not requisite for purposes of necessary revenue'. Such orientation towards government had already been anticipated in Birmingham in 1813 when the Chamber of Commerce was formed.

Also an organization of merchants and manufacturers, it defined its purpose as that of 'collecting and representing' their opinions, and 'of acting as a medium of communication between the community and the legislature on the subject of trade, and co-operating as the occasion may require with other parts of the United Kingdom'.

Religious associations differentiated for the purpose of grappling with the inequities of the visible world also remained on a (relatively) exclusive foundation, now wider, now narrower, but always Christian. Stimulated by a movement of the liberal clergy within the Establishment itself that had produced the Clerical Petition of 1772 (defeated by 217 votes to 71), the London Dissenting Ministers (of the Three Denominations) decided to apply to Parliament for relief not from their civil disabilities but from their religious ones under the Toleration Act itself (e.g., from having to subscribe to most of the Thirty-Nine Articles, which had caused their grandfathers no difficulty but now troubled them). To 'manage the affair' a committee of fifteen was appointed.[11] They and their parliamentary friends managed well in the Commons, gaining a large majority on the Second Reading, only to be put to rout in the Lords (by 'most of the temporal peers and all the bishops', according to a committee member). The Dissenting Ministers returned to the attack at a general meeting just before Christmas and conquered again in the Commons in the spring, only to be once more overcome in the Lords.

Despite these disappointments, some relief was granted in 1779. Partly for that reason, when the Dissenting Deputies assembled for a general meeting in 1787 they set out to right a civil not a religious wrong, i.e., they resumed the earlier attack on the Test and Corporations Acts. But these, according to Lord North, made up 'the corner-stone of the constitution', and 177 others (against 100 *for*) apparently agreed with him in defeating the motion. Two years later the majority against repeal fell to twenty. But across the Channel the Bastille fell too, and in the intoxication of that hour even the Dissenters of the rural areas were moved to act. Twenty large meetings were held throughout the country, helping to precipitate a counter-movement led by the Leeds clergy and sustained in the metropolis by the Society for Promoting Christian Knowledge. Spoken for in the Commons by Pitt and Burke in March 1790, their view prevailed by a majority of 189, the largest such majority on record.[12] 'Test Act 189' chalked up on the houses of Dissenters added insult to (the failure to relieve) injury, which in physical terms one of the leading Dissenters of the day, Joseph Priestley, was lucky to escape in Birmingham, where a mob smashed his scientific instruments, destroyed his records and burnt his house to the ground. The movement fell into the doldrums during the war years, not picking up until 1811, when Methodists joined hands with the traditional Dissenters in the Protestant Society for the Protection of Religious Liberty. That was an important landmark but not immediately productive.

Curiously enough, the older Dissenters had fared rather better in Ireland, in circumstances, however, that were more fortuitous. By 1763 the Catholic Association had collapsed, and was not replaced until 1773, by the Catholic Committee. But what then helped the cause of religious dissent in general was a secular body, the United Volunteers, which, under the leadership of Grattan, a Protestant, took advantage of the American War and consequent withdrawal of the militia from Ireland to recruit a large body of armed men. They cast a long shadow across the Irish Sea; in 1780 Dissenters (mainly Northern Presbyterians) were freed from their disabilities, and even Catholics gained some relief.

When, in 1792, the Catholic Committee called a Convention in Dublin for the purpose of petitioning Westminster, relations between Dissenters and Catholics were still good. The Protestant barrister, Wolfe Tone, who led the Society of United Irishmen formed the previous year with a membership of Dissenters as well as Catholics, became secretary of the Catholic Committee. The Catholic leader (and Dublin merchant) John Keogh reciprocated by joining the United Irishmen. A contingent including Protestant and Catholic was cheered in the streets of Dublin. Out of their agitation came (in 1793) the right to vote in Ireland. But the euphoria did not last. By 1795 the United Irishmen had narrowed down to Catholics only and the Orange Societies were being formed to pick up the gauntlet (or throw one down). The United Irishmen had dealings with the English enemy, France, and were taught a terrible lesson by English troops. The Catholic response in 1798 was rebellion, which was put down ruthlessly. The break-up of the Catholic Committee followed. Revived in 1805, its activists came to the view that the method of presenting petitions to Parliament (at Westminster) was an idea whose time had passed. Soon (1809) the Committee felt in its new constitution the transforming touch of Daniel O'Connell's hand. But his famous orator's voice and organizing skill would not be brought to bear until he had formed the Catholic Association in 1823.

Several of the principal Interests, then, gave rise to specializations for political purposes. 'Gave rise' rather than 'sloughed off' because these specializations all remained permanently attached to their parent bodies, and as such recruited only within the ascribed (or 'given') range. Nor was the political specialization invariably 100 per cent complete: some of the new formations, such as the General Chamber of Manufacturers, were political in origin and orientation, but not to the extent of ruling out the provision of some technical, or domestic, services for their members. The end of the 1760s saw the emergence of a new type of group, not only so differentiated as to have no other *raison d'être* than to pursue political objectives but also so 'free-floating', or 'loose' and, accordingly, so 'open-ended' in terms of recruitment as virtually to offer a standing invitation to join their ranks. These constituted the pure pressure groups (in the chemical-analysis rather than the ethical sense). In the long view of history, they represent a further stage beyond (a) that specialization on a basic societal task which nevertheless lends itself to some ventures in political influence, and (b) the (mainly) political extension of (a), such as the Committee of West India Planters and Merchants.

The first of the new species was the Society for Supporting the Bill of Rights (document 3) which the Wilkes case precipitated but which has to be seen against the background in general of the sharp rise of 'outside influence on Parliament and Ministries' and in particular of the acute frustration and commercial difficulties of the City merchants, notably the exporters to America, *pari passu* with the surging tide of popular radicalism, also a City phenomenon but more broadly based. John Wilkes would one day emerge as Alderman and then Chamberlain of the City; for the moment he was just that Member of Parliament who had made himself a thorn in the flesh of Ministry and King. The edition number 45 of his journal *The North Briton* was held to be libellous and brought about in 1764 his expulsion from the House of Commons. Wilkes slipped out of the country to Paris where he remained for four years as an outlaw but kept in touch with his political associates from whom he received financial assistance. Early in 1768 he defiantly returned and put himself up as a candidate for the City of London. Defeated on that occasion, he then put up for the County of Middlesex, which he won but, presenting himself in the courts, he found himself in prison for libel. From there he managed to attack the Government in the Press, for which he was again expelled from the House of Commons. The Middlesex voters re-elected him, whereupon he was once again expelled. After further vicissitudes, the Commons decided that Wilkes was incapable of membership and his opponent at the election was declared elected.

The repercussions of the Wilkes case were widespread but its immediate significance for our theme is that it catalyzed urban radicalism and produced the Society for Supporting the Bill of Rights. Sociologically, urban radicalism was a movement of the 'lower middle class' (the smaller merchants, shopkeepers, professional men), and its objectives were shorter Parliaments, bills to remove 'places and pensions', and a greater responsiveness on the part of Members of Parliament. The movement spread to Bristol where, by 1769, the M.P.s were being instructed to demand shorter Parliaments. Meanwhile in the City of London, where in January of that year Wilkes had been made an alderman, the Bill of Rights Society had been launched to redress his grievances. Radicalism also spread to Westminster, which enjoyed a large popular franchise, and there in 1770 Sir

Robert Bernard, a leader of the Society, was returned unopposed, the first candidate returned against the Government since 1741.[13] The movement, which was neither socialist nor particularly concerned with the lot of the labouring poor, spread in the mid- and later 1770s to Worcester and then to such other freeman boroughs as Newcastle upon Tyne, Bedford and Nottingham.

By now the idea of a specialized political association was being openly advocated by political theorists, quite against the grain of the political culture of the age. In 1775 the Scotsman, James Burgh, a Dissenting schoolmaster who had taught at Newington Green, published the third volume of his *Political Disquisitions*, advocating a Grand National Association (document 4). In the following year Major John Cartwright, a former naval officer whose military title came from service in the county militia, published his famous pamphlet *Take Your Choice!* (document 5). It called for annual elections on the basis of manhood suffrage by secret ballot in equal electoral districts; the second edition added the abolition of the property qualification for M.P.s, as well as a salary for them.[14] For these and many other reforms, such as the abolition of slavery, he advocated a national association along Burghian lines. This pamphlet obviously laid down the seedbed for the radical movement for the next hundred years. In December 1779 John Jebb, a former Cambridge don, carried the idea a stage further in presenting the Middlesex freeholders with a plan for a national body whose authority would be superior to that of the un-reformed House of Commons.

During the course of the American war, urban radicalism was succeeded by rural radicalism. Sociologically, it represented a revolt of the squirearchy against aristocratic electoral practice: the association that was to be its vehicle 'was a challenge to government by cousinhood and connection, by influence and patronage'.[15] But its current aims matched those of urban radicalism: the reduction of government expenditure and influence, and parliamentary reform. On the other hand, rural radicalism stemmed from and was still wedded to property as the basis for political rights, whereas in the larger freeman boroughs where urban radicalism flourished 'the majority of voters had no property.[16] Even this radicalism did not mean equal political rights for every Tom, Dick or Harry, but it did contain the germ of the idea. This was in the decade before the French Revolution, long thought to be the source of such ideas.

The antithesis between property and personality as the basis for political rights stood out even more plainly in 1780. Almost as the old year ended the Reverend Christopher Wyvill, an Anglican clergyman and considerable landowner, had, with friends and after carefully preparing the ground, launched at a county meeting the Yorkshire Association. Stimulated by the American war, they petitioned for a reduction in the 'gross abuses' in public expenditure and in royal influence. But the nub was the plan to enter into correspondence with other counties for the better prosecution of the object of the petition and other related goals, and so the creation of a national body. Helped on by the London Press, the plan prospered, spreading to the counties and gaining the support of even a few towns and cities.

Among these was Westminster, which, at a national meeting in London at Easter 1780, followed the Yorkshire line. But in trying as early as February to win over Essex as an ally, Westminster had shown itself ambitious to lead the movement. In March Charles James Fox, wishing to be elected for Westminster, had already made a bid to capture the leadership of the movement from Wyvill by appointing, as chairman of the Westminster Committee, a sub-committee of seven to discuss reform, and seeing that Cartwright, Jebb and Thomas Brand Hollis (son of Thomas Hollis, the republican) were on it. With that composition, the sub-committee naturally produced the sort of report that Fox at that moment wanted. However, their plan may have gone further than he really intended, so he kept it 'under wraps' for several months, meanwhile getting Westminster to accept the approach of the Yorkshire Association. In this fashion the City acquired a Westminster Association based on the local tax-payers. All the same the plan was released just before the Westminster election in July at which Fox was in fact elected.

Meanwhile, in April 1780, the men who had run the Westminster subcommittee had followed another path with the Society for Promoting Constitutional Information, which, under the title of the Society of Political Enquiry, Cartwright had proposed two years earlier. Rooted in the Bill of Rights Society, this had a touch of the later Fabian Society about it, providing tracts for the times with a view, ultimately, to parliamentary reform and so the restoration of ancient rights. Essentially a 'middle-class' organization, its keynote was liberty.

That general attitude entailed opposition to the proposal for a police force but also required removal of the civil disabilities of Roman Catholic and Protestant Dissenters, of whom there were many in membership. In that very year the development of the issue took an ugly turn. In 1779 the Catholic Relief Act (1778), technically an English measure, had stimulated a violent reaction in Scotland, where zealots within the (Presbyterian) Church of Scotland had been moved to prevent the extension of the Act north of the Border. But the campaign to win over the official Presbyterian machinery just failed, and the opposition had to proceed to mobilize, through *ad hoc* bodies (variously known as the Committee for the Protestant Interest and the Society of Friends to the Protestant Interest), the municipal authorities and some eighty private institutions in order to get its way. The campaign was carried to England where, in February, the Protestant Association was launched. Later that year Lord George Gordon, M.P., the perhaps mentally disturbed son of the Duke of Gordon, who had been active in the movement in Scotland, became its leader. By the spring of 1780 he was the spearhead of a revived campaign which took the form mainly of petitions against the supposed political influence of Roman Catholics. The presentation of one such petition in June was backed by the London mob; while Lord George was on his feet inside the House of Commons, members of both Houses were 'hustled and buffeted' outside to cries of 'No Popery!'[17] The mob then ran wild, looting private houses as well as chapels, blasting the distilleries in Holborn and breaking into Newgate prison. After other distilleries were sacked, spirits ran so freely that the water-supply of Lincoln's Inn turned into alcohol, and rioters were burned as they lay in their drunken stupors. The troops now began to shoot: over 450 persons were killed or wounded. Lord Gordon escaped a charge of high treason but ended his days in a prison cell.

Religious fervour was turned to a more constructive use in 1787 with the founding of the Committee for the Abolition of the Slave Trade (document 6). Launched in May, nine of the original twelve members of this Committee were Quakers, but already they had approached William Wilberforce to be their spokesman in the House of Commons. Wilberforce was, of course, one of the Evangelicals prominent in the House where they enjoyed in this period an influence out of all proportion to their numbers. A close working relationship developed in which 'the Slave Committee' dined each week at Wilberforce's house. A few of them visited Wilberforce so frequently that Mr Pitt, whom the Evangelicals followed, characterized them as Mr Wilberforce's 'white negroes'. Religious fervour, however, was not enough to secure abolition as they were up against what an M.P. called 'the great importance of our West Indian islands and the grandeur of Liverpool'. The work in fact took twenty years.

The year 1788 marked the centenary of the Glorious Revolution. In the ceremonies and dinners to commemorate the occasion Dissenters played a prominent part. In London the Friends of the British Constitution, a mainly Scottish body, went on to dinner after hearing a suitable sermon preached at the Scots Church, in London Wall. The Society for the Commemoration of the Glorious Revolution (the Revolution Society) also congregated on 4 November, proceeding from sermon to dinner and producing a statement of principles including the sovereignty of the people, the right of revolution, liberty of conscience and freedom of election.

Appropriately enough, this was the society which first welcomed the fall of the Bastille in 1789, an event which the Society for Constitutional Information was slow even to notice. On 4 November 1789, the Revolution Society provided a platform for Richard Price, the Dissenter who enjoyed membership of learned societies in Boston and Philadelphia, held an honorary degree from Yale and, like Winston Churchill in this century, had received citizenship from an admiring Congress. His speech welcoming the French Revolution was promptly published, reprinted in places as far apart as Boston and Paris, turning into a best-seller. Some three weeks later the Society for Constitutional Information endorsed Dr Price's approach, uttered a call to liberty and pledged itself to renewed efforts for parliamentary reform. Such an effort was made in 1790 through Henry Flood, M.P., and in association with the Revolution Society with which it had formed a joint action committee.

That set the scene for what became, organizationally, a kind of dialectic. In March 1790, a Church and King Club was formed in Manchester, rallying Anglicans against Dissenters as well as Tories against revolutionaries and reformers. It was itself countered the following autumn by the Manchester Constitutional Society, a Radical body (led however by an Anglican) that, judging by the middle term of its title, was not going to let the other side monopolize the best tune, or name. The Sheffield Constitutional Society appeared when Tom Paine started answering Burke in the great pamphleteering war, and Church and King groups began to be busy in the main provincial towns, running riot in some. That year also produced the London Correspond-ing Society (document 8). Organized by the Scottish-born shoe-maker, Thomas Hardy, it was composed of artisans, small shopkeepers and the like, who sought, by the joint action of affiliated groups throughout the nation, various political reforms, notably annual Parliaments and universal suffrage.

In 1792 the pattern grew more complex. In Manchester two other reformist bodies were established: the Patriotic Society and the Reformation Society. The last-mentioned later joined hands with the Constitutional Society, the London Corresponding Society and other radical groups in an approving address to the French Convention. The Society of the Friends of the People was formed in the same year but it was aristocratic and distrustful of popular movements, although also welcoming to the French Revolution. From the other side, the Loyalist Associations were launched in the name of John Reeves but 'with the explicit approval and active support'[18] not only of the Government but of a section of the Opposition. All the same, the movement, whose central pillar was the Association for the Preservation of Liberty and Property, spread so quickly and widely, eventually reaching even far-off Wales, that the Government's initiative must have commanded substantial general support.

The work of the loyalists was eventually reinforced by the full rigours of the law. In December 1792 a Royal Proclamation called out and embodied the militia. Ominously, the King's speech soon afterwards had as its theme 'the destruction of our happy constitution, and the subversion of all order and government'. The Courts then took up the running, and in 1794 the Government began to resort to the device of suspending *habeas corpus*, which was followed in 1795 by an Act striking at the roots of public meetings. In 1799 and 1800 came the blanket prohibitions on combinations, in the first one of which the London Corresponding Society was suppressed by name. This virtually brought to an end the first phase in the history of the 'pure' pressure group. For although the reform movement flickered into life in 1806–7, followed in 1812 by the Hampden Club (in which the indefatigable Cartwright was again prominent), the Union for Parliamentary Reform and, in 1818, the Political Protestants, it met the opposition not only of the Loyalist Associations but also the legal attacks of 1817 and then of the notorious Six Acts of 1819.

1823–59

By now those 'classical' interests that, although *functionally* specialized, had remained *politically* diffuse were evidently in decline. The great increase in the export of Lancashire cotton goods following the opening up of the India trade had whetted northern appetites for the abolition of the East India Company's monopoly of the China trade.[1] Again, as in 1812, Liverpool merchants took the lead in setting up an *ad hoc* committee, which, as before, launched pamphlets from a London headquarters and stimulated petitions, 257 of which were presented in the period 1829–30 alone. The Government responded in 1833, when the Company lost not only its China monopoly but also, as Marx observed, its whole 'commercial character'. In other words, as a commercial enterprise, it was nationalized, and on terms (by way of annuities charged against Indian revenues) that were not unfavourable to the proprietors (as bourgeois historians have noted, although Marx himself missed the opportunity). The Company still administered India but after the Mutiny in 1857 it yielded full control, including its troops, to the British Crown, thus ending the strange phenomenon of a private concern that had 'maintained armies and retailed tea'. As such, the Company had always constituted a special case, but the Levant Company also had to give up its monopoly (1825). Even the Bank of England, if safe, was not immune to the trend. It lost its monopoly of (English) joint-stock banking in 1826 when such banks were authorized within a sixty-five-mile radius of London. Seven years later, as the East India Company was being eclipsed commercially, the Bank suffered the intrusion of joint-stock banks into its own circle, although retaining the right of note issue.

As that part of the old order changed, what took its place? At the 'unit' or 'operating' level, the railway companies constituted a major replacement. Under way from 1825 and reaching their first construction peak in 1836, these companies were initially drawn into politics in order to beat down the opposition to their cutting a swath through the countryside. Having, as it were, recovered their strength in the period 1839–43 (when no new lines were opened), the companies took off again like comets in the mid-1840s: between 1844 and 1847 some 440 acts were passed and over 2,000 miles of track opened. This aptly known 'railway mania' invited Government regulation and received it, as from Gladstone in 1844, which in turn prompted co-ordinated political effort by the companies through an *ad hoc* steering committee of directors and managers whose wide-ranging attack proved fairly successful.[2] Organizations

c

of employers as such represent a further degree of functional differentiation, not yet political but potentially so. Such organizations were not new but had long ago been the subject of unflattering comment by Adam Smith. In his day the Master Printers was one association among many such. In 1803 the Master Spinners of Manchester had come together for the declared purpose of countering the 'dangerous and unjust combination' of working mule-spinners.[3] At the outset of the period now under review, the association of Master Shipwrights of Liverpool was reorganized and followed (in 1834) by the Master Builders of London, itself succeeded (during an industrial dispute in 1859–60) by a distinct body, the Central Association of Master Builders.[4] Specialization again, but on shaky foundations, and generally not yet infused with 'politics' in the pressure-group sense.

The earlier trade unions and co-operatives in this period also provide examples of evolving differentiation with a potentiality for pressure-group action. Resorting to a series of drastic simplifications, we may first recall that the repeal of the Combination Acts in 1824 was followed by such a burst of trade-union building, consolidation and activity that Parliament had second thoughts, resulting in the Act of 1825. Hard on its heels, further differentiation was attempted: the General Trades Union of the North, 1826, the National Association for the Protection of Labour, 1830 and the Grand National Consolidated Trades Union, 1833. The last of these embodied working-class disappointment with the Reform Act of 1832 and so might be characterized as negatively political. But none was a pressure group as here understood, nor was that creation of the 1840s, the National Association of United Trades for the Protection of Labour, although that might be regarded as another step on the long road to establishing one (the Trades Union Congress) in the succeeding period.

Meanwhile workers had been among those following the path of Co-operation under the spell of the Welsh manufacturer and social philosopher, Robert Owen. Working printers, in London in 1821, had helped to set up the Co-operative and Economical Society. In 1824 the running was taken up by the London Co-operative Society, which, at first a proselytizing body, turned to trading in 1827, the year when, fifty miles or so away, Dr William King was launching the Brighton Co-operative Movement (document 17) with some members drawn from the Brighton Mechanics' Institution, in whose establishment he – the 'poor man's doctor' – had also participated. Back in London, such trade-union activists as William Lovett, Benjamin Warden and George Foskitt were forming the British Association for Promoting Co-operative Knowledge (1829), particularly to impress 'on the working classes' the importance of Co-operative trading, but more broadly to adopt 'such parts' of Robert Owen's 'system as would be appreciated by the majority of the working classes' and bring reformers 'of every grade' together. If not itself a pressure group, it made a bridge to one – the National Union of the Working Classes and Others (1831), which falls for notice later.

As with the 'working classes' so with the aspiring professional men. In 1825 the Society of Attorneys, Solicitors Proctors, etc. replaced the earlier Society of Gentlemen Practisers, by now in the doldrums. Launched from the Inns of Court in 1851, the Council of Legal Education lived up to its name by arranging lectures and examinations. But these and scores of other new professional bodies were more 'domestic' than political, mainly devoting themselves to status and qualifications. Some, however, tended from the outset to act politically: of these, the elementary-school teachers and the local doctors constitute examples.

In England and Wales elementary education was still in the hands of two private bodies, the National Society for Promoting the Education of the Poor in the Principles of the Established Church (1811), and the British and Foreign School Society (1814), which was non-denominational. In 1833 they managed to swallow the first few drops (the celebrated £20,000 'for the purposes of education') from what proved to be the great fountain of State aid (which their rivalry had dammed). In the aftermath of that tentative first move the London teachers of the British and Foreign sought its help to launch an organization of their own and, not at first getting it, proceeded to form the British Teachers' Quarterly Association, more commonly known as the

British Teachers' Association or the British Society of Teachers.

In 1843, with the blessing and indirect financial support of the National Society, the Schoolmasters' Mutual Improvement Society was set up, which, after a change of name, turned into the Metropolitan Church Schoolmasters' Association in 1853.[5] By now a network of local and district associations extended over England and Wales.

Initially such bodies were not pressure groups but the entering wedge of State aid made it probable that they would soon become so. One issue that loomed up in the 1840s was the role of laymen (but members of the Church of England) in the management of the 'National schools'. The National Society opposed lay management (which included the appointment and dismissal of teachers) but was overborne by the supervising body (a Committee of the Privy Council), although it retained control, through the clergymen, of religious instruction. In 1852 it recovered lost ground, being now enabled, through the Bishop, to suspend and dismiss. The Metropolitan Church Schoolmasters' Association promptly dispatched a deputation to Lord John Russell; its memorial asked that Parliament should withhold approval of the change. As a mark of his disapproval of this adoption of a pressure-group (as against a mutual-improvement) role, its patron, the Bishop of London, withdrew his patronage, whereupon the Association repudiated its deputation. But politicization had begun. A ginger-group, the Committee of Metropolitan Church Schoolmasters, resumed the battle, stirring up their country cousins and organizing (in February 1853) a deputation to the Lord President of the Council. Two months later the offending Minute was cancelled. Burrowing from within the larger body, this group captured control the following year and committed it to 'the furtherance of education' as well as 'the improvement of schoolmasters', by implication a further step in politicization, although the Bishop of London may not have realized that, since he continued to confer his patronage.

Now the structure began to gain height. District associations were attempted from a Bristol base; a Western Union of Teachers (presumably West of England) also put in a

fleeting appearance. The national heights were scaled in
December 1853 by the General Associated Body of Church
Schoolmasters in England and Wales (A.B.C.S.), a provin-
cial initiative from which the Metropolitan Schoolmasters
stood aloof; and by the United Association of Schoolmasters
(U.A.S.), a non- or supra-denominational body led by
London training-college instructors and central-school
masters, with which the A.B.C.S. would have no truck.
The U.A.S. was more professional than political, as the
Social Science Association for Schoolmasters (1859) was
more technical, setting out (on the model of the National
Association for the Promotion of Social Science), to pursue
'the study of social science, and how to teach it' (a problem
not altogether resolved over a century later). By contrast,
the A.B.C.S. was soon treading the pressure-group path,
with its petitions and memorials and deputations to the
committee of the Privy Council. These representations,
however, were scarcely concerned with general policy.
Broader political roles were not assumed until early in the
succeeding period.

In these early strivings the tension and rivalry between
London and the provinces was manifest. With the doctors it
was proclaimed: the Provincial Medical and Surgical
Association (document 18), brought into the world in 1832
in Worcester by 'more than fifty medical gentlemen' in
conscious opposition to the two Royal Colleges (Physicians
and Surgeons) in London. The object was declared to be
the 'Maintenance of the Honour and Respectability of the
Profession generally in the Provinces' but engagement in
political action soon followed as a consequence of the
Association's very concern for the practice of medicine.
'Petitions to Parliament and negotiations with Ministers of
Government became a staple part of the Association's
business'.[6] But not it alone, for in 1836 a British Medical
Association was set up by doctors practising in London itself
(Southwark and Camberwell). This new body lasted long
enough to put its weight behind the campaign in 1841 ('a
Public General Meeting of the profession') to persuade
Parliament to undertake a number of medical reforms: of
the Royal Colleges, and for a single faculty of medicine for

Britain to control medical education and practice. The Association then faded away but its memory was preserved by the earlier body's unopposed decision in 1855 to adopt the broader title.

Like the professional men, manufacturers and merchants were busily organizing themselves, creating a network of chambers of commerce throughout the country: Bristol and Kirkcaldy at the beginning of the period; Leith, Swansea and Liverpool in the middle of it; Kendal and Sheffield towards the end. As with the professions, much of this development served domestic rather than political ends, yet some of it, too, was intensely political from the start. In 1824 the 'Manchester Chamber of Commerce became the centre of an organized agitation, which included not only Birmingham but also Liverpool, Glasgow, Leeds, Huddersfield and other towns', to keep up the old rules against the export of machinery, arguing that ' "the race [for economic supremacy] is begun, and we would not wantonly throw away any advantage"'.[7] They were rewarded by the Customs Regulation Act of 1825, which, with a later act in 1833, set out schedules of prohibited machinery. These could, however, be modified by Board of Trade licence, and so the Manchester Chamber took it on itself to police such waivers as well as to keep an eye open for out-and-out evasions. In 1820 Manchester, in order to relieve the credit stringency, co-operated with Glasgow and Liverpool in pressing the Government to authorize the issue of Exchequer Bills. A deputation from the Manchester Chamber attended the Treasury and presented its views in a memorial, although the outcome was not what it sought but a loan from the Bank of England to which the deputation had been referred.[8]

Opposition to the Corn Laws had long been expressed, e.g. in 1815. Among Chambers, Glasgow had then been quick off the mark, complaining in 1814 in anticipation of the measure. As soon as the Manchester Chamber was founded (in 1820) it threw its hat – a petition – into the ring. The Chamber was by no means monolithic, however, and divisions within its ranks remained obvious until the end of the following decade. But since Birmingham's corporate attitude was even more ambiguous, Manchester became for a time the core of the Chambers' opposition to the Corn Laws in their entirety and a considerable force in the general Free Trade movement. That took a generation to mature. Meanwhile the Manchester Chamber engaged in many a skirmish, e.g., supported originally by Liverpool and London, taking the side of the East Indian as against the West Indian interests in order to remove the latter's advantage of ten shillings a hundredweight in the customs duties on sugar. In 1836 the rates were equalized: as the Board of Directors of the Chamber put it, 'the sugar of the two hemispheres has now been brought into fair and advantageous competition in the British market', to which they might have added that the Indian peasant would now be better placed to pay for Lancashire cottons by sugar exports to this country.

That year saw the start of a greater movement into whose vortex the Manchester Chamber was drawn, much to its initial discomfort. The first manifestation appeared in London as the Anti-Corn Law Association, but made little headway until, in September–October 1838, the Mancunians showed them how to do it with another body then bearing the same title (documents 19 and 21). According to a Manchester University historian, 'it was generally recognized that the new Association was, in effect, the off-shoot from the Manchester Chamber of Commerce', there being an overlap in the new leadership of about forty considerable persons from the older body[9] [*Cf*. document 20]. The historian of the League, however, sees the Association as having captured the Chamber.[10] What is clear at least is that the Chamber's need to decide its policy *vis-à-vis* the Association brought to the surface the latent conflict about the Corn Laws in particular and by implication free trade in general. The Chamber's first special meeting had to be adjourned; at the second, the Sussex-born but locally prominent Radical (and member of the Chamber) Richard Cobden and his associates managed to put through a proposal (in the form of a petition)

to repeal all laws relating to the importation of foreign corn and other foreign articles of subsistence, and to carry out to the fullest extent, both as affects agriculture and manufactures, the true and peaceful principles of free trade, by removing all obstacles to the unrestricted employment of industry and capital.[11]

But the 'excited and heated discussions of December 1838' and the *coup* at the annual meeting early in the New Year, when the official slate was wiped clean by the election of the Cobdenite list, must have convinced many that the Chamber as such could be used for the Anti-Corn Law movement only at the risk of foundering. Thereafter the Chamber as such reserved its interventions for special occasions.

However politicized some Chambers of Commerce and professional bodies had proved to be, they had also been performing domestic services for their members. But some differentiation was essentially for political (or pressure-group) purposes. Of the older, functionally specialized groups that had generated specific associations for political purposes, the West Indian formations had survived: the Society of Merchants (to 1843) and the broader and more distinctly political Society of Planters and Merchants (to this day, as the West India Committee, now located, aptly enough, near that American territory in London, Grosvenor Square). But evidently their survival had not been enough to arrest their decline (document 10) or prevent their fortunes becoming the subject of parliamentary investigation. In accelerating that decline the anti-slavery movement was clearly significant; *how* significant – a controversial question – we need not discuss.[12] New specializations now appeared, such as the Licensed Victuallers' Defence League (document 37). Some of the liveliest action by (politically) specialized bodies, however, was not economic but religious in foundation. The Catholic Association of 1823 (documents 11, 12 and 13) revealed the potentialities of the 'medium'. The earlier Catholic Committee (set up in Dublin in 1809) had set out to persuade, but the organization for managing the petitions had been declared illegal on the ground that delegates or representatives were being appointed. The Catholic Association recruited the whole of Catholic Ireland and set itself up in Dublin as a quasi-Parliament, financed by a 'rent' upon every parish in Ireland, proceeding to appoint and receive petitions. In London the Government counter-attacked by way of a bill (1825) that prohibited the permanent sittings of political bodies, the raising of money for the redress of grievances and other features that were obviously the attributes of the Catholic Association. Dissolved in ostensible obedience, it promptly rose from the ashes as an association to advance the cause of education and other charitable objects and so conducted as to be outside the law, although permanent committees were still appointed and 'Catholic rent' still collected in every parish.

The cause of Catholic Emancipation did not remain confined to Ireland alone, nor even to Catholics alone. A more 'open-ended' group appeared, the Friends of Civil and Religious Liberty (document 14), embracing Protestants as well as those of the older faith. But some Protestants revealed a menacing as well as a smiling face. The circumscribing act of 1825 expired in 1828, whereupon the Catholic Association promptly reappeared, discarding its disguise. In the Catholic–Protestant 'dialectic' that followed Brunswick Clubs were established, as at Dublin University (document 15). In the North, the Orange Society, dating from 1795, was revived; in London the Duke of Cumberland was inaugurated as its Grand Master, and large subscriptions were collected. Faced with the possibility of a confrontation in the streets the British Government chose, once again, to suppress the Catholic Association but in the end gave way and with the Catholic Emancipation Act (1829) brought Catholics within the pale of the constitution.

Protestant Dissenters had already been admitted the previous year. Protestant activity of this kind had begun to revive towards the end of the Napoleonic wars: its principal manifestation was the Protestant Society for the Protection of Religious Liberty of 1811. In the Protestant realm this represented a substantial degree of 'aggregation' since it included for the first time the Methodists as well as the Three Denominations. Soon the new Society was trenching on the East India Company's power to keep missionaries out of India: the method was to influence the terms of the Company's Charter, then up for renewal. On the wider issue of political rights the Protestant Society was for some

time inhibited in its pressure-group role by internal disagreement, although it broke out of its strait-jacket in the
late 1820s, e.g., in 1828, encouraging 'without delay' the
flow of petitions that had been deferred rather 'than produce
any schism'. But the main instrument at this time was the
United Committee of Dissenters, formed in 1827 as the
pressure-group arm, although delegating some work (e.g.,
the preparation of petitions) to the Body of Ministers of the
Three Denominations established for over a century. In the
Commons Lord John Russell made the running, gaining
ground against the Government, which, taking 'the sense
of the house of commons, and, as was considered, of the
country at large' (as an Anglican journal remarked), was
forced to make the best of it. Using the Lords to salvage
something from the wreckage (as the Government perceived
the progress of the measure), it accepted the repeal of the
Test and Corporation Acts.

Dissenters were mollified, but not finally appeased.
Among many grievances was their continued exclusion from
Cambridge and Oxford; that they were still 'taxed, tithed,
and rated to the support of a system we abjure'; still 'governed by bishops', whom they wanted out of a House of Lords
still dominated by 'a corrupt state church', for which their
remedy was 'a total disconnection between church and
state'.[13] In order to consider such grievances 'with a view to
their Redress', the Protestant Dissenting Deputies (not
Ministers) formed in March 1833 a United Committee
principally made up of their own members with representatives of the General Body of Ministers and of the Protestant
Society. Summarizing the grievances, the United Committee
presented these to the Prime Minister by way of a deputation,
but came away empty-handed. In consequence the campaign was carried into 1834. Despite some individual
ministerial support, a bill to admit Dissenters to the two
ancient Universities was defeated in the House of Lords.
The Dissenting rank and file of the movement accused the
United Committee of timidity, and what had been a demand
for 'disconnection' turned into one for 'full and complete
separation of church and state', i.e., disestablishment. To
promote this, the Religious Freedom Society was founded in

1839, the *Nonconformist Weekly* in 1841, and three years later the British Anti-State Church Association recruited mainly from the Midlands and Scotland under the inspirations of Edward Miall, the Leicester Congregational Minister and later M.P. It was transformed in 1853 into the Liberation Society (shorthand for the 'Society for the Liberation of the Church from State Patronage and Control'). But much of the 'competition' expressed itself in educational terms, through the National Society on the one hand and the British and Foreign Society on the other, as already touched upon above, but also revolving around the compulsory education of children in the factories. This would have had (in the 1843 Bill) an Anglican flavour and so aroused widespread Dissenting opposition, as a result of which, despite some substantial support on both sides of the Commons, the Bill was abandoned as unworkable in the country even if successful in the division lobby.

Like its predecessor, the Anti-State Church Association, the Liberation Society represented a further stage in differentiation. The Dissenting and Catholic associations had 'given' memberships; even the Friends of Civil and Religious Liberty had united 'only' Protestants and Catholics. But the Liberation Society was in principle open to all who, following the 1851 census disclosures that the Anglicans commanded the support of little more than half the country (and only a fifth of the Welsh), favoured disestablishment; just as the National Sunday League (1855) and the Sunday Band Committees (1856) were open to all who favoured permitting the provision of some modest recreation, education (e.g., opening the National Gallery) and entertainment on the Sabbath. Actual recruitment to such bodies no doubt had a narrower range, as would have been true also of the United Kingdom Alliance (1853), which carried the Temperance issue into the election campaigns of the 1860s, and the Anti-Slavery Society formed in 1823 with the backing in particular of Evangelicals and Quakers. Rivalling its exact contemporary, the Catholic Association, in making a nation-wide appeal, the Society's task had been to consummate the earlier efforts, also Christian in inspiration and ethos, that had rid the British Empire of the slave trade but not of slavery. It gained its objective in 1833 but remained at its post (as it does to this day), casting a shadow across the path of less enlightened countries such as (at that time) Britain's European colonial rivals, who made hay while the sun shone, and the United States.

Another great political specialization of the period was the Political Union for the Protection of Public Rights, set on its way in Birmingham in December 1829 by Thomas Attwood and fifteen others, who were activated by the conviction that 'the rights and interests of the middle and lower classes of the people are not efficiently represented in the Commons House of Parliament'.14 If *The Times* is to be believed, some 12,000–15,000 others agreed with them, this being the number reported present at the inaugural meeting held in January. Whatever the truth of that, the Birmingham Political Union was launched, giving the country a nudge. Partly working-class in composition, it was led by middle-class persons in the direction of goals only too likely to serve some sections of the middle class – 'men engaged in trade, and actively concerned in it' as distinct from 'the landed interest, the church, the law, the moneyed interest' who had 'engrossed, as it were, the House of Commons, into their own hands'. By contrast, the National Union of the Working Classes had another perspective. Founded in the spring of 1831, it restored what the Birmingham Political Union had omitted from the traditional Reform programme: annual Parliaments, universal suffrage and the ballot. Such demands echoed old Major Cartwright but more immediately Tom Paine, although the National Union went beyond both of them in seeking to 'obtain for every working man . . . the full value of his labour, and the free disposal of the product of his labour'.

In the following October, at a critical stage in the parliamentary progress of the Reform Bill (its rejection in the Lords), the National Union of the Working Classes was joined by the *National* Political Union. Created by Francis Place and some middle-class Radicals but making room for working-class representatives, it set out against a background of disturbances and riots to crusade for 'the whole

Bill and nothing but the Bill'. That sounded Radical but represented (within the Radical sub-culture) a moderate position, falling far short of the goals (e.g., universal suffrage) of the National Union, which tried to call a protest meeting only to have it prohibited by royal proclamation.

After various vicissitudes, Reform came with the spring, although not as 'nothing but the Bill' nor with anything in it for 'the workers' except the seeds of their future enfranchisement. But the Act represented a kind of equilibrium, if not 'finality', and some trade unionists who had been active in the campaign now bent their energies towards a militant trade unionism flavoured with the ideas of Robert Owen. The Grand National Consolidated Trades Union was the constructive climax of that phase; its collapse in 1834 the anti-climax.

Trade unions were also busy in other ways, as in the movement to limit working hours. Robert Owen had earlier advocated for textile factories a maximum working day of ten and a half hours, not counting one and a half hours for meals. Other manufacturers were less generous; after long consultations with them, the Act of 1819 had provided a twelve-hour day, apart from breaks for meals. Now, in 1830, the Tory-Anglican Richard Oastler, in a letter to the *Leeds Mercury*, initiated a new campaign. In Yorkshire county meetings carried the campaign forward to a Ten Hours Bill. To this broad movement the trades unions were connected through the Short Time Committees set up in various parts of the country but especially in the north. Groups of workers in Lancashire and Yorkshire were more ambitious: their National Society for Promoting National Regeneration (1833) had the eight-hour day as one of its objectives, but the method of achieving it was not political but industrial action. In any case, it took much effort throughout the 1840s to produce even the ten-hour day (1847), and even that Act was in part nullified by the evasion of the employers and by judicial interpretation. The further Act of 1850 conceded a ten-and-a-half-hour day as a compromise between the aims of the Short Time Committees and the eleven hours sought by the employers.

From the middle 1830s the campaign for shorter working

hours had to some extent merged with that against the implementation of the New Poor Law. The centre of gravity was again the north of England, where the leadership again came from the 'Radical Right' in the persons of Richard Oastler and the Reverend J. R. Stephens. But whereas in the south the agricultural labourers, intimidated by their treatment at Tolpuddle in the year of the Poor Law Act (1834), did not put up a fight, the factory workers of Lancashire and Yorkshire strongly resisted. The combined efforts of 'Radical Right' and factory workers were embodied in Anti-Poor Law Associations. At Todmorden the Radical cotton-spinner John Fielden led the way; as long as he lived the Act was never fully implemented there.

Many an Anti-Poor Law Association acquired a new name if not a new local habitation as specific embodiments of Chartism, which also gained impetus from the movement for shorter working hours. Organizationally, Chartism dated from the London Working Men's Association of 1836, initially recruited in particular from those who had been active in Co-operation, trade unionism and the National Union of the Working Classes. Lovett, who spanned all these worlds, took on the secretaryship and drew up the Charter, essentially an expression of the traditional Radical demands from Cartwright onwards.

What London had initiated, Birmingham sustained. The old Political Union, resuscitated in 1837, gave the Charter its blessing, although its original demand had been for household, not universal (manhood) suffrage, that 'grand test of Radicalism', as Bronterre O'Brien, the Chartist leader, called it. Birmingham also invented the strategy of a great petition to Parliament in support of the Charter, and a great Convention in London in support of the petition.

The two streams converged in 1838 in vast meetings in Glasgow and elsewhere. The third stream – the Northern England – was far more turbulent, whipped up by Feargus O'Connor in the *Northern Star* and from the platform, and by J. R. Stephens. Even so the three elements held together long enough to stage the National Convention in London in February 1839, but dissensions precipitated the withdrawal of the Birmingham delegation. There was sniping, too, from (in shorthand) the Left, represented by the London Democratic Association, an 1837 splinter from the London Working Men's Association that espoused, or at least talked about, the politics of confrontation and violence. Through the mind of George Julian Harney, at least, passed the iconoclastic images of Marat, Babeuf and Buonarroti. Later, through the Society of Fraternal Democrats (1845), which had international aspirations, he touched hands with Marx and Engels, who had also been inspired by the French Revolution. But Marx cruelly dismissed him as 'Citizen Hip-hip-hurrah'. The constitutionalists suffered their own humiliations; in the House of Commons that summer of 1839 the Petition went down to a five-to-one defeat. On the Welsh border that autumn the militants fared worse. A Chartist force descended on Newport, bearing its pikes and sticks and muskets. Fourteen were shot by soldiers, better armed and quicker on the trigger; of the fifty wounded, ten succumbed later, all 'fallen in a noble cause' according to eighteen-year-old George Shell's premonition, writing to his parents from Pontypool on the eve of the affray:

'I shall this night be engaged in a glorious struggle for freedom, and should it please God to spare my life I shall see you soon; but, if not, grieve not for me, I shall have fallen in a noble cause. Farewell!   Yours truly . . .'

A fresh start was made in Manchester the following year with the founding of the National Charter Association, working-class and committed to constitutional methods in the form of the second Charter Petition. But soon the movement was at sixes and sevens. When O'Connor was released from York Castle, he took over the Charter Association and ran it for all it was worth, while building himself up in the pages of his *Northern Star*. But Lovett was busy with his National Association for Promoting the Political and Social Improvement of the People, articulating his abiding interest in educational reform as *the* vehicle of emancipation. Soon, in Birmingham, Joseph Sturge, the Quaker banker, was launching the Complete Suffrage Union [*Cf.* document 30], which, adopting almost the whole of the traditional Radical programme and hoping that the working-class would abjure violence, attracted several leading Chartists, including Lovett and O'Brien. In May 1842 the Charter Petition, despite its 3,000,000 signatures, was defeated by a majority nearer six to one than the five to one of 1839. In the wake of that defeat the Metropolitan Parliamentary Reform Association was founded, hoping to wield together both working-class and middle-class Radicals for a less ambitious programme, universal (manhood) suffrage and the ballot but triennial not the annual Parliaments of the Radical tradition. It seems barely to have got off the ground.

The virtual end of the Chartist road was reached in 1848. With the revolutionary crisis from across the Channel reverberating in London, the Chartists converged on the capital to present another Charter Petition. It was presented, and received just seventeen votes, after the celebrated march on Kennington Common had fizzled out and O'Connor had had to drive to Westminster by cab. Thus the episode concluded with a whimper, not a bang, with not enough 'romance' (or martyrdom) to create even a myth. Organizations, however, tend to live longer than the issues they originally encapsulated. Already in 1847 O'Brien had created the National Reform League for the purpose of propagating the faith; in the post-1848 period, he tried out a marriage of convenience with the Owenites, bringing forth the National Rational Society (document 31). Lovett with his People's League also trod the path of sweet reason and persuasion, but the main body, the National Chartist Association, was taken over by Ernest Jones, who, rejuvenated by a spell in jail, strove to commit the movement to Marxism and the class struggle. But before the decade was out he was ready to collaborate with the middle classes, some of whom had also been going it alone sporadically in the National Parliamentary and Financial Reform Association, of which Joseph Hume had been the catalyst. Now (in 1858) Jones proposed to 'meet the middle classes half-way', provided they would accept universal manhood suffrage and preferably the ballot. In the Northern Reform Union of 1858, based on Newcastle upon Tyne, the organized miners and ironworkers did work with some of the middle classes for both universal suffrage and the ballot, although taxation reform was also a major objective. In the same year the Reform Association made its appearance, launched by the Radical, J. A. Roebuck.

Reform of the relevant kind lay in the future, but some other ground had been gained. 1839 was the year of the great Chartist Petition and of the Newport 'shoot-out' that followed in the wake of its rejection; it was also the year of Harmony Hall in Hampshire, the Owenite experiment in communal living (document 31). This went the way of the earlier Harmony 'flesh' (in the United States), but in 1844 Owenite socialists connected with the Rational Society formed the Rochdale Pioneers' Society, some of whom had invested in Harmony Hall. Owenite in ethos, the Pioneers decided upon more limited goals, hence their Toad Lane retail store, but from that modest beginning came consumers' co-operation in this country. Producers' co-operation did not disappear but was practised (or sought) through the General Labour Redemption Societies, as at Leeds, Stockport and Bury in the mid-1840s. Towards the end of that decade Louis Blanc's celebrated attempt to put socialism into the workshop inspired on this side of the Channel other ventures of co-operative production. Even the hard-headed men of the New Model Unionism, the Amalgamated Society of Engineers, tried their hand at it with factories in the East End and at Liverpool. But the Society for Promoting Working Men's Associations (1850) was nearer to the Louis Blanc example, embodying a generically ethical, specifically Christian, socialism.

The efforts of the Christian Socialists, as of the Dissenters and the Chartists, were more than matched by those undertaken to eradicate the Corn Laws, dating in their modern form from 1815, which, overcoming opposition, forbade imports absolutely until the home price reached famine level, and 1828, which permitted imports but regulated these by way of a sliding scale. In a sense, Byron's *The Age of Bronze* (1823) prepares the ground, but the direct ideological attack on the Corn Laws may be dated from Thompson's *Catechism* in 1828; the organizational, from the Associations formed in London (1836), in Glasgow (summer, 1838), and in Manchester (autumn, 1838), the immediate stimuli coming from industrial depression and a series of bad harvests with consequent rising prices. Of the three early initiatives, only Manchester's was sustained, despite the initial awkwardness of its relationship to the Chamber of Commerce (document 20).[15] In February 1839, with a network extending to many of the great urban centres of the north, a conference was staged in London from which the Anti-Corn Law League emerged.

Despite this launching, and the establishment in 1840 of the Metropolitan Anti-Corn Law Association (document 23), the headquarters of the League was located in Manchester. The history of the League has been traced several times. Here one can note first the unswerving dedication to a single objective, a strategic decision made early on and rightly maintained despite the bad advice to the contrary, e.g., from Robert Owen writing on behalf of the Rational Society (document 31). The methods included initially a great propaganda and organizational drive interspersed with forays to and within the Commons, where Radicals presented petitions and opened debates; then, with the growing awareness that one had to cultivate and so organize the electorate itself, intervene in elections and even to qualify voters beforehand; the mobilization of prestigious allies, such as ministers of religion, who as Dissenters already disaffected, somehow managed to convey the flavour of a moral crusade that all right-thinking men should support; the mobilization of youthful energies (document 24); deputations to the Prime Minister (Peel from 1841) and other senior Ministers; all shot through with a massive attempt to influence public opinion by journalism (its organ came out weekly from 1842), public meetings and the distribution of bundles of tracts on an unprecedented scale.

In 1842 Peel took the wind out of the sails of the campaign by his new Corn Law sharply reducing the rates of the sliding scale of 1828. To what extent Peel was 'acting out' his free-trade tendencies at an opportune time as distinct from being responsive to the League's campaign, it is impossible to say. He had been a member of the Government in 1828, when, as one aspect of the free trade movement led by

Huskisson, the sliding scale had been introduced; and a Lewes journalist shrewdly remarked in 1843, commenting on the complaint that Peel had done little since coming into office: if Peel did legislate, he would follow Huskisson, of whom he was a disciple, so he would only 'carry the free trade and reciprocity policy of that foreigner-favouring statesman further'.[16] What is clear is that some combination of League activities and Peel's new Corn Law 'decomposed' for the first time the Landed Interest, until now so fundamental, pervasive and 'built into' government that (in accordance with the elucidation in the general introduction) it has not merited separate treatment in distinctive pressure-group terms. Such 'decomposition' took the form of Agricultural Protection Societies, planned at the Smithfield Show in December 1843, which was attended by agriculturalists from all over the country. Essex led the way, followed by Sussex, Warwickshire[17] and Lincolnshire. By January 1844 an editorial in the *Brighton Gazette* could claim that 'the counter-movement is in real existence' and anticipated that 'the whole may be ultimately amalgamated into one national and magnificent COUNTER-LEAGUE'[18] (document 26). In that anticipation the voice was that of a Brighton journalist but possibly an echo from the Duke of Richmond, whose seat was (and still is) nearby, who had been present at Smithfield and who had already emerged as a leader. In any event, within the month the newspaper was recording 'the intention of the Duke of Richmond and other members of both Houses to form a Metropolitan Society for the Protection of British Agriculture', which soon turned out to be the body known officially as the Central Agricultural Protection Society for the United Kingdom, and unofficially as the Anti-League.

Some proponents of the movement visualized it as 'a happy blending together of landlord and tenant' and even of 'the labourer' (document 25). Others presented it as a movement of tenant farmers: 'This is an Association, be it observed, got up, not by landlords, but by tenant farmers', pronounced the *Morning Herald*.[19] Such assertions as these have been accepted by some economic historians[20] but do not hold for Sussex at least, where 'a large proportion of the most influential landowners and land occupiers in the county'[21] had given the original impetus; while at the Chichester meeting, the support came not only from tenant farmers but proprietors, 'many' with 1000–1200 acres. At the inaugural meeting of the Sussex Society at Steyning towards the end of January, the chairman claimed that the meeting 'originated with the tenantry' but thought it necessary to deny that they had been 'incited by our land-lords to do this'.[22] The meeting was faithfully reported in the *Brighton Gazette* under 'Farmers, Tradesmen, and Others', but these 'Others' did not deserve to be treated on a level with 'miscellaneous'. In the running of the Society, the landed proprietors and tenant farmers shared equally in twenty-four of the places on the Central Committee of Management; the president (Duke of Richmond), vice-presidents (including the Earl of Egmont, Lord Gage, and the Earl of Sheffield) and three trustees (Sheffield again as well as the Earl of Abergavenny) were also members *ex officio*. No doubt the strategy was to give the appearance of a farmers' movement. Lord Henniker, M.P., self-described as a 'Suffolk landowner', rather gave the game away at a meeting of the East Suffolk Protection Society early in 1844, when he was at pains to explain his presence despite its having 'been said to him since he had arrived in town, and previously that this matter should be left in the hands of the tenant farmers'.[23] A reading of the Sussex newspapers for the period supports Miss Mary Lawson-Tancred's view that although 'the Anti-League was always referred to as a farmers' movement it was, in reality, a combination of country gentlemen, clergymen and the more important farmers'.[24]

What this 'combination' set out to achieve was to main-tain agricultural protection by hitting back at the Anti-Corn Law League in the rural areas through the M.P.s and by answering, or at least dealing with, the arguments on the League's own level. It was by no means ineffective, but it could scarcely turn back the tide that was washing away not only Protection but also, as many perceived the issue, the political power of aristocracy, quite apart from holding the dyke against the particular exigency in 1845 of another failure of the potato crop – the staple diet – in Ireland. Peel argued that to meet this crisis suspension of the Corn Laws was 'inevitable', but several of his major cabinet colleagues disagreed. He resigned in early December only to be recalled before Christmas. In the New Year he placed the repeal of the Corn Laws in the context of tariff reform in general, but did not escape the charge (by the Duke of Richmond) that what he proposed 'was contrary to every principle ever brought forward by the present government when they were seeking for office. These changes ought not to be made without an appeal to the country' (document 27). He could see 'no difference between the government of the country and the Anti-Corn Law League ... they were the authors of the whole of the change which the Minister was about to propose'.[25] Despite the Duke and his Anti-League, the deed was done, although it broke the party as well as Peel, 'a name, severely censured' by many, as he feared, but perhaps 'sometimes remembered with expressions of goodwill in the abodes of those whose lot it is to labour ... when they shall recruit their exhausted strength with abundant and untaxed food, the sweeter because it is no longer leavened by a sense of injustice'.[26]

1860–1970

Structural differentiation in this period proceeded rapidly and extensively. So far as concerns this inquiry, the central trends were the continued decline in terms of public policy-making of the functionally specialized but politically diffuse groups; the rise of new specializations, some 'merely' domestic, others in part politically oriented, many more the groundwork for 'peak' structures that were distinctly or presumptively political; the continued vitality for most of the period, but ultimate weakening, of the open-to-all specialization (or 'pure' pressure group). This was a weakening in several senses: in terms of its own past; of the newer, essentially occupational, groups and their peaks; and of the political parties as vehicles for the conveying of public policies.

At the very outset of the period, the banding together of individual chambers of commerce as the Associated British Chambers of Commerce (document 38) proved to be a portent. In a sense the original title was apt enough, since several of the major units (Glasgow, Manchester, Liverpool) kept aloof for about a generation. To a considerable extent, the A.B.C.C. (today, Association of British Chambers of Commerce) looked 'inward' to domestic duties, but it soon occupied itself with changes in the bankruptcy laws, the patent laws and other issues of public policy.

From the 1860s, too, employers continuously organized themselves to 'deal with' the trade unions, often in more senses than one. The resulting structures included, in the 1860s, the ironmasters of midland and northern England,[1] and the Clyde Shipbuilders and Engineers;[2] in the 1870s, the Iron Trades Employers, the National Federation of Associated Employers of Labour (document 47), and the National Association of Master Builders;[3] the Shipbuilding Employers' Federation of 1889, not to be confused with the Shipping Federation (anti-closed shop) of a year later, and in the succeeding decade, the Federation of Master Cotton Spinners Associations, and the Engineering Employers' Federation (to give it the title adopted only in 1899 and to which it reverted, after two later changes, only in 1961).

As if changing partners in a progressive dance, employers also disported themselves in other ways. Almost from the opening of this period they sought to temper the keen wind of competition to the lambs that stood in danger of being shorn. Their protective screens were the trade association and the cartel. In the sense of a simple selling 'arrangement', the cartel may perhaps be traced to the Newcastle upon Tyne Vend, a device (1770s to 1840) for ensuring that 'carrying coal' *to* London *from* Newcastle should be properly remunerative. Now the cartel became more common: in 1879, the Shipping *Conference* provided rebates on freight charges by a group of shippers in exchange for a group of merchants' giving exclusive dealing. By the 1890s cartelization was proceeding rapidly, especially in textiles:[4] the Bradford Dyers' Association is an example.

Trade associations had been tried earlier in the century,

in the form (e.g.) of the Booksellers' Association (1848), which failed four years later to enforce, with the help of some publishers, a net book agreement;[5] and of the Manchester Grocers (1855). Neither lasted long. In this period, the Soap Manufacturers' Association of 1867 marks the new beginning. By the 1880s 'almost every trade' was so organized, essentially for the purpose of setting minimum prices, often combined, however, with a territorial division of the market.[6] In 1888 the National Federation of Property Owners was formed to defend ownership and private enterprise. Retailing was not to be left out. At Birmingham as well as Manchester, the grocers revived (1873), reaching peak level in 1891 (Federation of Grocers' Associations of the United Kingdom). This was followed in 1896 by the Proprietary Articles Trade Association, by which time resale price maintenance had taken root. That decade also found the booksellers and publishers on the march again: in 1895 the Publishers' Association managed to establish a net book agreement. By a nice touch of irony, the first volume to which it was applied was Marshall's *Principles of Economics*. To this decade belongs the National Chamber of Trade (1897) (document 73), as well as the British or Employers' Parliamentary Council (1898) (document 52). This tried to get to grips with the Government, immediately over the Eight Hours' Bill but ultimately against its general regulating trend. It prepared the way through the Manufacturers' Association (1905) and other bodies for the Federation of British Industries (document 59). Meanwhile a different focus had been achieved through the setting-up of the Institute of Directors (1903), a sign perhaps of the growing tendency for management to be divorced (in the later phrase) from ownership.

This raising of the structural level combined with growing politicization can be discerned even in agriculture. Now the old landed interest (or country interest) was breaking up into its component parts. The Central Chamber of Agriculture tried to hold things together (1866), but by then the agricultural labourer was also astir, in Scotland and various parts of England, and was organized by 1872. In 1879 the tenant farmers followed suit with the Farmers' Alliance.[7]

What proved to be the last attempt to defeat this centrifugal tendency took the form in 1892 of the National Agricultural Union (document 51), yet another peak of this period, bringing together the landowners, tenants and labourers. Unlike the Central Chamber, which continued to exist but essentially in the market towns, the Agricultural Union penetrated into the villages, where the labourer was by now no longer organized, but the initial success (500 branches were claimed) was not sustained. At the turn of the century the Agricultural Union turned into the Agricultural Organization Society, and the 'threefold cord' (as Lord Winchelsea had called it) finally snapped. In 1904 tenant farmers set up the Lincolnshire Farmers' Union, which became the National Farmers' Union four years later (document 56). From the same geographical area, in 1906, came the Eastern Counties Agricultural and Small Holders Union; a national body followed in 1912 (the National Agricultural Labourers' and Rural Workers' Union). Meanwhile, in 1907, the Central Land Association had been formed. As these were the landowners (it is now the Country Landowners' Association) (document 79), the dissolution of the old country interest was complete, except that a Land Union (Lincolnshire again) soon broke away, apparently to the Right.

In industry in the conventional sense, unions had by then been long engaged in both raising the structural level and infusing it with 'politics'. Some part of the groundwork for this was laid in 1860, when the New Model Unionism was augmented by the arrival of the Amalgamated Society of Carpenters. Other unions revealed a disposition to undertake political influence. In 1861 a leader of the building trades attended the War Office in order to protest against the use of troops in strike-breaking. The miners continued to march to their own drummer, the Miners' National Association of 1863 being followed by the more militant Amalgamated Association of Miners (1869). Even when less well organized, the miners had undertaken political as well as industrial action. Now they sought to amend the law of Master and Servant, which bore more heavily on them than on other trade unionists, whose active support, however, was secured since the implications of its very title were generally regarded as objectionable. In this campaign the miners were joined by those new territorial entities, the trades councils. London's, set up in 1860, was the first to be permanently established: its purpose was 'to watch over the interests of labour, political and social, both in and out of Parliament'. The Glasgow Trades Council was in the van of the trades councils' contingent from 1864, convening the first ever trade-union delegate conference. Parliamentary lobbying, public meetings and newspaper articles helped to bring about the appointment of a Select Committee and, in 1867, an amending act removed the worst of the discrimination in the law of Master and Servant.

As bodies embracing unions within particular geographical areas, trades councils already represented some raising of the structural level, but in that very year, 1867, the tendency was strengthened. From Manchester, at the beginning of the year, the United Kingdom Alliance of Organized Trades was launched, with headquarters, however, in Sheffield. Curiously enough, other tendencies towards higher-level growth were also linked to Sheffield, which had been the scene (in 1866–7) of unpardonable violence by some trade unionists against 'blacklegs'. In that context the Queen's Bench judges decided (in January 1867) that trade unions could not, after all, prosecute officials who dipped their hands in the till, and even that trade unions were, after all, in restraint of trade and so were illegal if not criminal. The Government announced a Royal Commission, one response to which came from the London Working Men's Association, founded in 1866, its title echoing the body with the same name of a generation earlier. Uniting 'working men of different trades', this new L.W.M.A. set out to promote interests of the industrial classes, and to get a lodger clause inserted into the Reform Bill. Its leader, George Potter, soon waited upon the Home Secretary in the hope of influencing the membership of the Royal Commission. When, also in 1867, the London Trades Council, dominated by the 'Amalgamated' leaders, took fright at the public outcry that followed the Sheffield violence, the L.W.M.A. took up the reins. Its Conference attracted the Northerners but was boycotted by the 'Amalgamateds', who sponsored a Conference of Amalgamated Trades. However, since nothing concentrates the mind so much as the prospect of immediate execution, the trade unions trundled along in the direction of a united movement, reaching (at Manchester, in 1868) the Trades Union Congress (documents 45 and 46).

In 1870 the T.U.C. became more representative when it recruited most of the principal unions from the now declining U.K. Alliance of Organized Trades. The following year saw the entry of the 'Amalgamateds' into the fold. That the T.U.C. was 'only' an annual meeting and not a federation, however, was demonstrated in 1874, when, at the Liverpool Congress, the Carpenters and Joiners, the Ironworkers and the Boilermakers took time off to discuss greater unity, with the (paradoxical) result that early in the New Year they set up the Federation of Organized Trade Societies. Mainly drawing on some of the metal and building trades, it was to prepare the ground in particular for those 'struggles between capital and labour' that 'will probably be conducted in future on a far more gigantic scale than we have hitherto witnessed'.[8]

The T.U.C., meanwhile, had been engaged in a struggle along a more limited front. Initially intended neither to strengthen industrial bargaining power nor to be political like the L.W.M.A. but rather a forum for discussion, it was soon to be committed not only to 'bringing the trades into a closer alliance' but also to taking 'action in all parliamentary matters pertaining to the general interests of the working classes'. Opportunity to practise what had been passed (if not fervently preached) was not lacking, for the Royal Commission Report of 1869 contained unpalatable recommendations from the majority. Congress decided in March 1871 to oppose the consequential legislation; the body of five charged with the work turned into the Parliamentary Committee. The Trade Union Act of 1871 protected union funds as well as unions themselves, now declared not to be illegal because in restraint of trade. However, from its other sleeve, the Government plucked, in the very same year, the Criminal Law Amendment Act, which declared peaceful picketing, the standard means to the now approved end,

illegal. Against that the Parliamentary Committee organized
deputations and campaigns, which trade unions generally
joined in from 1873. Two years later the incoming (Conservative) Government not only legalized peaceful picketing
and made other concessions but also (by another Act)
converted Masters and Servants into Employers and
Workmen. The change was not merely symbolic but one
of substance, providing a new form of civil contract more in
keeping with the age.

For about the next quarter of a century the T.U.C.,
in so far as it was a pressure group, busied itself with industrial reform, notably amendments to the Factory Acts,
gaining a considerable victory at Asquith's hands in 1895.
But in 1901 the judiciary (in a House of Lords decision)
once again revealed itself to be a virtual part of the policy-
making process, conventionally ascribed to Government
and Parliament. The subsequent campaign by the Parliamentary Committee entailed drafting a Trades Dispute Bill,
for which it then lobbied M.P.s and intervened with determination in the convenient general election of January
1906. Sustained pressure on the new Government and
Parliament produced the Trades Disputes Act of 1906, which
gave the T.U.C. most of what it had asked for. In 1909,
however, yet another judicial decision undermined the assumption of a political role by trade unions, with the added
advantage of undermining the financial support by unions
for the young Labour Party, the original issue turning on the
spending of union funds for political purposes. The upshot
was a compromise embodied in the Trade Union Act of 1913.

The emergence of a trade-union peak and within it of a
pressure-group specialization (the Parliamentary Committee) never looked like excluding such activity at the lower
levels. In 1867 the textile unions had opened a campaign
for an eight-hour day in place of the ten and a half hours
then worked. Unsuccessful in that, they sponsored in 1869 a
Factory Acts Reform Association. Others pressed for the
intermediate goal of a nine-hour day. In the early 1870s in
the north-east rank-and-file engineers set up the Nine Hours
League. The movement spread and had some local success,
but in 1871 the cotton-spinners were appealing in a manifesto

for the same limitation, later broadening their goal to cover various industrial reforms. The Act of 1875 did not concede the nine hours but helped indirectly by making fifty-six and a half hours the maximum working week for women and children.

The miners, too, made their own running, lobbying M.P.s and waiting on Ministers. By such methods they gained much ground in a series of Acts between 1860 and 1887. In 1889 they even created a further specialization, the Miners' Federation of Great Britain, not, apparently, in response to the National Association of Colliery Managers founded the year before, but immediately for common industrial action, including, however, the objective of the eight-hour day.[9] This was more or less achieved in the Coal Mines Regulation Act of 1908. An even greater degree of political specialization was displayed in the late 1880s in the United Textile Factory Workers' Association, which drew together (1886) the cotton-spinners, weavers, card-room operatives and others purely for 'the removal of any grievances . . . for which Parliamentary or Governmental interference is required'. The same upward 'thrust', although less politicized, is discernible in the Federation of Engineering and Shipbuilding Trades, sponsored in 1891 by the Boilermakers, but from which the Amalgamated Engineers kept aloof.

Cutting less complicated patterns, white-collar workers were also forming organizations and, by virtue of their objectives, tending towards pressure-group activity. Thus, in the 1890s, the shop assistants began trying, through the good offices of M.P.s, to have shop hours regulated by Parliament. The London Municipal Officers of the same period led on to the National Association of Local Government Officers (1905), which had to be political to achieve, for example, its goal of superannuation. Nearer the professional end of the continuum, the schoolteachers had been organized since the mid-1860s, especially in the (General) Associated Body of Church School Masters (A.B.C.S.). Re-modelled and re-named, it proceeded in 1868 to join some miscellaneous groups in forming the London Association of Church Teachers, from the start a pressure group for improving the status of teachers and for supporting the Church in the growing controversy over elementary education. When, in 1870, that was resolved by the creation of a State system, a new body followed quickly on the heels of the Act – the National Union of Elementary Teachers (N.U.E.T.) (document 44). Growth was rapid: within two years it could boast of over 5,000 members; five years later the total had doubled. In 1902 (that year of a landmark Education Act) membership stood at some 47,000. From the very first the N.U.E.T. was political, exerting 'pressure'[10] on the Education Department and on Parliament, sometimes in a trade-union sense (as in the 1875 campaign for pensions for teachers) but also in terms of educational policy. By 1900 (now the N.U.T.) 'it had several substantial victories to its credit'.[11] But the climax for that era was reached in the Education Act of 1902. The Bill's provisions were scrutinized by the union's Parliamentary Committee, which secured a number of changes advocated in Conference resolutions. As a result, the act 'met the main demands' of the union (and of others) by abolishing the school boards and concentrating responsibility for both secondary and elementary education in Local Education Authorities (L.E.A.s) based on the principal local Government units and linked to the new (1899) Board of Education.

Some of the new professional bodies were less politicized than the schoolteachers, e.g., the Law Society, which arose in 1877 from the ashes of the Society of Attorneys, Solicitors, Proctors, etc., and the Bar Committee (1883), replaced in 1894 by the General Council of the Bar. On the other hand again, the British Medical Association (document 82) disclosed marked political propensities, if not continuously. From the late 1860s it had been growing rapidly, reaching 4,400 in 1871, twice the N.U.E.T.'s total at that (early) date. In the longer run, it was naturally outdistanced by the N.U.T., which in 1900 found itself with 43,000 members compared with the B.M.A.'s 18,000. The corresponding totals in 1911 were 72,400 and 25,000. But 'densities' (the proportion of actual members to the potential number available) had been increasing: from about 28 per cent (of the registered) in 1871 to 50–60 per cent (of the number in

practice) in 1911. On that basis, the B.M.A. engaged effectively in politics though its Parliamentary Bills Committee,
which, formed in 1863, operated through three M.P.s,
two of them doctors by training. A 'thriving'[12] pressure
group, this Committee offered in 1871 successful opposition
to one bill but support for several others. With other elements
in the profession, the B.M.A. exerted influence that resulted
in the establishment of the Royal Sanitary Commission of
1869, whose Report was productive of the Local Government
Act of 1871, which put public health and the Poor Law
under one roof. A year later the whole country was divided
into sanitary districts, each with a sanitary authority and a
Medical Officer of Health. But in 1911 an epic conflict
with the Government broke out over Lloyd George's
National Insurance Bill. As early as 1887 a B.M.A. committee had recommended that medical attendance on the
poorer classes should be undertaken on an insurance basis.
As recently as 1909 the Annual Representative Meeting had
called on the B.M.A. Council to draft a scheme for a comprehensive public health service. But the Government's
1911 version of such a scheme was indignantly opposed.
Under a threat of boycott, four of the B.M.A.'s 'Six Cardinal
Points' were conceded. Over the remainder a battle royal
ensued, from which the Government appeared to emerge
victorious, although there was point to the *Westminster
Gazette*'s comment: 'We all admire people who don't know
when they are beaten. The trouble with the B.M.A. is that
it doesn't know when it has won.'[13]

As the manual worker and the professional man continued
to build up their organizational structure to designs determined earlier, that 'other half of the human race' began to
discover for the first time nationally the joys and benefits of
associated action. Stimulated by observation of women's
trade unionism in the United States, Emma Paterson set
up on her return the Women's Protective and Provident
League of 1874, which later evolved into the Women's
Trade Union League. A peak, but for many different kinds
of women's organizations, was reached in 1895 in the
National Council of Women Workers, now the National

Council of Women. Meanwhile, Emma Paterson had spanned in her own person the two realms, industrial and political, in which a small number of courageous women were fighting for their elementary rights, for she had been active in the women's suffrage movement. Launched in Sheffield in 1851, this movement had accelerated during the 1860s. In 1866 women's suffrage committees blossomed in both Manchester and London, the first of which grew within the year into the first of the permanent societies. This, joining hands with London and Edinburgh, turned into a confederation – the National Society for Women's Suffrage (1867). Thirty years later the National Union of Women's Suffrage Societies (1897) kept up that tradition of quiet persuasion through Parliament, but the founding of the Women's Social and Political Union (W.S.P.U.) in 1903 marks the rising tide of impatience and the beginning of the resort to physical force. The breakaway Women's Freedom League (1907) disclaimed physical force but did adopt 'constitutional militancy', such as boycotting the 1911 Census Returns ('No Vote, No Census') and not only refusing to pay income tax but even to stamp the gardener's insurance card or take out a dog licence. (This is also the period, 1909, of the breakaway of the National Union of Women Teachers from the N.U.T. on the issue of equal pay.)

Despite the practical help (as distinct from expressions of goodwill) of such men as Richard Pankhurst, Frederick Pethick-Lawrence and others, the women's suffrage movement was essentially what the words convey and in that sense 'exclusive'. In principle the men's side of the suffrage movement was more open-ended in so far as it recruited those who already enjoyed the vote, but in practice it was less broadly based than it seemed, keeping itself not merely to men but to some extent attracting particular categories of men. Just before this period opened, the Northern Reform Union had received much support from the miners and ironworkers of the north-east. What the north-east initiated (or revived) in the late 1850s, London sustained in the 1860s. Out of two 'lock-outs' of the London building-trades workers (1859–61) came the belief that 'the working class could get little advancement until they had more political power'. In 1862 that flame was fanned by the American Civil War, 'the working classes as rule defending the Federalists'; in the autumn the Manhood Suffrage and Vote by Ballot Association was created. In composition it was essentially working-class, unlike the National Reform Union established in Manchester in 1864, whose leaders were for the most part middle-class. They accepted (among other policies) the Ballot but not Manhood Suffrage, preferring Household Suffrage, and so on occasion, even in the face of the common enemy, crossed swords with the other association and *its* successor, the National Reform League (1865). The centre of gravity of the League remained London and the South as its social composition remained largely working-class.

Unlike the International Working Men's Association (the 'First International') founded in London the year before, attracting some indigenous trade-union activists, the National Reform League relied on forming an iron fist within the velvet glove for voting rights. This was the time when, in England and Wales, five adult men out of six, and the great majority of the working class, had no vote. 'The consequence is, that our laws are partial, being made by a class, for a class' wrote George Howell, secretary of the Reform League, in 1865 addressing trade unionists throughout the land. The Liberal Government of that year wrestled with the issue of electoral reform but, failing to agree, subsided in June 1866 to the advantage of the Conservatives. In July the Reform League organized the famous Hyde Park demonstration; the collapse of the railings was rather less resounding than the fall of the Bastille, but, coupled with a nation-wide agitation, the event was claimed as a famous victory, 'which compelled the Tory Government to bring in a Reform Bill early in 1867'.

Certainly the act enfranchized the urban worker. It was a 'leap in the dark' in more senses than one. One latent, or unintended, consequence was a stimulus to independent working-class representation in Parliament, the road to which had already been cleared in 1858 by the Act abolishing the property qualification for M.P.s. Now came the vote itself for the urban workers. With that victory the scene changes. The middle-class National Reform Union kept going, aiming, among other things, for the county vote and the (secret) ballot, but spilling over into reform of the land laws, and so entering an area being ploughed by the Land and Labour League (1867), which sought nationalization of the land, and the Land Tenure Reform Association (1870) which, led by Mill, pursued several objectives, including the elimination of primogeniture. The working-class followed at least three main paths. In the north-east the Northern Reform Union was reconstituted, combining with the Miners' Franchise Union in pursuit of such goals as putting lodgers on the electoral roll. In London the (new) London Working Men's Association launched by George Potter (in 1866) was first off the mark, seeing in the 1867 Act the opportunity for extensive working-class represen-tation in Parliament. Three trade-union candidates tried their luck in the 1868 election, and gained experience if not seats. Meanwhile, the rival National Reform League had been closed down, but early in 1869 a Working Men's Parlia-mentary Association in effect prepared the ground for the Labour Representation League later in the year. By 1872, when the secret ballot was at last secured, the case for 'the direct representation of labour in Parliament' was argued in a pamphlet. Two years later two of the fifteen working-class candidates were successful in constituencies where Liberals had not put in an appearance. In one sense, this historic pair was hardly independent, having to sit with the Liberal Opposition in that 'Lib–Lab' arrangement which survived into the 1890s. All the same a step had been taken which was to lead to the creation of 'a distinct Labour Party in Parliament' (as even the Fabians advocated in 1887): it was achieved *de facto* at the 1892 election and organizationally, as an Independent Labour Party, the following year.

Initially, even the I.L.P. did not constitute a very distinct party in the Commons, if only because no more than three such Independents had been elected in 1892. Nor was it bound to the T.U.C. The watershed was reached in 1900, when the I.L.P., Fabians, Social Democratic Federation (S.D.F.) and trade-union spokesmen met in London to produce the Labour Representation Committee. The S.D.F.

D

wanted the working-class movement to form in the Commons 'a distinct party' embodying 'a recognition of the class war', but its motion was lost and the following year it went its own way. But the historic concept of 'a distinct Labour Party in Parliament' with its own Whips was accepted. What was lacking was money: the 1858 Act had removed the property qualification for election as M.P.s but M.P.s were still unpaid. In 1903 the Labour Representation Committee, whose constituent members were organizations, not individuals, started its own political fund with a modest *per capita* levy; trade unions sowed the wind of their own individual political funds only to reap the Osborne whirlwind in 1909 (as already noted). Meanwhile, in 1906, twenty-nine scions of the L.R.C. had been returned to Parliament, and the substitution of 'Labour Party' as the official title may be taken as marking Labour's coming of age in the House of Commons. But what made possible a successful career beyond a coming of age was the Liberal Government's readiness to overturn the Osborne Judgement by the Trade Union Act of 1913. Thereafter the Labour Party would be able to draw upon the trade-union purse; the terms for drawing would vary, but not the availability.

One theme underlying the rise of the Labour Party is the transmutation of pressure group into political party. The trend was not always in that direction: the Primrose League (document 49) divested itself of its party clothes in the hope of appearing to be more 'neutral', i.e., potentially more of a pressure group. On the other hand, in one of its main manifestations, the Liberal development paralleled Labour's. Its source was the continuing dispute about the role of State and Church in the organization of elementary education, in which the Nonconformists (descended, as it were, from Dissenters) naturally took a keen interest. In the 1860s discussion centred in Manchester, where the Education Aid Society, erected (in 1864) to buttress the voluntary system, learned from experience to give its reluctant support to State provision. But the national leadership was assumed by Birmingham, where the National Education League of 1869 came out for a system of elementary education that would be universal, compulsory, unsectarian and free, i.e., paid for out of public funds. On the other hand, the organizational model was still that forged in Manchester for the Anti-Corn Law League: a network of branches throughout the country kept in touch by a monthly journal; there were public meetings and pamphleteering on a grand scale. This was financed by local manufacturers, many of whom were Nonconformists. One of them was to be of outstanding importance, Joseph Chamberlain, whose Unitarianism was partly responsible for his entering into the politics of education as vice-chairman of the League.

Despite the efforts of the League, the Government in its 1870 Education Bill plumped for a compromise arrangement in which the State would make good the gaps in the voluntary system. Chamberlain mounted a campaign against the proposals, using the League machinery to generate petitions and deputations to local M.P.s; he also led a mass deputation of League members and M.P.s to Number 10 to wait upon Gladstone. Despite the parallel efforts of an *ad hoc* (Birmingham-based) campaign body, the Central Nonconformist Committee, whose national petition was signed by two Nonconformist Ministers out of three (in England and Wales), the Bill went through largely unamended, although the system was made compulsory in 1880 and free in 1891.

Long before that time, Chamberlain had been advocating not only 'Free Schools', but 'Free Church, Free Land, . . . Free Labour', a programme for the Liberals that could be taken as marking one aspect of the transition from pressure group to political party. From 1873 to 1874, Chamberlain, enjoying his vantage-point as mayor of Birmingham, had the map of England unrolled before his eyes. Attwood, of the Birmingham Political Union, had stood back from 'the system', exercising pressure on it; he, Chamberlain, would now work inside it. In 1874 he had remarked: 'I do not think the League will do', and went on to contemplate 'a new organization'.[14] This turned out, in 1877, to be the National Liberal Federation: the League had been buried a few months earlier.

Meanwhile a different kind of pure pressure group had been slowly developing, expressive of a concern for the

environment, the amenities, for those unable to help themselves. The charitable field is too vast even to sketch, but the
opening of our period was notable for the creation of the
Salvation Army, Dr Barnardo's, and the Charity Organization Society (now the Family Welfare Association), all in
the 1860s, followed by the British Red Cross in 1870.
Potentially more political was the National Society for the
Prevention of Cruelty to Children of 1884, a tardy com-
plement to the Royal Society for the Prevention of Cruelty to
Animals of just sixty years earlier.

Precipitated by a particular exigency, the Commons
Preservation Society appeared in 1865 (document 40). It
joined forces in 1899 with the National Footpaths Society,
adding 'Open Spaces', perhaps significantly, in 1910.
William Morris sponsored in 1877 the militant Society for
the Preservation of Ancient Buildings (S.P.A.B.). The 1880s
produced the Dartmoor Preservation Association and the
National Trust, which 'went public' in 1895 and statutory
in 1907 (document 54). The Society for Checking the Abuses
of Public Advertising (S.C.A.P.A.) was founded in 1893.
Five years later it launched an initiative to bring about a
peak organization for amenity groups, but in a decade when
so many peaks were successfully established, the attempt
failed. These are just samples of amenity bodies necessarily
oriented towards government. Of a different order but also
inevitably a pressure group was the Malthusian League
(1877), catalyzed by the Bradlaugh–Besant trials. Postulating
over-population but unwilling to rely upon abstinence to
rectify it, the founders began the public advocacy of birth-
control.[15] Up to 1913, they had only a small 'attentive
public', no doubt as middle-class as they were themselves,
but then they began to reach a wider public, including the
working class. Their immediate goal became the dispensation
of birth-control advice at Maternity and Child Welfare
Centres.

In the fifty years, then, between 1860 and the first decade
or so of this century, the secondary-group structure relevant
to this inquiry assumed its characteristic modern form of
great range capped with peaks of varying heights. What the

First World War and the consequential policies did was to 'fill in' the structure without greatly altering its general outline. The Government of a country that had become for the first time a nation in arms had to manage accordingly. Existing trade associations were drawn into a close embrace. Where trade associations did not exist, the Government saw to it that they were invented. This increasingly complex network required co-ordination at least. Some of this came from the National Union of Manufacturers (1915), but more from the Federation of British Industries the following year (document 59). Under the leadership of Dudley Docker, the industrialist, and William Peat, the chartered accountant, the F.B.I. joined Birmingham's British Manufacturers to Manchester's Employers' Parliamentary Association.[16] One consequence of this close working relationship between Government and industry was that, by the end of the war (an official committee would report), 'in every important branch of industry in the U.K. there is an increasing tendency to the formation of trade associations and combinations', and a survey of the work of the thirty sub-committees studying specific industries prompted the conclusion that 'free competition no longer governs the business world'.[17] Within a decade or so, even the economic theorists would discover 'imperfect competition'.

Industry, manufacturing especially, had now found its own voice. Soon the significance of the F.B.I. would be marked by the granting of a Royal Charter (document 59). Since chambers of commerce had always included manufacturers, the A.B.C.C. was indeed weakened by these developments, as its official historian has remarked.[18] All the same, as a peak for a base of 101 chambers with a membership that had risen from 25,000 to 45,000 by the end of the war, its representative position was not inconsiderable. On the other hand, the F.B.I. itself proved to be a lesser peak than had been intended. By 1915 some 1,200 employers' organizations extended across the land for labour-relations purposes. The F.B.I. was meant to encompass them as well as the trade associations. But the intention was not pursued, or was thwarted, and the gap was filled in 1919 by the founding of the National Confederation of Employers'

Organizations (better remembered as the British Employers' Confederation) (documents 67 and 69).

What the war years had accelerated, the post-war years sustained. Seventy-six trade associations were registered between 1920 and 1939.[19] One of the most important of these covered the steel industry (documents 64 and 48). After Free Trade had been finally abandoned in 1932, a number of trade associations were drawn closer to, and the main peak, the F.B.I., almost 'dove-tailed' into, government through the Import Duties Advisory Committee, a quasi-public body empowered to add customs duties over and above the general 10 per cent *ad valorem* imposition. Even apart from that, trade associations felt a centripetal pull towards, or propelled themselves into, close relations with government by means of consultation, traceable to the 1880s, but systematized during the course of the First World War. But Business as a whole did not enjoy a sense of security. The Bolshevik Revolution and the trend towards socialism at home made them apprehensive, prompting the formation in 1919 of the Economic League, devoted to propagating the virtues of private enterprise (document 76).

During the Second World War, anticipating further political attack, a number of great industrial and commercial concerns launched Aims of Industry (1942). It went quickly into action, defending the British Sugar-Refiners' Association generally and Tate & Lyle in particular (one of its founding firms) from the Labour Party's proposal to nationalize the industry. Apparently successful then, it later came to the support of a more significant industry, steel (document 75), although some companies fought on their own account. In the end, the steel industry was brought into public ownership. To the surprise of many, the Conservatives launched an attack of their own, on retail price maintenance but inevitably on trade associations as well. That, too, was pressed home. On the other hand, Business won a resounding victory in setting up commercial television in 1954. They did not succeed without allies (a curious medley of forces), but they (the industrial, advertising and public-relations concerns) did supply most of the drive and the money.

In the 1960s the fuller development of trade associations in the distributive trades was significant (document 74). Meanwhile employers' organizations had continued to develop (documents 66 and 65). In 1965 their central body amalgamated with the F.B.I. and the National Association of British Manufacturers (as the N.U.M. had become) to form the Confederation of British Industry (documents 69 and 70). Despite the emergence of an inner group (document 71), the C.B.I. is a unified peak, the first in British history. It even contains the N.F.U. Prospering during the First World War, the N.F.U. later weakened, although remaining strong enough to undermine the Council of Agriculture, a public body established in 1919 for consultation and advice to government. Another great accession of strength came from the Second World War. It was sustained by economic prosperity and by Labour's Agriculture Act of 1947, providing support from public funds and systematic consultation. But some branches of the Union sometimes expressed themselves more openly and vigorously.

Consultation of the interests, however, remained throughout a fundamental theme, not merely for trade associations, other business groups and the N.F.U., but far more broadly, so that 'interests' must be interpreted broadly too. The tendency towards central and regional planning serves only to strengthen it.[20]

War had proved to be an excellent recruiting sergeant not only for employers in various guises but also for the trade unions. In the early years of the century their membership had been of the order of 1,500,000, rising to some 4,000,000 by 1913. By 1919 the total had almost doubled; by 1920, the moment of pride before the fall, it had more than doubled. Future giants such as the Transport and General Workers Union and the Amalgamated Engineering Union were created in their modern form. The co-ordinating power of the union peak was strengthened by the invention of a General Council of the T.U.C. in replacement of the Parliamentary Committee (1921). Among professional workers, the N.U.T. (document 83) advanced in membership from about 88,000 in 1913 to almost 102,000 in 1918, although defections on the issue of equal pay for women led to a breakaway, the National Association of Schoolmasters (document 84). Prodded by G. D. H. Cole, professionals of another kind banded together in 1920 to produce the National Federation of Professional Workers.

The Second World War had the effect of 'integrating' the trade union movement. Notable mergers took place, such as that linking foundry workers to engineers. In 1947 the engineers put their weight behind or into the Confederation of Shipbuilding and Engineering Unions, which in 1936 had replaced the Federation of Engineering and Shipbuilding Trades. In 1936 the National Association of Local Government Officers joined the National Federation of Professional Workers. By 1970 not only N.A.L.G.O. but the N.U.T. had thrown in their lot with the T.U.C., which already loomed larger as a result of its war-time role. Now it became as broadly based and representative as it can ever be (document 81).

Even before the Representation of the People Act, 1918, conceded the right to vote to women aged thirty and over (as to men aged twenty-one), women's organizations had begun to change their character. In 1915 seeds blown from Canada took root in Wales in the town boasting a fifty-eight-letter name (said to be unpronounceable by Englishmen): the Women's Institutes (document 58). Two years later these were harnessed by the National Federation of Women's Institutes. Some of the old suffragette spirit, however, survived in the Minerva Club, 1920, and later (1929) in the National Federation of Townswomen's Guilds.

War service produced another species of 'exclusive' organization, that of the ex-servicemen (or veterans). Service in the old regular Army and Navy had given rise to organizations *for* those who had laid down their arms; but the men returning with mud on their boots from the trenches wanted organizations of their own, and had grievances enough to sustain them. Contrary to M. René Rémond's assumption that ex-servicemen's associations are always right-wing,[21] some of these in England and Wales in the period 1916–20 belonged to the left of the spectrum (documents 60 and 61). But the work of Sir Frederick

Maurice (document 62) and others had clipped both left and right wings, leaving their new creation, the British Legion, to occupy the centre (document 63). The left wing continued to flap for a while; later, in those militant years culminating in the 1926 General Strike, a communist ex-service association successfully pinned its colours to the mast. But the Legion was not to be successfully challenged except, after the second of the century's great wars, on the specialized ground of organizing the very severely disabled. Meanwhile the Legion, in pursuing its policies, had made vigorous use of standard pressure-group methods, but these, such as the submission of questionnaires during general elections, were now getting somewhat old-fashioned. This gave offence in high quarters, and cost one of their leaders 'his' knighthood (happily 'restored' thirty years later).[22] Gradually the Legion did become less political, but also because in the post-1945 period much of what it sought was achieved.

Open in one sense, the ex-servicemen's associations were obviously 'exclusive' in another. The other important new association of that type but with an ethnic base appeared only in the 1930s – the League of Coloured Peoples, which survived into the 1950s, and the Indian Workers' Association (1938) which, by contrast, having gone into a decline, was being successfully revived in the 1950s, at Coventry (the original home) and elsewhere.[23] But the objective was changed. The League seems to have been general-purpose; the Workers' Association specifically out to further the cause of Independence for India. Now the goals were broadened to include the improvement of working conditions, keeping in touch with India and fighting against 'all forms of discrimination'. The great 'Third World' influx of the 1960s produced a number of other such bodies, including the West Midlands Caribbean Association, the Pakistan Workers Union and even a peak – the National Federation of Pakistani Associations (document 97). Even the shadow of American Black Power (document 98) was briefly seen in the later 1960s. No doubt the chronic English–Irish conflict had had an ethnic edge to it, but the appearance in England of permanent associations of Indians, West Indians and Pakistanis was a new phenomenon. From the late 1960s

'Women's Lib.', too, was under way (document 95); whether it would make a good landfall, or any, was not clear.

As to the pure pressure groups, and the part they had played in public-policy-making, echoes of the great campaigns were still heard after 1918. Tariff Reform and imperial preference were kept before the public eye through the Empire Industries Association (1924). A prominent member of it was a son of Joseph Chamberlain, Neville, to whom, aptly enough, fell the task of introducing in 1932 the Bill that his father had vainly sought – a general customs tariff encompassing imperial preference. In 1933 the India Defence League tried to beat off an earlier wind of change, Baldwin's proposals for Indian constitutional reform. In the mid-1960s the Campaign for Education and its successor were noteworthy. The fight for the 1965 Race Relations Act was of greater human significance. It was led by a sub-committee of the Society of Labour Lawyers and backed by C.A.R.D. (the Campaign Against Racial Discrimination),[24] whose hand was played by Equal Rights to win the Race Relations Act of 1968. The most long-drawn-out campaign was that for equal pay for women. Open to masculine support and receiving some, individual and corporate, this campaign extended over about twenty years, first tackling the public services, then industry. One of the few such manifestations in the great tradition arose out of the Peace Movement, traceable in our period to the Union of Democratic Control (U.D.C.), which in those hot August days of 1914 set itself the ambitious task of securing democratic control of foreign and defence policy (document 57). It lived on into the age of nuclear annihilation when its original task both deepened and broadened into the survival of mankind. Under the shadow of the billowing nuclear cloud, the new legions of the Campaign for Nuclear Disarmament (C.N.D.) foregathered at Easter, hoping for secular redemption and a new beginning (document 87). Part of a Peace Movement (document 89) that the old U.D.C. could not have dreamt of, C.N.D. won over a party but never a government, and even the party victory was promptly reversed under the influence of the Campaign for Democratic Socialism (C.D.S.), by Oxford out of Westminster (document 88). This was matched as to the importance of the issue by the several Common Market campaigns (document 101), but hardly as campaigns, these being essentially 'reflexive' to Government policy and apparently causing little stir or commotion. Associations concerned for the Arab cause or for the fate of Soviet Jewry (documents 99 and 100) may embody more goodwill than effectiveness, although the pro-Israel groups are commonly judged more influential. Skirmishes as distinct from pitched battles have been common, as with the 1957 fight of the Workers' Educational Association against the proposed policy of 'block grants' to local authorities in place of specific grants (including education), and by others against the fluoridation of the water supply.[25]

Within these limits, a kind of 'privatization' or 'personalization' of the pure pressure group has been discernible. Dating, as we saw, from the charitable bodies and the Commons Preservation Society, etc., of the 1860s, it developed more strongly after the First World War. The National Council for the Unmarried Mother and her Child (1918) sought legislative reforms. What had been Charity was co-ordinated in 1919 in a peak significantly named the National Council of Social Service. The R.S.P.C.A. continued its political work (document 90). Eventually, in the 1960s, the N.S.P.C.C. was supplemented by the more crusading Child Poverty Action Group (document 92). Shelter crusaded for better housing (document 91).

In 1921 the Howard League for Penal Reform arose from the ashes of two earlier bodies. Four years later it joined hands with nine other associations to form a specific peak, the Central Consultative Council for the Abolition of Capital Punishment, which in turn gave rise to a 'working' body, the National Council for the Abolition of the Death Penalty. This survived the Second World War, but not the peace, expiring in 1948.[26] In 1955 the running was taken up by the National Campaign for the Abolition of Capital Punishment (N.C.A.C.P.), a creation of the fertile mind of the publisher Victor Gollancz. The Howard League had additional goals (document 85) but like the N.C.A.C.P., which undertook the public campaign, helped Sidney

Silverman in the successful Parliamentary drive. In other campaigns, the law was reformed to permit homosexual practices between consenting adults in private, and abortion under certain conditions (document 93). The second result had been long sought: the Abortion Law Reform Association (A.L.R.A.) was formed in 1936.[27] But in a sense the pedigree extends to the Malthusian League of the late 1870s, which in 1922 turned into the New Generation League. By now Marie Stopes's Society for Constructive Birth Control was on its way. By 1924 even the workers had been recruited (Workers' Birth-Control Group). A number of these organizations merged in 1930 to produce the National Birth-Control Association,[28] some of whose prominent members joined and assumed leadership roles in the A.L.R.A.

The conservation and amenity societies survived the First World War: they, too, eventually (1926) 'peaked' as the Council for Rural Amenities, now the Council for the Protection of Rural England. The Georgian Group appeared, somewhat belatedly, in 1937. The Lewisham Society was a later example. With a somewhat different focus, the National Smoke Abatement Society was formed in 1929, sixty years after a Royal Commission had declared that the requisites of a civilized life included the prevention and removal of nuisances, of which air pollution was (for the first time in this country) defined as one. Now the National Society for Clean Air, it enjoyed some success in the mid-1950s.[29] On the same tack have been the Anti-Concorde Project (document 94), the various groups combating the location of the third airport for the south, and the perhaps less structured groups of tenants protesting against the Westway Motorway (document 96). Here, as elsewhere, a certain 'volatility' was evident, some tendency towards a 'politics of the streets'.

3
Interpretation

What does all this sound and fury signify, over the years? At one level it means what it plainly says – the strivings of men and women, through government, to gain advantage and to right wrongs. The deeper meaning, however, is that what they undertook and in part achieved contributed importantly to the modernization of the British polity. In seeking their own objectives, they eased the transition from (in shorthand) oligarchy to democracy. That was certainly not accomplished without violence, but it was relatively peaceful for a period of rapid economic development, which we now recognize as a potentially dangerous phase for any nation, the strains and stresses, tensions and conflicts, discontinuities and incompatabilities tending towards extremist 'solutions' to current suffering and only-too-probable injustice. Credit for such a deliverance has been given to a number of entities and factors; pressure groups in general as distinct from religious groups in particular (e.g., the Evangelicals) have received less than their due (*Cf.* document 29). They organized and acted, and in acting served to satisfy the actors in some degree even when they did not fully succeed; in acting they also served by adding their mite to social learning. Structural differentiation does not proceed by endless novelty alone but in part by imitation, as the pure pressure groups so often reproduced the weekly 'class' meetings and penny subscriptions invented by the Wesleyan Methodists, indeed by Wesley himself (documents 33 and 34). So, too, men, having learned their fighting trade in one good cause, carried their banner into the next jousting-field.

It would be a mistake, however, to think of political

modernization in terms of the cause (or pure) pressure groups alone. The motives of the more 'grounded' groups may be more questionable, but in effect they too helped to weaken and then break the crust of oligarchy and to produce, if not a whole new political culture, then one in which democractic values and beliefs loom much larger than they did in the eighteenth and early nineteenth centuries. Group representations may begin as assertions but are susceptible to debate; in granting a limited right, the public authorities tend to have to concede a wider one. There is no finality in fair play: having expressed the hope that the extension of the vote to the middle class in 1832 was the 'final' reform, which would have left the whole of the working class permanently outside the pale of the Constitution, poor old 'Finality Jack' lives on as a figure of fun.

There one touches mind, not form; ethos, not organization. Whether conceived of as an aspect of political modernization or autonomously, the secularization of British politics owes much to pressure groups. This is obviously true of the efforts of the Dissenters, Catholic as well as Protestant. It took them about a century and a half (depending on the dates judged significant), but (in effect) they did it, squeezing most (not all) of the religion out of British politics. They managed that in at least two senses. Originally, religious society had (in principle) fitted or matched political society: to be outside the Anglican Church was to be outside the Constitution. The later caricature – that the Anglican Church was the Tory Party at prayer – catches in a scaled-down version one segment of the once wider ideal. What the groups in effect did was to sever the link between believer and citizen, a crucial attribute of secularization. Secondly, their efforts also had the effect (in Britain although not in the United Kingdom) of eliminating religion as an important variable, or factor, shaping political action. In Britain, social class is known to play a more important role in shaping voting habits than in Australia, the United States and Canada (in descending order).[1] In a sense that is because it is residual, and it is residual partly as an unanticipated result of pressure-group strivings and attainments.

Those are specific senses in which the groups helped to

secularize British politics. There is a broader sense. For all the drum-beating and the marching, pressure politics has a core of argument and so of rationality and 'scientific' calculation. In the silence of the inner sanctum, bluster and rhetoric fall away in the moment of rising: one has to proceed from premise to conclusion by the accepted rules of the mind, making use of whatever 'hard data' can be mustered. If one cannot be convincing, one must at least appear plausible, for the only other alternative is to appear stupid, which would not do. Even plausibility is 'of this world', the world of evidence, calculation and logic, the secularized world.

If a strain towards equality is also taken to be a feature of modernization, then to assess what the groups have contributed is ultimately more ambiguous. The general topic has often been discussed along lines set by T. H. Marshall: citizenship as a quest for equality in the several classes of rights and gained sequentially, first civil, then political, finally social.[2] If that sequence is suspiciously neat, it will serve as a peg for saying that, along those dimensions, the groups served equality well. They contributed something to civil rights (e.g., those of trade unionists as such), and much to both political and social rights.

In time, however, structural differentiation played a trick on the pressure groups, on the one hand cutting short their exclusive contribution to social rights (and so to equality), on the other coming in themselves to embody, without malice aforethought, some anti-egalitarian tendencies. Appearing as organizations (the political clubs) in our third period (1823–59), the parties tended in the succeeding one to become 'programmatic'. As a result, much of the load previously carried by the great campaign groups began to be carried by the parties. Why that should have happened when it did (it coincides more or less with the creation of the peak structure) itself requires analysis. Here one can merely draw attention to a point or two. The already noted transition of National Education League to National Liberal Federation is significant. Even if the Federation were to be taken merely as a ginger-group within the Liberal Party, the point is that it was *within*, and that in the eyes of some participants it was intended to serve what has now come to be known as the aggregative function of political parties. As a delegate to the inaugural meeting expressed it: why should reformers have to establish an Education League, a (parliamentary) Reform Union, a (religious) Liberation Society, a Land Reform Association, especially when so many of them appear and re-appear wearing different hats? Why should there not be a single body to collect the voices and speak with full authority? Such an aggregative function was exactly what Chamberlain visualized for the National Liberal Federation: in what now seems commonplace enough but was then novel, it meant a party with a broad programme. The appointment of Francis Schnadhorst to the secretaryship of the Federation was apt and even symbolic. He had been secretary of the Central Nonconformist Committee, which faded away after the election of 1874. But he had been installed a year earlier as secretary of the Birmingham Liberal Association, itself the product (1865) of the Liberal Registration Association set up in London in 1860 by the Liberal Whip, H. B. W. Brand (better remembered as Viscount Hampden). This progression from pressure group to party service culminated in his appointment as secretary to the National Liberal Federation, immediate successor to a pressure group, the National Education League, which for its method of operation had itself been cast in the image of the Anti-Corn Law League.

To say this is not to perpetuate the Ostrogorski 'caucus' myth: it is clear that he exaggerated the power of the National Liberal Federation, and so the danger to Parliamentary government. It is rather that the transition from Education League to Liberal Federation so brightly illuminates the changing 'balance' between the roles played by a certain kind of pressure group on the one hand and the political parties on the other. The Liberal Federation is part of that change, if only because, as one of the leading authorities, Professor H. J. Hanham, remarks, it did permit 'a measure of local initiative'.[3] But if there were space for it, the story would also take in the U.K. Alliance, discussing whether to align itself and the Temperance cause with a political party (1869), and then (1874) officially expressing sympathy with the Liberal Party.[4] It would take in the

Liberation Society (if not the Working Men's Committee for Promoting the Separation of Church and State that sprang from it in 1871). Of the 343 Liberals elected in 1880, 100 were Nonconformists, including sixteen members of the executive committee of the Liberation Society. The story could also with advantage be extended to Tariff Reform campaigning, in which the first shots were fired, say, by the Association of the 'Revivers' of British Industry (1869), the Fiscal Reform League (1870) and the Reciprocity Free Trade Association (1871), which in 1880 intervened in the general election. The following year saw the emergence of the National Free Trade League, but in 1883 its leadership – the presidency – passed to Lord Dunraven, 'rising rapidly in Tory circles'.[5] Too much should not be made of that, but it symbolizes, or marks a stage in, the process by which the issue gradually passed from the hands of pressure groups into the political parties. Early in this century, the Tariff Reform League was ostensibly non-party, but one of those non-party organizations of Tory inspiration (L. S. Amery's). Joseph Chamberlain took hold of it, and the result if not the intention was a great party battle. Slowly (say, 1913–23) the Conservative Party took on a commitment to tariffs that it had jettisoned in 1852. In 1924 the Empire Industries Association was founded (Amery again prominent). By 1931–2 the policy was implemented. It was only poetic justice that the hand was that of Neville Chamberlain, who introduced the Bill 'complete with pious reference to his father'.[6] Neither this nor other connected themes can be pursued here, but they are probably enough to make the general point convincing – that political parties were tending to replace one type of pressure group.

The latter part of the fourth period 1860–1970 may have seen some weakening in the impetus that earlier seemed to be carrying the political parties towards an exclusive or even an essentially programmatic role in British politics. Specifically, too, there are some rights, arguably to be defined as 'social', that the parties perfer not to pursue, thus still 'allowing' the pure pressure groups room to act, e.g., the Abortion Law Reform Association (document 93) and the Society for the Protection of Unborn

Children; the Homosexual Law Reform Society and the Kenric Society (whose goals would be the more recognizable had it been entitled the Sapphic Society). Still, over the broad acres of social rights as in some adjoining meadows, political parties have tended to displace groups of the great campaigning variety, thus diminishing the role of groups as a whole in the general push towards equality.

Meanwhile, both the parties and the groups, dual-purpose as well as single-purpose, had been getting so differentiated *internally* that they could in themselves be reckoned to work in a counter-clockwise direction, setting hierarchy against the general egalitarian trends of the time (or, closely related to that if not identical, oligarchy against democracy, thus modifying the earlier generalization). Among business enterprises, the limited liability provisions of the 1850s have been at work, partially separating ownership from control. During the last quarter of the nineteenth century, trade unions began to take on full-time staffs (document 50). Even the most unlikely groups, such as the charitable associations, were not immune to the bureaucratic trend: charity became – had to become – something of a business.[7] What it all portended is still not easy to determine. When the observers caught up with the facts, they produced a so-called theory of bureaucracy (as in Max Weber), also a so-called iron law of oligarchy (as in Robert Michels), which had claims to universality but (significantly for us) had its source mainly in German party politics and in German trade unionism. The truth may be that when structural differentiation generally reaches a 'critical' point, it can be serviced or managed only by internal oligarchy, so that this 'micro-oligarchy' may even be a condition of continued differentiation (itself presumably indispensable in complex societies). In any event, the net contribution of the groups to the egalitarian component of modernization seems difficult to assess.

On the other hand, the main thread running through modernization is believed by some to be the increasing capacity of government,[8] its range and effectiveness. One index of it in Britain in our fourth period, when parties were becoming programmatic and groups were developing peaks, would be the creation of the modern Civil Service after 1870. One could count the numbers engaged in, or the units of, central government, the startling addition in the First World War of a baker's dozen to the sixteen principal departments that had shouldered the burden until the lights went out all over Europe in 1914. Contraction came with the peace but was succeeded by another great expansion when the war was 'resumed' in 1939. This time the post-war shrinkage was smaller, leaving eight more departments (mid-1950s) and about half a million more (non-industrial) civil servants than there existed in 1911.

So now the theme becomes: differentiation conducing towards increasing government capacity. Where, now, stand the groups? Having increased equality in some important respects if diminishing it in others, the groups undoubtedly enable government to make the most of its increased capacity. The tell-tale sign came in the First World War when the burgeoning public authorities themselves deliberately called forth groups (e.g., trade associations) that had not yet been invented.[9] But generally the private realm has been innovative enough, building its own bridges to government, through regional and district structures to national organizations, or peaks. Private groups generally but those peaks in particular have been drawn more and more into the orbit of government through advisory committees, planning agencies, regular consultation and exchanges of a more informal kind. A considerable part of their time is given over to acting as the eyes and ears of the departments, even from time to time becoming *de facto* administrative extensions of them.

There high-level group differentiation serves government capacity by bridging the gap caused by the lower-level differentiation: it is commonly called vertical integration. In following their own objectives, the groups also bring about horizontal integration. This theme could well be elucidated as yet another facet of modernization: the tension, or conflict, between centre and periphery; in English terms, between London and the provinces. The decline of the provinces as bases for pressure-group activity has already been well explored by Donald Read,[10] but it may also be painted into the picture of modernization. What has occurred is the enhancement of London at the expense of Norfolk and the eastern counties, of Sheffield and Leeds, Glasgow and Edinburgh, and above all Manchester and Birmingham. Groups, dual-purpose as well as single, have been drawn into the vortex of London for general as well as political purposes, a move facilitated originally by the railways, the penny post and the telegraph and now by motorway and telephone, but corresponding largely to the increased capacity of London-based government itself. The reality of horizontal integration may well be less impressive than the appearance, as may also be true (I at least come increasingly to believe) of vertical integration. Taken together, however, they are surely indispensable for putting government capacity to practical use.

In all this one perceives the kernel of good sense within the husk of such glib phrases as 'the new feudalism' and 'the new Mercantilism'. Obviously, the line of demarcation between society and State, private and public, has become blurred along some lengths of the frontier: some elements of economic and political power exhibit a tendency to fuse. Whether that should yet be a matter for serious public concern is difficult to judge: so much depends upon the exact nature of the interplay, about which the public stock of information is very small. We do know that Parliament has lost ground to the groups, which are often consulted before a bill is read, even at times before it has been drafted. Within Whitehall and along Victoria Street, are government-group relations too cosy for the public good? Is one side manipulating the other: if so who is jollying whom along? Is government squaring the groups, partly by patronage, partly by sleight of hand? Are the groups at times colonizing the departments (e.g., the Ministry of Agriculture, Department of Health)? Do groups exercise a veto? Everyone has his own dearly cherished horror story, but over a long span, it hardly seems to add up to enough. Do the groups, then, induce 'pluralistic stagnation'? The potentially vigorous opposition of groups may have kept some good things locked away in the strongroom of the unthinkable. That is indeed a plausible explanation of the failure of the British politico-economic system to adapt successfully to the post-war, post-colonial situation. But the general issue is hard to resolve without more evidence.

What is clear is that the theory of all this, at least, has not been adapted to the rise and current role of pressure groups. To accommodate them a new political theory (and probably a new political economy) is required. It is obviously true, as has often been said, that what we have now is a system of functional representation, making good the deficiencies of geographical representation, in which one is thrown together with others merely on the often slim foundation of residential propinquity. The meaning of neighbourhood and community has so far changed that occupation and so place of work may well be a more important basis for cohesion and some political activity than the merely territorial; certainly that will be an important supplement. There, reading occupations as estates or local communities or local interests is a way of making sense of 'the new feudalism'. But it is easily overlooked that the theory of representation most appropriate to the era of feudalism was the 'attorney' theory – a representative, as in Parliament, was deemed to be an attorney for local interests.[11] Traceable at least to the fourteenth century, that theory of representation reappeared in the seventeenth and eighteenth centuries, when it was successfully challenged in a series of engagements in which Coke, Walpole and Hume took part as well as Edmund Burke. Coke's version is perhaps less familiar than Burke's: 'though one be chosen for one particular county or borough, yet when he is returned, and sits in Parliament, he serveth for the whole realm'.[12]

As formulated by Burke for the benefit of his Bristol constituents, that view was adopted by other jurists, by the university opinion-makers and endlessly repeated by their followers, thus becoming the nearest thing we have had to an 'official' theory of representation appropriate to our system of government. By a strange turn of the wheel, however, the older theory of representation lived on in the minds of those who launched the pure pressure groups of the late eighteenth century and who passed it on like an Olympic torch to their successors. Now the attorney theory of representation suits not only groups of that kind, which have relatively declined in importance, but also those that have greatly gained in importance and still straddle the scene at this time: the 'estates', the occupationally based groups, especially at peak level, as they treat with both government and Parliament. So at the present time at least two theories of representation are in effective use, but between them tension has not yet been creative. One reason for that may be the compartmentalization of political studies; another, the convenient but misleading label, 'functional representation'. That, one is slow to realize, is not only *not* what Burke taught but subversive of it. The problem has to be left to the theorist. A mere under-labourer in the field may simply be allowed to wonder whether the 'reconciliation' ought not to follow these lines. The ideal is still 'for the whole realm', yet what is miscalled 'functional representation' is both necessary for the authorities and apparently legitimate for the private realm. So we need that kind of structure or institution which embodies 'function' in the contemporary occupational sense yet provides opportunities for transcending it, for widening the ambit of group loyalties if not exactly serving 'the whole realm'. If that turns out to be an old solution – some sort of occupational House – it seems to have been reached by a not very familiar path, the recognition that the theories of representation underlying our political practice are contradictory.

Another element in the structure of traditional political thinking that seems to have been weakened is the theory of consent, one of the replacements of the divine right of kings for eliciting political obligation (or for legitimizing the exercise of political authority). Many factors are responsible for the current confusion, but the role of the groups is clearly contributory. Elections confer legitimacy; 'governing' antici- pates the next election, having become, in Professor Bernard Crick's words, 'a prolonged election campaign'.[13] Wherein lies the legitimacy, present or projected, of the T.U.C., C.B.I. or B.M.A.? Who among us consented to the first two being consulted about the Race Relations Bill, 1968, before Parliament was even informed? But perhaps such questions are beside the point. The traditional theory of consent (a construct that does not exist but has to be invented) implied some flow *from* the public *to* the authorities. Suppose there is not, cannot be, any such flow, except fitfully, at the margins? Then consent has to be mobilized, answers the Eaton Professor of the Science of Government at Harvard (and sometime Rhodes Scholar at Balliol), Professor Samuel Beer.[14] The Cabinet (constitutionally, the Government) occupy the foreground: they are perturbed, besieged, but they are doing their best. Dismissing or merely ignoring the insuperable, they try their hand at the apparently possible (granted the many assumptions of the Cabinet Memoranda on which their Conclusions have to be based). To carry the day, they have to carry Parliament and the party (in several senses), and through them and the mass media (via the lobby correspondents) try to persuade the wider public: but they also have to win over the particular publics, the groups. So they set to work, mobilizing (indeed) consent.

If this is how it works, then the outraged questions ('who consented to . . .?') tend to be irrelevant. But if so, we are living by more than one theory of consent, neither of which fits as in tongue and groove our actual, operative theories of representation. Do such 'double' discrepancies matter? Perhaps even (physically) small nations can never quite pull off a common political culture (of which theories of representation and theories of consent are basic ingredients). Or incongruity may simply be the price of modernization, yet another example of 'failure of fit'. Still the resources of reason are not exhausted, do not even, in this respect, seem under strain: it ought to be possible to minimize what we cannot altogether avoid, and perhaps help the British political system to work more effectively. For Kurt Lewin, the German-American founder of 'group dynamics', was surely right: there is nothing so practical as a sound theory. And that goes for 'theory' as ideal as well as for 'theory' as validated relationship.

However, our theme here is that the groups, in pursuing (1720–1970) their own objectives, furthered both structural differentiation and integration. In the course of doing so, they did much to adapt a political system not entirely inappropriate for a small, simple, relatively static, agrarian society to one that was on the way to becoming large, complex, rapidly changing and industrial. In so adapting they helped to keep down at least one of the costs (the bloodshed) that other nations have paid for rapid economic development. Directly and indirectly, they served to secularize British politics, and if secularization is deemed a theological or cultural loss, nonetheless it, too, helped to minimize bloodshed. When religious dogma, seriously entertained, is projected into politics, then politics tends to be zero-sum (as the 'game theorists' say), i.e., your gain is bound to be at my expense. In other words, secularization reduces the all-or-nothing, winner-take-all component of political conflict, a consummation devoutly to be wished (other things, as always, being equal). Besides, secularization, by requiring argument supported by evidence, increases the element of rationality in public-policy-making.

As to equality in Britain, the *net* contribution of the pressure groups is perhaps more ambiguous: so much depends upon the conclusions of research probably not even under way. On the other hand, no one can doubt that the groups have done (and do) much to sustain, even to some extent make possible, the effective use of the greatly increased capacity of government. That has been accomplished by way of both vertical and horizontal integration, thus including, in the end, the enhancement of the centre at the expense of the periphery, i.e., London at the expense of the provinces. This whole process has entailed more differentiation, not less, and so we come full circle.

If, in their private purposes, then, the groups 'meant well, tried a little, failed much', their public achievement, consequential although unintended, was greater – a substantial role in the modernization of the British polity. Their role in its current working remains substantial, but has perhaps yet to be satisfactorily assimilated to traditional theory. That, in the eighteenth century and later, the newer groups at least (fundamentally, those actually called 'self-created') received a cold reception was noted at the outset of this essay, but it cannot be said that their great development after 1823 and significant current role have conjured up any serious attempt at legitimization by British political thinkers. Thus, the *denotation* of 'pressure group' may now be clearer than it was at the outset, but its *connotation* – its aura – may remain unattractive to many. There lies part of the challenge to the theorists: they would do the State some service by discussing at length its relationship to the groups, bringing to bear the traditional concerns (as with political obligation, authority, legitimacy, representation and consent, and, if deciding to make a virtue of present necessity, then prescribing the proper limits, as to means and ends, of group activity in our time.

Notes

I GENERAL INTRODUCTION

1. Graham Wootton, *Interest-Groups* (Hemel Hempstead: Prentice-Hall International, 1970), pp. 1–3.
2. Mary E. Dillon, *American Political Science Review*, Vol. xxxvi, (June 1942).
3. *British Journal of Sociology*, Vol. vi, (June 1955).
4. *Government and Industry in Britain* (Longmans, 1962), p. 126, n. 1.
5. *Modern Democracies* (Macmillan, 1921), Vol. ii, p. 529; *American Commonwealth* (Macmillan, 2nd rev. edn, 1891), Vol. i, p. 647.
6. Belle Zeller, ed., *American State Legislatures* (New York: Crowell, 1954), p. 215.
7. Wootton, op. cit., p. 9, n. 7.
8. (New York: Bartlett & Welford, 1848.)
9. (London: G. Routledge), Vol. ii, p. 89.
10. 6 January 1862, p. 10.
11. 22 February 1873.
12. James A. H. Murray, ed., *A New English Dictionary on Historical Principles* (Oxford University Press, 1908), Vol. vi.
13. ibid.
14. ibid.
15. V. L. Allen, *Trade Unions and the Government* (Longmans, 1960), p. 16.
16. ibid.
17. *Brighton Herald*, 6 January 1844.
18. E. S. Beesly, in the *Bee-Hive*, quoted by F. M. Leventhal, *Respectable Radical: George Howell and Victorian Working-Class Politics* (Weidenfeld & Nicolson, 1971), p. 153.
19. A. R. Ilersic assisted by P. F. B. Liddle, *Parliament of Commerce* (Association of British Chambers of Commerce and Newman Neame, 1960), p. 141.
20. Annual Register, quoted by Donald Read, *The English Provinces: 1760–1960* (Edward Arnold, 1964), p. 228.
21. Henry Jephson, *The Platform: Its Rise and Progress* (London and New York, Macmillan and Co., 1892), Vol. ii, p. 135.
22. Quoted in Asher Tropp, *The School Teachers* (Heinemann, 1957), p. 137 and n. 4.
23. *Industrial Democracy* (Longmans, 2nd edn, 1911), p. 259.
24. Ilersic, op. cit., p. 143.

25. ibid.

26. Robert E. Dowse and John Peel, *Political Studies*, Vol. XIII (June 1965), p. 185.

27. W. L. Guttsman, *The British Political Élite* (MacGibbon & Kee, 1963), p. 299.

28. *How Britain is Governed*, 1933 edn, (Macmillan, 1970), pp. 306–10.

29. *The People and the Constitution*, (Oxford University Press, 2nd edn, 1962), p. 99.

30. In the United States, 'pressure group' has been said (see n. 3 above) to have been 'well established by 1928'. But it was not listed in Edward Conrad Smith's *A Dictionary of American Politics* (New York: A. L. Burt, 1924). And in 1929 when the book cited by Professor Mackenzie was reviewed, the groups dealt with were referred to as 'interest groups' (*The Annals of the American Academy of Political and Social Science*, July 1929, p. 160), and the Academy's special review of the field was called *Lobbying*. In 1931 a Chicago conference was indeed called 'Pressure Groups and Propaganda', but judging by the time spent on exchanging definitions and the variety thus disclosed, a number of the participants must have been inclined to echo the brisk if discouraging announcement by a famous psychologist: 'I don't know what is meant by ''pressure group'' so I can't talk about that.' By 1935, when the American Academy again reviewed the field, it did resort to 'pressure group', which four years later, however, was not included in the new edition of a specialist volume that had recognized words of the 'lobby' family since 1912 (Richard H. Thornton, *An American Glossary*, Philadelphia: Lippincott, and London: Francis and Co., 1912; Madison, Wis.: American Dialect Society, 1939).

31. Graham Wootton, *The Politics of Influence: British Ex-Servicemen, Cabinet Decisions and Cultural Change, 1917–57* (Routledge & Kegan Paul; Cambridge, Mass.: Harvard University Press, 1963), pp. 133–4; Stephen R. Ward, 'The British Veterans' Ticket of 1918', *Journal of British Studies* (November 1968).

32. *King George III and the Politicians* (Clarendon Press: Oxford University Press, 1953), p. 54.

33. Wootton, *Interest-Groups*, pp. 2–5.

II INTRODUCTION TO THE RISE AND DEVELOPMENT OF PRESSURE GROUPS

1720–61

1. George Rudé, *Wilkes and Liberty* (Oxford University Press, 1962), p. 1.

2. E. N. Williams, *The Eighteenth Century Constitution, Documents and Commentary* (Cambridge University Press, 1960), p. 309.

3. Williams, op. cit., p. 309.

4. Rudé, op. cit., p. 150.
5. Lucy Sutherland, in Richard Pares and A. J. P. Taylor, eds., *Essays Presented to Sir Lewis Namier* (Macmillan, 1956), p. 49 and n. 1.
6. Charles Wilson, *England's Apprenticeship: 1603–1763* (Longmans, 1956), p. 329.
7. Christopher Hill, *Reformation to Industrial Revolution* (New York: Pantheon Books Inc., 1967, p. 147; Weidenfeld & Nicolson, 1967).
8. ibid., p. 200.
9. Sutherland, in Pares and Taylor, eds., op. cit., p. 50, n. 2.
10. Hill, op. cit., p. 147.
11. Wilson, op. cit., pp. 173–4.
12. ibid., p. 271.
13. Lewis Namier and John Brooke, *The House of Commons: 1754–1790* (H.M.S.O. 1964), Vol. i, p. 156.
14. Douglas Hall, *A brief history of the West India Committee* (Barbados: Caribbean Universities Press, 1971), p. 2.
15. Lillian M. Penson, *English Historical Review*, Vol. xxxvi (July 1921), p. 381.
16. ibid., pp. 378–82.
17. Norman Hunt, *Two Early Political Associations* (Clarendon Press: Oxford University Press, 1961), p. 3.
18. ibid., p. 113.
19. J. J. Auchmuty, *Sir Thomas Wyse 1791–1862* (P. S. King, 1939), pp. 3–6. Great-grandson of 1760 namesake. *Cf.* document 1.
20. Peter Mathias, *The First Industrial Nation: Economic History of Britain: 1700–1914* (Methuen, 1969), p. 85.
21. Hill, op. cit., p. 61.
22. L. S. Sutherland, *The East India Company in Eighteenth-Century Politics* (Oxford University Press, 1952), p. 30.
23. P. J. Marshall, *Problems of Empire: Britain and India: 1757–1813* (Allen & Unwin, 1968), p. 79.
24. S. B. Clough and C. W. Cole, *Economic History of Europe* (Farnborough: Heath, 1947), p. 263.
25. Mathias, op. cit., p. 89, n. 1.
26. G. M. Trevelyan, *English Social History* (Longmans, 1945), p. 323.
27. Norman Hunt, *Oxford Slavonic Papers*, Vol. vii (1957), p. 58.
28. Patrick Richardson, *Empire and Slavery* (Longmans, 1968), pp. 11–12, 14.
29. Wilson, op. cit., pp. 175–6.
30. Richardson, op. cit., p. 17.
31. L(ucy) Stuart Sutherland, *English Historical Review*, Vol. xlvii (January 1932), p. 49.
32. ibid.
33. Merrill Jensen, *English Historical Documents: American Colonial Documents to 1776*, Vol. ix (Eyre & Spottiswoode, 1955), p. 354.
34. D. B. Horn and Mary Ransome, *English Historical Documents: 1714–83*, Vol. x, (Eyre & Spottiswoode, 1957), p. 776.
35. Penson, op. cit., p. 79.

36. ibid., p. 381.
37. Wilson, op. cit., p. 319.
38. John Craig, *A History of Red Tape* (Macdonald & Evans, 1955), pp. 100–1, believes that the Parliamentary draughtsman was confused, this really being 'a customs measure'.
39. George Rudé, *The Crowd in History: Study of Popular Disturbances in France and England, 1730–1848* (Wiley, 1964), p. 51.
40. J. H. Plumb, *England in the Eighteenth Century* (Penguin Books, 1964), p. 66.
41. Rudé, *The Crowd in History*, p. 51.
42. ibid.
43. Lucy Sutherland, in Pares and Taylor, eds., op. cit., p. 54.
44. ibid., p. 60.
45. Mathias, op. cit., p. 34.
46. Wilson, op. cit., p. 316.
47. Rudé, *The Crowd in History*, p. 67.
48. Geoffrey Millerson, *The Qualifying Associations* (Routledge & Kegan Paul, 1964), p. 19.
49. Plumb, op. cit., p. 181.
50. *The Catholic Encyclopedia* (New York, 1913), pp. 125–6.
51. E. Raymond Turner, *English Historical Review*, Vol. XLII (January 1927), p. 45.

1762–1822

1. George Rudé, *The Crowd in History: Study of Popular Disturbances in France and England, 1730–1848* (Wiley, 1964), p. 67.
2. V. L. Allen, *Trade Unions and the Government* (Longmans, 1960), pp. 14–15 and n. 1, citing J. D. Chambers.
3. Asa Briggs, *The Age of Improvement 1783–1867* (Longmans, 1960), p. 136 and n. 2.
4. P. J. Marshall, *Problems of Empire: Britain and India: 1757–1813* (Allen & Unwin, 1968), pp. 89–90.
5. Lewis Namier and John Brooke, *The House of Commons 1750–1790* (H.M.S.O., 1964), Vol. I, pp. 150–2.
6. Marshall, op. cit., p. 100.
7. Lucy Sutherland, in Richard Pares and A. J. P. Taylor, eds., *Essays Presented to Sir Lewis Namier* (Macmillan, 1956), p. 63.
8. Douglas Hall, *A brief history of the West India Committee* (Barbados: Caribbean Universities Press, 1971), p. 4.
9. Namier and Brooke, op. cit., p. 157.
10. Witt Bowden, *Industrial Society in England towards the end of the Eighteenth Century* (New York: Barnes & Noble, 2nd edn, 1965), p. 202.
11. Anthony (Handley) Lincoln, *Some Political and Social Ideas of English Dissent 1763–80* (Cambridge University Press, 1938), p. 225.
12. ibid., p. 266.
13. Namier and Brooke, op. cit., p. 336.

14. Naomi Churgin Miller, *English Historical Review*, Vol. LXXXIII (October, 1968), Document 5, this volume.
15. Eugene Black, *The Association: British Extra-Parliamentary Organization 1769–1793* (Cambridge, Mass.: Harvard University Press, 1963), p. 49.
16. Namier and Brooke, op. cit., p. 17.
17. George Rudé, *Paris and London in the Eighteenth Century* (New York: Viking Press, 1973, p. 270; Fontana, 1970).
18. Donald E. Ginter, *Historical Journal*, Vol. IX (1966), p. 179.

1823–59

1. Peter Mathias, *The First Industrial Nation: Economic History of Britain: 1700–1914* (Methuen, 1969), p. 295.
2. Geoffrey K. Roberts, *Political Parties and Pressure Groups in Britain* (New York: St Martin's Press, 1971, p. 84; Weidenfeld & Nicolson, 1970).
3. Arthur Redford, *Manchester Merchants and Foreign Trade: 1850–1939*, Vol. I, (Manchester University Press, 1934), pp. 66–7.
4. H. A. Clegg, *The System of Industrial Relations in Great Britain* (Oxford: Blackwell, 1970), pp. 120–1.
5. Asher Tropp, *The School Teachers* (Heinemann, 1957), p. 45, nn. 2 and 3.
6. Paul Vaughan, *Doctors' Commons: A Short History of the British Medical Association* (Heinemann, 1959), p. 9.
7. Redford, op. cit., Vol. I, pp. 131–2.
8. ibid., pp. 76–7.
9. ibid., p. 154.
10. Norman McCord, *The Anti-Corn Law League, 1838–46* (Allen & Unwin, 1958), p. 38.
11. *Proceedings*, 20 December 1838, quoted in Redford, op. cit., Vol. I, pp. 151–2 and n. 1.
12. See, initially, Eric Williams, *Capitalism and Slavery* (André Deutsch, 1964). Powerful *economic* rivals to the West India Interest had long been at work. The turning-point may have been reached somewhere between 1807 and 1812. See François Crouzet (Lille), 'Groupes de pression et politiques de blocus . . .', *Revue historique*, Vol. 228 (July–December, 1962).
13. Norman Gash, *The Age of Peel: Documents of Modern History* (Edward Arnold, 1958), p. 54.
14. Henry Jephson, *The Platform: Its Rise and Progress* (London and New York, Macmillan and Co., 1892), Vol. II, p. 48.
15. See above, pp. 60–62.
16. *Sussex Agricultural Express*, 2 September 1843, editorial.
17. Mary Tancred-Lawson, *Historical Journal*, Vol. III (1960), p. 168.
18. *Brighton Gazette*, 11 January 1844.
19. As quoted in *Brighton Gazette*, ibid.
20. George L. Mosse, *Economic History Review*, Vol. XVII, no. 2, (1947), p. 134.

21. *Brighton Gazette,* ibid.
22. *Brighton Gazette,* 1 February 1844.
23. Quoted in *Brighton Gazette,* 25 January 1844.
24. ibid. and n. 30.
25. *Brighton Guardian,* 28 January 1846.
26. The peroration of Peel's speech of 29 June, in Gash, op. cit., pp. 133–4.

1860–1970

1. H. A. Clegg, *The System of Industrial Relations in Great Britain* (Oxford: Blackwell, 1970), p. 121.
2. Arthur Marsh, *Collection of Teaching Documents and Case Studies for Industrial Relations in Engineering* (Pergamon Press, 1965), p. 8.
3. Now the National Federation of Building Trade Employers.
4. Peter Mathias, *The First Industrial Nation: Economic History of Britain: 1700–1914* (Methuen, 1969), p. 390; W. H. B. Court, *British Economic History, 1870–1914: Commentary and Documents* (Cambridge University Press, 1965), pp. 252–3.
5. *The Author,* summer 1964, pp. 23–4.
6. Mathias, op. cit., p. 388.
7. Peter Self and Herbert J. Storing, *The State and the Farmer* (Allen & Unwin, 1963), p. 38.
8. B. C. Roberts, *The Trades Union Congress, 1868–1921* (Allen & Unwin, 1958), pp. 48–9.
9. H. A. Clegg, Alan Fox and A. F. Thompson, *A History of British Trade Unions since 1889* (Clarendon Press: Oxford University Press, 1964), Vol. I, pp. 89–99, 240.
10. Asher Tropp, *The School Teachers* (Heinemann, 1957), p. 137.
11. ibid., p. 151.
12. Jeanne L. Brand, *Doctors and the State: The British Medical Profession and Government Action in Public Health, 1870–1912* (Baltimore: Johns Hopkins University Press, 1965), p. 162.
13. Quoted in Paul Vaughan, *Doctors' Commons: A Short History of the British Medical Association* (Heinemann, 1959), p. 209.
14. Donald Read, *The English Provinces: 1760–1960* (Edward Arnold, 1964), p. 177.
15. Robert E. Dowse and John Peel, *Political Studies,* Vol. XIII, (June 1965), p. 180 and n. 5.
16. *The Times,* 29 August 1916; Stephen Blank, *Industry and the State: The Changing Relationship of Government and Industry in Britain,* Harvard University doctoral thesis, 1968, pp. 63–4.
17. Cd. 9236.
18. A. R. Ilersic assisted by P. F. B. Liddle, *Parliament of Commerce* (Association of British Chambers of Commerce and Newman Neame, 1960), p. 170.
19. J. H. Dunning and C. J. Thomas, *British Industry* (Hutchinson, 1963), pp. 46–7.

20. The consultation of interests was central to the pioneering book by a British author, J. D. Stewart's *British Pressure Groups* (Clarendon Press: Oxford University Press, 1958). See also J. W. Grove, *Government and Industry in Britain* (Longmans, 1962), ch. 5.

21. *Revue française de science politique*, Vol. v, 1955, pp. 287–8.

22. A more important form of social control was the threat to have royal patronage withdrawn. Another, ante-natal, was embodied in the conditions prescribed by the Privy Council as the 'price' to be paid for the Royal Charter.

23. De Witt John, *Indian Workers' Associations in Britain* (Oxford University Press, 1969), p. 45.

24. Keith Hindell, *Political Quarterly*, Vol. xxxvi (1965), pp. 390–405, and *Observer*, 30 May 1965 (on whose report, however, Hindell has cast some doubt).

25. J. A. Brand, *Political Studies*, Vol. xix, December 1971.

26. J. B. Christoph, *Capital Punishment and British Politics* (Allen & Unwin, 1962), pp. 30–1, 113.

27. Madeleine Simms and Keith Hindell, *Abortion Law Reformed* (London: Peter Owen, 1971), p. 57. For the pressure groups 'on moral issues', see Bridget A. Pym, *Political Quarterly*, Vol. 43, July-September 1972.

28. Dowse and Peel, op. cit., p. 192.

29. J. B. Sanderson, *Political Studies*, Vol. ix, October 1961.

III INTERPRETATION

1. Robert R. Alford, *Party and Society* (Chicago: Rand McNally, 1963).

2. *Citizenship and Social Class* (Cambridge University Press, 1950).

3. *The Nineteenth-Century Constitution: Documents and Commentary* (Cambridge University Press, 1969), p. 227.

4. Brian Harrison, *Drink and the Victorians* (Faber & Faber, 1971), ch. 10 and p. 243.

5. Benjamin H. Brown, *The Tariff Reform Movement in Great Britain, 1881–95* (New York: Columbia University Press, 1943), p. 61.

6. A. J. P. Taylor, *English History, 1914–45* (Oxford University Press, 1965), p. 330.

7. Graham Wootton, *The Politics of Influence: British Ex-Servicemen, Cabinet Decisions, and Cultural Change, 1917–57* (Routledge & Kegan Paul; Cambridge, Mass.: Harvard University Press, 1963), chs. 3 and 10.

8. Leonard Binder, James S. Coleman, Joseph LaPalombara, Lucian W. Pye, Sidney Verba and Myron Weiner, *Crises and Sequences in Political Development* (Princeton: Princeton University Press, 1971).

9. Graham Wootton, *Interest-Groups* (Hemel Hempstead: Prentice-Hall International, 1970), pp. 96–7.

10. *The English Provinces: 1760–1960* (Edward Arnold, 1964).

11. Isaac Kramnick, 'An Augustan Debate: Notes on the History of Representation', in James Roland Pennock and John W. Chapman, *Representation* (New York: Atherton Press, 1968), pp. 86–7.

12. Cecil S. Emden, *The People and the Constitution* (Oxford University Press, 2nd edn, 1956), p. 23. On the changing conceptions of representation, with special reference to groups, consult Samuel H. Beer, *British Politics in the Collectivist Age* (New York: Vintage, 1969).

13. *The Reform of Parliament* (Weidenfeld & Nicolson, 1964), pp. 25–6.

14. 'The British Legislature and the Problem of Mobilizing Consent', in Elke Frank, ed., *Lawmakers in a Changing World* (Hemel Hempstead: Prentice-Hall International, 1966).

E

List of Documents

Documents

I
The First Catholic Association, 1760
Thomas Wyse, Jr, *Historical Sketch of the Late Catholic Association of Ireland*, London, 1829, Vol. I, pp. 67–9

To him [Mr Wyse] the Catholic body is indebted for the first uniform or general plan of a convention or association. He fully saw (as appears from his private correspondence) its numerous inconveniencies, but he was still more deeply impressed with its absolute necessity . . . He conceived the project of a great representative body, formed on general and permanent principles, and which, far from affecting to limit its representation to the interests of the aristocratic class, or to that of the merchants only, should extend its delegation to every rank of the community. The plan, after having been matured in solitude, was finally submitted to the few gentlemen Mr Wyse could collect together in Dublin, in March and April, 1760. The first meetings were held in the Elephant tavern, Essex Street. Not more than three or four were found willing to attend them. The walls of Rome were not yet built; a child could leap over the intrenchments. In how few years these three or four persons were destined to increase to hundreds, the hundreds to thousands, the thousands to millions, until they at last took in an entire people! At one of these meetings Mr Wyse proposed his plan. It was adopted with some slight alterations. The reader will see later how far it formed the principle of the various associations, boards, and committees, which were afterwards successively adopted. It particularly suggested the improved one of 1793.

2
Molasses and the American Colonists, 1765
Observations on the Present State of American Trade, 1765.
Goodwood MS 183, West Sussex Record Office

... 'tis inconceivable to think how much they are distressed by the Manacles with which these Laws have so severely, as well as injudiciously fettered up their Molasses, except a trifling Part indeed which the poorer Sort of People make Use of instead of Sugar, is constantly distilled into Rum, which, with that imported from the English & Foreign Islands, is generally consumed in carrying on the Fishery, in bartering for Fish, and in trafficking with the Indians for Furs & Skins. These are the Branches of Commerce which were formerly extremely lucrative to the Colonists, & consequently extremely profitable to the Mother Country. But these Branches are no longer to be exercised and all the Advantages with which they were once opened, are now pretty nearly at an End. The Colonies being now no longer allowed to import Molasses from the foreign Islands, they are utterly unable to get a Sufficiency of Rum for their most necessary use; hence Fisheries are in a manner ruined, and the Indian Trade almost wholly given up. In the Indian Trade particularly, Rum is an Article so very essential, that the Savages will scarcely deal without it. Besides this, the Article of Rum, 'tille the late Restrictions, made up a principal part of the Cargoes which the American merchants employed in the Guinea Trade, and brought them home Slaves, Bees-Wax, Gold & Ivory which they sold to a prodigious Advantage, and from which they gained new Resources of discharging the astonishing Sums in which they stood indebted to the Merchants of England. These resources being cut off, as well as their Fisheries, and their Indian Trade, they are left with no Prospects but Despair, and that Despair it is, which has rendered them so impatient under the late Stamp Duty . . .

3
Society for Supporting the Bill of Rights, 1769
Alexander Stephens, *Memoirs of John Horne Tooke*,
London, 1813, Vol. I, pp. 163–4

. . . it was at length determined, in 1769, to form one, which should have for its main object the preservation of the constitution, as it had been established at the Revolution, and at the suggestion of Mr Horne, who may be considered as the founder, it assumed the denomination of the 'Society for supporting the Bill of Rights'. This met at stated times at the London Tavern . . .

This Society was originally instituted for the express purpose of supporting all those whose rights had been violated, whose fortunes had been injured, or whose persons had been seized and imprisoned, in opposition to the laws of the land. The members were few at first, but respectable for wealth and talents. Their meetings, their speeches, their resolutions and, above all, their subscriptions, were attended with powerful effects. They inflamed the zeal of each other; they inspired the public mind with energy, vigour, and resentment; they supported those who were doomed to expiate their political offences by a rigorous imprisonment; and they found means to agitate some critical questions in the courts of justice, the decision of which was attended with wonderful effect. Mr Horne, as has already been intimated, was a leading man in this society; and there is reason to suppose that he either drew up the whole or part of the following instructions, intended to be presented by way of *test*, to all candidates, before their election to serve in parliament.

4
Need for a Grand National Association, 1775
James Burgh, *Political Disquisitions; or, an Enquiry into public Errors, Defects, and Abuses*, Philadelphia, 1775, Vol. III, pp. 428–9, 432 and 455–6

Before all other things, there must be established a GRAND NATIONAL ASSOCIATION FOR RESTORING THE CONSTITUTION. Into this must be invited all men of property, all friends to liberty, all able commanders, &c. There must be a copy of the ASSOCIATION for every parish, and a parochial committee to procure subscriptions from all persons whose names are in any tax book, and who are willing to join the Association. And there must be a grand committee for every county in the three kingdoms, and in the colonies of *America* . . .

The court was glad to encourage such an association of the people in a time of danger. They did not then insist, as has been done since, that the people are annihilated, or absorbed into parliament; that the voice of the people is nowhere to be heard but in parliament; that members of parliament are not responsible to their constituents, &c. . . .

Instructing, petitioning, remonstrating, and the like, are good diversion for a court; because they know, that, in such ways, nothing will be done against their power.

5
The Radical Programme, 1776
John Cartwright, *Take Your Choice!*, London, 1776, pp. 88–9

CONCLUSION

I cannot but feel the strongest persuasion that the *facility* of annually electing our lower house of parliament, and of restoring a full, equal and perfect representation to the commons, is in the foregoing pages demonstrated: and I hope my reader agrees with me, in the idea of its being absolutely necessary to make these reforms immediately. . . . Now it only remains to inspire him with a confidence that they may be effected, even against the whole force and fraud of ministerial opposition; and to adjure him, as he shall answer it hereafter, not to be wanting to his country on this great occasion: but to do his duty to that, I had almost said divine constitution, under which he lives, and under which he looks for peace and protection. No man can plead impotency without confessing disinclination. The poorest peasant of our state, I have shewn to be an important member of it; and he that hath as high a title to liberty as the most illustrious nobleman. I have shewn likewise that, in justice, the voice of the peasant goes as far as that of the richest commoner towards the nomination of a member of a parliament. The name of a peasant will consequently, be of as much value in a petition to the throne, or any public act of the commons in their social capacity, as that of any freeholder or borough voter whatever. It will be the signature of a freeman: of a man every way intitled to the protection of the laws, and competent to a share in the framing of them. To vindicate this right is doubtless of the last importance; for liberty, like learning, is best preserved by its being widely diffused through society. *Numbers* are its health, strength and life. But, to return, let my reader, if he have a wish for reformation, either recollect or read what is proposed in the conclusion of the political disquisitions, concerning a GRAND NATIONAL ASSOCIATION FOR RESTORING THE CONSTITUTION. It would be impertinent to repeat what is there written. I will only endeavour to throw in my small contribution towards removing the difficulties of carrying such a noble scheme into practice. As soon as leaders worthy of such a cause shall have made themselves known to the public (and such I have reason to believe will soon appear) it may be presumed that they will be provided with a concise and clear state, of the evils flowing from long parliaments; of the injustice and absurdity of such parliaments themselves; of the infinite advantages from their removal; and of the method proposed for this salutary work . . .

6

Committee for effecting the Abolition of the Slave Trade: the Quaker initiative, May–June 1787

Thomas Clarkson, *The History of the Rise, Progress, and Accomplishment of the Abolition of the African Slave-Trade by the British Parliament*, Philadelphia, 1808, Vol. 1, pp. 206–7, 209

. . . While such conversation was passing, and when all appeared to be interested in the cause, Mr Langton put the question, about the proposal of which I had been so diffident, to Mr Wilberforce, in the shape of a delicate compliment. The latter replied, that he had no objection to bring forward the measure in parliament, when he was better prepared for it, and provided no person more proper could be found. Upon this, Mr Hawkins Browne and Mr Windham both said they would support him there. Before I left the company, I took Mr Wilberforce aside, and asked him if I might mention this his resolution to those of my friends in the city, of whom he had often heard me speak, as desirous of aiding him by becoming a committee for the purpose. He replied, I might. I then asked Mr Langton, privately, if he had any objection to belong to a society of which there might be a committee for the abolition of the Slave-trade. He said he should be pleased to become a member of it. Having received these satisfactory answers, I returned home.

The next day, having peviously [*sic*] taken down the substance of the conversation at the dinner, I went to James Phillips, and desired that our friends might be called together as soon as they conveniently could, to hear my report. In the interim I wrote to Dr Peckard, and waited upon lord Scarsdale, Dr Baker, and others, to know (supposing a society were formed for the abolition of the Slave-trade) if I might say they would belong to it? All of them replied in the affirmative, and desired me to represent them, if there should be any meeting for this purpose.

At the time appointed, I met my friends. I read over the sub-

stance of the conversation which had taken place at Mr Langton's.
No difficulty occurred. All were unanimous for the formation of a
committee. On the next day we met by agreement for this
purpose. It was then resolved unanimously, among other things,
That the Slave-trade was both impolitic and unjust. It was
resolved also, That the following persons be a committee for
procuring such information and evidence, and publishing the
same, as may tend to the abolition of the Slave-trade, and for
directing the application of such moneys as have been already,
and may hereafter be collected for the above purpose.

Granville Sharp	Thomas Clarkson
William Dillwyn	Richard Phillips
Samuel Hoare	John Barton
George Harrison	Joseph Hooper
John Lloyd	James Phillips
Joseph Woods	Philip Sansom

All these were present... on the twenty-second of May, 1787...
After the formation of the committee,[1] notice was sent to Mr
Wilberforce of the event, and a friendship began, which has
continued uninterruptedly between them, from that to the present day.

7
Response of other religious bodies to the Quaker initiative

Thomas Clarkson, *The History of the Rise, Progress, and Accomplishment
of the Abolition of the African Slave-Trade by the British Parliament*,
Vol. I, pp. 353–7

... The committee having dispersed five hundred circular letters,
giving an account of their institution, in London and its neighbourhood, the Quakers were the first to notice it. This they did in
their yearly epistle, of which the following is an extract: 'We
have also thankfully to believe there is a growing attention in
many, not of our religious Society, to the subject of Negro-
slavery; and that the minds of the people are more and more
enlarged to consider it as an aggregate of every species of evil, and

1. All the members were of the society of the Quakers, except Mr Sharp,
Sansom, and myself. Joseph Gurney Bevan was present on the day before this
meeting. He desired to belong to the society, but to be excused from belonging
to the committee.

to see the utter inconsistency of upholding it by the authority of any nation whatever, especially of such as punish, with loss of life, crimes whose magnitude bears scarce any proportion to this complicated iniquity.'

The General Baptists were the next; for on the twenty-second of June, Stephen Lowdell and Dan Taylor attended as a deputation from the annual meeting of that religious body, to inform the committee, that those, whom they represented, approved their proceedings, and that they would countenance the object of their institution.

The first individual, who addressed the committee, was Mr William Smith, the present member for Norwich. In his letter he expressed the pleasure he had received in finding persons associated in the support of a cause, in which he himself had taken a deep interest. He gave them advice as to their future plans. He promised them all the co-operation in his power: and he exhorted them not to despair, even if their first attempt should be unsuccessful; 'for consolation,' says he, 'will not be wanting. You may rest satisfied that the attempt will be productive of some good; that the fervent wishes of the righteous will be on your side, and that the blessing of those who are ready to perish will fall upon you.' And as Mr Smith was the first person to address the committee as an individual after its formation, so, next to Mr Wilberforce and the members of it, he gave the most time and attention to the promotion of the cause.

On the fifth of July, the committee opened a correspondence, by means of William Dillwyn, with the societies of Philadelphia and New York . . .

On the twenty-seventh of August . . . This sitting was distinguished by the receipt of letters from two celebrated persons . . . The second was from Mr John Wesley, whose useful labours as a minister of the Gospel are so well known to our countrymen . . .

Mr Wesley, whose letter was read next, informed the committee of the great satisfaction which he also had experienced, when he heard of their formation. He conceived that their design, while it would destroy the Slave-trade, would also strike at the root of the shocking abomination of slavery also. He desired to forewarn them that they must expect difficulties and great opposition from those who were interested in the system; that these were a powerful body; and that they would raise all their forces, when they perceived their craft to be in danger. They would employ hireling writers, who would have neither justice nor mercy. But the committee were not to be dismayed by such treatment, nor even if some of those, who professed good-will towards them . . .

8

The London Corresponding Society : origins, 1791–2

Letter from Thomas Hardy to *The Examiner*, 1816, in Henry Jephson,
The Platform: its Rise and Progress, London, 1892, Vol. i, pp. 193–4

The London Corresponding Society began in the latter end of
1791, in consequence of a conversation I had with a friend res-
pecting the unequal representation of the people in Parliament.
That conversation suggested the propriety of instituting a society
with the view of ascertaining the opinion of the people on that
question by corresponding with other societies that might be
formed, having the same object in view. The idea was mentioned
to another friend or two. At last a society was formed. Its first
meeting was held on the 25th of January 1792, consisting of
eight persons . . .

The first Address and Resolutions which the Society published
were dated 2d [*sic*] April 1792. From that time the Society became known to the public. Societies were formed in different parts
of England, Scotland and Ireland, in quick succession for the
same laudable object . . .

[After recalling the County Associations of 1780] The lapse of
ten years took place, when another class of reformers started up,
unknown to those who preceded them. They were of the lower
and middling class of society *called the people*. They dared to
associate to demand a restitution of their long-lost rights. Those
two classes of reformers being almost total strangers to each
other, some of those who were strenuous for reform in 1782
scarcely knew those who were associated for a reform in 1792.
Many of them were so dreadfully alarmed at the uncommon
appearance of the reformers in 1792 that they fled for shelter
under the all-protecting wings of the Crown.

9

Address from a Society established at Newington to the French National Convention in their sitting of 10 November 1792

Goodwood MS 183, West Sussex Record Office

Frenchmen and Citizens of the World . . .

We congratulate you however on the total defeat and expulsion
of the combined Armies of the senseless Despots and those impious
Rebels, who came to desolate your fields ravage your Towns and
massacre the innocent Inhabitants; The goodness of your cause

must be crowned with success. Your Wisdom and Valour have ensured it, Your wise decrees have enlightened Europe and like the Rays of the Sun they will enlighten the four Parts of the World. The two great Bulwarks of human Liberty are the Legislative and judiciary bodies, by organising with the latter, you have ensured to yourselves the Efficacious Advantages of the former. You have since given a Proof of your Consummate wisdom by keeping the Legislative judiciary and Executive Powers entirely distinct, and by declaring that the two latter should be respectively responsible to the Grand Council of the Nation . . .

President's answer to five English societies

The National Convention has heard with the warmest sensibility the generous declaration of the English Citizens who cordially unite with us in our Labours.

The Sentiments of 600 Britons devoted openly to the cause of Mankind are without doubt in the hearts of all the free Men in England.

10

The West India Interest: decline of influence acknowledged, 1823

Minutes of the Standing Committee of the West India Planters and Merchants, 26 June 1823. Douglas Hall, *A brief history of the West India Committee*, Barbados: Caribbean Universities Press, 1971, p. 9

. . . it is idle to disguise from ourselves, that the various parties who from different motives are hostile to the West India Interest, are at least as powerful, and act upon a more extensive system, and have greater means of influence on the public mind, than the Proprietors and Merchants connected with the Colonies . . . we cannot, therefore, beat them by influence – we must trust to reason – and the only way of getting that weapon into our hands, is by doing of ourselves, all that is right to be done – and doing it speedily and effectually . . .

11

The Catholic Association of Ireland: Rules and Regulations, 24 May 1823

Thomas Wyse, Jr, *Historical Sketch of the late Catholic Association of Ireland*, London, 1829, Vol. II, p. xxxvii

. . . the following resolutions were adopted:

That the Catholic Association be formed to adopt all such

legal and constitutional measures as may be most useful to obtain Catholic emancipation.

That the Association is not a representative or delegated body; and that it will not assume any representative or delegated authority or quality . . .

That all reporters for newspapers, &c. be at liberty to attend all the meetings of the Association.

12
The Catholic Association of Ireland : pressure from without

Thomas Wyse, Jr, *Historical Sketch of the late Catholic Association of Ireland*, London, 1829, Vol. i, pp. 5–6

. . . the Catholic Association was a coalition of a very different order: it had a method in its madness, and an object in its tumult, which a close observer and a constant attention only could discern . . . its strength was not known, until it had been brought into direct collision with the government; it was not even fully appreciated by the very hands which wielded it, until its temper had been brought out by hostile attack. It was then suddenly perceived, that a body had been growing up unnoticed, *without* the constitution, which might in its due season disturb from its foundations the constitution itself, co-extensive with the immense majority of the population, and reflecting, in its utmost energy, the entire form and pressure of the popular mind.

13
The Catholic Association of Ireland : Secretary's circular about Petitions to Parliament, 1 January 1829

Thomas Wyse, Jr, *Historical Sketch of the late Catholic Association of Ireland*, London, 1829, Vol. ii, pp. cclxxvii–cclxxix

Reverend Sir,

It is deemed of vital importance to the Catholic cause, that petitions should be presented in the ensuing session of parliament from *every parish in Ireland*. To facilitate the attainment of this great end, it has been considered expedient to furnish you with the annexed models of petitions, from which you may select one that appears to you most suitable. These models are not transmitted with the view of dictating to any individual, or set of men, but merely saving them trouble. It is not deemed necessary, that any of these models should be selected by you, or at the meeting at which you may preside. All may be rejected – and when this can be done with convenience, it is decidedly the better course; sentences may be taken from each – corrections or alterations may be made in them – passages may be introduced, and passages omitted – in short, any thing may be done with these models, which may be thought desirable; and the Association only entreat, that at all events *some* form of petition may be adopted in each parish throughout Ireland . . .

To some clerk, or scrivener, or schoolmaster, this form should be given, without delay, to be by him copied on a large sheet of paper, or any sized sheet of paper that will contain the words – the heading should invariably be . . .

Care should always be taken to have some signatures on the sheet containing the form of words of the petition, otherwise it will not be received by the House. The greatest exertions should be made to obtain a number of signatures. Every person in the chapel, or in the parish, who can write, should be called upon to subscribe his name.

The most effective mode of procuring signatures is to place a table, with pen and ink, at each chapel door, and to apprise each congregation of the circumstance from the altar. Another mode is to appoint some person to take the ruled sheets about from house to house.

14
Society of the Friends of Civil and Religious Liberty: Objects, 1829

Thomas Wyse, Jr, *Historical Sketch of the late Catholic Association of Ireland*, London, 1829, Vol. II, pp. cclxvi–cclxviii

. . . we recommend that a committee of forty persons, twenty Protestants and twenty Catholics, be now appointed, and be selected from the list of nobility and gentry of both persuasions, who concurred in those proceedings, for the purpose of considering the most effectual means for establishing a permanent junction of Catholics and Protestants, in order to insure a continuance of their exertions for the success of the cause in which we are all engaged, 'the religious peace of Ireland' . . .

RESOLVED That the committee is of opinion, that for the sake of our common country, as well as of the empire at large, all party and sectarian distinctions and jealousies should be buried in oblivion, and that all persons should be invited to advance and uphold the great cause of civil and religious freedom.

RESOLVED That it is the universal sentiment of this meeting, that no member of the committee is or shall be deemed to be bound by any resolution or proceeding to which he does not personally assent.

RESOLVED That no question be decided on its first mention, but that notice be inserted in the summons for a subsequent meeting that such a measure would be considered.

RESOLVED That it is expressly understood, that the proceedings of this committee are to have no publicity, farther than what may be sanctioned by a resolution of the committee.

15
Dublin University Brunswick Club : Objects
Thomas Wyse, Jr, *Historical Sketch of the late Catholic Association of Ireland*, London, 1829, Vol. II, p. ccxxi

1st Resolution . . . That the graduates of the University of Dublin feel themselves called on to unite, at the present important crisis, not from any principle of offence, but solely for defence; and that it is the bounden duty of every graduate of the University to stand fearlessly forward in defence of that church which the University was established to support – in defence of those laws, the dispensers of which that University was established to provide, and in defence of that religion, which that University was established to inculcate and disseminate.

2nd Resolution . . . That a society be now formed, entitled the Brunswick Constitutional Club of the Graduates of the University of Dublin; the principles of the club to be such as necessarily flow from a determination to preserve our Protestant constitution, and maintain the Protestant institutions of the country in their present integrity.

16
The Orange Order
Thomas Wyse, Jr, *Historical Sketch of the late Catholic Association of Ireland*, London, 1829, Vol. II, pp. ccxxiii–ccxxiv

It is not less the interest than the duty of Protestants to support, by every lawful means, the religious and civil establishments of their country. By these the honour of God and the happiness of man are most effectually secured. In the present era, our religion is menaced by the attacks of Popery and Infidelity, while our constitution is assailed by faction and sedition.

Against the double danger the Orange institution was formed, being so named in honour of King William the Third, Prince of Orange, the illustrious champion to whom Great Britain owes her deliverance from thraldom, spiritual and political, the establishment of the Protestant religion, and the inheritance of the Brunswick throne.

We lay no claim to exclusive loyalty, or exclusive Protestantism; but no man, unless his creed be Protestant, and his principles loyal, can associate with us. We recognise no other exclusions. Our institution receives, nay, solicits into its circle, every man whose religion and character can stand these tests.

We reject also an intolerant spirit . . .

17
The Brighton Co-operative Movement: A Co-operative Society, or Working Union: Objects, 1827
Dr William King's *The Co-operator*, 1 October 1828

The Objects of such a Society are, first, the mutual protection of the members against POVERTY: secondly, the attainment of a greater share of the COMFORTS of life: thirdly, the attainment of INDEPENDENCE by means of a common capital.

18
Provincial Medical and Surgical Association 1832: Prospectus and Rules
Ernest Muirhead Little, *History of the B.M.A., 1832–1932*, London: B.M.A., 1932, pp. 20-21; *Journal*, Vol. I, 1833, pp. iii–iv

The diligent collection of facts, accurately observed and faithfully recorded, supplies the foundation of all natural science.

From these are deduced general truths, which constitute the principles by which Science is rendered practically available. From their multiplication additional light is continually derived, new truths being elicited, or those which had been inferred from a too hasty or inadequate induction being rendered more accurate and precise. In Medicine the benefits of inductive science have been long felt and acknowledged. But great as is the store of facts accumulated by the labour of ages, and many and various as have been the attempts to generalise them into a consistent and harmonious system of principles, much remains yet to be done for giving to the Science of Medicine the perfection which it is capable of attaining. Nature is perfect in all her works, acting by general laws which are immutable. Man has the power of discovering those laws and of applying them to the uses of life, as is amply exemplified in the history of Physics. The laws of animal life may not admit of being ascertained with the same precision as those to which inanimate matter is obedient – yet by patient observation of facts, and a cautious induction, unbiassed by hypothesis, great accuracy may be attained in determining the inherent powers by which the animal frame lives, moves, and has its being.

In order that facts should be sufficiently abundant, it is necessary that they be derived from a wide field, and from numerous contributors. But the duties and cares of life prevent many from paying their mite into the general treasury, unless where arrangements are made for inciting to industry, and facilitating communication. Association ministers to these ends more effectually than any other means hitherto devised; and on this ground it is proposed to associate the Provincial Medical Practitioners of England, or at least as many as can be brought to rally round a common centre, on a comprehensive co-operative Institution, which by collecting the results of individual experience, and bringing the energies of many minds to bear on those unsettled points which have subjected Medicine to the imputation of being a conjectural art, may contribute to redeem its character, and to give to its operations more precision and greater certainty.

The foregoing views having, through private correspondence, been favoured with very general approval, and with promises of very extensive co-operation, it is now proposed to realise the conception, by founding 'A Provincial Medical and Surgical Association' for the purpose of collecting useful knowledge, and publishing 'Transactions' at such intervals as the matter furnished may warrant.

The objects of the Association, so far as they have yet been canvassed, are recited in the following paragraphs:

1. Collection of useful information, whether speculative or practical, through original Essays or Reports of Cases occurring in Provincial Hospitals, Infirmaries, or Dispensaries; or in Private Practice.

2. Increase of knowledge of the Medical Topography of England, through Statistical, Meteorological, Geological, and Botanical Inquiries.

3. Investigation of the Modifications of Endemic and Epidemic Diseases, on different situations, and at various periods, so as to trace so far as the present imperfect state of the art will permit, their connexions with peculiarities of soil or climate, or with the localities, habits, or occupations of the people.

4. Advancement of Medico-legal Science, through succinct Reports of whatever cases may occur in the Provincial Courts of Judicature.

5. Maintenance of the Honour and Respectability of the Profession generally, in the Provinces, by promoting friendly intercourse and free communication of its Members; and by establishing the harmony and good feeling which ought ever to characterize a liberal profession . . .

RULES

On Thursday, July 19th, 1832, a Meeting of more than fifty Medical Gentlemen took place, agreeably to advertisement, in the Board Room of the Worcester Infirmary, for the purpose of forming an Association under the above name. The venerable Dr Johnstone, of Birmingham, was unanimously called to the Chair; there were also present the following eminent individuals: Dr Kidd, Regius Professor of Physic, Oxford; Dr Barlow, of Bath; Dr Conolly, of Warwick; Dr W. Conolly, of Cheltenham; Dr Corrie, of Birmingham; Dr Evans, jun. of Ross; Dr Thomas, of Rose Lawn; Mr Hodgson, of Birmingham; Mr W. Sands Cox, of Birmingham; Mr Soden, of Bath; Mr Hetling, of Bristol; and many others, including most of the resident Faculty of Worcester and the neighbouring towns.

The following resolutions were passed unanimously:

1st. That a Provincial Medical and Surgical Association be now formed.

2nd. That the management of the Association be conducted by a President and Council, and two Secretaries, to be elected annually, agreeably to the following Provisional Constitution:

The Association to be managed by a President, two Secretaries, and a Council.

The several officers to be appointed annually, by a general meeting of members convened for that purpose, at whichever of the principal towns may be appointed; the place of such meeting being prospectively notified each year.

At this meeting shall be presented a Report, prepared by the Secretaries, of the general state of the Association, its proceedings, and pecuniary accounts; the Report to be afterwards printed, and a copy supplied to every member.

At this meeting it is also proposed, that one of the members shall be appointed to give, at the next Annual Meeting, an account of the state or progress of Medical Science during the last year, or an Oration on some subject connected with Medical Science, or a Biographical Memoir of some eminent cultivator of Medical Science, who may have resided in the Provinces.

President

The office of President to be honorary, and conferred on some senior Physician or Surgeon of eminence, resident in any of the provincial towns comprised in the circle of the Association.

Secretaries

The two Secretaries to be resident in Worcester, the place of publication, their duties being to attend to the printing of the transactions, and to correct the press; to be present at the meetings of the Council, and to keep the minutes thereof; to correspond with the members of the Association; to receive and submit to the Council all papers transmitted for publication; and to keep the financial accounts of the Association.

Council

The Council to consist of – members, to be selected from the principal provincial towns. The Council, with whom must rest the chief responsibility of publication, to have full power of deciding on all papers transmitted, and the consent of three of its members must be obtained before any paper can be published. It shall also be the duty of the Council to receive the subscriptions, when due, in their respective districts. Each member of the Association to pay one guinea on admission, and the same amount, annually, afterwards; the subscription to commence from the 1st of January each year, and to be considered as due, unless notice of its being withdrawn be given to one of the Secretaries, antecedently to the year for which it would be payable; for such subscription each member shall receive a copy of each part of the transactions published. Each volume to contain a list of all the members.

3rd. That Dr Johnstone, of Birmingham, be elected President of the Association for the ensuing year; that Dr Carrick, of Bristol, be elected President for the year 1833–4.

4th. That Dr Hastings and Mr Sheppard be Secretaries.

5th. That the following Members, with power to add to their number, do constitute the Council for the ensuing year.

6th. That each Member of the Association do pay the sum of one guinea per annum, towards printing the transactions of the Association, and defraying the incidental expenses, and that subscriptions do commence from the 1st of January, 1832.

19
The Manchester Anti-Corn Law Association, September 1838 : Objects

Archibald Prentice, *History of the Anti-Corn-Law League,*
Vol. 1, 1853, p. 75

. . . About seven o'clock the Committee of the Anti-Corn-Law Association took their seats on the platform, and J. B. Smith, Esq., having been called upon to preside, in introducing Mr Paulton, said he would take the opportunity of stating the objects for which the association had been established:

It had been established on the same righteous principle as the Anti-Slavery Society. The object of that society was to obtain the free right for the negroes to possess their own flesh and blood – the object of this was to obtain the free right of the people to exchange their labour for as much food as could be got for it; that we might no longer be obliged by law to buy our food at one shop, and that the dearest in the world, but be at liberty to go to that at which it can be obtained cheapest. It was an object in which men of all political opinions might unite without compromising those principles, and it was a fundamental rule of the association that no party politics should be mixed up in the discussion of the question . . .

20
The Manchester Anti-Corn Law Association and the Manchester Chamber of Commerce

(a) Henry Ashworth, *Recollections of Richard Cobden M.P., and the Anti-Corn-Law League,* London, Paris and New York, n.d. (preface 1876), pp. 32–5

(b) Archibald Prentice, *History of the Anti-Corn-Law League,*
Vol. I, 1853, pp. 108–9

(a)

Agreeably to a requisition to the President of the Manchester
Chamber of Commerce (Mr George Wm Wood, M.P. for Kendal), a General Meeting of the members was held on the 13th
December, 1838, to consider the effect of the law on the importation of Corn, and, if thought advisable, to petition Parliament for
its repeal. At the meeting, the President read a petition which he
had drawn up, setting forth very fully the evils occasioned by the
operations of the Corn Law; but during the discussion which
followed, it became evident that he and some of the directors
were divided in opinion, and that the President was more inclined to *modify* than to *repeal* the existing Law, and the prayer of
the petition which he had prepared was accordingly to that
effect. It was the largest meeting of the Chamber which had
ever assembled, and the discussion, after continuing for some
hours, was adjourned to the following week, (the 20th December,) when the attendance was still more numerous, and comprised the most eminent manufacturers and merchants of the
district. During the interval, Mr Cobden, Mr J. B. Smith, and I,
prepared another petition, praying for '*the Repeal of all Laws
relating to the Importation of Foreign Corn and other Foreign articles of
subsistence*', which was submitted to the meeting for approval.
The debate again extended over five hours, and the merits of the
rival petitions were amply discussed. During the whole of this
protracted sitting there was evidence of a deep and concentrated
interest, amounting even to a feeling of solemnity. The amended
form of petition was moved by Mr Cobden, and seconded by
Mr R. H. Greg, and was carried by a majority of about six to one,
and this was followed by the resignation of the President of the
Chamber, and the appointment of Mr J. B. Smith to the office.
   It was now seen to be necessary to follow up the action of the
Chamber of Commerce by a special organisation, and a small
body of thoughtful men, under the influence of Mr John Benjamin Smith and Mr Archibald Prentice, including Mr Cobden,
Mr Thos Bazley, Mr William Rawson, Mr W. R. Callender, my
brother Edmund, and myself, met for consultation. This little
company was very soon joined by other influential gentlemen,
and assumed the title of the 'Anti-Corn-Law Association'; and
on the 10th January, 1839, a meeting was held at the York Hotel,
'To consider the proper mode of carrying forward the proceedings

of the Anti-Corn-Law Association, in a manner commensurate with the magnitude of the obstacles to be surmounted, and worthy of the object for which it has been established.' Mr Cobden recommended to those present, an investment of part of their property, to save the rest from confiscation; and subscriptions were at once put down in the room for £1,800, and in the course of a month they had reached £6,136 10s. 0d. These proceedings gave vitality to the Association, which was soon enlarged, and adopted the title of 'The National Anti-Corn-Law League'. A small narrow room, in Newall's Buildings, Market-street, was hired for our meetings, or 'League Room', as we called it, and when first opened, there were usually not more than seven or eight members present, and the room being very cold, we had a red blanket hung up to mitigate the severity of the draughts of wind. When it became publicly known that an Association was in existence having in view the repeal of the Corn Law, people came from far and near, in the greatest anxiety, giving most doleful accounts of mills and other works which were standing idle, whilst the operatives were dependent on charity or on their various parishes for support. The Association had no funds to relieve this distress, and could only advance the object of the distressed by the publication of properly authenticated statements in the newspapers.

These statements brought the League into notice, and led to many small donations of money to advance its usefulness. The first subscription of the amount of ten pounds came from Mr Robert Stuart, of Ardwick, and was hailed as an omen of success; other and larger subscriptions soon began to pour in, and as it became necessary to make a show of organisation, we appointed Mr John Benjamin Smith, President; Mr William Rawson, Treasurer; and a few of our most energetic members were formed into an Executive Council for conducting the transactions of the Body . . .

(b)

. . . The Queen's speech made no allusion to the Corn Laws. Mr E. Buller, the mover of the address in the Commons, admitted the impossibility of sustaining high prices by the existing laws. The seconder, Mr George William Wood, President of the Manchester Chamber of Commerce, in obedience to instructions received from his constituents at Kendal, stated the injurious effects to manufacturers and labourers produced by the exclusion of foreign corn; but, elated by the honour conferred upon him by ministers, he thought he could not well fulfil his mission without adverting to the usual topic of address movers – the prosperity of the country – and in doing so, struck at the then main argument for repeal.

There was something [said the London *Examiner*] at once painful and ludicrous in the effect which this part of Mr Wood's speech produced. The astonishment of the advocates of free trade in the house – the nervous anxiety of the delegates under the gallery – the whispered assurances of the sagacious that 'Wood was a deep fellow, and would wind it all round before he sat down' – the respectful attention of Sir Robert Peel – the startling applause of the country gentlemen – and the unconscious, earnest, and solemn complacency with which the orator himself continued, brick by brick, to demolish the foundations of the castle he was commissioned to garrison – made what play writers call 'a situation', that would have been irresistibly droll, if the House of Commons were the Adelphi Theatre, and the Corn Laws a farce, instead of a question involving the interests of millions, and, perhaps, fraught with a fearful tragedy. Sir Robert Peel adroitly availed himself of Mr Wood's statements. With cutting irony, he thanked the honourable member for Kendal for the very able speech he had delivered in favour of the existing system, and, with all the art of the practised debater, expressed his hope that the house would pause before it acceded to any propositions which would have the effect of exchanging a law thus proved to be beneficial, and which would materially affect the agricultural interests of this country, having received from the President of the Chamber of Commerce at Manchester the account which had been given them of the *stable and secure* position of our commerce and manufactures!

This was availing himself, with a vengeance, of Mr Wood's unfortunate affection for 'prosperity' tables; but Mr Villiers at once cut down both the prosperity statist and the Tamworth baronet, by proofs of the worthlessness of the alleged proofs of an improvement in trade. Mr Brotherton had previously, in a plain and manly way, contradicted the statements made by Mr Wood, and shown the mischievous operation of the Corn Laws in diminishing the demand for labour. Lord John Russell left it in doubt whether he leaned to Mr Villiers or to Sir Robert Peel. He thought the subject of the Corn Laws deserved *investigation*. In the House of Lords, Lord Melbourne gave assurance that he was neither pledged to maintain nor to change the laws . . .

21
The Manchester Anti-Corn Law Association,
January 1839 : Rules

Archibald Prentice, *History of the Anti-Corn-Law League,*
Vol. I, 1853, pp. 104–5

... A meeting of the Manchester Association was held in Newall's Buildings, on the 28th of January [1839], J. B. Smith, Esq., in the chair, at which it was resolved:

1. That the association be called 'The Manchester Anti-Corn-Law Association', and its object is hereby declared to be, to obtain by all legal and constitutional means, such as the formation of local Anti-Corn-Law Associations, the delivery of lectures, the distribution of tracts, the insertion of articles in the public papers, and forwarding petitions to Parliament, the total and immediate repeal of the corn and provision laws.

2. No party political discussions shall, on any account be allowed at any of the general or committee meetings of the association; nor shall any resolution be proposed, or subject entertained which shall be at variance with the declared object of the association.

3. Every person who shall pay in advance an annual subscription shall be a member of the association.

4. Every person on paying a subscription of five shillings or upwards, per annum, shall receive from the secretary a ticket, which shall entitle the subscriber to attend all general meetings of the association, and to take part in the proceedings of the same.

5. The management of the officers of the association shall be vested in a council, to consist of a president, vice president, treasurer, and not less than one hundred members, to be chosen by the members out of their own body.

6. The council shall elect out of its own body an 'Executive Committee', consisting of twelve members, three to be a quorum, and other committees if necessary, whose duty shall be to conduct the business of the association.

7. The council shall also select out of its own body, a 'Finance Committee', consisting of eight members, three to be a quorum, whose duty shall be to receive all moneys on account of the association, and to pay the same to the treasurer, to examine all accounts and to direct payment by the treasurer.

8. The president, vice-president, and treasurer of the association shall be, *ex-officio*, members of every committee.

9. Every committee, at its first meeting, shall appoint out of its own body a chairman and deputy-chairman.

10. The council shall meet at least once a fortnight, to receive the reports of the sub-committees, and for the transaction of the general business of the association.

11. No alteration shall be made in the rules of the association, except at a general meeting of the members, convened for that purpose, of which a week's notice shall be given by public advertisement, in at least two of the Manchester newspapers . . .

22
The Anti-Corn Law League : a 'permanent union' formed 20 March 1839

Archibald Prentice, *History of the Anti-Corn-Law League,*
Vol. I, 1853, pp. 124–5

The delegates met again on Wednesday, the 20th, not convinced by the arguments which had been brought against their object in the 'collective wisdom of the nation', not disheartened by the numbers arrayed against them, but with fresh determination to go on in their great purpose. They could not conceal from themselves that a great number of the 195 who had voted in favour of considering the question, would fall off when a total repeal should be asked for; and that it was necessary, before that demand could be made with any reasonable prospect of success, that the constituencies and the country in general should be further instructed and aroused. An address to the public was agreed upon, in which the following, amongst other measures, were recommended and adopted:

The formation of a permanent union, to be called the Anti-Corn-Law League, composed of all the towns and districts represented in the delegation, and as many others as might be induced to form Anti-Corn-Law Associations and to join the League.

Delegates from the different local associations to meet for business, from time to time, at the principal towns represented.

With the view to secure the unity of action, the central office of the League shall be established in Manchester, to which body shall be entrusted, among other duties, that of engaging and recommending competent lecturers, the obtaining the co-operation of the public press, and the establishing and conducting of a stamped circular, for the purpose of keeping a constant correspondence with the local associations.

That, in addition to the funds subscribed for local purposes by the several associations, at least £5,000 should be raised to defray the expenses of the general League for the ensuing year, and that every sum of £50 entitle the individual, or association subscribing it, to one vote in the appropriation of the funds of the League, and that on all other questions the votes of the persons present be equal.

That this meeting adjourn, subject to the call of the Manchester Anti-Corn-Law Association; that it be left to their discretion at what time to bring forward the substantive question for the total abolition of the Corn Laws before Parliament, and to adopt any other measures to secure the great object of the association which they may think fit.

The delegates then separated to agitate the question in all their various localities, not many of them, perhaps, thinking that they should have to meet again and again, often in every year, during a seven years' struggle, but all determined, whether the contest were to be short or long, to enter upon it with spirit, and to persevere until its accomplishment; and many of them disposed to combine with their demand for free-trade a demand for a more fair and free representation, although they saw the propriety of confining the movement to one easily defined object, for which all honest politicians could unite. Meetings were immediately held in nearly all the great towns which had sent representatives to the London conference, and the delegates became so many local missionaries to spread the doctrines that had been enunciated in the metropolis . . .

23
Metropolitan Anti-Corn Law Association: Repeal of the Corn Laws

Leaflet No. 8, n.d. Cobden Papers 422, West Sussex Record Office

On Friday, March 27, 1840, the DUKE OF RICHMOND, in the House of Lords, complained that 'year after year this question was agitated, and thereby no landowner could sell his land, nor any tenant think it safe to take a lease, while certain paid parties went about the country teaching the labourer not to look with confidence to his employer, and preaching that the interest of the landlord and the tenant was not the same'. – *Morning Chronicle*.

Unhappily, the employers alluded to, and the landlords, have made it impossible for the 'labourers to look with confidence to their employers'.

The Duke must be very ignorant if he does not know that tenants very generally think that their interests, and those of their landlords, are not the same.

In 1815, the landlords obtained an Act of Parliament, to prevent – so they intended – the price of wheat from ever falling below 80/- a quarter, or that the price of the QUARTERN LOAF should ever be less than A SHILLING.

This Act was intended to secure to the landlords the double and treble rents which they had forced the farmer to pay during many years of war.

The Act was to prevent the rent of land from falling, as the price of every thing else fell.

The wages of the labourer might fall – the price of every kind of goods might fall – but neither the price nor the rent of land was to fall – so said the landowners then; so says the *Duke of Richmond* now.

The Duke says, 'The landowner cannot sell his land.'

The Duke says, 'Tenants will not take leases of landowners.'

These are two exaggerations, to say the least of them.

There are many persons who are able and willing to buy land at its fair value.

But the landowners are not content with the fair natural price, they want the war price – the Act of Parliament monopoly price; which no one who knows what he is about will give them.

There are plenty of farmers ready to take land at a fair rent, but the landowners are not content with a fair rent, they want a war rent – an Act of Parliament monopoly rent, which no one who knows what he is about will give them.

The evils of the Corn Laws are now understood; but the land-owners will resist their appeal as long as they can.

The people must therefore go on unweariedly.

The people must continue to petition.

Steady perseverance will compel the

REPEAL OF THE CORN LAWS

24
Young Men's Anti-Monopoly Association: Address, 1841
Cobden Papers 433, West Sussex Record Office

Young Men,

A righteous and a patriotic cause demands our assistance. Our Manufactures paralysed, our Commerce oppressed, the finances of the country embarrassed, proclaim a crisis too serious to be trifled with. Our country groans under the oppression of Monopoly! A momentous conflict has begun. Shall WE stand idly by?

During the last fifty years our country has increased in population, in wealth, and in national resources in a degree unparalleled in the annals of History. Agriculture has improved, and the value of land has increased in an unprecedented ratio. To the rise and progress of Manufactures, and of the industrial arts, aided by modern science, must this increase be attributed. Without our manufactures, agriculture, in its present extent, could not subsist a single day; and without their aid, the fertile plains of England would recur to pristine rudeness. Agriculture and Manufactures united by Commerce – such is the law of God and nature! What God hath joined let no man put asunder.

To embarrass or impede the extension of our manufactures and commerce is a national suicide – as insane in its character, as it must be awful in its results. The spell of our greatness would be broken, and a starved population and ruined capital would indicate to the nations of the earth the wreck of former prosperity and the beacon of future ages. Yet such is the prospect which now threatens us! A wicked and unjust spirit of monopoly pervades our commercial legislation, and already does the rapid increase of poverty and crime point to the abyss which yawns upon us.

We hold that all government, wherever placed, or by whomsoever wielded, is a sacred duty held in trust for the happiness of all; and that it is unjust, as well as impolitic, to interfere, in any degree, with the liberty or property of the subject, for the exclusive benefit of a class. But monopoly denies to us the liberty of frequenting the cheapest market for the supply of our wants, and of exercising our industry in the most profitable manner. It thus robs us of the wealth which we are compelled to pay in the shape of increased price to the monopolist, and prevents the further creation of an indefinite amount of wealth which would otherwise be produced, and which would be a fresh guarantee of Peace and Plenty to Mankind. It is equivalent to the extension of the Pension List to the whole body of monopolists, or to the annual destruction, by fire or wreck, of the whole amount of wealth thus lost to the nation. Some faint idea may be formed of the extent of this loss when we state, on no less an authority than John Deacon Hume, one of the secretaries of the Board of Trade, that from one monopoly alone, viz., the corn and provision laws, the direct annual loss is estimated at no less than THIRTY-SIX MILLIONS per annum!

Monopoly, stripped of the sophistry in which self-interested advocates have disguised it, means the spoliation of the Many, whose wealth has been accumulated by *industry*, for the exclusive benefit of a class whose wealth is increased *without industry*. It is thus a national premium upon Idleness and its attendant vices, and is one of the principal causes of the contempt with which the industrial class is too frequently regarded. There are not, however, wanting those who attempt to justify monopoly under the plea of protection; but if protection by Act of Parliament be of any pecuniary benefit, such benefit must be obtained at the expense of some other party. 'Protection' is but a smoother name for robbery, and is the policy of the sharper who puts his hands into his neighbours' pockets for the 'protection' of his own interests.

That 'Honesty is the best Policy' is a maxim as true of nations as it is of individuals; and the disastrous reaction of monopolies upon the very interests they were intended to *protect*, is an instructive warning to us for our future guidance. Not a single branch of industry but labours under the general depression; not a market but is glutted with our products. Monopoly refuses us the liberty of exchanging them for the products of other climes, and we are now famishing in the midst of Plenty – the Laughing-stock of nations – and this for the especial benefit of a few powerful monopolists!

But this supremacy of monopoly must not – shall not last! As young men, struggling for the enjoyment of a profitable and honourable subsistence, we feel that we have far too deep a stake in our country's prosperity to remain idle or indifferent spectators. The increasing scarcity of situations, the small remuneration for talent and industry, and the increasing embarrassments of our employers, prove how greatly our own interests are at stake, and how deeply we are involved in the common weal. Yet, powerful as these considerations may be, addressing themselves, as they do, to our private interests, we are not insensible to motives of a yet higher character.

The obstruction which monopoly opposes to the onward progress of Humanity is a consideration pregnant with interest in the estimation of those who watch with anxiety the ameliorating influence of civilization, and who love to cherish high hopes for the future destinies of our species.

The past history of our race proclaims the supremacy of force, the selfishness of empire, and the subjugation of mankind, as the prevailing aspect of society. But the rise and progress of the industrial arts, and the extension of a beneficent Commerce, indicate, in terms too plain to be misunderstood, the real Destiny of society and the existence of a new Epoch which shall substitute the ploughshare for the sword, and the loom for the battery. The cause of Industry is the cause of Humanity. Instead of the subjugation of mankind, and the devastation of the earth, let peaceful and attractive industry propose, as its highest aim, the *enrichment of all* by the *civilization and embellishment of the globe*.

But, if this be our aim, we must unshackle industry from the chains with which monopoly has fettered it, and we must vindicate the principle of *freedom of industry and security of property*, without which, the tide of human progress will be stayed.

The time has arrived when we are called upon to choose between the artificial interests of monopolies and the interests of humanity at large. If monopoly continue we shall witness the rise of a commercial feudalism more dreadful than the feudalism of the middle ages. Self-preservation is the first law of nature, and if we tamely yield our right to freedom of industry we become the slaves of a few overgrown monopolists from whom we shall be compelled to receive a paltry pittance for our subsistence in return for our base treachery to ourselves and our fellow-creatures. The proclamation has gone forth. WE MUST DESTROY MONOPOLY, OR MONOPOLY WILL DESTROY US! Already have the young men of Manchester assembled to prepare for the conflict. We have established a Young Man's Anti-Monopoly Association for the purpose of combining our energies more effectually in the approaching struggle. Our subscription is small, and our organization is simple. We place our reliance not so much on the extent of our funds as on the Righteousness of our Cause, and on the numbers and devotion of our fellow-members. We have to do the work Ourselves, each according to his ability, whether by lecturing, by discussion, by writing for the press, by conversation, or by distribution of tracts. Personal influence and Personal energy are the weapons we depend on for success in our cause.

The campaign has begun, and we summon to our aid every young man who, with true heart and fervent devotion to the cause of Industrial Emancipation, is anxious to make battle against the tyrant of Monopoly, and to protect the interests of himself, and of those he holds dearer than himself, from the ruin which threatens us. Manchester has taken the lead, and now calls aloud for help! Let every town, and village, and hamlet bestir itself, and send forth its youth in this glorious and peaceful crusade.

By Order of the Provisional Committee,
Edward Herford, Chairman
June, 1841

25
Association for the Protection of Agriculture: letter to Secretary, 2 January 1844 from Sir Edward Dering, a landowner

Brighton Gazette, 11 January 1844, quoting the *Maidstone Journal*

If the Government mean to act fairly by us (which I hope and believe will be the case) the formation of these Associations for the protection of agriculture throughout the kingdom will strengthen their hands, and show them that if on one side they have to contend against the pressure of the League, on the other they have the broad shoulders of the agriculturalists, on which they may confidently rely for support. If again we have anything to apprehend from the Government, and the farmer is to be thrown overboard, how much better will we be prepared to resist an attack, if by a happy blending together of landlord and tenant (and, I may in truth add, the labourer) in one common bond of union, we can come forward united in behalf of those great interests, which have ever been justly considered the foundation of national prosperity?

26
The Anti-League, 1844

Why are the Anti-Corn-Law League like the letter M? Because they make *Masses* of *asses*.

Brighton Gazette, 11 January 1844

Sir C. Knightley at a meeting of tenant-farmers at Northampton:
'Amongst our enemies are ranked the whole of the Radicals, Jacobins, and the whole refuse of mankind. The League, called the Anti-Corn Law League, is, I think, the most pestiferous

F

Society that has ever been formed since the days of the Jacobin Club during the French Revolution.' (Cheers)
Brighton Herald, 27 January 1844

It is the intention of the Duke of Richmond and other members of both Houses to form a Metropolitan Society for the Protection of British agriculture.
Brighton Gazette, 8 February 1844

'. . . all room for doubt is past. The counter-movement is in real existence.' A leader of it in Lincolnshire had proposed 'a committee of gentlemen be appointed to correspond with the Societies formed in Essex and Sussex, so that a common mode of action might be adopted for counteracting the poison circulated by the Anti-Corn-Law Agitators; and we take for granted that this hint will be acted upon generally, until perhaps the whole may be ultimately amalgamated into one national and magnificent COUNTER-LEAGUE'.
Editorial in *Brighton Gazette*, 11 January 1844

27
The Anti-League 1846
The Duke of Richmond in the House of Lords, January 1846, quoted in the *Brighton Guardian*, 28 January 1846

He saw no difference between the government of the country and the Anti-Corn Law League. (Laughter.) He could not see any reason why Mr Cobden should not be created a peer of the realm. The course of the League had been most unconstitutional; they were the authors of the whole of the change which the Minister was about to propose, but which he hoped the House would not sanction, for he trusted that the house would never so far abandon its duty to the country as to be intimidated by the Anti-Corn Law League, or its money (Cheers) . . .

It was contrary to every principle ever brought forward by the present government when they were seeking for office. These changes ought not to be made without an appeal to the country.

28
The Agriculturists : through a journalist's eyes, 1846
Editorial in *Brighton Guardian*, 21 January 1846

. . . the landlord-ridden, landlord-enfeebled and deteriorated agriculturists. They have basked so long in the *far niente* (do

nothing) rays of protection, that, like the lazzaroni, they dread
the vigorous competition which excites the energies and promotes
the happiness of men liable to the stirring changes of wind and
storm and rain and fine weather.

29
The Anti-Corn Law League: its significance
for politics assessed by John Bright
Henry Ashworth, *Recollections of Cobden and the League*, pp. 324–31

. . . I am, at this moment, impressed with a feeling of the greatest
possible delight, that the object, for which we have been banded
together, is at length accomplished; but that feeling is tinged with
one of another character, when I remember that in all probability
we are about to separate finally from friends with whom we have
been long connected, and that we have no longer in pursuit an
object, which has been the most cherished of our lives. At such
a meeting as this, and in such circumstances, I would be the very
last man to utter one syllable of unworthy exultation over those
who have been defeated. (Hear, hear.) But I am of opinion that
this final meeting may have some result beyond that of merely
determining to wind up the affairs of the League; that by it we
may point a moral, and learn a lesson; that we may contemplate
the past, and to some extent look into the future. (Hear, hear.)
To the public, to those men especially, who don't think very
deeply, the object of the League is accomplished when the Corn
Law is repealed; but if a thinking and philosophic mind were
asked what the League has done, I am of opinion that his answer
would include many other points and many other things, beyond
the repeal of a particular statute. (Hear, hear.) The public have
learned that there is nothing that can be held out to the intelligent
people of this kingdom, which is so calculated to stimulate them
to action, to united and persevering action, as a great and sacred
principle like that which was espoused by the League. (Hear,
hear.) They have learned that there is in public opinion, a
power much greater than that which resides in any particular
form of government; that although you have in this kingdom a
system of government which is called 'popular' and 'representative' – a system which is somewhat clumsily contrived, and which
works with many jars and joltings – this still, under the impulse
of a great principle, with great labour, and with great sacrifices,
all those obstacles are overcome, so that out of a machine especially contrived for the contrary, justice and freedom is at

length achieved for the nation; and the people have learned something beyond this, namely, that the way to freedom is henceforward not through violence and bloodshed. (Hear, hear, and loud cheers.) This Anti-Corn-Law League will henceforth stand before the world as the sign of a new order of things. Until now, this country has been ruled by the class of great proprietors of the soil. Everyone must have foreseen that as trade and manufactures extended, the balance of power would, at some time or other, be thrown into another scale. Well, that time has come – (hear, hear) – and the rising of this League seven years ago, was sufficient to have pointed out to any statesmen that the power of the landed aristocracy had reached its height, and that henceforth it would find a rival to which eventually it must become subjected. (Cheers.) We have been living through a revolution without knowing it. In 1833 the House of Lords deemed itself a power in the state irresponsible except to heaven, and able to say absolutely whether a law should pass or not. The House of Lords now makes no such pretensions. Lord Stanley declared, 'God forbid, that your lordships should set yourselves against the clearly expressed will of the people'; and I heard (for I listened to most of their debates on this question) – I heard several other members of the House of Peers make use of very similar expressions. I say that the vast population of Lancashire and Yorkshire – with their interests, their morality, and their union – must exercise an immense influence upon all future legislation in this kingdom, and that the direction of future legislation must be in accordance with the prevailing sentiments of those two counties; and there is not a man in the kingdom knows this better than Sir Robert Peel. There is no man more likely to know it, for he was born amongst us, and I confess that in looking at the course which he has pursued during the last session, I have felt some satisfaction that the man, who came forward to give the finishing stroke to that gigantic monopoly which we have opposed, should have been a man born amongst us, sprung from the trade of this district, of a family who have done much to create and extend the industry of this district, and the wealth of whose family has to be traced entirely to that industry. (Hear, hear.) At the commencement of the present session, Sir Robert Peel showed that he knew where lay the power of this kingdom. When the address was to be moved, an address almost pledging the House of Commons to sanction some great measure of commercial reform, the members chosen to move and second that address, were the members for the West Riding of Yorkshire, and for South Lancashire – (hear, hear) –

and I am certain that henceforth a representative from these districts will have a large influence in the House of Commons; and that as the spirit, which is now originated, extends and becomes perpetual, we shall have a much better representation for these districts than we ever had before; and that members for these counties will take the position in the House of Commons, as well as in the country, which their constituents take out of doors. I said we have been living in a revolution, and I am prepared to maintain it. Not such a revolution as that which we were charged with wishing to make. We all recollect the seditions, the conspiracies, and the ulterior objects, the democracy, the revolution, the destruction of property, and all the other things, which were laid to the charge of this National Anti-Corn-Law League. I put it to the meeting, – is the crown less popular now, than it was seven years ago? (Cries of 'no', and cheers.) Is not the Queen as safe in the occupation of her throne without any aspirant – without anyone to envy, or to slander her, as she ever was at any time? (Hear, hear.) Even the House of Lords itself, I believe, stands at this moment infinitely better, in the respect and the affections of the people, than it has done for many years. (Cheers.) We don't look at the House of Lords now, as a body which is either ignorantly or wickedly maintaining a law, which we believe to be unjust to millions of the people. We look upon it as a house, tending – unfortunately sometimes too much – to moderate the legislation of another House, which nobody, I think, will contend goes on too fast for us; but I must confess that I have a greater respect for the House of Lords, from watching their passing of this Bill, and the manner in which they have passed it, than I ever had at any former period. (Cheers.) . . . In conclusion, I would briefly refer to the period when we were first banded together. For several years previous to 1837, we had abundant harvests, good trade, prosperity, and comfort; and for several years after, we had the reverse of that state of things. We found merchants and manufacturers engaged in trade, who, without any cause or sensible reason, so far as they themselves were concerned, found their prosperity wasted, their business destroyed, and themselves driven into the *Gazette*, without any charge of dishonesty; and in this way a wreck of property took place, which was painful to behold. (Hear, hear.) And we saw also, that the working classes were brought to want and suffering. In fact, then was the time, when it was said 'human food was very dear, and flesh and blood were cheap'. (Hear, hear.) At that time, we associated together, for the purpose of repealing the laws, which, we believed, brought those inflictions upon us. It may appear that seven or eight years is a long time to be engaged in controversy, in order to bring about what was merely an act of justice – (hear, hear) – but, let us consider the elements we have had at command to effect our object. We were an association formed for the most part of commercial people, unlearned in agitation and unskilled in logic and rhetoric, and lacking those arts of oratory which our opponents possessed; and therefore it was hardly to be expected that we should accomplish a result such as we have now achieved in even so short a time as eight years. (Applause.) Gentlemen, it is now seen that business industry, with a good cause, can beat titled power with a bad one. (Cheers.) We now know our strength, – it behoves us not to use it heedlessly and improperly, but, at the same time, not to hesitate to use it on all proper occasions. The League has now finished its work, and in taking leave of it, I will adopt the language used by one of our distinguished converts on a recent occasion, namely, that the name of the League will live in the execration of monopolists, but that it will be gratefully remembered in the homes of toiling labour (hear, hear); and that when the workman comes to refresh his strength with food, it may be all the sweeter because it has not been leavened with taxation. (Cheers.)

30
The Manchester Complete Suffrage Union
Objects and Rules, n.d. (c. 1842)

OBJECTS

I *Universal Suffrage*
To obtain for each Man of twenty-one years of age, the right of Voting for Representatives to serve in the Common's House of Parliament.

II *Electoral Districts*
That for the purpose of securing a fair and equal representation of the people, it is necessary that the whole country be divided into districts, each containing as nearly as may be an equal number of Electors.

III *Annual Parliaments*
That it is of great importance to secure and maintain the responsibility of Members to their Constituents, and that Annual Parliaments are a proper means for securing this object.

IV *No Property Qualification*

That every Elector shall be eligible to be Elected.

V *The Ballot*

That the Right of Voting for a Representative, shall be exercised secretly by Ballot.

VI *Payment of Members*

That each Representative of the People shall be paid for his services.

It will be the duty of the Society to adopt all legal means by which these objects may be promoted.

RULES

Members

1. All persons are admitted Members of this Association upon enrolment of their names and addresses in the books of the Association, and on Payment of a Subscription for the current year of One Shilling, but no person's name shall be so entered until such Subscription is paid.

Every person, upon becoming a Member, is requested to make a donation of such further sum of Money as he may think proper.

General Meetings

1. An Annual General Meeting of the whole of the Member, shall be held on the last Wednesday in the month of June, 1843 and so on, from year to year, until the object proposed shall be obtained.

2. General Meetings of the Members may, at any time, be called by order of the Executive Committee, or on a requisition signed by twelve Members of the General Committee, or by fifty Members of the Association.

3. At the Annual General Meeting, the Secretary shall produce the books in his possession, and shall read the statement of accounts signed by the Auditors.

4. No alteration shall be made in any of the Rules of the Association except by a Majority of the Members present at a General Meeting, notice of the intention to propose such alteration having been given at the preceding General Meeting, and a Copy of such notice having been sent to the Members at least a week prior to the Meeting being held.

Management

The general management of the Association shall be in the General Committee, the details to be carried out by the Executive Committee.

General Committee

1. The General Committee shall consist of fifty Members, and shall be elected at the Annual Meeting for one year.

2. The General Committee shall meet once a quarter, and as much oftener as it may deem necessary.

3. It shall appoint from its own body an Executive Committee, consisting of Twenty Members, for twelve months, and fill up such vacancies as may occur.

4. It shall appoint two Auditors to inspect the accounts, and certify their correctness or incorrectness to the Annual General Meeting of the Association.

Executive Committee

1. It shall meet, at least, once a fortnight, and as much oftener as may be necessary; three to form a quorum.

2. It shall have the power to employ such persons as the business may require, and at such rates as may be necessary.

3. It shall keep accounts and minutes of its proceedings, and shall lay them before the General Committee at its Meetings.

The Secretary

1. He shall keep the minute-books, the account-books, and such other books as may be necessary, either by his own hands, or by those of his Assistants.

2. He shall be responsible for the accuracy of all the Books.

3. He shall produce all the books which may be required at every Meeting of the General and Executive Committees.

4. He shall produce all the books, vouchers, &c. which may be necessary, or may be required by the Auditors, and shall give them whatever assistance they may require, in making up the accounts.

Finance

1. All Money shall be received by the Secretary, and be by him paid to the Treasurer at least once a week.

2. No accounts or Money shall be paid by the Treasurer, except by order of the Executive Committee, signed by two Members of the Executive, and countersigned by the Secretary.

3. The Secretary shall lay his accounts before the Executive Committee, at each of its Meetings.

31
Robert Owen, Chairman of the Rational Society's Congress at Harmony, Hampshire to Richard Cobden, M.P.: Address, 25 May 1843

Cobden Papers 586, West Sussex Record Office

Sir and Gentlemen and Fellow Men,

The Congress of the Rational Society met in its Annual Session in the Hall of the Society at Harmony, Hants, to address you at this critical period in the affairs of our common Country in which you Gentlemen and this Congress have so deep an interest.

You desire to terminate the system of Monopoly, which of course includes the monopoly of the corn and other provision laws, herein we perfectly agree with you; and while you remain true to your own stated principles, we will, as a society, give you our most cordial support, to the full extent of the principles which you have leagued to advocate. If we understand you aright in this case it is to abolish for ever the principles and practice of monopoly, not merely of the corn and other provisions, but through all the ramifications of society in which monopoly can be found. It is a just and beneficient principle, and will prove ultimately most beneficial for the Human race, as such it will allways [sic] have our most decided approval and aid.

Will you now fellowmen of every class which constitute your league, consent to adopt the shortest, easiest and as we believe the most just and best course to ensure success to your views? . . .

But you appear to give an importance to the mere repeal of the corn laws greatly beyond any result, which can be reasonably anticipated from their abolition. For without 'Free Trade in all things with all the World' and the appendages which such an altered state of society will require, the repeal alone of the Corn laws can effect but little in the social condition of society, which requires to be new modelled. And why do you desire now a repeal of the corn laws? To give, as you say, remunerating wages for labor [sic]. But Gentlemen are you sure, that the mere repeal of the corn laws would give this employment in the strangely altered condition of our country, and the rapidly altering condition of other countries; a change produced by the extensive introduction of scientific power upon the magnificent scale in which it is now advancing throughout the civilized world.

It will be well for you to pause and deliberate with care and circumspection, before you come to any such hasty conclusion upon this now all important question.

Signed by order and on behalf of the Congress of the Rational Society

Robert Owen, President of the Rational Society and Chairman of Congress

32
Rochdale Equitable Pioneers' Co-operative Store: progress, 1843–60

Rev. W. N. Molesworth's Paper to the British Association, 1861. Cobden Papers 437, West Sussex Record Office

The progress of co-operation in Rochdale has excited much attention and interest . . . The first thing that seems to be requisite, is to give some sort of definition of the principle which is embodied in these societies, and I cannot do this better than by copying their own statement of their objects.

The objects of this society are the social and intellectual advancement of its members; it provides them with groceries, butcher's meat, drapery goods, clothing, shoes, clogs, &c. There are competent workmen on the premises, to do the work of the members, and execute all repairs. The capital is raised in £1 shares; each member being allowed to take not less than five, and not more than one hundred, payable at once or by instalments of three shillings and threepence per quarter. The profits are divided quarterly as follows: 1st. Interest at 5 per cent per annum, on all paid-up shares; 2nd. $2\frac{1}{2}$ per cent of net profits for educational purposes, the remainder divided amongst the members in proportion to money expended. For the intellectual improvement of the members, there is a library consisting of more than 3,000 volumes. The librarian is in attendance every Wednesday and Saturday evening, from seven to half-past eight o'clock. The newsroom is well supplied with newspapers and periodicals, fitted up in a neat and careful manner, and furnished with maps, globes, microscope, telescope, &c. The newsroom and library are free to all members. A branch reading room has been opened at Oldham-road, the readers of which meet every second Monday in January, April, July, and October, to choose and sell the papers. . . .

It may, perhaps, provoke a smile to find in the above-cited statement of objects, 'social and intellectual advancement', placed in such close juxtaposition with 'groceries, butcher's meat, drapery goods, clothing, shoes and clogs'. But there is a real and very close connection between these two classes of things. Men must be provided with the necessaries of life, or they will be unable to devote attention to their social and intellectual advancement; and the more abundantly their material wants are supplied, and the more they are released from care and anxiety about these wants, the more time will they have at their disposal to devote to their mental and spiritual improvement; and the greater, as a general rule, will be their intellectual, social, moral, aye, and I would even add, their religious progress.

There are, no doubt, instances in every class, and in every society, in which the increase of national prosperity is attended by an indulgence of the lowest passions and vices of our nature; but all experience shows that such cases are rare and exceptional, and that for one instance in which the leisure and opportunities which increased prosperity brings, are abused and perverted, there are thousands in which they are rightly and beneficially used.

I know that it is a sort of moral and philosophical common place to associate wealth with licentiousness, corruption, and decay – to point to Tyre and Babylon, and Rome as instances and proofs that the acquisition of unbounded wealth, and the consequent command of all the necessaries of life, and a vast abundance of superfluities is the harbinger of decay, and the cause of the most frightful moral and political dissolution. But it was not the wealth of these cities, but the excessive inequality of its distribution that produced their downfal [sic]. When the opulence of the few stands in ominous contrast with the squalidness and misery of the multitude – when on the one hand there is superabundance and on the other starvation, here riotous licentiousness, and there cowering downtrodden sullen servility – when every Dives looks with an indifferent eye on thousands of Lazaruses – then it is that the wealth of a state is the cause of its dissolution, and the forerunner of its fall. But when the wealth of a society is, not equally but equitably distributed through all its various classes, when in fact it is allowed to take its normal and natural course, then the material progress, becomes the instrument and the condition of every other description of progress.

I have dwelt on this point at a length somewhat out of proportion to the size of the paper, because it is one with regard to which a good deal of error and misconception prevails, and because the principle of making material progress, the basis of intellectual and social progress is, I believe, a fundamental principle of co-operation. . . .

33
Methodist organization: the class meeting, 1741
Robert Southey, *The Life of Wesley and the Rise and Progress of Methodism*, London, 1820, Vol. 1, pp. 391–5

. . . The organization of Methodism, which, at this time [1741], may vie with that of any society that has ever been instituted, for the admirable adaptation of the means to the end proposed, was slowly developed, and assisted in its progress by accidental circumstances. When the meeting-house was built at Bristol, Wesley had made himself responsible for the expenses of the building: subscriptions and public collections had been made at the time, but they fell short. As the building, however, was for their public use, the Methodists at Bristol properly regarded the debt as public also; and Wesley was consulting with them concerning measures for discharging it, when one of the members proposed that every person in the society should contribute a penny a week, till the whole was paid. It was observed that many of them were poor, and could not afford it. 'Then,' said the proposer, 'put eleven of the poorest with me, and if they can give any thing, well; I will call on them weekly, and if they can give nothing, I will give for them as well as for myself. And each of you call upon eleven of your neighbours weekly, receive what they give, and make up what is wanting.' The contribution of class-money thus began, and the same accident led to a perfect system of inspection. In the course of their weekly calls the persons who had under-taken for a class, as these divisions were called, discovered some irregularities among those for whose contributions they were responsible, and reported it to Wesley. Immediately he saw the whole advantage that might be derived from such an arrange-ment. This was the very thing which he had long wanted to effect. He called together the leaders, and desired that each would make a particular inquiry into the behaviour of those under his care. 'They did so,' he says; 'many disorderly walkers were detected; some turned from the evil of their ways; some were put away from us; many saw it with fear, and rejoiced unto God with reverence.' A few weeks afterwards, as soon as Wesley arrived in London, he called together some of his leading disciples, and explained to them the great difficulty under which he had hither-to laboured, of properly knowing the people who desired to be under his care. They agreed that there could be no better way to come at a sure and thorough knowledge of every individual, than by dividing them into classes, under the direction of those who could be trusted, as had been done at Bristol. Thenceforth, whenever a society of Methodists was formed, this arrangement was followed: a scheme for which Wesley says he could never sufficiently praise God, its unspeakable usefulness having ever since been more and more manifest.

The business of the leaders was to see every person in his class at least once a week, in order to inquire how their souls prospered; to advise, reprove, comfort or exhort, as occasion might require; and to receive what they were willing to give toward the expenses of the society, and the relief of the poor. They were also to meet the minister and the stewards of the society, that they might inform the minister of any that were sick, and of any that were disorderly, and would not be reproved, and pay to the stewards what they had collected from their several classes in the week preceding. At first they visited each person at his own house, but this was soon found, on many accounts, to be inexpedient, and even impracticable. It required more time than the leaders could spare; many persons lived with masters, mistresses, or relations, who would not suffer them to be thus visited; and when this frequent and natural objection did not exist, it often happened that no opportunity could be had of speaking to them, except in the presence of persons who did not belong to the society, so that the purpose of the visit was rendered useless. Differences, also, and misunderstandings between members of the same class could not be cleared up, unless the parties were brought face to face. For these reasons it was soon determined that every class should assemble weekly. Advice or reproof was then given, as need required; quarrels were made up, misunderstandings were removed; and after an hour or two had thus been passed, the meeting concluded with prayer and singing.[1] 'It can scarcely be conceived,' says Wesley, 'what advantages have been reaped from this little prudential regulation. Many now happily experienced that Christian fellowship, of which they had not so

1. The leader has a class paper, upon which he marks, opposite to the name of each member, upon every day of meeting, whether the person has attended or not; and if absent, whether the absence was owing to distance of abode, business, sickness, or neglect. And every member has a printed class ticket, with a text of scripture upon it, and a letter. These tickets must be renewed every quarter, the text being changed, and the letter also, till all the alphabet has been gone through, and then it begins again. One shilling is paid by every member upon receiving a new ticket; and no person, without a proper ticket, is considered a member of the society. These were later regulations; but the main system of finance and inspection, for which the class meetings provide, was established at this time, in consequence of the debt incurred for the first meeting-house.

much as an idea before. They began to bear one another's burdens, and naturally to care for each other. As they had daily a more intimate acquaintance with, so they had a more endeared affection for each other. Evil men were detected and reproved: they were borne with for a season; if they forsook their sins we received them gladly; if they obstinately persisted therein, it was openly declared that they were not of us. The rest mourned and prayed for them, and yet rejoiced, that as far as in us lay the scandal was rolled away from the society.'

34
Significance of Methodist organization
for working-class associations

Robert Southey, *The Life of Wesley and the Rise and Progress of Methodism*, Vol. II, pp. 533–4

. . . Some evil also, as well as some good, the Methodists have indirectly caused. Though they became careful in admitting lay-preachers themselves, the bad example of suffering any ignorant enthusiast to proclaim himself a minister of the gospel, found numerous imitators. The number of roving adventurers[1] in all the intermediate grades between knavery and madness, who took to preaching as a thriving trade, brought an opprobrium upon religion itself; and when an attempt was made at last to put an end to this scandal, a most outrageous and unreasonable cry was raised, as if the rights of conscience were invaded.[2] Perhaps the manner in which Methodism has familiarized the

1. One magistrate in the county of Middlesex licensed fourteen hundred preachers in the course of five years. Of six-and-thirty persons who obtained licences at one session, six spelled 'ministers of the gospel' in six different ways, and seven signed their mark! One fellow, who applied for a licence, being asked if he could read, replied, 'Mother reads, and I 'spounds and 'splains.'

2. A writer in the Gospel Magazine says, concerning Lord Sidmouth's well-meant bill, 'By the grace of God I can speak for one. If in any place I am called to preach, and cannot obtain a licence, I shall feel myself called upon to break through all restrictions, even if death be the consequence; for I know that God will avenge his own elect against their persecutors, let them be who they may. The men that are sent of God must deliver their message, whether men will hear, or whether they will forbear; whether they can obtain a licence or not. If God opens their mouths, none can shut them.' – Every man his own Pope, and his own lawgiver! These are days in which authority may safely be defied in such cases; but there is no reason to doubt that the man who speaks thus plainly would not have been as ready to break the laws as to defy them. Had he been born in the right place and time, he would have enjoyed a glorification in the Grass Market.

lower classes to the work of combining in associations, making rules for their own governance, raising funds, and communicating from one part of the kingdom to another, may be reckoned among the incidental evils which have resulted from it; but in this respect it has only facilitated a process to which other causes had given birth . . .

35
The East India Company: as viewed by Karl Marx, 1853
New York Daily Tribune, 22 June and 15 July 1853. In Marx and Engels, *On Colonialism*, Moscow, 1968, pp. 30-4 and 70-4

The last India Bill of 1783 proved fatal to the Coalition Cabinet of Mr Fox and Lord North. The new India Bill of 1853 is likely to prove fatal for the Coalition Cabinet of Mr Gladstone and Lord John Russell. But if the former were thrown overboard, because of their attempt to abolish the Courts of Directors and of Proprietors, the latter are threatened with a similar fate for the opposite reason. On June 3, Sir Charles Wood moved for leave to bring in a bill to provide for the Government of India. Sir Charles commenced by excusing the anomalous length of the speech he was about to deliver, by the 'magnitude of the subject', and 'the 150,000,000 of souls he had to deal with'. For every 30,000,000 of his fellow-subjects, Sir Charles could do no less than sacrifice one hour's breath. But why this precipitate legislation on that 'great subject', while you postpone it 'for even the most trifling matters'? Because the Charter of the East India Company expires on the 30th April, 1854. But why not pass a temporary continuance bill, reserving to future discussion more permanent legislation? Because it cannot be expected that we shall ever find again 'such an opportunity of dealing quietly with this vast and important question' – i.e., of burking it in a Parliamentary way. Besides, we are fully informed on the matter, the Directors of the East India Company express the opinion that it is necessary to legislate in the course of the present session, and the Governor-General of India, Lord Dalhousie, summons the Government by an express letter by all means to conclude our legislation at once. But the most striking argument wherewith Sir Charles justifies his immediate legislation, is that, prepared as he may appear to speak of a world of questions, 'not comprised in the bill he proposed to bring in', the '*measure* which he has to submit is, so far as legislation goes, *comprised in a very small compass*'.

After this introduction Sir Charles delivered himself of an

apology for the administration of India for the last twenty years. 'We must look at India with somewhat of an Indian eye' – which Indian eye seems to have the particular gift of seeing everything bright on the part of England and everything black on the side of India. 'In India you have a race of people slow of change, bound up by religious prejudices and antiquated customs. There are, in fact, all obstacles to rapid progress.' (Perhaps there is a Whig Coalition party in India.)

'The points,' said Sir Charles Wood, 'upon which the greatest stress has been laid, and which are the heads of the complaints contained in the petitions presented to the Committee, relate to the administration of justice, the want of public works, and the tenure of land.' . . . The clauses of the India Bill are passing one by one, the debate scarcely offering any remarkable features, except the inconsistency of the so-called India Reformers. There is, for instance, my Lord Jocelyn, M.P., who has made a kind of political livelihood by his periodical denunciation of Indian wrongs, and of the maladministration of the East India Company. What do you think his amendment amounted to? To give the East India Company a lease for ten years. Happily, it compromised no one but himself. There is another professional 'Reformer', Mr Jos. Hume, who, during his long parliamentary life, has succeeded in transforming opposition itself into a particular manner of supporting the Ministry. He proposed not to reduce the number of East India Directors from twenty-four to eighteen. The only amendment of common sense, yet agreed to, was that of Mr Bright, exempting Directors nominated by the Government from the qualification in East India Stock, imposed upon the Directors elected by the Court of Proprietors . . .

36
North of England Anti-Slavery and India Reform League: Conference at Manchester, 1 August 1854

Report of the Proceedings, revised from the *Manchester Examiner and Times*, 2 and 5 August 1854, London and Manchester, 1854

An Anti-Slavery Conference, in commemoration of West India emancipation, was held in the Athenæum yesterday (the anniversary of that event), under the auspices of the North of England Anti-Slavery and India Reform League, 'to review the result of the abolition of slavery in the British colonies; to consider the present aspects of negro slavery in Brazil, Cuba, and especially in the United States of America; and to discuss the various means by which the British anti-slavery party may aid in the abolition of slavery and the slave trade'. . . .

The Rev. Francis Bishop, of Liverpool, briefly moved the first resolution:

That all persons who believe slaveholding to be a sin, and immediate emancipation to be the right of the slave and the duty of the master, shall be eligible to be members of this conference, and to take part in its deliberations.

The Rev. S. R. Ward (coloured minister), of Canada, had great pleasure in seconding the resolution, because he believed it to be true to the great basis on which this movement was to be carried, whether we had regard to any or all of the phases of the anti-slavery agitation.

The resolution was carried unanimously.

Mr George Thompson then rose, and said: I have been appointed to submit to this conference a resolution, commemorative of the abolition of slavery throughout the colonies of Great Britain. Had this meeting been convened for the sole purpose of celebrating this great national event, I might have considered myself justified in addressing you at greater length than I feel authorised to do under existing circumstances. As it is, the duty which has been assigned me shall be discharged with as much brevity as the nature of the subject and the terms of the resolution will permit. The theme is a tempting one; but we are here, I conceive, less for the purpose of reviewing the past, than of forming plans for the future, and of drawing from the past lessons of duty, and motives of encouragement, in reference to the millions, who, while we are commemorating the triumphs of liberty in the West Indies, are extending their manacled hands towards us, and imploring our aid to deliver them also from the galling yoke of slavery. God grant that the deliberations of this sacred day may tend to this result!

> God give ye strength to run
>   Unawed by earth or hell,
> The race ye have begun,
>   So gloriously and well!
> Until the trumpet call
>   Of freedom has gone forth,
> With joy and life, to ALL
>   The bondsmen of the earth!
> Until no captive one
>   Murmurs on land or wave,
> And in his course, the Sun
>   Looks down upon no slave!

In the year 1807, after the slave trade had been suffered for three centuries to desolate Africa and disgrace mankind, and after a struggle of nearly forty years' duration – a struggle which has made the names of Granville Sharp, Thomas Clarkson, and William Wilberforce immortal, an act of parliament was passed abolishing the inhuman traffic, and declaring it piracy punishable by death. Slavery, however, the root and parent of the foul enormity, was permitted to survive. The hopes of the friends of humanity were, nevertheless, sanguine that the overthrow of the foreign supply would lead to an immediate mitigation of the rigours of slavery, and at no distant day to its banishment from the West Indies. These hopes and expectations were doomed to experience a bitter and complete disappointment. No improvement in the treatment of the slaves followed the cessation of the horrors of the middle passage. At the end of twenty years, notwithstanding the unremitting efforts of the friends of the negro, the system remained one of almost unmitigated cruelty, tending in some of the colonies to the extinction of the injured race. The influence of slavery upon the colonial communities in which it was fostered was scarcely less appalling than its effect upon the slaves themselves. In spite of prodigal bounties and prohibitory duties, the planters and proprietors were involved in inextricable embarrassment, or brought to utter ruin. In every colony the press cowered under a withering censorship; the freedom of speech was struck dumb by proscription; a standing army of patrols was necessary to awe down insurrection; the mechanic arts, and all vigorous enterprise lay crushed under an incubus; a thriftless agriculture hurried the richest lands to barrenness and decay; industry, in any but a slave, was held up to scorn; idleness was the badge of dignity; profligacy was no barrier to respectability; lust was emboldened by impunity; profuseness, in lavishing upon others the plundered earnings of the poor, was accounted high-souled generosity; sympathy was deadened by scenes of cruelty rendered familiar; and even female amiableness was often transformed into fury, by habits of despotic sway. Such was the general state of society in the slave colonies of Britain, where power had no effectual restraint, and weakness no potential succour. The friends of education and religion who are old enough, will well remember in what way their efforts were treated by the advocates of slavery in the West Indies. Thus far nothing had been demanded of the legislature beyond measures for the melioration of the condition of the slave and the gradual extinction of the system. So late as 1823, Mr Clarkson put forth a work entitled *Thoughts on the Necessity of Improving the Condition of the*

Slaves, with a View to their Ultimate Emancipation. To an English-woman belongs the honour of having been the first to call the attention of her countrymen to the duty of immediate abolition, and to the doctrine of immediatism as the only right foundation of their efforts for the deliverance of the slave. That woman was Eliz. Heyrick, a member of the Society of Friends, who, about 1826, published a tract with the title of 'Immediate not Gradual Emancipation'. In the year 1830, two speeches were made, which, in their influence upon the public mind, and for the direction they gave to the future labours of the anti-slavery party, were of the highest value and importance, The first of these was delivered in the House of Commons, on the 13th of July, by Henry, now Lord Brougham. It was a speech worthy of its author, and worthy of the cause it advocated – remarkable throughout for power and brilliancy, but chiefly influential and decisive in giving tone to all future anti-slavery addresses, in consequence of one passage – a passage as nobly eloquent as any with which I am acquainted within the range of human oratory. Here it is:

Tell me not of rights – talk not of the property of the planter in his slaves. I deny the right – I acknowledge not the property. The principles, the feelings of our common nature rise in rebellion against it. Be the appeal made to the understanding or to the heart, the sentence is the same that rejects it. In vain you tell me of laws that sanction such a claim! There is a law above all the enactments of human codes – the same throughout the world, the same in all times – such as it was before the daring genius of Columbus pierced the night of ages, and opened to one world the sources of power, wealth, and knowledge; to another, all unutterable woes; – such it is at this day: it is the law written by the finger of God on the heart of man; and by that law, unchangeable and eternal, while men despise fraud, and loathe rapine, and abhor blood, they will reject with indignation the wild and guilty phantasy, that man can hold property in man!

I am old enough to remember the effect which this almost unrivalled climax of eloquence produced upon the public mind, and I can never forget the effect which it had upon my own. 'Man can hold no property in man' became, from that day, the watchword of the anti-slavery hosts. The second of the speeches to which I have alluded was delivered in the assembly room of the city of Edinburgh, by the late Dr Andrew Thomson, one of the most distinguished ornaments of the Church of Scotland. I name Dr Thomson with the greater respect and reverence, because I owe to the speech made by him, on the 19th of October, 1830, the completion of my own conversion to the doctrine of immediatism. In the course of that speech, which was in support of a petition to the House of Commons, praying for the *immediate* and total abolition of slavery, – the first with such a prayer ever sent to parliament, he said:

But if you push me, and still urge the argument of insurrection and of bloodshed, for which you are far more indebted to fancy than to fact – (how true the doctor was in asserting this I shall presently demonstrate) – then I say be it so. I repeat that maxim taken from a heathen book, but pervading the whole book of God, – *Fiat justitia – ruat cœlum*. Righteousness is the pillar of the universe. Break down that pillar, and the universe falls into ruin and desolation; but preserve it, and though the fair fabric may sustain partial dilapidations, it may be rebuilt and repaired – it *will* be rebuilt and repaired, and restored to all its pristine strength, and magnificence, and beauty. If there must be violence, let it even come, for it will soon pass away – let it come and rage its little power, since it is to be succeeded by lasting freedom, and prosperity, and happiness. Give me the hurricane rather than the pestilence. Give me the hurricane, with its thunder, and its lightning, and its tempest; – give me the hurricane, with its partial and temporary devastations, awful though they be; give me the hurricane, with its purifying, healthful, salutary effects; – give me that hurricane, infinitely rather than the noisome pestilence, whose path is never crossed, whose silence is never disturbed, whose progress is never arrested, by one sweeping blast from the heavens; which walks peacefully and sullenly through the length and breadth of the land, breathing poison into every heart, and carrying havoc into every home, enervating all that is strong, defacing all that is beautiful, and casting its blight over the fairest and happiest scenes of human life – and which, from day to day, and from year to year, with intolerant and interminable malignity, sends its thousands and its tens of thousands of hapless victims into the ever yawning and never satisfied grave.

This speech, the effect of which was electrical upon the audience privileged to listen to it, exploded at once the doctrine of gradualism, and 'immediate emancipation' became the motto of the true abolitionist. It was this speech that completed my conversion to immediatism. The close of the year saw the establishment, by the London Anti-slavery Society, of a new branch of operations. A highly influential committee of gentlemen was formed, called the Agency committee, with a liberal fund at their disposal for the employment of lecturers, the holding of public meetings, and the publication of stirring appeals to the people of this country. I had the honour to be one of the first persons engaged by that committee to go forth and enlist the sympathies of this nation in behalf of eight hundred thousand of our enslaved fellow-subjects. My instructions were, 'Your judgment must be guided by principle alone; this principle must be, that the system of Colonial slavery is a crime in the sight of God, and ought to be immediately and for ever abolished.' . . .

37
Licensed Victuallers Defence League, 1855
Cobden Papers 436, West Sussex Record Office

Sir,

The present critical position in which the trade of the LICENSED VICTUALLERS has been placed by the recent proceedings in Parliament, has caused the members of that body in Lancashire to form themselves into the above Society for the protection of their interests; and they are of opinion that they cannot effect that, in a more legitimate manner than by laying before the members of the Legislature and the public their case, and the objections they entertain to the Resolutions of the Select Committee of the House of Commons on Public Houses, and they entreat your attentive consideration of the following Statement.

The Select Committee which was appointed in the Session of 1853, met in that year and in the beginning of 1854, and took Evidence; and on the 14th July last, they reported to the House of Commons certain resolutions, amongst which are the following:

That Licenses for the Sale of Intoxicating Drinks should be issued by the Magistrates at sessions holden for that purpose; that it should be open to all persons of good character to obtain such license, on compliance with certain conditions and the payment of a certain annual sum, that every person previous to obtaining a license should himself give bond and find two sureties to be bound with him, for the due observance of the laws and conditions upon which the license shall be granted; that in large towns and populous places there should be appointed Inspectors of Public Houses and all places of public refreshment and entertainment, as in the case of Common Lodging Houses, and that such inspectors should constantly visit and report upon the condition and conduct of all such houses and places; and that, with the exception of the hours of from 1 to 2 o'clock, P.M., and of from 6 to 9 P.M., all places for the sale of intoxicating drinks should be closed on Sundays, and that on week-days all such houses should be closed from 11 o'clock, P.M., until 4 A.M.

That the said Select Committee did not publish any reasons which operated on their minds to induce them to recommend such resolutions, and we can therefore only offer our objections to the resolutions as they stand, there being no arguments to grapple with.

That the effect of such resolutions would, if embodied in an Act of Parliament, render it imperative on Magistrates to grant a license to every applicant who could comply with the conditions to be annexed, without any regard to the wants of the public, or to the character of the property in the neighbourhood. We consider that such a change would be not only impolitic, but is totally unnecessary; impolitic, because it would take away that discretionary power so well vested in the Magistrates by the present law – that of judging not only of the character of the applicant, but the requirements of the public and the nature of the premises sought to be licensed; and unnecessary, because the powers granted to Magistrates under the 9th Geo. iv., c. 61, are unlimited, and it is perfectly open now to any Bench of Magistrates to grant, if they should so think fit, any number of licenses whatever.

That the Resolution of the Select Committee suggesting that applicants for licenses should give bonds with sureties for the observance of the law and the tenor of the license, would be perfectly inoperative for the purpose intended. We do not assert this without having just grounds for it, and we beg respectfully to point out that this very system of giving bonds has been tried under the existing Beer Acts, and has been universally acknowledged to be a perfect failure in securing either good conduct or observance of the law.

That the change sought to be effected by the carrying out of the Resolutions of the Select Committee has not been called for by any demonstrations of public opinion; and that no petition praying for any such change had ever been presented to either branch of the Legislature before the Select Committee reported their Resolutions.

That on the other hand, very many petitions have been presented to both Houses of Parliament praying for restrictions on the sale of spirituous liquors, and for the total repeal of the Acts relating to the sale of Beer.

That the Acts for the sale of Beer, however well-intentioned they might have been by the authors and promoters of the system, have been not only an entire failure as regards the objects which their framers had in view in their promotion, but the Beer-houses have been universally condemned by every Judge on the Bench, as being the incentive to every vice and the focus of every crime; and also especially by the Chief Constables of Police and the Chaplains of Gaols throughout the kingdom, who have had the best opportunities – the one of watching the character of the Beer-shops and of those who frequent them, the other, of tracing the causes of crime and the career of criminals. . . .

In conclusion, we hope that the above candid and fair Statement will meet with your approval, and that you will aid in resisting any measures which may be brought forward in Parliament to carry out so much of the resolutions of the Select Committee as we trust we have shewn to be injurious to the welfare of the people at large.

I have the honour to remain, Sir,
Your very obedient Servant,
CHARLES RIDINGS
Chairman of the Licensed Victuallers' Defence League
11*th January*, 1855

38
Associated British Chambers of Commerce: Objects, 1860

A. R. Ilersic, *Parliament of Commerce*, London: A.B.C.C. and Newman Neame Ltd, 1960, p. 18

1. To discuss and consider various commercial questions at Meetings of delegates from Chambers of Commerce, and to disseminate mutual information from time to time, on matters affecting the common and separate interests of such Chambers.

2. To attain those advantages by united action (where that is practicable), which each Chamber would have more difficulty in accomplishing in its separate capacity.

3. To establish an Office in London, with an Agent there, in order to ensure to the various Chambers early and reliable information on matters affecting their interests, and to facilitate communication between the Association or individual Chambers and the Government or other public bodies.

39
National Association of Ireland, Dublin: Objects and Rules, December 1864

Cobden Papers 438, West Sussex Record Office

Committee Rooms,
No. 7 Lower Ormond Quay, Dublin,
16th February, 1865
Sir,
Should the objects and policy of the National Association of Ireland, as stated in the following documents, meet with your

approval, we trust the Association will have the benefit of your coöperation and advocacy.

John B. Dillon,
R. J. Devitt, } Hon. Secs.

RESOLUTIONS

Passed at an Aggregate Meeting held in Dublin on Thursday, December 29th, 1864

I. That the entire ecclesiastical revenues of Ireland, amounting to upwards of £580,000 annually, are appropriated to the maintenance of a Church which (according to the latest census) counts amongst its members only 691,872 persons – being less than one-seventh of the entire population of this island. That this singular institution was originally established, and has been always maintained, by force, in opposition to reason and justice, and in defiance of the will of the great majority of the Irish people. That we, therefore, resent it as a badge of national servitude, offensive and degrading alike to all Irishmen, Protestant as well as Catholic.

II. That we demand the disendowment of the Established Church in Ireland as the sole condition on which social peace and stability, general respect for the laws, and unity of sentiment and of action for national objects, can ever prevail in Ireland. And in making this demand, we emphatically disavow any intention to interfere with vested rights, or to injure or offend any portion of our fellow-countrymen; our desire being rather to remove a most prolific source of civil discord, by placing all religious denominations on a footing of perfect equality, and leaving each Church to be maintained by the voluntary contributions of its members.

III. That as a general rule all agricultural improvements in Ireland have been and are effected by the occupiers of land; and that the law, by denying the right to compensation for such improvements, prevents the application of capital to the soil, and paralyses industry by taking away its motive and its reward.

IV. That the enactment of a law securing compensation to improving tenants would promote more amicable relations between landlord and tenant, and would lead the latter to respect the law which he now (with too much reason) regards as partial and oppressive. That no class would derive more advantage from such an enactment than the proprietors of the soil, who, more than all others, are interested in social stability and order, in the improvement of agriculture, and in the growth of national wealth and prosperity.

V. That the interference of the State in public education should be confined to rendering impartial aid towards the establishment and maintenance of schools, and ensuring their efficiency by a well-regulated inspection. But that when the State assumes to control the course of teaching and training in public schools or colleges – still more when it establishes and endows schools which are managed and conducted by its own nominees – it not only ignores the claims of religion and its ministers, but also usurps one of the most sacred of human rights, that of a parent to determine the education which shall be given to his child. That where the Government is unfriendly to the religion and the nationality of the people, the assumption of such a right is especially noxious, as tending to poison the fountains of knowledge, and to make of education a temptation and a snare.

RULES OF THE NATIONAL ASSOCIATION OF IRELAND

i. The Association shall be called The National Association of Ireland. Its objects shall be: 1st, To secure by law to occupiers of land in Ireland compensation for all valuable improvements effected by them. 2nd, The disendowment of the Irish Protestant Church, and the application of its revenues to purposes of national utility, saving all vested rights. 3rd, Freedom and equality of education for the several denominations and classes in Ireland.

ii. The Association will seek to realise its objects by convincing, as far as possible, all men of their fairness and utility, by fostering a rational and intelligent patriotism, by uniting the people for mutual aid and protection, and by placing in representative positions, both imperial and local, men from whose principles and character they may anticipate a disinterested and effective support.

iii. The Association will not support any political party which shall not in good faith coöperate with it, in accomplishing one or more of its objects. Neither will it recommend, or assist in the election of, any candidate, who will not pledge himself to act on the same principle.

iv. No member of the Association shall be bound by, or answerable for, any opinion expressed, or language uttered, by any other member at any of the meetings thereof.

v. The affairs of the Association shall be managed by a committee, who shall appoint such officers as they may deem necessary, shall fix the times and places for holding public meetings, and shall appoint a chairman to preside at each such meeting.

VI. The Committee shall also have power to make bye-laws for the regulation of their own proceedings and of the general business of the Association, provided that such bye-laws shall accord with the general scope and objects of the Association, and that no such bye-law shall contravene any of these fundamental rules and provided that such bye-laws shall be passed at a meeting of not less than ten members.

VII. At the public meetings of the Association it shall be the duty of the chairman to prevent violent or illegal discussion; and if any member shall, in defiance of the decision of the chairman, persist in such discussion, the chairman shall thereupon have power to declare the meeting adjourned, and shall bring the conduct of the member so offending under the notice of the committee at its next meeting.

VIII. The Committee, at a meeting to be specially convened for that purpose, shall have power to expunge from the list of members and associates the name of any person so offending; and the person whose name shall be so expunged shall thereupon cease to be a member or an associate, as the case may be.

IX. The accounts of the Association shall be audited and published at such intervals as the committee may deem expedient – such intervals not to exceed six months.

X. Every person approving of the objects of the Association, and accepting its rules, whose admission shall be moved and seconded at a public meeting thereof, may be admitted and remain a member, on handing in to the secretary an annual sum of one pound, and may be admitted and remain an associate on paying an annual subscription of one shilling.

XI. These fundamental rules shall not be abrogated, added to or in any respect altered, unless by vote of the Committee passed at two successive meetings (called by special notice for the purpose), and confirmed by the Association at a public meeting thereof.

40
Commons (Open Spaces and Footpaths) Preservation Society, 1865 : Origin and Objects

The Future of Common Lands, n.d.

The Society's Origin

The Society was founded in 1865 to save from inclosure some well-known London commons, including Wimbledon Common,

Hampstead Heath and Epping Forest. Its success in these early fights encouraged the Society to widen the scope of its work to include not only metropolitan commons, but all commons in England and Wales.

The Society's Objects

The Society's objects include the following: to preserve for the public use commons and village greens, and to advise those who have rights over these lands; to advise local authorities and others on securing and preserving public open spaces; to protect road-side wastes; to preserve public rights of way over footpaths, bridleways and carriage ways used mainly as public paths; and to assist local authorities and the public on any questions arising from these objects.

The Society's Achievements

During the years of its existence, the Society has helped to pro-tect a million and half acres (two thousand square miles) of commons, the chief open spaces of the country from inclosure or encroachment and has assisted commoners and owners to main-tain their rights over them. It has helped to secure a legal right of public access to half a million acres of these commons. It has inspired or promoted the acquisition of land for open spaces in all parts of the country. It has been largely responsible for the insertion, in innumerable statutes dealing with the acquisition of land for public purposes, of provisions designed to prevent inter-ference with commons, village green, recreation grounds and other public spaces. It has prevented an incalculable number of public rights of way from being unwarrantably extinguished or unlawfully obstructed and it has helped to obtain statutory powers for their protection.

41
The Interests : as represented in Parliament, 1865

Bernard Cracraft, in *Essays on Reform*, 1867, Analytical Table, pp. 328–9

Authors	78
Lawyers	100
Queen's Councillors	24
Magistrates	175
Deputy Lieutenants	235
High Sheriffs	28

Railway Directors	179
Insurance Office Directors	53
Bankers	78
Brewers	12

Trade:	
Ship-Owners	7
East India Merchants	4
Iron Masters	10
Cotton Merchants and Calico Printers	7
Worsted and Carpet Manufacturers	5
Silk Manufacturers	2
Miscellaneous	87

Total	122

42
The Corn Laws linked to Class Interests, 1865

James Aytoun in letter to the *Morning Advertiser*, 22 March 1865.
Cobden Papers 428, West Sussex Record Office

A more unjust tax there could not be. It is the last remnant of
the iniquitous corn laws . . . the allowing this heavy tax, or rather
protective duty, to remain a single session proves that the class
interests of the majority of the members of the House of Commons
are attended to as much as ever, and demonstrates to the great
body of the people the absolute necessity of a further reform in
Parliament.

43
The Central and Associated Chambers of Agriculture, 1866: origins

A. H. H. Matthews, *Fifty Years of Agricultural Politics, being the History
of the Central Chamber of Agriculture, 1865–1915*, 1915, appendix 2

Walton, near Wakefield, December 5th, 1865

PROPOSAL FOR A FARMERS' LEAGUE OR CENTRAL
CHAMBER OF AGRICULTURE

Sir, the idea of a general meeting in London of deputations from
all the Farmers' Clubs and Agricultural Societies in the Kingdom,
to consider the questions arising out of the Cattle Plague – which

I had the pleasure of suggesting and proposing to the members of the Wakefield and West Riding Farmers' Club – having been so well received throughout the country, induces me (after mentioning it to a few friends) to venture upon another subject which has for some years appeared to my mind to be a great want, and which (if properly carried out) would tend greatly towards the efficient management of agricultural affairs. My present suggestion is embraced in the title of 'A Farmers' League'. The means of forming such an Association are so ready to hand that I almost wonder it has not been carried out long ago. I would adopt the same plan as suggested for the Cattle Plague Meeting, viz., forming the Chairman and Secretaries, for the time being, of every Farmers' Club and Society – with such other members as it may be found desirable to enrol – into one central 'Farmers' League or Association', each Club paying, say, £5 5s. to the funds of the League annually, which (as there are some 400) would give at once about £2,000 per annum. With such pecuniary means and such extensive influence capable of being exerted at any moment over the whole country, and brought to bear with all its force upon any and every measure affecting the farmer, it cannot but be evident, I think, that the agricultural interest would thereby have a power ready at command which it does not possess at present, simply because there is no organisation; each Club exhausts its influence locally – with, I admit, corresponding local benefit – whilst the more exalted Societies devote their whole attention, in accordance with their rules, to the improvement of stock and agricultural machinery, a field sufficiently large for their useful labours. All these are specially excluded by their regulations from entering upon politico-economical subjects – whether wisely so it is not requisite to ask; therefore, the formation of a League could not possibly interfere with any existing Society, but would rather tend to stimulate their formation and action, as every one would have a claim to send their Chairman and Secretary to the League, on paying the subscriptions, and, of course, their own deputation's expenses.

As to the management of the League, that could easily be arranged if the idea itself should meet with approbation – say, by the election at the annual meeting, which might be held in the Smithfield Show week, of a Council consisting of twenty-four members, one-third retiring annually; with an efficient well-paid Secretary, resident in London, whose whole time should be given to the duties of his office, and with such legal assistance as may be required; and also the establishment of a comprehensive and expansive code of rules to enable the League to adapt itself to the various alterations necessitated by change of time and circumstances.

The special object of the League would be to undertake duties now much neglected and beyond the rules of all existing societies; viz., the charge of measures in the Houses of Parliament and before the Government, calculated to benefit agriculture, as well as to oppose or modify any movement detrimental to that important interest. It cannot be denied that more attention to such matters would result in some improvement, and might *eventually lead to the appointment of a Minister or Board of Agriculture*, which is much needed; for although the present House of Commons contains many members who are friendly to the farmer, yet the prominence with which his younger but more energetic brother, 'The Manufacturer', has contrived to push forward his own measures seems to be obliterating the fact that there is such an interest in agriculture – which equally requires and fully deserves the application of those free trade and progressive principles which have been of so much benefit to commercial enterprise.

This state of things need not be, if agriculturists and their friends would make up their minds to set fairly about altering it; and if the idea of a 'Farmers' League' as here proposed, appears to meet the case, and should find sufficient favour to lead to its formation, I shall be glad to assist, if requisite, in my humble way. But my object just at present in addressing this letter to you is to excite discussion in the first place, in the hope that, if worthy of notice, some more prominent member of society may be induced to take up the subject and carry it to the successful issue which, in my opinion, the importance of the interests more directly concerned, as well as the general benefit to the country, seem fully to deserve.

I shall be glad to have your opinion on this subject, and remain,

Yours very truly,

Chas. Clay

Walton, Wakefield,
January 26th, 1866

Sir, In December last I addressed a letter to you on this subject, which has since then found its way into almost all the agricultural papers in the kingdom, and has, apparently, been well received, at least I have numerous correspondents who request and even urge me to take steps for carrying out the scheme proposed for

forming a 'Farmers' League' or 'Central Chamber of Agriculture', the latter title being perhaps more acceptable to the
public than the former, I propose to adopt it in preference to the
name of 'League'.

This first question suggests itself – How shall a Central Chamber of Agriculture be formed? I confess my own influence is but
very small for organizing such a powerful body; but what I can do
and what I now propose as a further step towards the end is –
that if all those who are willing to meet in London on an early
day (say, if possible, on the 6th of February next, the day after
the great Anti-Malt Tax Meeting), will send me their names and
full addresses immediately, I will, if sufficient support appears –
of which there is not much doubt – convene a meeting, 'for the
purpose of considering the desirability of launching this or some
other scheme for forming a "Central Chamber of Agriculture,"
whose duties shall be as already proposed – to take charge of
measures in the Houses of Parliament, and before the Government, calculated to benefit agriculture, as well as to oppose or
modify any movement detrimental to that important interest'.

If those favourable to this mode of proceeding will oblige me
with their names as early as possible, I will, if the list is not too
long, add them as supporters to the notice calling the meeting,
that some idea may be obtained of the position of the movement
by persons unavoidably prevented attending in London.

Yours very truly,
Chas. Clay

Note. The meeting above alluded to was held on the 6th of February, 1866, at the Salisbury Hotel, Fleet Street, London, when
the Central Chamber of Agriculture was formally established.

44
National Union of Elementary Teachers:
Objects and Rules, 1871
Annual Report for the year, 1871

OBJECTS OF THE UNION

The aim of the Union is to unite together, by means of Local
Associations, Public Elementary Teachers throughout the
kingdom, in order to provide a machinery by means of which
Teachers may give expression to their opinions when occasion
requires, and may also take united action in any matter affecting
their interests. The character of the Union will be more fully

seen when it is fairly established, but the following topics will receive its immediate attention:

1. The Revision of the New Code.
2. The working of the New Education Act.
3. The Establishment of a Pension Scheme.
4. The throwing open of higher Educational Posts to Elementary Teachers.
5. The proposal to raise Teaching to the dignity of a Profession by means of a Public Register of duly qualified Teachers for every class of Schools.

W. Lawson,
St Mark's College, Chelsea, Hon. Sec.

RULES

I. That the various Associations of Teachers throughout England be formed into a Union, to be called the 'National Union of Elementary Teachers'.

II. That a Central Council be established, consisting of Representatives from the various Associations, and that this Council meet in Conference annually.

III. The Conference be held at Easter in each year, at the place agreed upon at the previous Annual Conference; but that Special Conferences may be held at such times and places as the Standing Committee may deem expedient.

IV. That each Association be permitted to send one Representative for every ten members up to a limit of ten Representatives; but that any one Representative may vote for his absent colleagues.

V. That the amount contributed to the Central Fund by each Association, numbering one hundred members and upwards, be five pounds; and that Associations with less than one hundred members contribute at the rate of one shilling per annum for each member.

VI. That the Central Council in Conference elect a President, Vice-President, Treasurer, Secretary, and Standing Committee of twenty-four members, all of whom shall be ex-officio members of the Council.

VII. That the Secretaries of Associations in the Union be ex-officio members of the Standing Committee.

VIII. That the Standing Committee meet Quarterly, and at such other times as the Secretary may deem fit; and that the Secretary be required to summon a meeting at any time on receiving a requisition signed by four members.

IX. That seven members duly summoned form a quorum.

X. That the General Officers and Standing Committee be elected annually; but that all of them, with the exception of the President and Vice-President, be eligible for re-election.

XI. That no alteration in, or addition to, these Rules be made except at the Annual Conference; and that notice of such alteration or addition be sent to the Standing Committee, at least six weeks before the Annual Conference.

45
Trades Union Congress: committee to draw up Standing Orders, 1872
T.U.C. archives

'That a Committee of five, exclusive of the President and Secretary, be appointed to draw up Standing Orders for the Congress, and to prepare the order of business of each day.'

(Carried)

Mr Ashton (Oldham) moved, and Mr Walton seconded 'That the Report of the London Committee as read be accepted'. Mr Nicholson spoke in favour of waiting for Mr McDonald, he, it was understood, having some remarks to make upon it.

(Carried)

Mr Potter spoke upon a meeting that had been suggested to be held on Thursday evening, and moved 'That a public meeting be held on Thursday evening', Mr Archer seconding the proposal.

(Carried)

Messrs Leigh, Nicholson, Graham, Higham and Halliday were constituted the Standing Orders Committee.

46
Trades Union Congress: Standing Orders, as approved in 1873
T.U.C. archives

STANDING ORDERS

The following are the Standing Orders as agreed to at the last Congress. The Committee have thought it desirable to reprint them as many of the Delegates may not have their copies with them for reference.

G

1. The Congress shall consist only of Delegates representing *bona fide* Trade Societies, and Trades Councils, and similar bodies, by whatever name they may, for the time being, be called.

2. Each Delegate shall come provided with a credential signed by the officers of the society or council he represents, certifying to his appointment, such credential to be given up to the Secretary immediately on his arrival at the Congress.

3. The time of meeting shall be as follows:– On the first day to assemble at 12 o'clock noon, prompt; on all other days at 9.30 a.m.; adjourn at 1, re-assemble at 2, and adjourn at 5 o'clock each day.

4. The roll shall be called promptly to time morning and afternoon, the names of all Delegates late or absent to be read over with the minutes each morning.

5. At the opening of the Annual Congress, the Chairman of the Parliamentary Committee shall take the chair *pro forma* until the Congress has elected its own President, which shall be its first business.

6. The Trades Council of the town where the Congress is being held shall elect a Committee of three to examine the credentials, and report thereon to the meeting.

7. The Delegates shall then proceed to elect the President of the Congress, preference being given to a delegate of the town where the Congress is being held.

8. The Congress shall then elect a Secretary, a like preference being given.

9. The Congress shall then elect a Treasurer, a Vice-President, two Auditors, a Doorkeeper, and a Messenger.

10. A Standing Committee of five shall then be elected, to whom shall be remitted the whole business of the Congress; the order of, and subjects for, discussion, together with the whole financial arrangements of the Congress. The Vice-President to be the chairman of the committee.

11. After the routine business of election of officers and committee, the President shall formally open the Congress.

12. Each Delegate shall pay to the Treasurer, on the first day of his arrival, the sum of 10s. towards the expenses of the Congress; and in case he represents more than one society, 10s. for every such society he is delegated to represent. Trades Councils to be taken as a unit, and pay 10s. for each delegate sent. The names of those who have, and those who have not paid, to be read over when the roll is called on the following **morning**. No person shall be deemed a member of Congress until his levy is paid.

13. The reader of a paper shall be allowed twenty minutes;

the mover of a resolution fifteen minutes; succeeding speakers ten minutes each; no one shall speak more than once on any one question. After the reply, no one shall be allowed to speak on the question before the chair, but it shall be at once put to the vote by the chairman.

14. No second amendment, or rider to an original proposition, shall be put to the vote until the first amendment is disposed of.

15. The voting shall be by show of hands; but in case of a dispute, the chairman may order a division.

16. Two tellers shall be appointed by the Congress, and their ruling shall be final.

17. No delegate shall be allowed to read a second paper until after all other Papers, of which notice has been previously given, have been read.[1]

18. In the selection of Papers to be read, preference shall be given to those of which notice has been given, and in the order in which they have been received by the Committee.

19. No delegate shall leave the room without the consent of the Vice-President; and Delegates absent one whole sitting without leave of absence, shall be named by the Chairman.

20. A General or Parliamentary Committee of nine shall be elected on the last day of each Congress, who shall continue in office until they are re-elected, or their successors are appointed. They shall elect from among themselves a President, Treasurer, and Secretary for the ensuing year; and they also shall remain in office until they are re-elected, or their successors are appointed.

21. All surplus monies, after payment of the expenses of the Congress, shall be handed over to the Treasurer of the Parliamentary Committee for the general purposes of such Committee.

22. The duties of the Parliamentary Committee shall be (1) to watch all legislative measures directly affecting the questions of labour, and (2) to initiate, whenever necessary, such legislative action as Congress may direct, or as the exigencies of the time and circumstances may demand.

23. The officers, under the direction of the Committee, shall have authority to solicit subscriptions, donations, or levies, for the purpose of defraying the expenses incurred by such Committee; but the mode of payment shall be left optional with each society as to whether it shall pay by levy or donation.

24. The Congress having been formally opened by the President, after the usual routine business of electing Officers and Committee, the Parliamentary Committee shall present their

1. No. 17 is rendered null and void by No. 28 – Note by the Parliamentary Committee.

report for the past year, which shall be read by the Parliamentary Secretary, and shall be laid on the table for discussion by the Congress.

25. The Parliamentary Committee shall assist and co-operate with the Local Committee of the town where the next Congress is to be held, for the purpose of making the arrangements as complete as possible, and preparing the questions to be discussed, and together to take such joint action as the business or other special circumstances of the time may render necessary or desirable.

26. The Parliamentary Committee, in conjunction with the Local Committee, shall be empowered to invite persons to attend the sittings of the Congress whose presence they may deem advisable and desirable, such persons to be allowed to address the Congress on the invitation of the Chairman. The above to be acted upon only in exceptional cases.

27. That papers in defence of Trades Unions are unnecessary.

28. That no papers should be read excepting those which are required for Parliamentary legislative purposes. No member to read more than one paper.

29. That all papers should be sent to the Secretary of the Parliamentary Committee two weeks before the meeting of the ensuing Congress. The same to be read and arranged by the Committee to facilitate the business of the Congress.

30. That a sub-committee of the Parliamentary Committee should meet a week before the meeting of each Congress to arrange matters for the Congress.

31. That no candidate shall be eligible for election on the Parliamentary Committee unless the society which he represents has contributed towards payment of the expenses of that Committee during the year previous to his nomination.

32. That it be an instruction to the Parliamentary Committee that Clauses 9 and 10 in the amended Truck Bill be incorporated in any Truck Bill which may be introduced.

Resolved – 'That the standing orders, as amended, be adopted.'

47
National Federation of Associated Employers of Labour, 1873 : Objects

George Howell, *Labour Legislation, Labour Movements, Labour Leaders,* London, 1902, pp. 308–10

Early in April, 1873, I heard of a project to establish a great federation of Employers' Associations, whose object was said to be to resist, by all lawful means, the demands of the workmen for the repeal of certain laws, and the amendment of others, deemed by them to be adverse to labour. A circular was sent out, dated April 25th, convening a conference of employers, at the Westminster Palace Hotel, on April 30th, at 2.30 P.M. Another circular, by another body, was issued on April 26th, urging the attendance at such conference of all employers in the cotton trades . . .

Objects of Employers' Federation

(a) The circular (No. 1) adds: 'Under these circumstances the Iron Trades Employers' Association have called upon this Committee to take measures to resist the trade unionists in their attempts to efface from the Statute Book such laws as experience is daily showing to be of paramount importance for the safety of capital, the protection of labour, and the prosperity of the country.' The circular goes on to say that 'the Committee are acting conjointly with other important organizations of employers in the cotton, flax, iron, coal, and building trades', and they therefore 'call a private meeting with a view to secure the assistance of members of Parliament, in protecting the enterprise of the country against the aggressive movements about to be made upon it'.

(b) Circular No. 2, after setting forth the programme of the Trades Congress Parliamentary Committee, and adding a paragraph from the Committee's circular, as to the national importance of the measures described, adds: 'In the presence of such declarations as these, it appears to your Committee that the safety of capital, the protection of labour, and the prosperity of the country, alike call upon the leading employers to take council together.' Other reasons are urged in favour of joint action at the conference to be convened. One association mentions that it represents employers of 7,000 workmen, the other of 250,000. The circulars state that 'the conference is called irrespective of political party, in the interests of employers of labour'.

48
British Iron Trade Association, 1875

An account of the principal trade associations in the steel industry:
British Iron and Steel Federation, 1963, Appendix 1

In order to understand more fully the part played by the Federation in the steel industry today, it is useful to have some knowledge of the political and historical forces which have shaped the development of the present organization. This appendix gives a brief historical sketch of the industry's central organizations and traces the growth of the Federation from its formation up to the present day.

Earlier central organizations in the steel industry

Most trade associations were created because the individuals or companies in the trade at some time came to see a need for co-operative action in certain spheres; the iron and steel industry was no exception to this general rule, though its first ventures in central organization were unambitious by modern standards. This is explained by the fact that the industry was very early in the field: the iron trade – the steel age had not yet arrived – was forming associations before the end of the eighteenth century. Each of these associations was normally confined to the iron-masters in a particular district, and often their purpose was vaguely defined as 'the discussion of matters of mutual interest'.

The first association which covered the industry throughout the country was the British Iron Trade Association, established in 1875. (The Iron and Steel Institute, which had been formed six years earlier, was, and remains, the industry's scientific and technical society for the increase and dissemination of scientific knowledge.) The B.I.T.A. was concerned with tariffs, legislation, commercial treaties and, generally, with considering 'proper measures for advancing the interests' of the British iron and steel trades.

One of its chief aims, however, was to 'procure and circulate detailed statistics of the iron and steel trades both at home and abroad'. From 1877 onwards, the B.I.T.A. published a series of Annual Statistical Reports giving information on the British iron- and steel-producing and consuming industries, on overseas trade and on overseas iron and steel production. The statistics in these Reports were subject to many limitations, but they form an indispensable source of information about the early development of the industry, and they were made possible by the co-operation of iron and steel producers in supplying information about their works.

This statistical service was transferred, when the B.I.T.A. came to an end in 1915, to the Iron, Steel and Allied Trades Federation of Middlesbrough (I.S.A.T.F.). In 1918, however, I.S.A.T.F. itself was dissolved; but in the same year – on Armistice Day – was formed a more representative and comprehensive organization than any which had existed in the industry up to that time. This organization, the immediate predecessor of the British Iron and Steel Federation, was called the National Federation of Iron and Steel Manufacturers.

The National Federation had its genesis in the recognition by the industry and the Government that the First World War and its aftermath had created problems which could not be dealt with satisfactorily without the help of a stronger central organization. The concept of the National Federation had the full support of the Government of the day, and during the 1920s and early 1930s the National Federation was acknowledged as the industry's spokesman, particularly in connection with the case – which became overwhelming – for the introduction of a tariff.

The National Federation was also notable for the marked improvements it made in the industry's statistical service, and for its help to the industry in the spheres of standardization, transport, fuel efficiency and research.

49
The Primrose League: Resolutions and Original Statutes of 1883

Janet Henderson Robb, *The Primrose League 1883–1906*, New York: Columbia University Press, 1942, Appendix 1

It may be interesting to Primrose Leaguers, as showing how future circumstances can alter and develop primary ideas, if there are here set out *verbatim* the resolutions of the first meeting of the Council, held 17 November 1883, together with the original statutes then promulgated.

RESOLUTIONS

1. That a political society be and is hereby founded under the title of the 'Primrose Tory League'.

2. That — constitute the Ruling Council of the League, and have power to establish branches in all parts of the British Empire.

3. That the objects of the League are the promotion of Tory principles – viz. the maintenance of religion, of the estates of the realm, and of the 'Imperial Ascendancy of Great Britain'.

4. That — be the first Grand Councillor, and that in the event of any vacancy in that office the Ruling Council have power to fill the same.

5. That the form of admission to the League and the powers of the various branches shall be determined from time to time by the Ruling Council.

6. That the motto of the League be '*Imperium et Libertas*', the seal 'Three Primroses', and the badge 'An Imperial Crown encircled by Primroses'.

ORIGINAL STATUTES

I. The League will be governed by the Ruling Council. In case of any vacancy the Ruling Council within the space of three months shall select a fresh Councillor.

II. The President of the Council will be called the Grand Councillor. His appointment will last for three years. He will be assisted by three Executive Councillors, to be elected annually.

III. There shall be a Central Office for communications, with a Registrar.

IV. In every town and district in the United Kingdom where there are thirteen Knights of the League a Habitation can be established by a warrant from the Ruling Council. The warrant shall be marked with the mark of the Grand Councillor, stamped with the seal of the Order, and testified by the Registrar. Every Habitation shall have a number assigned to it by the Ruling Council, by which it shall be always designated.

V. Every Habitation shall be governed by a Ruling Councillor and three Executive Councillors, who shall regulate the admission and initiation of Knights. It is not necessary that the Ruling Councillor of a Habitation should be a member of the Ruling Council. Every Member of the League shall have a number at the time of enrolment, which shall appear on his warrant.

VI. Every Habitation shall keep a roll of its Members. The name of every Member initiated shall be immediately sent for enrolment to the Registrar in London, together with a fee of one crown, which shall include the tribute for the first year. A Diploma of Knighthood shall thereupon be sent to the Ruling Councillor of the Habitation containing the name of the new Knight, marked with the mark of the Grand Councillor, stamped with the seal of the League, and testified by the Registrar.

VII. The annual tribute of each member to the funds of the League shall be a half-a-crown, payable on 19 April (Primrose Day). This amount will be remitted by the Ruling Councillor of each Habitation annually to the Secretary. Each Habitation will regulate the local tributes of its Members. The Diploma of each Knight shall be stamped annually by the Ruling Councillor on payment of the tribute.

VIII. Every Knight shall pay his own tribute, and shall himself pay for any refreshment consumed by him in the Habitation, whether occasional or at a banquet.

IX. The Knights shall be divided into two classes – Knight Companions and Knight Harbingers. After probation of one year a Knight Harbinger may be promoted by the Ruling Councillor of his Habitation to the rank of Knight Companion, and his warrant shall be stamped accordingly. Members in holy orders shall be designated Knights Almoners. Knights Almoners shall rank with Knights Companions. Seniority of Knighthood shall govern the precedence of Knights in the several grades.

X. In all towns and districts under a Habitation one or more Knights shall be assigned to sub-districts. Such sub-districts shall not contain more than one hundred houses. It will be the duty of such Knights to promote to the best of their ability the doctrines of the League throughout their sub-district, to obtain information as to the views and position of each inhabitant, details useful for registration, and to make reports on these and other subjects of importance at the meetings of the Habitation. During any public election the Habitation will meet every evening, each Knight bringing a report of his proceedings during the day. Monthly reports of the Habitation, and during election time daily reports shall be forwarded by the Ruling Councils of the Habitations to the Registrar.

XI. Every Knight shall be entitled to wear the badge of the order attached to a ribbon. The ribbon of a Councillor shall be all primrose; of a Knight Companion or Knight Almoner, primrose on violet; of a Knight Harbinger, primrose centre with violet borders. The badges must be worn by Knights at all the meetings of Habitations. On Primrose Day all members of the League shall wear a bunch of Primroses.

XII. Any Knight or Councillor who during an election has been found guilty of any corrupt or illegal practice shall be degraded and expelled from the League. His name shall be erased from the roll of the Habitation and from the roll of the Ruling Council, and the reason of such erasure shall be entered on the books. The same course shall be adopted in the case of any Knight or Councillor divulging the secrets of the League or acting in a manner unbecoming a Knight or gentleman.

XIII. No Knight not a member of a Habitation shall be admitted to any meeting except on the responsibility of two Knights, members of the Habitation. There shall be no strange guests at any banquet, and stranger Knights shall be required equally with members to pay for their own refreshments.

xiv. The Ruling Council may withdraw the warrant of any Habitation.

xv. Every communication from the Ruling Council to the Habitation shall be called a Precept. It shall be headed by the word 'Precept', shall bear the seal of the order, the mark of the Grand Councillor, and shall be testified by the Registrar. Every communication from a Habitation to the Ruling Council shall be termed a 'Representation', whether originating with the Habitation or in answer to a Precept. It shall bear the stamp of the local seal, which shall be the same as the seal of the Ruling Council, together with the number of the Habitation. On the receipt of a Precept a meeting of the Habitation shall be summoned within two days, for the purpose of considering it and returning an answer to the Registrar, and as far as possible complying with the requirements of the Precept.

xvi. Every Member on his initiation shall make the declaration hereto annexed and signify his adhesion to the bye-laws of the League by subscribing his signature to a copy thereof. He shall also sign his name in a book to be kept for the purpose.

FORM OF DECLARATION

This obligation may be administered to any person by a member of the Ruling Council or by a Habitation, which shall be responsible to the Ruling Council for his fitness.

xvii. The Ruling Council and the Habitation shall conform to all the requirements of the law regulating societies of this character.

xviii. Gentlemen wishing to become Knights of the League must, until further steps be taken, apply in writing to the Registrar, accompanying their application with a fee of a crown and a reference. They will announce their readiness to subscribe to the statutes and ordinances, and to take the declaration. No applicant can be accepted except upon the approval of the Ruling Council. In case of non-approval the fee will be returned. No application will be received by the Registrar from any town or district where a Habitation has been constituted, but the applicant will be informed to whom he can apply in the town or district of his residence. The Ruling Council may reward either by Diplomas of Honour, or the presentation of special badges or clasps, any distinguished services rendered by Knights.

xix. The Ruling Council shall be entitled to receive monies both from the Habitations and from individuals, to be spent for the advancement of the purposes of the League. An account shall be kept of receipts and expenditure, and such account shall be annually audited by chartered accountants. Any Ruling Councillor of a Habitation may at any time have access to the Auditor's report. These rules can be altered or added to by the Ruling Council.

50
Trade Unions : form of central government, late nineteenth century

Royal Commission on Labour, 1891–4, Rules of Associations of Employers and of Employed, C. 6795 – xii, *Memorandum*, introduction, p. x

The form of the central government is very similar in all the different societies. The transaction of ordinary business is generally in the hands of an executive, which consists of certain officers and a committee or council; while the supreme government of the society is vested in a larger body, which in the case of the more extensive unions is usually a conference or delegate meeting, and in the smaller ones is often a general meeting of members . . .

The general control and direction of the society is usually in the hands of the executive, which makes provision for the establishment of new branches, expels members and removes or suspends officers who act contrary to the interests of the society, and arranges all matters that are not of sufficient importance to be brought before a general or delegate meeting . . .

With the exception of the general secretary, the officers are usually elected by ballot or show of hands at a general or delegate meeting. In some cases the members of the executive council or committee choose a chairman by co-option, and occasionally they have power to elect the other principal officers. The election of the general secretary is, as a rule, determined by the votes of the whole body of members, and in many of the more important societies the office is permanent, subject to the continued approval of the members. The other officers serve for very different periods in the various societies. In some cases elections take place quarterly, in others half-yearly, annually, or at longer intervals; and the officers, like the members of the council, are generally eligible for re-election.

In almost every society the principal officers receive some payment for their services. This takes the form in some cases of a fixed yearly or weekly salary, in others of a salary regulated by the number of members and in others of payment for each meeting attended. The rules of some societies again merely state that the salaries of the officers are fixed by the executive council or by a general or delegate meeting. The amounts of the salaries given in the rules vary greatly in the different societies, but that of the secretary is usually considerably larger than that of the other officers.

51
The National Agricultural Union, 1892

A. H. H. Matthews, *Fifty Years of Agricultural Politics, being the history of the Central Chamber of Agriculture, 1865–1915*, 1915, pp. 379–82

THE NATIONAL AGRICULTURAL UNION

Agricultural depression had become so acute, and the leaders of both political parties seemed so entirely heedless of its general conditions, that when, in November, 1892, the Lancashire Federation of Farmers' Associations suggested that a national conference should be convened, the proposal was warmly taken up. Invitations were issued to every known agricultural society to send delegates, and on 7th and 8th December of that year there was held what was probably the largest, and was certainly the most representative agricultural gathering that has ever been got together in this country. The Chairman of the Central Chamber (the Right Hon. James Lowther, M.P.) presided, and resolutions were adopted on the following subjects:

1. Pointing out that the extreme depression had become very critical; that it was due to a continuous fall in prices; that land was going out of cultivation; and that it was a matter of the highest national concern that the progress of this calamity should be arrested.

2. That all competing imports should pay a duty not less than the rates and taxes levied on home production.

3. Supporting bimetallism.

4. Local taxation.

5. Compensation for unexhausted improvements; abolition of the law of distress; equal division of local rates between owners and occupiers.

6. Approving the principle of co-operation.

7. The extirpation of tuberculosis.

8. The formation of an Agricultural Union to give effect to the foregoing resolutions, to frame measures needed in the agricultural interest, and to organize voters in every constituency,

pledged to return, without distinction of party, candidates who agree to support such measures.

The last resolution aroused more enthusiasm than any of the others, although Lord Winchilsea's speech in introducing it was very brief. The Committee which arranged the conference were instructed to prepare a draft scheme to give effect to the proposal, and a special meeting of the Council was held in the following February to consider it. This was sent to local Chambers and came again before the Council on 28th February, when, after a long discussion in which considerable opposition was apparent, the debate was deferred. When the matter came again before the Council in April the National Agricultural Union (the N.A.U.) had been launched by Lord Winchilsea, and a provisional council formed; Mr R. H. Rew holding an extremely delicate position as Secretary for both parties. In October, when the rules of the N.A.U. came for the last time before the Council, it was resolved that though regretting that the rules and organization prevented the fusion of the two bodies, it was hoped that they would work harmoniously side by side. Mr Rew then resigned his connection with the N.A.U. and Mr A. T. Matthews (father of the present writer) was appointed Secretary of that body. Thereafter, until 1900, there were in existence two societies working for the same ends, having practically the same parliamentary programme, composed to a considerable extent of the same individuals, and, though not 'associated' in any way, always maintaining harmonious relations with each other. In 1900 the N.A.U. came to an end . . .

There was no fundamental difference in the organization of the two societies. The N.A.U., in order to reach the labourers, went into the villages, while the Chambers seldom got further than the market towns. The Union insisted that its executive must consist of an equal number of landowners, tenant farmers, and labourers, so that each class should have its full voice in directing its policy, whereas the Chambers had no rule of the kind. The Union had a scale of subscriptions based on the acreage owned or occupied, with a nominal subscription of 1s. per annum for labourers, while local Chambers fixed their own scale in each case. The great attraction possessed by the N.A.U. lay in the eloquence, the charm of manner, and the personality of its founder. There was, of course, the magic of a new name. There are today hundreds of fairly intelligent men who belong to no agricultural organization. Yet if one with a new name, but still advocating the most ancient programme, were started tomorrow, many of them would come in, and they would be joined by numbers who would leave the old ones, believing that they had at last found salvation. This may not mean altogether wasted effort, though it is certainly a waste of money, and it sometimes enables the mere politican to make much of the want of unanimity among agriculturists. However, for good or ill, this peculiarity appears to be inherent in the human mind; perhaps especially in the agricultural mind.

The N.A.U. succeeded in starting some 500 local branches in England, many of which developed surprising activity. As the writer of this history was Organizing Secretary to the Union for some years, and during that period visited every county in England and attended several hundreds of meetings of branches, he had an opportunity of knowing how effective the organization was. *The Cable*, a weekly agricultural paper, which Lord Winchilsea started, was of great assistance in educating members and in keeping the branches informed of the work of the Union, and was a decided factor in spreading the movement. A sufficient number of branches were successful enough to prove the correctness of Lord Winchilsea's theory, viz., that 'the threefold cord' *could* be twined, that harmony among the three sections was attainable and could be maintained, and that the organization as a whole was not the Utopian idea which so many onlookers considered it. The only reason why the Association did not survive was that means were lacking. One of the main causes of its demise was the growing fear of its strength prevalent among the party political wirepullers.

The British Produce Supply Association was never connected in any way with the N.A.U., except that Lord Winchilsea and one or two others worked actively for both. The one was purely commercial, the other political and educational. The work done by its founder was not wasted, for though the machine of which he was so proud eventually broke down, he had infused a spirit into agricultural combinations which has never died out. Many organizations have since sprung into existence as an indirect result of his efforts. The organization of agriculture was the cause for which he eventually sacrificed his life.

52
Employers' (or British) Parliamentary Council, 15 November 1898 : Objects
Robert A. Brady, *Business as a System of Power*, New York: Columbia University Press, 1943, pp. 154–6

To take action with respect to any bills introduced in either House of Parliament, affecting the interests of trade, of free contract and of labour, or with respect to the action of imperial or local authorities affecting in any way the said interests . . .

1. It is not, and ought not to be, the duty or business of Parliament to fix the hours during which adults may work.

2. [hours of work should be separately negotiated within industry]

3. The system of inspection necessary for the enforcement of State regulation of labour would be vexatious and intolerable.

4. The function of the State is to protect, and not to restrain, the liberty of the subject, and a legal eight-hour day is an infringement of the liberty of an individual to make his own labour contract.

5. The growing tendency, as evidenced by the divisions on the Mines (eight-hour) Bill, to look to the Legislature or Government to supply immediate remedies for all evils, however arising, in the struggle for existence, is of a most dangerous character and destructive of the spirit of sturdy independence which characterizes the British nation.

6. Former Acts of Parliament, which were intended to regulate hours of labour, only provoked evasions and resistance on the part of employers and employed.

7. [eight-hour-day laws in thirteen of the United States had become a dead letter because not enforced]

8. [the reform ought to come about by voluntary effort and negotiation, which had not been exhausted]

9. [hours of work are not identical with hours of duty]

10. [Many workmen prefer five days a week with longer hours so as to get a weekly holiday]

11. When Parliament interfered to limit the hours of women and children in factories, both were being taxed beyond their strength, amid surroundings that were not generally as sanitary as they should have been. The hours of labour were much longer than they are now; the education of the children was being neglected; the health and maternity of the women were being injured; and other objectionable features were common. No one, however, can claim that nine or ten hours of work are inhealthful or oppressive.

12. [reduction of the hours of labour would bear most heavily on those who could not stand the increased pace]

13. If the principle of State interference with working hours is conceded, the Legislature may also seek to control the use of a man's leisure.

14. The logical sequence to State regulation of hours is State regulation of wages.

53
Trade Unions: 'pressure' on M.P.s by Post Office workers, 1905

H. C. Deb., 6 July 1905, C. 1354–5

. . . Now [Lord Stanley, Postmaster General] came to the Bradford Committee and he hoped the House would allow him to put his case to the best of his ability and as fully as he could. The House must allow him to go back to the beginning of this agitation. It began with applications in this House for a Parliamentary Committee to deal with the question of Post Office wages. It was refused by his right hon. friend the present Chancellor of the Exchequer for reasons which he then considered adequate, and he felt perfectly certain that recent events would not have made him see any cause to differ from the opinion he then expressed. He must be allowed to quote his words. Speaking on April 30th, he said 'I hold as strongly as I have ever done that a House of Commons Committee is not a body for such an inquiry. No one can have a higher respect for this House or its reputation, and for the spirit which leads so many Gentlemen to give up so much time to public work, and it is therefore with no disrespect for the House of Commons or its Committee that I repeat for myself and my colleagues that we are unalterably opposed to anything in the nature of a Select Committee of the House of Commons for a decision of this Question. Hon. Members know and it is no use blinking our eyes to, the amount of pressure which is brought to bear or is attempted to be brought to bear upon Members on both sides of the House by public servants and by Post Office servants especially, . . . and even if the machinery by which Select Committees are appointed were such as to enable us to secure a Select Committee composed of thoroughly impartial men who had committed themselves by no expression of opinion to one side or the other, I still think it would not be fair to pick out fifteen Members of this House and make them marked men for the pressure which is now exercised more or less over the whole Assembly.'

That was the reason for which his right hon. friend rightly refused to give a Parliamentary Committee to inquire into these grievances. At the same time he recognised that there were certain anomalies which wanted looking into, and that there might be certain points of hardship which ought to be met. With that view he appointed a Committee which was now known as the

Bradford Committee to report to him, and to give him the
benefit of their advice . . .

54
The National Trust Act, 1907

An Act to Incorporate and Confer Powers upon the
National Trust for Places of Historic Interest or Natural Beauty.
21 August 1907

Whereas the National Trust for Places of Historic Interest or
Natural Beauty (hereinafter referred to as 'the Association')
was in the year 1894 incorporated as an Association not for profit
under the Companies Acts 1862 to 1890 with a liability of the
members limited by guarantee:

And whereas the Association was incorporated for the purposes
of promoting the permanent preservation for the benefit of the
nation of lands and tenements (including buildings) of beauty or
historic interest and as regards lands for the preservation (so far as
practicable) of their natural aspect features and animal and
plant life:

And whereas the Association in furtherance of those purposes
have acquired considerable property comprising common park
and mountain land and buildings and are or are reputed to be the
owners of or interested in the properties specified in the First
Schedule to this Act to the extent and in the manner therein
specified:

And whereas the public are admitted to the enjoyment of the
lands buildings and property held by the Association but no
adequate powers exist for regulating the use of or protecting the
property of the Association or for controlling the persons using
the same or resorting thereto:

And whereas with a view to the continuance of the work of the
Association for obtaining and preserving lands and buildings as
aforesaid and for the permanent holding and maintenance
thereof and for the preventing as far as possible their destruction
or disfigurement and for promoting the permanent preservation
of buildings places or property having historic associations or
being celebrated for their natural beauty it is expedient that the
Association should be dissolved and re-incorporated as in this
Act provided and that the powers of this Act should be conferred:

And whereas the objects of this Act cannot be obtained without
the authority of Parliament:

May it therefore please Your Majesty that it may be enacted
and be it enacted by the King's most Excellent Majesty by and

with the advice and consent of the Lords Spiritual and Temporal and Commons in this present Parliament assembled and by the authority of the same as follows (that is to say):

1. This Act may be cited as the National Trust Act 1907 . . .

3. From and after the passing of this Act the Association shall be dissolved and the several persons who immediately before the passing of this Act were members thereof and all other persons who shall subscribe to or who shall hereafter become members of the National Trust in accordance with the provisions of this Act and their executors administrators successors and assigns respectively shall be and they are hereby incorporated for the purposes hereinafter mentioned by the name of 'The National Trust for Places of Historic Interest or Natural Beauty' and by that name shall be a body corporate with perpetual succession and a common seal and with power to purchase take hold deal with and dispose of lands and other property without licence in mortmain.

4. (1) The National Trust shall be established for the purposes of promoting the permanent preservation for the benefit of the nation of lands and tenements (including buildings) of beauty or historic interest and as regards lands for the preservation (so far as practicable) of their natural aspect features and animal and plant life . . .

55
Towards an Agricultural Party, 1907

A. H. H. Matthews, *Fifty Years of Agricultural Politics, being the History of the Central Chamber of Agriculture, 1865–1915*, 1915, pp. 341–8

REPORT OF THE ORGANIZATION COMMITTEE

November 1907

1. The Staffordshire Chamber of Agriculture passed a resolution on 25 May urging the Central Chamber to take seriously into consideration the formation of a real, Independent Agricultural Parliamentary Party. This resolution was sent to all affiliated Chambers, and the principle it embodied has since been adopted by Canterbury, Lincolnshire, Monmouthshire, Totnes, Worcestershire Chambers, Chester, Holderness, Liverpool, Wadhurst Farmers' Clubs. This resolution formed the chief subject for discussion at the meeting of Secretaries at Lincoln on 26 June. This was attended by fourteen Secretaries and several members of the Organization Committee, and the following resolution was unanimously carried:

This meeting of Secretaries is strongly of opinion that an Independent Agricultural Party is *absolutely necessary and could be formed*, and asks the Central Chamber to devote a day to its discussion, and, if advisable, appoint a Committee to consider the best mode of creating and maintaining such a Party, and to send its suggestions to the local Chambers for consideration. Further, this meeting considers that to get as immediate results as possible much can be done by using the means already existing, by forming a joint Committee of Agricultural Members in the House composed of all political parties, which should be in close touch with the Central Chamber, its Business Committee, and Parliamentary Committee.

2. Any action in favour of the formation of an Agricultural Party in Parliament is quite within the province of the Chambers, Rule 1 providing that:

The object of the Chambers shall be . . . to take such action on all matters, both in and out of Parliament, as may seem desirable for the benefit of agriculture.

3. Your Committee are of opinion, and they believe it is one generally held, that the industry of agriculture is not represented in the Legislature in the degree that its relative importance, industrially and politically, demands, and therefore it does not receive the consideration that is necessary for its advancement that is so freely offered to it – with such marked results – in other countries. In making this statement your Committee desire to recall that there are about 150 parliamentary divisions in which the voters are chiefly agricultural, and it is therefore not through any lack of material that there has been this marked inactivity. The question your Committee are asked to consider is how can the present representation be shaped into a working party, and how can it be so effectively increased that agriculture can demand more attention from Parliament and from the Government of the day. On a matter of such importance it is necessary that some definite line of action should be decided upon by those interested without loss of time.

4. Your Committee have no hesitation in saying that the obvious answer to the question laid before them is by strengthening and consolidating existing agricultural organizations, and by the formation of others in unorganized districts. It is, however, unfortunately the case that the continued efforts of forty years have failed to bring more than a moderate percentage of agriculturists into line, and this forces your Committee to the conclusion that more attractive proposals are necessary to bring about the requisite combination than those hitherto laid before the farming community.

5. The Lincoln resolution given above proposes the formation of a distinct Agricultural Party. Your Committee feel that this is the ideal for which to strive, despite the financial consideration such a policy would involve. It must be obvious that with a section of the House of Commons returned as agricultural members by agriculturists, pledged to promote beneficial measures and to resist injurious legislation, and quite independent of the Whips of other sections of the House, agriculture will receive more of its due share of attention than it does now or has ever done in the past. The need of such a section has especially been apparent during the past decade.

6. One of the chief duties of an Agricultural Party was referred to in the last paragraph as 'resistance to injurious legislation'. The necessity of unceasing vigilance in this connection hardly needs demonstration; but to show that this is not an idle figure of speech the fact may be mentioned that in the years 1869 to 1896 inclusive eighty-four separate Acts were passed authorizing new or additional local taxation in England and Wales. (Appendix to Report of Local Taxation Commission, C. 8764, 1898, pp. x–xii, 54, 76.) Forty more such Acts were passed between 1896 and 1903, and this policy of adding to the local burdens of agriculturists still continues, whichever party happens to be in power.

7. For many years there have been a Conservative and a Liberal agricultural group in the House of Commons, which have met from time to time and elected chairmen and secretaries; but their activity as a rule has only become apparent when their respective parties have been in opposition. Such groups might as well be non-existent.

8. It may be urged that an individual cannot sit in the Imperial Parliament simply as an agricultural member, since wider and more important matters than even British agriculture must claim the attention of Parliament. But there are numerous precedents of members who nominally represent particular divisions, but in reality represent particular interests which may or may not exist in their respective constituencies. Moreover, every parliamentary candidate will always have to give expression to his views on Imperial and general questions, and unless those views commend themselves to the voters he will fail to be returned.

9. The second part of this resolution suggests the formation of a Joint Committee, composed of members drawn from all parties. Your Committee would point out, however, that the Parliamentary Committee of the Central Chamber is potentially all

that is required. It is composed of members drawn from the two great parties, and there is nothing to prevent other parties being represented upon it. The Parliamentary Committee has never been influenced by party considerations, and there are manifest objections to multiplying unattached committees. The one fault that can be found with the present Parliamentary Committee is that, collectively, it might show more activity, and that its individual members ought to attend its meetings more regularly. If this can be said of a Committee which has the stimulating force of the Central Chamber to stir it into action, there is no reason for supposing that one which has not this impetus behind it will be more active. There is also the danger that with two Committees – if the second one be formed – there would be overlapping, and therefore waste of time, possibly friction, and, more particularly, many things that are at present well done would be left undone, as they might fall between the two Committees in a well-intentioned endeavour not to interfere with each other's work.

10. One proposal laid before your Committee is that agriculturists should select their own candidate, subject to the approval of the Central Chamber, and inform the 'party' associations that they have done so, and claim their support. It is further suggested that in a division where the predominant vote is Liberal a candidate acceptable to the Liberals should be chosen, and conversely in the case of a Conservative constituency. It is claimed that this course would involve a minimum of expenditure, though it is pointed out that a central fund would, of course, be a necessity to fight a battle in some semi-rural districts, and in certain cases to aid suitable and successful candidates to bear the expenditure of Parliamentary life. Your Committee record this proposal without comment.

11. Another method has been the old practice of putting questions to candidates at or before elections and endeavouring to hold them to their pledges; but in practice it is found impossible to state the needs of an industry in a sufficiently definite form to make a candidate's reply in any way binding.

12. To give definite examples: At the General Election in 1905 the local Chambers put the following questions, among others, to all candidates:

Local Taxation

(a) that a permanent and comprehensive measure be passed, giving adequate relief from the excessive and unfair burdens at present imposed upon agriculture.

(b) That steps be taken to remedy the anomalies disclosed by the First Report of the Royal Commission on Local Taxation of 16 December 1898, and especially to provide one uniform assessment for all purposes both Imperial and local.

The first four replies, taking them in alphabetical order, two of which were Unionist and two Liberal, were:

(a) Strongly in favour. I have advocated this for the last two and a half years most keenly.

(b) Local taxation undoubtedly requires revision. Agricultural Rating Act gives temporary relief.

(c) Expressed approval of the programme of the Central Chamber.

(d) In favour of practically the whole of your proposals, and, if returned to Parliament, the agriculturists would find in me one ready to watch or to safeguard their interests whenever possible.

These replies had to be taken as satisfactory, but there is nothing in any one of them to prevent the writer voting against any Bill for revising local taxation, explaining his action with the greatest ease, and claiming that he kept within his pledge.

13. As this report deals with a matter which affects so vitally the future of agriculture in this country, your Committee recommend that before any decision is recorded by the Council it should be referred to the local Chambers for their immediate consideration. With regard to the suggestions in the present report, your Committee desire to support the first part of the Lincoln resolution advocating the formation of an 'Independent Agricultural Party'. They are of opinion, however, that the second suggestion of the Secretaries would only end in disappointment and in waste of time and money. Your Committee consider that it is better boldly to face all the difficulties involved in the creation of a new parliamentary party, and recommend the formation at once of a central fund for electioneering purposes. This fund should be kept quite distinct from the current account of the Central Chamber, and should be administered by a Special Committee nominated by, and consisting of members of, the Central Chamber.

14. Your Committee think that if care is taken much expense may be avoided by selecting constituencies where a Central Chamber candidate would be generally acceptable, and would, therefore, not be opposed.

15. In conclusion, your Committee are strongly of opinion that the value of such a party as that proposed depends far more on its absolute independence and singleness of aim than on its numerical strength, and recommend that the efforts to establish it shall at first be concentrated on those constituencies whence it

would be possible to secure a thoroughly compact and reliable body.

AGRICULTURAL REPRESENTATION COMMITTEE

April 1908

1. At the Council meeting on 11th December the following resolution was carried with four dissentients, and the Special Committee was appointed:

That in the opinion of this Council an Independent Agricultural Parliamentary Party should be formed, and other steps taken to strengthen the representation of agriculture in Parliament, and that with this object in view immediate steps should be taken to appoint a Committee to consider the matter and report to the Council.

2. Your Committee felt that their inquiries should follow the lines suggested by the report of the Organization Committee adopted on 5 November last, since that report met with such warm approval by the local Chambers.

3. The proposal to form an Independent Agricultural Party has, naturally, attracted a good deal of attention from the Press, from politicians, and from other quarters, and the statements made in the report just referred to have been subjected to much criticism, friendly and otherwise. As was expected, the unfriendly criticism came from strong party politicians, and this has, of course, been reflected in the columns of those local papers whose *raison d'etre* is the advocacy of certain political views. These have, of course, been followed by those (who still exist, though in greatly diminished numbers) who hold that blind obedience to their party at all cost is the one redeeming virtue. On the other hand, a considerable section of the Press, a large number of individual agriculturists, and a few members of Parliament have expressed warm approval of the formation of such a party.

4. The statement that 'there were 150 constituencies in which the voters were chiefly agricultural' has been called in question; but your Committee's inquiry shows that it was perfectly correct. They find, moreover, that in fully half of these the agricultural vote so largely predominates that (other circumstances being favourable) there is no reason why agricultural candidates should not be returned for that number of divisions. Assuming for a moment that a group of candidates standing for such divisions were returned as Independent Agricultural Members, your Committee wish to point out that this by no means represents the limit of the voting strength upon which agriculture might count,

as there would still remain a large number of members representing divisions in which agriculture is a considerable factor, and in many of which the agricultural vote, if properly organized, would hold the balance of power. Moreover, there are some members whose sympathies are with agriculture, though they may sit for purely urban constituencies, and these members might often be relied upon to exercise a benevolent neutrality even if they would not support the Agricultural Party. But it is not merely the number of possible votes that have to be looked at so much as the fact that a group of members existed to watch over and further agricultural interests: for your Committee are convinced that the mere knowledge of the existence of such a party would prevent agriculture being played with or neglected as has been the case in the past.

5. Another statement which raised some comment was that two party agricultural groups already existed in the House of Commons, but that, in the opinion of the Organization Committee, such party groups were useless. Our opponents have used the existence of these groups in an endeavour to show that an Agricultural Party is 'unnecessary'. In this connection we quote the remarks of two well-known Unionist members of Parliament.

In the *Southern Daily News* of the 21 December 1907, Lord Edmund Talbot, M.P., is reported as having said:

... There was at this moment in the House an Agricultural Committee to which he had the honour to belong, and which met to consider every agricultural question which was brought forward in the House, and he believed it would be wisest to leave this question of the Agricultural Party in the hands of that Committee.

But in the *Hampshire Chronicle* of 7 December 1907, and in other local papers of that date, Mr A. H. Lee, M.P., is reported to have said:

He had been a member for several years, representing what was largely an agricultural constituency, but he had never been invited to the meeting of any such Committee, and he did not know until he read this report of the Central Chamber that there was supposed to be an Agricultural Committee of members of the House of Commons – it had never been brought to his notice, he had never been invited to it.

In the opinion of your Committee, if these groups ever did anything to justify their existence their use has long since entirely vanished.

6. Many critics have said that the agriculturists have not made out sufficient need for an Agricultural Party, and that we should remain satisfied with the present representation of agri-

cultural constituencies. Your Committee, therefore, think it worth while to state a few recent facts connected with agriculture in Parliament which have come before them.

7. In the last Parliament there were about 110 M.P.s who were members of the Central Chamber; in the present Parliament there are about eighty. Every year these members have been asked to ballot for private members' Bills at the beginning of each session. On an average barely twenty have replied at all, and of those only three or four have promised their ballot. Recently twelve members were asked to put their names on the back of a certain Bill; only one took the trouble to reply. The attendance of members at meetings of the Parliamentary Committee of the Central Chamber is deplorable – usually three or four out of fifteen; yet these meetings are always held in the House of Commons in order to meet the convenience of members. The late Government allowed six hours for the discussion of agricultural questions in five sessions, but the only protest came from *outside* the House of Commons. Last session the Government gave a day to the vote for the Board of Agriculture; only one agricultural member had any question to raise, and the day was occupied on matters outside agriculture, while scarcely a score of members representing agricultural divisions took the trouble to attend. There have been more than 100 Acts passed during the past thirty-eight years which increased the burden of local taxation; but, with the exception of the action taken against the Education Bill of 1902, they have passed almost without protest. Nearly one hundred M.P.s were specifically requested (during the session of 1907) to urge that the cost of administering the Destructive Insects Act should be defrayed by the National Exchequer instead of out of the rates; not one single member raised the matter in the House. This sort of example can be multiplied indefinitely.

8. One of the most important aspects of the whole question is the class of candidates brought forward and the way in which these candidates are forced upon some agricultural constituencies. In the course of their inquiry your Committee have come across several instances where the party organizations have selected carpet-baggers when they might have nominated a suitable candidate for an agricultural constituency.

9. It will be found in practice that there is no one method which will bring about the formation of an Agricultural Party, nor must it be expected that a strong party will develop in a short time. There is much work to be done in many directions, and a considerable expenditure will be required. We are of

opinion that the best way to carry out this will be by the appointment of a Special Standing Committee, *having a separate entity and yet working in accord with the Central Chamber, holding a position somewhat analogous to the late Local Taxation Committee. In order to ensure complete harmony prevailing between the Central Chamber and such Committee, we suggest that at least one half of the Executive should be nominated annually by the Central Chamber.* For the purposes of this Committee a fund shall be started, which should be kept distinct from the current account of the Central Chamber, and local Chambers and others are now invited to subscribe to this fund without delay.

10. Your Committee have in the course of several meetings considered the details of future action with a view to getting a better representation of agriculture in the House of Commons. They consider it would be unwise to set out in detail the methods to be adopted; but the Committee can see their way to materially improve the present position in several directions:

(a) By putting forward absolutely independent agriculturists, standing as third candidates if necessary, and, though giving a general statement on current politics, making agriculture the paramount question.

(b) By approaching the 'Party' organizations of both political parties with a view of selecting or approving candidates that will be acceptable to the parties.

(c) By local influence in each constituency, so that proper candidates are adopted by the executive of each 'Party' organization.

(d) By taking part in elections in agricultural constituencies and by questioning candidates on agricultural matters.

(e) By constant and active work among members of the House of Commons.

56
The National Farmers' Union, 1908

(a) Rules (1910) (b) Programme and Policy (1910) (c) Parliamentary Lobbyist (1913) (d) Representation in Parliament (1923) (e) Questionnaire to candidates (1924)

Yearbooks 1910, 1913, 1923, 1925

(a)

RULES

I Title. The title shall be the National Farmers' Union.

II Objects. To secure Parliamentary and other support of

British Agriculture, and to protect and further the interests of British farmers individually and collectively.

III Methods.

1. The promotion of united action throughout the country.
2. The organization of Farmers' Associations upon the adopted rules of the affiliated Unions.
3. To secure the representation of farmers by practical men in the Legislative and Administrative Councils of the Kingdom.

IV Membership. Farmers' Unions, Clubs, and kindred associations (consisting of farmers in actual practice only), hereafter called Branches, may become members of the National Farmers' Union on paying an affiliation fee of One Shilling a member, such amount to be computed on the numbers shown on their annual balance-sheet. Affiliation fees are due in advance on 1 January of each year, and if not paid by 31 March such Unions, etc., will be debarred until all arrears are paid, from taking part in any meeting of the National Farmers' Union, but will not be relieved of their liability until duly resigning under Rule VI. Any difference in membership to be adjusted on 31 December following.

V. Associate Societies.

1. All Societies adopting the encouragement of British agriculture (as defined in Rule II.) as one of their principles may join the Union as Associates.
2. An Annual Subscription of not less than One Guinea shall be paid by each Associate Society.
3. Each Associate Society shall receive a copy of all literature issued by the Union, but shall have no vote or right to speak (without consent) at any meeting of the National Farmers' Union.

VI Resignations. Any Branch wishing to retire from the National Farmers' Union must give notice of such intention in writing to the Secretary by 31 October each year; such resignation will not be accepted unless all fees due to the National Farmers' Union are paid.

VII Constitution. The affairs of the National Farmers' Union shall be managed by a General Executive Committee (working through the County Executive Committees), who shall have control of funds of the Union, and shall report to the Annual General Meeting.

VIII General Executive Committee.

1. The General Executive Committee shall be composed of members elected annually by the County Executive Committees, subject to confirmation by the Annual General Meeting, and shall consist of one representative for 500 members, and one extra for every additional 1,000 members in the county. Such names shall be sent to the Secretary of the National Farmers' Union at least twenty-one days before the Annual General Meeting.

2. The General Executive Committee shall, from time to time, make its own by-laws.

3. Vacancies on the General Executive Committee shall be filled up by referring to the County Executive Committee in which the vacancy occurs.

4. The General Executive Committee shall appoint the paid Officers of the Union.

5. Out-of-pocket expenses to be paid by the National Farmers' Union to Members of the General Executive Committee.

6. The General Executive Committee shall appoint an Hon. Treasurer.

IX County Executive Committees. For the purpose of electing members to serve on the General Executive Committee and transacting any other business, each county (or Amalgamation of Counties, or other areas having not less than 1,000 members, with the assent of the General Executive Committee) shall form County Executive Committees duly elected by the Branches within the Counties.

The Branches shall adopt their own method of electing the County Executives.

County Executive Committees shall submit to the Annual General Meeting names of such members they elect to serve on the General Executive Committee.

X Annual General Meeting. An Annual General Meeting shall be held every year in February, consisting of duly elected delegates of the Branches which are members of the National Farmers' Union.

1. Each of such Branches shall be entitled to send representatives to the Annual General Meeting as follows: One for each Branch, and one extra for every 250 members.

2. To receive reports of the work done by the General Executive Committee and by members of the Union, and to transact other business of which fourteen days' notice has

been given to the Secretaries of the different Branches. Business for which urgency is voted may also be considered.

3. To adopt, if approved, the Balance Sheet for the year as presented by the General Executive Committee.

4. To confirm the Election of the General Executive Committee as submitted by the County Executive Committees. In the event of a County Branch qualifying for representation on the General Executive after the date of the Annual Meeting, and electing its representative, the General Executive Committee shall have power to confirm such election.

5. To elect the President and Vice-President for the ensuing year from the General Executive Committee.

6. Special General Meetings may be called by the General Executive Committee, and shall be called at any time at the request of three of the County Executive Committees.

7. At such meetings, of which seven days' notice must be given to the Secretaries of the Branches, no other business shall be taken except that specified in the notice calling the meeting, unless urgency is voted.

8. Notice of each General or Annual Meeting shall be sent to each secretary of affiliated Branches, detailing the business of the meeting, and for the Annual General Meeting the attendances of the General Executive Committee during the past year, and also the names of members submitted by the County Executive Committee for the ensuing year.

xi Accounts. The Accounts shall be audited annually by an Auditor or Auditors appointed by the Annual General Meeting.

xii Alteration of Rules. No Rule shall be made or altered except by a majority of votes given at the Annual General Meeting or a Special General Meeting of the National Farmers' Union called under Rule X. (6), and after twenty-one days' notice of such proposed rule or alteration has been given to the Secretary of the National Farmers' Union in writing.

Basis of rules for constituted branches of the N.F.U.

1. The Union is formed for the purpose of watching over and defending matters affecting farmers, and to take such action as may be thought desirable for their welfare. All party politics and all sectarian matters, except those bearing on agriculture, shall be avoided.

2. The annual subscription to be at the rate of $\frac{1}{2}$d. per acre on

land farmed, maximum subscription £3. No one to be eligible as a member unless he is carrying on the business of a farmer in actual practice, and farming not less than two acres of land. The minimum subscription to be 2s.

No member is entitled to vote who is in arrears with his subscription.

Honorary members accepted at a minimum subscription of 2s., and allowed to attend meetings and join in discussions, but not allowed to vote.

Renewal subscriptions are payable on the anniversary of the first payment.

3. The business of the Union to be managed by a Central Committee of twenty members, with power to add to their number, six of whom shall form a quorum; in case of a tie, the Chairman to have the casting vote. The Central Committee to be elected at the Annual General Meeting, and eligible for re-election provided they have attended at least two-thirds of the meetings during the year, with the exception of cases of illness or absence from the country of which notice has been given to the Secretary.

(b)

N.F.U. Yearbook 1910

PROGRAMME AND POLICY OF

THE NATIONAL FARMERS' UNION BRIEFLY REVIEWED

By the Secretary

In reviewing the work, aims and policy of the National Farmers' Union, it is as well first to consider the reasons that brought it into existence and how far it differs from other organizations, too numerous to mention, promoted for the benefit of the farming industry. The chief element in its success is, undoubtedly, due to the fact that the Farmers' Union is the first genuine effort on the part of farmers themselves to combine for their own protection and benefit. Other attempts have been made in the past – notably the late Lord Winchelsea's [sic] Agricultural Union, but this embraced the three classes, landlord, farmer and labourer, and though ideal in theory it was found impossible in practice. The Farmers' Union fully realizes that in most instances the interests of the three classes are identical, but instead of one body to represent the three, its gospel is that there should be three organizations representing each class, and from time to time the Executives of the Landlords' Association, the Farmers' Union and the Labourers' Union should meet at a round table conference and discuss a common ground of policy. But this can only be brought about provided that the separate Associations are free from party politics; for apart from the first essential of the Farmers' Union that its members should be farmers in actual practice – not necessarily tenant farmers – the second essential is that the Union's members should place agricultural questions above party, and so keep the Union free from all party questions; in other words, to lift politics out of agriculture, and uplift agriculture above politics.

It should be distinctly understood that the Farmers' Union is in no way antagonistic to either landlord or labourer – but the time has come – in these days of Unions for all other industries, when the farmers should voice their own opinions alone and unaided. Surely a Government or a Board of Agriculture would give greater attention to the voice of the farmers on farming questions than to that of a mixed body – a body possibly where the tenant farmer would necessarily have but a limited chance of speaking his mind.

The Farmers' Union would have no *raison d'être* if everything was going satisfactorily for the agricultural industry. Are farmers likely to be satisfied with the work and usefulness of the Board of Agriculture, knowing that its income is less than half that of the Board of Agriculture for Ireland. Again, the Agricultural Ratings Act has not yet been made a permanent Measure, although 'the half' paid today is in many cases greater than 'the whole' one fifteen years ago; although local rates pay something like 70 per cent towards the maintenance of Police, Highways, Poor, Lunatics and Education, and from the latter the farmer knows his labourers' and his own children are being given an education – so-called – which will be useless in agricultural life. Again, on such questions as the Milk Bill, the Beer Bill, the Hops Bill, and the Fertilizers and Feeding Stuffs Act, farmers feel, and not without reason, that Parliament has legislated for anybody but them, and they *now* know that had they been directly represented in Parliament, the last-named Act, at least, would not have been the absurdity it is today.

That the farming interest has been neglected by both parties cannot be denied, and the reason is not far to seek, to quote a pamphlet issued in 1907 by the Lincolnshire Farmers' Union, the pioneer in the movement:

It must be remembered that, however bitterly the two great parties of the State were opposed on many questions, as regards agriculture they were equally indifferent; the one side counting on the unreasoning support, and the other side on the bitter opposition of the farmers. The one felt confident they would not lose support, and the other that they were unlikely to gain any.

Taking the important question now before the Country – Tariff Reform – the National Farmers' Union's attitude is expressed in a resolution recently passed by the Executive, viz.:– The Union makes no pronouncement on the merits or demerits of Tariff Reform, but strongly urges its members and farmers generally, to make their combination so powerful that if a definite scheme of Tariff Reform is promulgated, the industry of agriculture in all its branches shall receive an equal share of any benefit that may accrue to other industries.

As the Union asks its members to place their industry above party considerations, is it not essential that they should see to it they are not left out if any benefits are to be conferred on other industries on this question?

Up to now those responsible for explaining the Fiscal Policy have failed to show that the farmer will receive any substantial benefit – many exponents have not even attempted the task. Before the next General Election a responsible pronouncement must be made on this subject, if it is to receive the support of the general body of farmers.

And as to Small Holdings. In principle this is admitted as useful, but for every thirty-three acres so taken, one agricultural labourer is done away with, and who takes his place? In many cases, a man with no agricultural knowledge, and not likely to make a farmer. And again, the farmer is dispossessed of the most useful part of the farm, although some County Councils have been sensible enough to only purchase such farms as are vacant.

The alternative of Small Holdings for Army pensioners will mean dispossession in much the same way.

Again, under the Development Act, certain funds are to be allocated for the benefit of agriculture, and it behoves farmers, through their Combination, to put before the County Councils their needs and desires.

On broad lines then, the combination of farmers, as such, is highly necessary, and an organization run on popular lines like the National Farmers' Union should appeal to all farmers great and small. The Union desires to work through county areas giving representation in its Executive to all Societies when membership exceeds 500, and further it asks each County

Union to form branches in each market town in its area, and give to each Branch representation on its own Executive, and asks each one to do its own share of work. It recognizes that however strong an Association may be in its own area, a combination of strong Associations will do far more in a national sense. Locally, one of the strongest points is protection in a legal sense.

Alone, a farmer can do nothing against railway companies, insurance companies, or merchants who are combined. United, the position is entirely different. As an instance, strong Unions have been able to make excellent terms with an insurance company, and it is no secret that when the Tariff Offices raised their rates in other risks in Employers' Liability Insurance last spring, farmers' rates were not raised, owing to the opposition of those Tariff Companies in districts where the Union was strong.

In legal aid to members the advantage of membership and the advice received has not only brought about satisfactory settlements in hundreds of cases, but has saved 'feeding the lawyers' in many others.

It may be said that apathy, due in a measure to the isolated lives they live, militates against the possibility of farmers forming a really powerful combination, but, already, in a few years, in at least three counties, the Unions have reached a membership of over 2,000. In these districts, indeed, the fact has been grasped that it is in the farmers' own hands to redress their grievances, protect themselves, and do away with the neglect from which they have too long suffered.

Much has been said about forming an independent Agricultural Party in the House of Commons. The National Farmers' Union does not aim at this, but rather it desires to get members for Agricultural Constituencies pledged to its very reasonable programme – a programme advocating reasonable local rates, a Beer Bill, feeding the Army on home-fed meat, keeping out live foreign cattle, etc. – and backing up these pledged members by a few practical men from themselves representing both sides in politics. The idea is, perhaps, new, and as such will be regarded as impossible; but already party whips have promised support, and common-sense and patience will bring it about.

Already the influence of the Union has extended into more than twenty counties, and the importance of joining the combination is being realized by farmers throughout the land.

The energy and enthusiasm of its pioneers has not flagged, and with the sound policy with which it started and its continuity assured, together with the fact of the organization being run on

H

popular lines, there is every hope that in the near future we shall see a combination worthy of the noble industry it represents.

(c)

. . . introduced the question of Parliamentary Lobbyist. He explained that as the outcome of a conversation between two or three members of the Parliamentary Committee and the chairman, it was decided by way of an experiment to put an anonymous advertisement in *The Times* for a Parliamentary Lobbyist. It was considered that one of the weakest links in the chain was the fact that the Union was not brought regularly into direct touch with those members of Parliament who had pledged themselves to support the National Farmers' Union programme, and it was considered how best to overcome the difficulty, and the advertisement was the result. A very considerable number of replies were sent in, and were carefully gone into by the president, the vice-president, and secretary, and were brought down to one. This applicant was Mr G. Weller Kent, who was present, and he replied in such terms as to show that he possessed better qualifications than any of the others for filling the post. He was a member of the bar, practising on the South-Eastern circuit, and had been, he believed, for some years past Parliamentary correspondent of *The Times*. Furthermore, though he did not lay any claim to agricultural knowledge, he possessed intimate acquaintance with many members of the House of Commons, and methods of Parliamentary procedure which should prove of great advantage to the National Farmers' Union. It was felt that it would be a very good thing to engage his services, and he was sure that he would give expression to their views, and would keep a watchful eye over the members who had promised to support them. This, as he had said, had always been a weak point with the Farmers' Union, but there was no reason at all why the weakness should not to a very large extent disappear. Mr Kent was very generous as to remuneration, as he was willing to accept a nominal sum by way of fees, in fact, whatever they could afford. He thought the Executive should agree to the provisional agreement entered into by the Parliamentary Committee and that it should only be a question of arranging the final details.

The Chairman moved that the recommendation be received and adopted. Mr Padwick seconded, and this was carried.

Mr Kent, returning thanks, said he understood they were a very vigorous body and a very rapidly growing Union. It would be his duty as well as his pleasure to attend as many of their meetings as he could to gather their views. He had been at the House for over twenty years, and knew a good many members and the procedure of the House. The Government had thrown over in 'the slaughter of the innocents' (laughter) the Milk and Dairy Bill for England, and many other Bills, and he thought that when next session opened the Government would be very busy with a life and death struggle to keep itself in office a few months, and would not have very much time to devote itself to agricultural subjects.

(d)

PARLIAMENTARY REPRESENTATION

89. The past year has seen the labours of the Committee crowned by the election to the House of Commons of four direct representatives of the Union – the first occasion on which the organized working farmers of England and Wales have secured representation by men from their own ranks. At the commencement of the year the series of Parliamentary Demonstrations arranged in co-operation with the County Branches proved that members everywhere were alive to the importance of paying due regard to the furtherance of their interests in the House of Commons, and subsequent happenings only accentuated the feeling that it would be folly to neglect any opportunity of strengthening their position.

Thus, when the General Election was sprung upon the country, the Union's machinery was in a state of complete preparedness.

At the October meeting of the Council of the Union the Parliamentary Committee was given executive powers in respect of the Political Fund, and it was agreed that the Committee should be convened immediately the necessity arose. Three meetings of the full Committee were held during the short period of the election, and matters that arose in the intervals were dealt with by the Chairman (Mr Bradshaw), the President and the Vice-President, with the Parliamentary Secretary.

The Committee met as soon as the dissolution was announced, and the Agenda covered the entire range of the Union's election activities. The first matter dealt with was the issuing of a letter to the County Branches directing their attention to the legal restrictions placed upon the work at elections of 'outside' organizations by the Representation of the People Act (1918), and this was done in consultation with the Union's Legal Adviser. The Committee decided to send a letter to the Party Leaders with a view to ascertaining their policy in regard to the existing and prospective condition of Agriculture. This letter was dispatched at once and the replies received were communicated to the Press in due course.

The next business before the Committee was to consider the Union's Election Programme. This duty was carried out with the utmost care and with due regard to the subjects on which the Council of the Union had from time to time expressed an opinion. It was necessary, of course, to restrict the length of the Programme and to include so far as possible only matters of importance to the Union as a whole. The various items to be included were agreed upon unanimously, and the Programme was embodied in a pledge form for submission to Parliamentary candidates.

Two thousand copies of this form were printed and circulated – the intention being to provide two copies of the form for each candidate, so that the original reply might be transmitted to headquarters for filing and a duplicate be retained in the County Office. County Branches were free, of course, to question candidates on matters of interest to their members not included in the national Programme and many did so.

A special leaflet (No. 20) was approved for publication for the purpose of emphasizing the importance of casting a solid 'agricultural vote'. The terms of a manifesto on the agricultural situation were endorsed, and this manifesto was also issued as a leaflet (No. 21). The Committee decided that, in addition to the publication of these leaflets, an advertising campaign should be conducted in order to direct the attention of the electorate to the importance of the agricultural issue from the standpoint of the welfare of the nation. Accordingly, leaflet No. 20 was used as 'copy' for an advertisement in the agricultural Press, while space was taken for the manifesto in many of the leading newspapers, the Union's case being thus brought immediately before many millions of electors. The value of this publicity was perfectly apparent, and a direct result was that the position of agriculture formed the theme of many leading articles in the Press.

The record of votes given by M.P.s in divisions in the House of Commons on questions affecting Agriculture was brought up to date and supplies were dispatched to all the County Branches for distribution. One hundred thousand copies of each leaflet and 20,000 copies of the record of votes were printed and distributed to the County Branches.

When the dissolution came, the Committee had six prospective candidates in the field – five in England and one in Wales. At the eleventh hour, however, the number was added to in consequence of the decision of the East Riding Executive to bring out a candidate in opposition to Lt-Col the Hon. F. S. Jackson in the Howdenshire Division.

The successful candidates were:

Mr F. N. Blundell	Lancashire, Ormskirk
Mr Robert Bruford	Somerset, Wells
Mr J. Q. Lamb	Staffs, Stone
Mr E. W. Shepperson	Hereford, Leominster

The unsuccessful candidates were:

Mr E. Clark	Rutland and Stamford
Mr D. Johns	Carmarthen
Mr H. J. Winn	Yorks., East Riding, Howdenshire

The replies received to the Union's *questionnaire* were analysed at headquarters immediately the polls were declared and the position in the House of Commons is that:

159 M.P.s have undertaken to join an Agricultural Committee on the basis of the first item in the Union's Programme, and seventy-four of them support the Programme in its entirety.

(e)

GENERAL ELECTION

90. As already stated, the Union's Election Programme and Manifesto were approved at a joint meeting of the General Purposes and Parliamentary Committees. In spite of the short time available the County Branches were highly successful in their efforts to get the Union's programme placed before all parliamentary candidates, and an analysis of the replies received show that over 120 members of the new Parliament have undertaken to support the Union's programme, wholly or in part. In view of the great preponderance of Conservative representation of agricultural constituencies, it was not thought worth while to publish an analysis of the support given to the Union's programme, but the information will be used by Headquarters as occasion arises.

Amongst the candidates again returned were Mr J. Q. Lamb (Stone Division, Staffs) and Mr E. W. Shepperson, (North Hereford), who both secured very substantial majorities. The Committee take this opportunity of recording their high appreciation of Mr Lamb's work in the late Parliament as Hon. Secretary to the Parliamentary Agricultural Committee.

57
Union of Democratic Control, 1914

Leaflet No. 1, n.d. (1914). In Marvin Swartz, *The Union of Democratic Control in British Politics during the First World War*: Oxford: Clarendon Press, 1971, Appendix D, ©️ 1971

Why should democracy control foreign policy? Because it is unwise and dangerous in a democratically governed country to exclude any large body of people from having any voice in the control of their most vital interest. Because the tendency of the people is more and more to desire peace and to see in the foreigner not an enemy but a fellow-worker and a fellow-sufferer. Because the people desire to turn their attention to the improvement of conditions at home and to fighting the real enemies – Ignorance and Poverty. Because they would not be influenced by the personal and petty quarrels that disturb the intercourse of ministers and diplomats. Because the Foreign Secretary, with the full sanction and approval of the people behind him, would be in a far stronger position than he is now. Because the people would no longer be deluded by the Press, which now trades on their ignorance. Because frankness and publicity are better securities for peace than secrecy and intrigue. Because aristocratic control of foreign affairs has failed. Because the highest moral sense of a nation resides in the people rather than in the Government. Because by democracy alone can the power of vested interests be counteracted.

How can democracy gain control? By more frequent discussion of foreign policy in Parliament. By the sanction of Parliament being obtained for all treaties, commitments and engagements with foreign nations. By the periodic revision of treaties by Parliament. By the establishment of a Foreign Affairs Committee. By the democratization of the Diplomatic Service and the Foreign Office. By the abolition of secret treaties, secret clauses to treaties and secret engagements. By the frequent publication in the Press of official news.

Make your M.P. press for these reforms.

Join the Union of Democratic Control.

58
The Women's Institutes, 1915 : in retrospect

Barbara Kaye, *Home and Country, 1915–65*, May 1965

For the first great occasion in the history of the Women's Institutes one must, without question, go back to an afternoon in

September 1915 when, in a small Welsh village with a fifty-eight letter name, the first British W.I. came into being.

Although at the time it can hardly have seemed an occasion to merit the word 'great', for the little group of countrywomen who came together that autumn afternoon to form the Llanfair P.G. Women's Institute, there must certainly have been a sense of occasion, of adventure, combined with pride in the knowledge that they were pioneers.

The meeting was held in Mrs W. E. Jones's summer house and the formidable Mrs Alfred Watt was there. This was an exciting day for her; the formation of Llanfair P.G. W.I. was the first fruit from the seed she had energetically been sowing ever since her arrival from Canada two years previously. Not long before she had spoken at a conference in Bangor, arranged by the Agricultural Organization Society, a body that had given her a short-term appointment to organize Women's Institutes in England and Wales. Local big-wigs had attended the conference, including Colonel Stapleford-Cotton, a Governor of the A.O.S., and his wife, who became Llanfair P.G.'s first President.

By October 1917, when the first A.G.M. was held in London, there were 137 W.I.s in existence. Some 200 members of the Movement, including sixty delegates, attended. Lady Denman, who was already directing the W.I. Sub-Committee, set up by the A.O.S., took the Chair, and was subsequently elected Chairman of the first N.F.W.I. Executive Committee, an office she was to hold for the next twenty-nine years. At this meeting, the delegates were asked to accept that the responsibility for the Institutes (and their financing) should be transferred from the A.O.S. to the Board of Agriculture. In fact, they had little option but to agree, but they did make it clear that they intended to be free to manage their own affairs!

The following year was one of tremendous expansion with an average of twenty new Institutes formed each week. By this time Mrs Watt had five full-time organizers working with her, but even so more help was badly needed. So in May 1919, she set up the first residential V.C.O. school at Wyberlye in Sussex. 'The atmosphere was one of exaltation', wrote one of those who took the first course. 'It was a condensed training in living.' Presumably all eight students were dedicated to the cause, and it is clear that they found Mrs Watt's personality impressive and her missionary zeal inspiring. A pattern for training V.C.O.s was thus established.

In 1919 came a royal occasion, the formation of a W.I. at

Sandringham, with H.M. Queen Mary graciously consenting to be President. It was Mrs Watt who had the task of picking her way through the protocol that preceded the formation. Later she described the event in the first issue of *Home and Country* (March 1919). Princess Mary was also at the meeting which was well attended by women from the village and the royal estate. Another memorable royal occasion was the garden party at Buckingham Palace, also in 1919, to which the N.F.W.I. Executive were invited. One sees this invitation as a gracious recognition of the part the W.I.s played in helping the war effort.

The A.G.M. of that year was an important landmark in the Movement's history, for the Board of Agriculture had already announced that it could no longer be responsible for the formation of new Institutes. This decision was softened, however, by the Government's promise to pay the N.F.W.I. a grant of £10,000, and no tears were shed by the 600 delegates (representing 1,405 Institutes) at the prospect of having to accept responsibility for their own destiny. The previous day there had been a lively Special General Meeting at which it had been decided that the N.F.W.I. Executive should continue to be elected by direct vote of the Institutes and that there should be a Consultative Council of County Federation representatives to advise the Executive and keep them in touch with the Counties. So, five months later, the first Consultative Council meeting took place in Leicester.

59
British Industries Federation, or Federation of British Industries Association, 1916

The main object of the new organization is to investigate and carry into effect a definite line of policy in regard to various matters affecting British industry both now and after the war.

F. Dudley Docker, President; Sir William Peat, Chairman.

The Times, 29 August 1916

Royal Charter, 1923.

George the Fifth, by the Grace of God, of the United Kingdom of Great Britain and Ireland and of the British Dominions beyond the Seas King Defender of the Faith Emperor of India;

TO ALL TO WHOM THESE PRESENTS SHALL COME, GREETING!

Whereas Colonel Oliver Carleton Armstrong D.S.O. of 98 Gloucester Place in the County of London lately President of the Voluntary

Society called 'The Federation of British Industries' (hereinafter referred to as 'the Association') Sir William Barclay Peat of 11 Ironmonger Lane in the City of London Knight c.v.o. the Chairman of the Council of the Association Sir Ernest Fitzjohn Oldham of 51 Lincoln's Inn Fields in the County of London Knight the Deputy Chairman of the Association and Roland Thomas Nugent of 21 Egerton Gardens Kensington in the said County of London the Director of the Association and others Our Loving Subjects Members of the Association have by their Petition represented to Us:

(a) That the Association was founded in the year 1916 as a Voluntary Unincorporated Society consisting of British individuals or companies corporations partnerships and associations established in any part of Our Dominions (whether in the United Kingdom or overseas) being to a substantial extent (either themselves or by their Members) producers of goods and commodities for sale or mainly engaged in an industry serving or providing for the needs of manufacturers or producers with the view of promoting the welfare and extension of British Industries when the war should end and in particular of promoting encouraging and protecting the interests of manufacturers and producers of all kinds of goods and commodities and the establishment and development of industries of all kinds;

(b) That the Association is not a trading association nor formed for the purpose of gain to its Members but is merely an association for the encouragement promotion and protection of British Industries of all kinds and the development thereof and the establishment of closer communications between manufacturers producers workmen and customers and the improvement standardization and simplification of commercial law in all parts of Our Dominion;

(c) That the aggregate numbers of Members of the Association is upwards of 1,887 consisting of 176 associations or companies and 1,711 firms and individuals;

(d) That the funds of the Association are at present mainly derived from the donations and annual subscriptions of Members although it is contemplated that certain of the departments shall be self-supporting and that for that purpose a charge will be made for services rendered by any such department;

(e) That it is believed that the Association has already assisted and will still more in the future greatly assist in the extension of British Industries throughout the world and that it would greatly promote the objects of the Association and would also be for the public benefit if the Association were incorporated by the exercise of our Royal Prerogative; AND WHEREAS by their said Petition the Petitioners pray that We would be graciously pleased in the exercise of Our Royal Prerogative to grant to them a Charter of Incorporation in terms of the draft thereunto annexed or such other terms as to Us should seem proper;

AND WHEREAS it appears to Us that the Association is doing important national work and that it would tend to improve its status and usefulness if the prayer of the said Petitioners was granted:

NOW THEREFORE WE having taken the said Petition into Our Royal consideration and being satisfied that the intentions of the Petitioners are laudable and deserving of encouragement have constituted erected and incorporated and We by Our Prerogative Royal and of Our Especial Grace and certain knowledge and mere Motion by these Presents for Us and Our Heirs and Successors do hereby grant appoint and declare as o llows:

INCORPORATION

1. We do constitute erect and incorporate into one Body Politic and Corporate by the name of 'The Federation of British Industries' the Petitioners and such other associations companies firms and persons as are by this Our Charter made or declared to be Members or shall hereafter be admitted as Members thereof with perpetual succession and a Common Seal and with power to alter and renew the same at discretion willing and ordaining that the said body corporate (hereinafter referred to as 'the Federation') shall and may sue and be sued in all Courts and be capable in law to take and hold any personal property and do all matters and things incidental or appertaining to a body corporate but so that the Federation shall apply its profits (if any) or other income in promoting its objects and shall not at any time pay any dividends to its Members . . .

OBJECTS OF THE FEDERATION

4. The objects for which the Federation is established and incorporated are:

(a) The establishment of a federation consisting of persons who are British subjects and of British companies corporations partnerships firms or associations which are formed or incorporated under the laws of the United Kingdom or any British Dominion Commonwealth Union Colony or Dependency and carrying on business in any part of the United Kingdom or any British

Dominion Commonwealth Union Colony or Dependency and being to a substantial extent (or in the case of an association by its members) producers of goods or commodities for sale or mainly engaged in an industry serving or providing for the needs of manufacturers or producers;

Provided always that although a British company or firm constituted under the laws of England shall not be incapacitated for membership by reason of its being controlled by foreign shareholders or partners yet nevertheless the Federation shall always remain British in character and free from foreign control and shall have its domicile and principal place of business in England.

(b) The promotion and encouragement of free and unrestricted communication and discussion between masters and workmen with a view to the establishment of amicable arrangements and relations between masters and workmen and to the avoidance and settlement of strikes and all other forms of industrial warfare between masters and workmen.

(c) The encouragement promotion and protection of the interests of manufacturers and producers of all kinds of goods and commodities and the assistance promotion and encouragement by all lawful means of the organization of industries of all kinds and in particular with the view to the establishment promotion and development of industries of all kinds.

In particular and without prejudice to the generality of the above objects and in the furtherance thereof.

(d) The promotion and development of any schemes or movements having for their object the establishment and maintenance of communication between manufacturers and producers of goods and commodities and customers desiring to purchase acquire and deal in such goods and commodities or of bringing such persons into closer relation with one another.

(e) The affording of facilities for the communication and interchange of views between manufacturers and producers and the governments government departments and public bodies and institutions and associations of all kinds in all parts of the world with a view to the ascertainment and the communication to such governments government departments public bodies institutions and associations of the views of manufacturers and producers and others with regard to matters directly or indirectly affecting the industries in which they are engaged.

(f) The promotion of improvements in the law and the consolidation standardization and simplification of laws in any part of the world and to promote support or oppose alterations in existing laws or proposed legislation and to effect improvements in administration and to co-operate with governments in establishing a more efficient commercial consular service throughout the world.

(g) The provision of legal aid to Members for the protection of copyrights rights in patents trade marks and trade names and similar rights and in any case where in the opinion of the Grand Council the interests of the Federation pecuniary or otherwise are involved and generally in any case in which the Grand Council deem it desirable that legal aid should be provided . . .

MEMBERS

5. The Members of the Federation shall consist of:

(a) The several persons companies corporations partnerships and associations who immediately before Our execution of these Presents were Members of the Association.

(b) All persons from time to time elected in accordance with the Bye-laws of the Federation for the time being in force.

6. If any person ceases for any cause whatever to be a Member of the Federation he shall not nor shall his heirs executors or administrators have any interest in or any claim against the funds or property of the Federation.

THE GRAND COUNCIL

7. The affairs of the Federation shall be managed by a body to be called 'the Grand Council' which shall be the Governing Body of the Federation.

8. The Grand Council shall consist of such numbers of persons possessing such qualifications and holding office for such periods and retiring therefrom in such rotation as may be prescribed by the Bye-laws for the time being in force.

Provided that no person shall as from the First General Meeting of the Federation to be held in October or November 1923 be qualified for membership of the Grand Council (or of the Executive Committee) who is not a British subject . . .

60
National Federation of Discharged and Demobilized Sailors and Soldiers, 1917

(a) Achievements claimed, 1919 (Leaflet Series No. 7)
(b) National Demonstration (Circular, 30 March 1920)
(c) Letter to M.P.s about Disability Pensions (19 February 1921)

(a)

WHAT WE HAVE DONE FOR EX-SERVICE MEN, WIDOWS AND DEPENDANTS	WHAT OTHER ORGANIZATIONS HAVE DONE

Gained substantial increases of Pensions.

Were the only organization to make a clear case for *statutory right to Pension, with independent Court of Appeal.* See Report of Select Committee on Pensions. *Federation evidence* quoted on ELEVEN questions. ALL other organizations ONCE.

? ?

Secured Disability Pensions FREE from Income Tax.

Secured *preferential consideration* to Ex-service Men for employment in Government Departments.

QUERY

Secured the acceptance by the Government of the *Federation Scheme* for employment of Disabled, now known as *The National Scheme* supported by the King.

? ?

Secured *extension* of Unemployment Donation to *disabled men.*

Secured *direct representation* on *Local War Pension and Local Advisory Committees.*

Secured *larger representation* on all Committees dealing with Ex-service Men.

Secured *right to represent* Ex-service Men, Widows and Dependants at *Appeal Tribunals.*

Secured *Navy and Army Canteen profits* from being commandeered by the Treasury. Responsible for funds being handed over to Independent Committee.

Secured *right to represent* Ex-service Men before Umpire on Appeals against stoppage of Unemployment Donation.

Secured *representation on National Industrial Conference*, dealing with questions of wages and hours.

Secured *representation on Whitley Councils* set up in all Government Departments.

Secured *higher pay* for Serving Men.

Secured *hundreds of other benefits* for Ex-service Men, Widows and Dependants.

EVERY DISCHARGED AND DEMOBILIZED MAN OR WOMAN SHOULD JOIN THE FEDERATION WITHOUT DELAY

(b)

Dear Sir and Brother,

National Demonstration

Further to the preliminary notice published in the 'Bulletin', I have to inform you that the National Executive Council have decided to hold a National Demonstration on Sunday 18 April, to protest against the attitude of the Prime Minister and the present Government towards the claims of ex-service men as put forward by the Deputation which waited upon him on 6 February.

I need hardly impress upon you the necessity of making this Demonstration a success. We must show our strength in numbers on this occasion and raise public opinion to support us in our admittedly just claims.

Branches are requested to send as large a contingent as possible. Where it is only possible to send a small contingent, local Demonstrations should be organized on the same day and a similar resolution to that enclosed should be sent to the local Members of Parliament and to the Prime Minister.

All London Branches should send markers to report to the Chief Marshal (Mr H. J. Trevillyan) or Assistant Marshals at 1.30 P.M. to take up position of Branch in the procession.

Positions will be allocated to Provincial Branches on arrival on reporting to the Chief Marshal.

The contingents will assemble at 2.0 P.M. and march off at 2.30 P.M. via Norfolk Street, Strand, Trafalgar Square, Pall Mall, Regent Street, Oxford Street, Marble Arch, Hyde Park.

There will be five platforms and a bugle will sound at about 4.45 when the resolution will be put simultaneously from each.

Bring your Bands and Banners and turn out in full force to demand fair treatment and justice.

General Secretary

(c)

19 February 1921
Sent to all M.P.s

Dear Sir,

Re. Disability Pensions

You are no doubt aware as to the present unrest and dissatisfaction which exists amongst widows, dependants and disabled men, in connection with the present rates of disability pensions.

The question has from time to time been raised with the Minister of Pensions and the Prime Minister, who refuse to do anything in connection with the matter.

The present flat-rate disability pension of £2 for a disabled man and 26s. 8d. for a war widow is, I am sure you will agree, quite inadequate, when one takes into account the fact that when this flat-rate pension was fixed the cost of living figure was 115.

I am quite sure you will agree that the people in whose name this organization speaks have the right to expect that while it is not possible to compensate them in pounds, shillings and pence for the disabilities and sufferings incurred, they shall be awarded pensions which will allow them to live in decency and comfort.

I have been instructed by my National Executive Council to ask you to be good enough to use your influence during the present Parliamentary Session to agitate for an increase in the present flat-rate pension.

We, as an organization, are quite prepared to have this matter placed before an independent Tribunal for consideration, but, unfortunately, this request has been refused by the Prime Minister.

It would appear that in many instances public men are now losing sight of the position of these men who are still disabled, and of the widows and children who have been left behind by those who fell.

The necessity for economy in National Expenditure is appreciated, but surely these women and children and disabled men are the last persons at whose expense economy should be practised.

I sincerely trust that it will be possible for you personally to raise this question in the House of Commons at an opportune moment.

General Secretary

61
National Union of Ex-service Men (N.U.X.) : statement, 1920

The New World, Glasgow, Journal of the N.U.X., Vol. 1, No. 11, January 1920

. . . is a fighting organization of discharged and demobilized men *inside*, and in closest sympathy with the general Labour movement. *It exists to fight for the special interests of the Ex-service Men, to secure justice for the disabled, and to look after the Dependants of the fallen.*

In fighting for the special interests of the Ex-service Men, the Union is assured of the wholehearted support of organized Labour.

But the Union exists also to emphasize the fact that *the general interests of the Ex-service Men are absolutely identical with those of all their fellow workers.* It will therefore fight shoulder-to-shoulder with organized Labour in the common struggle for the common good of all.

62
Ex-Servicemen's 'pressure' on the Government : General Sir Frederick Maurice, 1920

The 'unity' negotiations, *Proceedings*, 7 August 1920, p. 29

Everyone who has spoken up to the present has rather put up the Government as our natural enemy. I am not for a minute denying that that is the case, but I would point out that there is a great deal to be done in other ways besides bringing pressure to bear upon the Government, and that if we can get a united body which is going to represent the whole of the Ex-service opinion in this country we can do a great deal in those other directions.

63
The British Legion : Principles and Policy, and National Constructive Programme 1921

Graham Wootton, *Official History of the British Legion*, 1956, appendices 1 and 2

BRITISH LEGION

Rule 1 Principles and policy

(a) The Legion shall be democratic non-sectarian and not affiliated to or connected directly or indirectly with any political party or political organizations.

(b) The Legion shall be created to inaugurate and maintain in a strong stimulating united and democratic comradeship all those who have served in His Majesty's Navy Army Air Force or any Auxiliary Forces so that neither their efforts nor their interests shall be forgotten that their welfare and that of the dependants of the fallen may be safeguarded and that just and equitable treatment shall be secured to them in respect of the difficulties caused in their lives as a result of their services.

(c) The Legion shall exist to perpetuate in the civil life of the Empire and the World the principles for which the Nation stands to inculcate a sense of loyalty to the Crown Community and Nation to promote unity amongst all classes to make right the master of might to secure peace and goodwill on earth to safeguard and transmit to posterity the principles of justice freedom and democracy and to consecrate and sanctify our comradeship by our devotion to mutual service and helpfulness.

(d) There shall be nothing to prevent the Legion from adopting a definite policy on any question directly or indirectly affecting ex-service men and women nor from taking any constitutional action considered necessary in pursuance of such policy provided that the policy and proposed action have been considered and endorsed by a majority of the Area Conferences after due notice to the branches of the Legion and also providing that such policy or action is strictly in accordance with the principles laid down above and with the objects of the Legion as set out in the Charter of the Legion. Nothing in this Rule shall prevent Branches from exercising full local autonomy or from adopting and declaring a definite policy or taking any action considered necessary in pursuance of it upon local matters always providing that such action is constitutional and in accordance with the aims objects and programme of the Legion. The decision as to what are or are not local matters shall rest with the National Council of the Legion.

NATIONAL CONSTRUCTIVE PROGRAMME 1921

Imperial objects

1. To institute throughout the Empire a National Day of Commemoration for those who fell in the Great War, and to press upon the Governments concerned the desirability of instituting such a day as a General Holiday.

2. To co-operate and federate with ex-service organizations of a character similar to the British Legion throughout the Empire and our Allied Countries (The British Empire Services League

and the Fédération Interalliée des Anciens Combattants of France), and to encourage the interchange of visits and ideas between the members of the British Legion and such organizations.

3. To support actively all direct efforts for peace, primarily the League of Nations, while taking care that the defence of the Empire is adequately provided for.

National objects

1. To secure that the Government, Municipal, and Local Authorities, and other employers of labour shall give a preference in employment to ex-service men and women seeking employment and, in particular, that women who replaced men in employment, owing to war pressure and are not dependants of service men or actual bread-winners, shall be replaced in such employment by ex-service men or ex-service women.

2. To take active steps to obtain the co-operation of the Government, public and private employers, and of the Trade Unions in securing the fullest possible facilities for the training of ex-service men and women, and, when trained, their admission to the different organizations of skilled labour.

3. To support and encourage by financial and other means suitable undertakings by ex-service men and women conducted on business lines and for that purpose, and generally in order to help to re-establish ex-service men and women in civilian occupations, to secure Government assistance and voluntary aid, and to extend the principle of co-partnership in all such undertakings, and further to take action to prevent the exploitation of the employment of ex-service men in firms which have for their apparent object the benefit only of ex-service men.

4. To urge upon the Government and the community the necessity of providing for ex-service men and women, genuinely anxious and unable to obtain employment, reasonable maintenance until such time as they are absorbed into industry.

5. To emphasize the importance of the King's Roll, and to insist that, in the allotment of contracts by the Government and Local Authorities, preference be given to firms whose names are on the Roll. To undertake a Publicity Campaign to compel all private employers and public companies who should be on the King's Roll, but are not, to take immediate steps to qualify for admission to that Roll.

6. To secure the removal of the severely incapacitated or disabled ex-service men or women from the ordinary competitive

market by the scientific and compulsory distribution of the severely incapacitated or disabled ex-service men and women amongst the industries of the country.

7. To obtain special preference for all seriously disabled ex-service men and women as regards travelling and admission to places of recreation and entertainment.

8. To guard jealously the right to Pension of disabled and incapacitated ex-service men, and of the widows and dependants of ex-service men; to endeavour to remedy injustices and abolish anomalies.

Domestic objects

1. To make the British Legion truly National by drawing into or affiliating with it all existing ex-service men's and women's associations, benevolent funds, clubs, etc.

2. In co-operation with the United Services' Fund to provide in convenient centres for all Branches, facilities for social intercourse, recreation, and recreational education, acquiring, where not already in existence, permanent halls, club premises, or meeting rooms for the use of members.

3. To make the existence of the British Legion more widely known, by arranging for periodical group rallies of members of all Branches of the British Legion in convenient centres.

64
The British Iron and Steel Federation, 1934
An account of the principal trade associations in the steel industry,
British Iron and Steel Federation, 1963, pp. 28–9

For several years after the First World War, the steel industry operated under conditions of extreme difficulty. Demand for its products fluctuated sharply, and the industry was a particular victim of the economic uncertainty of the times. Many of its men were unemployed, the value of its assets had to be written down and serious capital losses were suffered. In these circumstances, it was impossible for the industry to install new plant or take adequate advantage of technical improvements. The way to recovery was prepared by the introduction of tariff protection under the Import Duties Act, 1932, and the appointment of the Import Duties Advisory Committee (I.D.A.C.) to advise the Government on the application of the tariff to British industry.

From the start, I.D.A.C. gave special attention to the position of the iron and steel industry, and the continuance of the tariff was made conditional on the industry carrying out measures of re-organization satisfactory to I.D.A.C. For this purpose the industry's own central organization had to be strengthened and greater co-ordination and co-operation secured.

Accordingly, the industry decided to adapt and improve the existing machinery, consisting of assocations and the National Federation of Iron and Steel Manufacturers. The association structure was revised and in April 1934 a new central organization – the present British Iron and Steel Federation – was set up, with the support of the Government, and with wider powers to co-ordinate the industry's policy.

The constructive work of the new Federation proceeded within a framework of public supervision, which has been maintained, in one form or another, ever since. I.D.A.C., as guardian of the public interest, was kept informed of the industry's plans and policies, particularly in the fields of development and prices. These arrangements, with the general improvement in trade, brought the industry and the country large benefits during the later 1930s. By 1939, much of the damage of the depression had been repaired, and the outbreak of war found the country well equipped in this vital industry.

During the war the industry operated under the close control exercised through the Iron and Steel Control of the Ministry of Supply.

The post-war period

In 1944, a special committee of the Federation examined the form which its future organization should take, and a new Constitution was adopted in the following year. That Constitution has remained substantially unaltered throughout the post-war period. Whereas, before 1945, the members of the Federation consisted of Associations, regional representatives and individual companies, from 1945 membership has been confined to 'Conferences' organized on a product basis . . . Many of the war-time Government controls over the industry, including price controls, continued for several years after 1945. The Labour Government announced its intention to nationalize the industry, and in 1946 appointed an Iron and Steel Board to supervise the industry pending nationalization. The Board was responsible to the Minister of Supply, in particular for watching over the industry's prices, production and development, and its creation marked a further stage in the public supervision of the industry.

This first Iron and Steel Board was dissolved in 1949, when the nationalization Act was passed. In February 1951 the shares of the main producing companies in the industry were vested in a new body set up under the Act, the Iron and Steel Corporation of Great Britain. This Corporation was charged with the general duty of managing the nationalized companies in the public interest.

The Federation, however, as the central trade association of both nationalized and independent companies, continued to operate the machinery for providing common services, etc., for the different sections of the industry . . .

65
Engineering Employers' Federation : structure and policy, late 1950s

Looking at Industrial Relations, Engineering and Allied Employers' National Federation, n.d. (1959), pp. 5–9

HOW THE FEDERATION WORKS

In 1896 pressure by the engineering unions to secure an eight-hour day, and to restrict the right of employers to manage their own establishments as they thought fit, led to the formation of the Engineering Employers' Federation.

Today it still pursues as vigorously as ever its original objective of safeguarding the interests of member firms. But over the past sixty years the Federation has striven consistently to become something more than a partisan body, concerned only with striking a bargain with the unions round the negotiating table.

It has sought and has contrived to develop a sound and durable system of negotiation and conciliation between employers and the unions.

Any deterioration in labour relations in an industry which employs one out of every seven workers in the country, and is responsible for about one half of our exports, could quickly wreck the national economy. Apart from the partial stoppage of work in the spring of 1957 and the one-day token strike in 1953, the majority of disputes involving withdrawal of labour since the last war have been unofficial.

The industry has an enviable record of industrial peace. This has not been achieved by accident. The Federation can claim to have established a code of relations with the unions at a time when in many big industries the workers were still either un-organized or fighting for recognition.

When the Federation was formed it had a membership of 180 firms. Now it has over 4,300 member firms employing nearly 2 million people. It has forty-six local Associations throughout the country, autonomous but working under the leadership of the Federation.

Wage Settlements between the Federation and the Confederation of Shipbuilding and Engineering Unions affect, directly or indirectly, 3 million engineering and allied workers.

The four main objectives of the Federation are:

to maintain, by agreement with the trade unions, a code of wages and working conditions appropriate to the industry;

to secure the settlement of labour disputes;

to counter movements detrimental to the industry; and

to afford assistance to constituent Associations and their members in all matters affecting labour.

Engineering firms join the Federation after becoming members of the appropriate local federated Association. These Associations, numbering forty-six, are grouped in eleven regional organizations. In addition to paying subscriptions to their local Associations, member firms make a contribution to the National Federation based on their annual wages bill.

Each federated Association is constitutionally autonomous and offers a direct service to its member firms, who take a part, through their nominated representatives, in the control and policy of the Association.

In addition to offering assistance on labour questions, the federated Associations handle all negotiations with local trade union officials and, on behalf of their members, make the necessary contacts with the Regional Offices of Government Departments, Local Authorities and other local bodies.

The federated Associations are in constant contact with the Federation, which is in a position to advise them on matters of national policy and in regard to any questions upon which the views of the Federation are desired.

The day-to-day work of the Associations is very considerable, comprising not only the formal negotiations referred to above, but also many informal discussions with local union representatives. The overall number of meetings, formal and informal, amounts to many thousands each year.

The Federation, which represents the bulk of engineering production in the country, is recognized by the Government as the national body representing the interests of employers of labour in the engineering industry. It is consulted by the various

Government Departments where these interests are affected and has, furthermore, full opportunity for making the appropriate Government contacts where it is desired to draw Government attention to matters in any way prejudicing the industry or a constituent firm.

The Federation takes an important part in the work of the British Employers' Confederation, which is mainly concerned with dealing at Government level with labour matters, national and international, on behalf of most of the private sections of industry, and through the Confederation is represented on various Departmental and other Government Committees concerned with prospective legislation, general inquiries and other matters.

Through its administrative and legal staff the Federation is able to offer to federated Associations and their members specialist advice on all problems directly relating to labour relations and labour legislation, and full information from official or other competent sources in regard to associated matters.

The interests of the federated Associations and their member firms are directly represented in the management of the Federation through their nominees on its General Council and Management Board, on its National Technical Committees which deal with problems affecting particular sections of the industry, on the various *ad hoc* Committees appointed from time to time to deal with special questions, and on the Regional Committees which co-ordinate Association matters on an area basis.

The General Council is the managing body of the Federation. It has about 120 members. It consists of the President, two Deputy Presidents, the Chairman of the Finance Committee who is also a Deputy President, nine Trustees, ten Vice-Presidents, the Director, the Chairmen of eleven Regional Committees, co-opted members of the Management Board, and members elected annually by the Associations.

The Management Board, composed of about ninety members and which normally meets monthly, is the executive committee of the Federation and is composed of *ex officio* members of the General Council and members appointed by the Council from its elected members on the basis of a formula calculated on the wages bill of the manual workers in each of the eleven regions.

The Director and a permanent staff carry out the administrative work of the Federation.

As part of the procedure for avoiding disputes in the industry, the Conference Committee plays a key role. Each month it meets the union leaders in York at Central Conference to operate the final stage of the agreed procedure.

Federated firms whose workpeople take strike action, or who adopt 'go-slow' tactics, are entitled to claim payment of indemnity in respect of loss sustained through the action of their workers. The payments are made out of an Indemnity Fund to which all federated firms contribute. The basis of contributions and the amount of indemnity payable are in accordance with the rules laid down for the regulation and administration of the Fund.

Details of membership of the Federation are supplied by local Associations. Names of all firms submitted for membership must be approved by the General Council. Data on wages bills are submitted annually to the Federation to enable voting rights to be assessed. Voting power, which is exercised in the event of questions relating to, for example, national wages applications being remitted to meetings of members of federated Associations, is assessed on wages bills on a basis laid down constitutionally.

The Federation has national agreements with forty-four trade unions, covering wages and working conditions such as overtime, shift working, systems of payment by results and holidays.

66
Employers' Associations: structure and main activities (other than industrial relations), mid-1960s

Royal Commission on Trade Unions and Employers' Associations, Research Paper No. 7, H.M.S.O., 1967, pp. 17–19, 53–5

The organizations selected for inclusion in the survey are as follows:

Engineering
The Engineering Employers' Federation
The Coventry and District Engineering Employers' Association
The Border Counties Engineering Employers' Association[1]
The North-East Coast Engineering Employers' Association[1]

Shipbuilding
The Shipbuilding Employers' Federation[2]
The Clyde Shipbuilders' Association
The Tyne Shipbuilders Association[1]
The North-East Coast Ship Repairers' Association[1]

1. These Associations in Engineering and Shipbuilding share a common secretariat and office.
2. Now combined with the Shipbuilding Conference and the Ship Repairers' Central Council to form the Shipbuilders' and Repairers' National Association.

Printing
The British Federation of Master Printers
The London Master Printers' Association
The South-Western Alliance of Master Printers

Building
The National Federation of Building Trade Employers
The London Region of the N.F.B.T.E. (formerly the London Master Builders' Association)
The North-Western Region of the N.F.B.T.E.
The Bolton and District Association of Building Trade Employers[1]
The Chorley and District Association of Building Trade Employers[1]
The Leigh and District Association of Building Trade Employers[1]
The St Helens and District Association of Building Trade Employers[1]

Civil Engineering
The Federation of Civil Engineering Contractors

Electrical Contracting
The National Federated Electrical Association

Multiple retailing
The Multiple Shops Federation
The National Association of Multiple Grocers
The Multiple Shoe Retailers' Association
The Association of Multiple Retail Meat Traders
The Multiple Wine Merchants' Association
The Multiple Tailors' Association
(NOTE: The Multiple Shops Federation provides staff and offices for the five Associations representing different branches of the industry.)

Smaller associations in other industries
Seven small associations in other industries who have appointed a firm of chartered accountants as their secretaries

Types of organization

93. In the first four of the industries selected the employers' organizations consist of local associations covering geographical areas which are affiliated to national federations. In all of these except shipbuilding there is also some kind of regional grouping, but there are considerable differences in the importance of the regional group and its function in the organization.

1. These Associations in the building industry are served by an Area Secretary at Bolton.

94. In civil engineering and electrical contracting the organizations consist of a single national association which maintains branches throughout the country.

95. The other associations are generally single organizations with a national coverage, although in some cases the industry may tend to be concentrated in one part of the country. The multiple retailers' associations have joined together in a Federation on the basis of similar industrial activity.

96. All of the organizations employ permanent staff except the smaller associations who use the services of the firm of chartered accountants.

Relationship with trade associations

97. All but three of the organizations are trade associations as well as dealing with industrial relations matters. The three exceptions are the engineering, shipbuilding and electrical contracting organizations.

98. The Engineering Employers' Federation covers a wide range of industrial activity whose trade interests are looked after by a large number of separate trade associations with whom there is no organizational link other than through the C.B.I. although informal contacts are maintained. The Shipbuilding Employers' Federation deals with employment matters for both the shipbuilding and ship-repairing sections of the industry. Trade matters for the shipbuilders are covered by the Shipbuilding Conference, and for the ship-repairers by the Repairers' Central Council.[1] In electrical contracting there are three organizations: the Electrical Contractors' Association deals with legal questions, contracts and technical matters; the National Electrical Contractors' Trading Association covers trading and retailing; and the National Federated Electrical Association covers employment and industrial relations. In practice these three associations are so closely linked as to be virtually indistinguishable from one another since they share the same office and the same permanent staff, the management structure and office-bearers are identical and there is a common membership with the exception of some retailers who are members of N.E.C.T.A. but not of the other two associations.

99. Among the organizations selected, therefore, the only industry in which the employers' organization can be accurately

---

1. Since the material for this study was collected these three organizations, which have always been closely associated, have combined to form the Shipbuilders' and Repairers' National Association.

described as confined to employment and industrial relations matters is the engineering industry.

Size and scope of industrial coverage

100. The organizations included in the survey provide a cross section of the great variety of employers' associations in the size of their membership, the number of employees of member firms and the range of industrial activity.

101. *Engineering*: The Engineering Employers' Federation is the largest and at the same time the most diverse. The thirty-nine associations affiliated to the Federation have in total approximately 4,600 members who between them employ about 2 million workers. This is estimated to be in the region of 60 per cent of the potential membership in terms of numbers employed. However, the individual associations include both large and small organizations. The Coventry and District Association is of medium size, having ninety-five members employing about 90,000 workers, representing 80 per cent of engineering employment in the city of Coventry, where most of the employment is concentrated, and 50 per cent in the rest of the district. The Border Counties Association has twenty members and the North-East Coast 250 members. The joint membership of the two associations employ about 80,000 workers representing 90 per cent of engineering employment in the area. While the Federation itself embraces the whole range of manufacturing of metal goods except the building of ships, the local associations visited naturally cover a slightly smaller range, with a strong emphasis on particular branches, such as motor-vehicle manufacture in Coventry and marine and general engineering on the Tyne.

102. Some of the employers not in membership of affiliated associations belong to other smaller associations dealing with a specified field, such as the National Light Castings Ironfounders Associations, or the National Federation of Vehicle Trade Employers, who manufacture specialist car bodies. The greater proportion of non-membership, however, consists of firms who are not members of any employers' associations in the engineering field including a number of large employers such as Ford, Vauxhall, National Cash Register and I.B.M. and some medium-sized employers such as Rubery Owen of Darlaston. Although many of the large non-members are American-owned, the Federation does not think that the American connection has much influence on the question of association membership, since other American firms with establishments in Britain are in membership. While

each company will have its own reasons for remaining unfederated it is likely that the desire to manage its own affairs independently is a more important factor than disagreements about particular policies or organizational questions . . .

MAIN ACTIVITIES OTHER THAN INDUSTRIAL RELATIONS

232. This chapter summarizes the main services provided by the associations included in the survey other than those concerned with industrial relations indicating significant variations in scale and content as between industries and between national and local organizations in the same industry. The relative importance of each service is also shown and current tendencies towards growth or decline.

233. The activities discussed in this Chapter are grouped as follows:

(a) The representation of employers' interests to Government and other bodies.

(b) The provision of information services.

(c) The collection of information and statistics.

(d) Assistance in manpower matters, such as the efficient use of manpower, labour supply and demand, recruitment and selection, education and training, and safety, health and welfare.

(e) Assistance in trade and commercial matters.

(f) Social activities.

Representation to Government

234. All of the national organizations regard the representation of members' views to Government as an important and growing part of their function. The general importance arises from the fact that much legislation has a direct bearing on industrial affairs, and associations take very seriously their responsibility to seek amendments to existing or proposed legislation which would have a harmful effect on their members, or to improve the practical execution of the Government's intentions. The growth in importance of this function results from the recent increase in the areas of activity covered by legislation particularly in the labour field represented by the Industrial Training Act, the Contracts of Employment Act and the Redundancy Payments Act among others.

235. The role of the associations is not however confined to that of a watchdog. The associations have also become the means by which industry co-operates with Government to achieve the goals of national economic policy, and this aspect has also grown

in recent years with the development of economic planning and the formation of Economic Development Committees for different industries. It also exists in a number of departmental committees, usually those of the Ministry of Public Buildings and Works and the Ministry of Labour.

236. This activity is important not only as a means of bringing the experience of industry to bear on Government thinking, but also because of its effect on the relationship of associations with their own members. The process of representing the industry involves not only the collection of facts and opinions from members, making the association better informed about the industry than individual members; it also puts the association in the position of adviser and guide to members on the interpretation of Government policy and legislation. Members expect their association to be able to answer their questions about the meaning of legislation and also, in effect, to tell them what they ought to do in particular circumstances. The legislation on prices and incomes policy is a good example of this. Associations dealt with a great number of inquiries from their members when the 'wage freeze' was announced in July 1966, and many of these inquiries asked for guidance on the action they should take, for instance whether annual review of salaries of managerial staff should or should not be carried out before 1 January 1967. The value to employers of having a sympathetic source of information is obvious. It is also interesting to note how this increases the influence of the association over its members. Most association officials are confident that the advice they give is acted upon.

237. The representational function also embraces the representing of the views of the industry to the general public and both national and local associations exercise public relations functions.

Information services

238. The provision of information to members is an important function of all the associations whether national or local. There is however some variation in the way the job is tackled and in the range of subjects covered.

239. Some of the smaller local associations fulfil this function almost entirely by word of mouth, through meetings of members (supplemented by the circulation of minutes of those meetings) and by answering individual inquiries made by members. The Clyde Shipbuilders' Association for example, which has a homogeneous membership of under two dozen firms, relies heavily on these means of communication with its members. Moreover, this

association, like others in shipbuilding and engineering, is concerned only with labour matters, and its members' trade and commercial interests are catered for by the Shipbuilding Conference or the Repairers' Central Conference. The Association, while it may deal with individual problems of this nature at the request of members, does not have the responsibility to keep its members informed of general developments outside the labour field.

240. The London Region of the National Federation of Building Trades Employers, on the other hand, which has more than 1,000 members of varying size and activity, has built up a more complex structure of information services embracing not only the holding of meetings and the provision of an inquiry service, but also the publication of regular bulletins and occasional papers. The bulletins include monthly circulars intended to keep members up-to-date with topical information and a two-monthly publication, the *L.M.B.A. News*, which contains longer articles and comment as well as news items. The occasional papers are more specialized and deal with particular subjects such as apprenticeship or technical building matters, on which leaflets and booklets are prepared by Association staff and made available to members.

241. Associations which circularize information to members usually cover such subjects as legislation, the progress of wage negotiations and reports on the activities of the association. Some go a stage further and act to some extent as a clearing-house of information between members. The Coventry Engineering Employers' Association, for instance, circularizes its members with detailed information about earnings levels in the locality obtained by the collection and analysis of information provided by the individual members themselves.

242. The variation in the method of approach of different associations appears to be mainly indicative of the different circumstances of their members rather than of differing attitudes to the importance of the function of keeping members informed, to which all the officials interviewed gave more or less equal prominence. Officials of several associations were clearly concerned with the efficiency of their lines of communication and were keeping the problems involved under regular review to try to ensure that their members' needs were satisfied. The effectiveness of particular methods of communication is always difficult to assess, but the associations visited were clearly aware of the problems and attempting to find their own solution. The importance of this function seems likely to be maintained.

Collection of information

243. As a subsidiary activity supporting a number of their functions, employers' associations act as collectors and repositories of information about their industries or localities. The extent to which this activity is engaged in depends on a number of factors including:

(a) the extent to which the association attempts to decide policy for the industry;
(b) the demand by members for particular types of information;
(c) the need for factual information to support a case – e.g. for representation to Government about the state of trade, or negotiations with a trade union on wages;
(d) the readiness of members to supply information.

244. Since the attitudes of these associations and the circumstances of their industries are by no means identical, it is to be expected that their activities in this field will be diverse. There are however some common features. Firstly, all association officials seem to be conscious that every request for information addressed to a member firm will involve that member in unproductive work, and that requests have to be kept to a minimum and serve a clearly useful purpose from the members' point of view. Secondly, perhaps partly for this reason, the collection of information is still generally an *ad hoc* matter – to obtain information required for a particular purpose – rather than a tool of management involving regular collection and assessment of trends. However, some regular collection of statistics takes place, for example, the Quarterly State of Trade Inquiry in the building industry . . .

67
British Employers' Confederation (the former National Confederation of Employers' Organizations)
(a) Objects, 1963 (b) Governing body, 1963

Report on the Formation of a National Industrial Organization, April 1964. By Sir Henry Benson, C.B.E., and Sir Sam Brown

(a)

. . . The main objects of the B.E.C. are set out in Article 2 of the Constitution and Conditions of Membership in the following terms:

The object of the Confederation shall be to promote the interests of employers in the United Kingdom of Great Britain and Northern Ireland in all matters affecting their relations with their workpeople and in particular:

(a) To provide for consultation between Employers' Organizations, to ascertain their views on matters of common concern, and to take steps to give effect thereto.

(b) To collect, collate and circulate information for the guidance of these Organizations, and to keep them informed on the national and international industrial position and on the operation of existing laws, legislative proposals and the activities of Government Departments which may affect the interests of employers.

(c) To undertake the functions of the industrial Organization most representative of employers in the United Knigdom of Great Britain and Northern Ireland under the constitution of the International Labour Organization.

Article 2 contains a proviso to the effect that the Confederation shall do nothing in pursuance of its objects which would constitute an interference with any member of the Confederation in the conduct or management of its own affairs . . .

(b)

The Governing body of the B.E.C. is the Council, which is composed of:

(a) one representative appointed by each member employers' federation and one additional representative for each member in respect of each complete £600 paid in the last annual subscription,

(b) the office-bearers comprising the honorary president, president, not more than six vice-presidents and the past presidents, who are all *ex officio* members.

In addition, each member federation may nominate one executive officer to attend meetings of the Council but such nominee has no right to vote.

60. At 31 December 1963 the Council numbered 160, of which 148 were representatives appointed by the employers' federations and twelve were office-bearers. The Council meets quarterly and the average attendance at meetings held recently has been about fifty-five.

61. The representatives of the employers' federations remain on the Council until they are replaced by their sponsors.

68

**National Association of British Manufacturers
(the former National Union of Manufacturers)**

(a) Objects, 1963 (b) Governing Body, 1963

Report on the Formation of a National Industrial Organization,
April 1964

. . . 11. The main objects of the N.A.B.M. are defined in its
Memorandum of Association as being:

(a) to promote the trade, commerce and manufactures of
British industries, and the home, colonial and foreign trades of
the United Kingdom;

(b) to originate, promote, support or oppose legislative or other
measures affecting British industries;

(c) to effect co-operation and mutual help amongst British
manufacturers and producers of all kinds of goods and commodities;

(d) to encourage free and unrestricted communication between masters and workmen, with a view to the establishment of
amicable arrangements and relations between them, and to the
avoidance and settlement of strikes and all other forms of industrial warfare between masters and workmen, and to undertake by
arbitration the settlement of disputes arising out of trade, commerce or manufacture . . .

(b)

50. The governing body of the N.A.B.M. is the Executive
Council which is composed of:

(a) one representative nominated by each affiliated trade
association,

(b) a maximum of fifteen individual members elected at the
annual general meeting,

(c) two representatives nominated by each regional branch
and an additional representative in respect of every 300 members
of such branch in excess of the first 300,

(d) the president, the elected vice-presidents, the past presidents and the treasurer, who are all *ex officio* members,

(e) the president or chairman of each branch on the nomination of the branch.

In addition, the Executive Council may co-opt members who it
considers would be useful, but such members have no voting
rights.

I

51. At 30 June 1963, which is the N.A.B.M.'s most recent year-end and therefore the latest date at which figures are available, the Executive Council numbered ninety-four of which forty-one were representatives of trade associations who normally attend only if there is an item on the agenda of particular interest to their associations. The Executive Council meets monthly and the average attendance at meetings held recently has been about thirty.

52. The elected members of the Executive Council retire annually but are eligible for re-election. The association and branch nominees remain until their sponsors decide to replace them.

69
National Association of British Manufacturers, Federation of British Industries, British Employers' Confederation

(a) Membership, 30 June 1963 (b) Income and expenditure accounts 1961–3 (c) Composition of subscription income (d) Representation on Government, national and local committees

Report on the Formation of a National Industrial Organization, April 1964

(a)

MEMBERSHIP OF THE EXISTING ORGANIZATIONS AT 30 JUNE 1963 AND THE INITIAL MEMBERSHIP OF N.I.O.

	N.A.B.M.	F.B.I.	B.E.C.	Total	Overlap in membership	N.I.O.
Employers' federations			53	53		53
Trade associations	53	280		333	30	303
Individual membership: Companies, firms and individual members	5,110	8,607		13,717	1,000	12,717
Less: Subsidiary companies sharing in group subscriptions	155	4,535		4,690	155	4,535
	4,955	4,072		9,027	845	8,182

NOTES

The overlap deducted from trade associations gives effect to [a] common membership of trade associations and employers' federations . . .

The overlap of 1,000 individual members is estimated. It has been assumed that, as regards the N.A.B.M., all the subsidiary companies sharing in group subscriptions are included in the overlap.

(b)

Detailed Income and Expenditure Accounts for the Last Three Years
(Deficits are shown in italics and in brackets)

N.A.B.M.

Year ended 30 June
(£)

	1961	1962	1963
Subscription income	64,851	63,692	63,458
Other income	30,142	29,992	23,833
	94,993	93,684	87,291
Salaries, commissions, pension contributions, etc.	46,505	49,849	54,208
Travelling expenses	5,225	4,249	4,672
Accommodation expenses	15,871	15,989	14,708
Administration expenses	18,881	16,024	8,645
Publicity and trade promotion expenses	2,735	4,471	3,153
Provision for new offices, and repairs and dilapidations of leasehold premises	3,173	3,953	4,582
	92,390	94,535	89,968
Surplus (*deficit*) before taxation	2,603	(*851*)	(*2,677*)
Taxation chargeable	2,100	1,011	1,229
Net surplus (*deficit*)	503	(*1,862*)	(*3,906*)

F.B.I.

Year ended 31 December
(£)

	1961	1962	1963
Subscription income	414,507	414,938	481,954
Other income	57,893	58,611	59,840
	472,400	473,549	541,794

Salaries, pension contributions, etc.	296,725	322,153	352,537
Travelling and entertaining expenses	42,493	39,228	40,445
Accommodation expenses	37,827	41,417	40,203
Administration expenses	89,280	90,460	101,177
Subscriptions	9,613	10,117	11,508
Depreciation and Amortization	11,000	11,000	8,000
Interest	4,882	4,722	4,562
	491,820	519,097	558,432
(Deficit) before taxation	*(19,420)*	*(45,548)*	*(16,638)*
Taxation chargeable *(recoverable)*	*(5,134)*	85	—
Net *(deficit)*	*(14,286)*	*(45,633)*	*(16,638)*

B.E.C.

	Year ended 31 December (£)		
	1961	1962	1963
Subscription income	101,029	104,663	111,062
Other income	3,679	3,673	3,630
	104,708	108,336	114,692
Salaries, pension contributions, etc.	64,703	68,978	72,457
Travelling expenses	931	1,348	1,214
Accommodation expenses	15,040	13,950	13,742
Administration expenses	9,890	11,055	12,786
Subscriptions and meetings	10,319	10,711	13,789
Depreciation	123	678	666
	101,006	106,720	114,654
Surplus before taxation	3,702	1,616	38
Taxation chargeable	3,225	1,550	—
Net surplus	477	66	38

NOTES

1. The 'other income' of the N.A.B.M. and the F.B.I. is mainly advertising revenue and rents receivable. The 'other income' of the B.E.C. is mainly investment income. In the audited accounts of the F.B.I. advertising revenue and charges for secretarial services have been deducted from the relevant expenses; for the purposes of the above statement however we have added them to 'other income' so that the figures may be comparable with the figures presented by the N.A.B.M.

2. In the year ended 30 June 1963 the N.A.B.M. entered into a contract for the publication of the *British Manufacturer* which it had formerly published itself. The publication costs and the advertising revenue had in the past been shown under 'administration expenses' and 'other income' respectively, which accounts for the reduction in the amounts of these two items for the year ended 30 June 1963. It is not possible to put the figures of the two earlier years on to a comparable basis.

(c)

Composition of the Current Subscription Income of the Existing Organizations and the Proposed Subscription Income of N.I.O. at Stage One

(£)

Subscribers	N.A.B.M.	F.B.I.	B.E.C.	Total	N.I.O.
Employers' federations			130,000	130,000	130,000
Trade associations	1,500	39,500		41,000	75,000
Nationalized industries					40,000
Individual members: Paying at normal rates	78,500	499,000		577,500	574,000
Paying at special rates		12,500		12,500	13,00
	80,000	551,000	130,000	761,000	832,000

(d)

Representation on Committees

180. The N.A.B.M., the F.B.I. and the B.E.C. are widely represented on Government, national and local committees. Representatives of the existing organizations sit on 184 such committees and an analysis of the position is set out below.

Number of
Committees

One only of the existing organizations is represented on   130
Two of the existing organizations are represented on   51
All three of the existing organizations are represented on   3

   184

181. If and when N.I.O. is formed, there will obviously be scope for eliminating overlapping and the number of persons who in future will be needed to sit on these committees will be reduced. As regards those committees which are concerned with matters which might affect small manufacturers, N.I.O. will doubtless ensure, in view of the clause which it is proposed should be included in the Royal Charter . . . that the person or persons selected will represent the views of the small manufacturers effectively.

70
Confederation of British Industry

(a) Royal Charter, 1965
(b) Membership at 31 December 1970
(c) Income and expenditure account for the year ended 31 December 1970; balance sheet at 31 December 1970; C.B.I.'s finances during the year: report by Sir Stephen Brown, Chairman of the Finance Committee

Annual Report, 1970

(a)

Elizabeth the Second by the Grace of God of the United Kingdom of Great Britain and Northern Ireland and of Our other Realms and Territories Queen, Head of the Commonwealth, Defender of the Faith:

TO ALL TO WHOM THESE PRESENTS SHALL COME, GREETING!

Whereas His Majesty King George the Fifth in the year of our Lord One thousand nine hundred and twenty-three by Royal Charter (hereinafter called 'the Original Charter') dated the twenty-eighth day of May in the fourteenth year of His Reign constituted a Body Corporate and Politic by the name of 'The

Federation of British Industries' (hereinafter called 'the Federation') with perpetual succession and a Common Seal:

AND WHEREAS the Federation has presented an humble Petition unto Us setting forth:

That the National Association of British Manufacturers (hereinafter called 'the Association') is a company limited by guarantee having amongst its main objects the promotion of the trade, commerce and manufactures of British industries and the home, colonial and foreign trades of Our United Kingdom of Great Britain and Northern Ireland, the origination, promotion, support of and opposition to legislative or other measures affecting British industries, and the effecting of co-operation and mutual help amongst British manufacturers and producers of all kinds of goods and commodities.

That the British Employers' Confederation (hereinafter called 'the Employers' Confederation') is a voluntary unincorporated society having as its main object the promotion of the interests of employers in Our said United Kingdom in all matters affecting their relations with their workpeople.

That in July one thousand nine hundred and sixty-three the respective Presidents of the Association, the Federation and the Employers' Confederation appointed two Commissioners to undertake the task of proposing the constitution of a national industrial organization which could embrace the activities of the three named existing organizations.

That the said Commissioners recommended that the three named existing organizations should be integrated into a single national industrial organization and that such integration could most readily be achieved by adapting the constitution of the Federation so as, under a new name, to provide the single organization which was required to enable such integration to be effected.

That the Federation, being desirous of furthering the aforesaid object and of thereby serving the public interest, desires that We should be graciously pleased to grant it a Charter supplemental to the Original Charter, re-naming the Federation as 'The Confederation of British Industry'.

That with a view to preparing for and facilitating the integration of the three named existing organizations, the Association, the Federation and the Employers' Confederation have entered into an Agreement (hereinafter called 'the Integration Agreement') dated the twelfth day of February One thousand nine hundred and sixty-five which provides, among other things (conditionally upon and subject to the grant of the said Supplemental Charter), for the transfer to the Federation, under its new name as aforesaid, of the assets and liabilities of the Association and the Employers' Confederation and for their subsequent winding up and dissolution.

Now KNOW YE that We, having taken the said Petition into Our Royal Consideration and moved by Our desire to further the objects of the Federation, of Our Royal Will and pleasure for Ourselves, Our Heirs and Successors have granted, ordained and declared and are graciously pleased to grant, ordain and declare as follows namely:

1. The Federation shall henceforth be known by the name of 'The Confederation of British Industry' (hereinafter referred to as 'the Confederation'). Subject as aforesaid the Original Charter (other than Article 1 thereof) shall be and is hereby revoked; but nothing in this revocation shall affect the validity or legality of any act, deed or thing lawfully done or executed under or pursuant to the provisions of the Original Charter . . .

3. The principal objects of the Confederation shall be as follows:

(a) To implement and carry into effect the Integration Agreement.

(b) To provide for British industry the means of formulating, making known and influencing general policy in regard to industrial, economic, fiscal, commercial, labour, social, legal and technical questions, and to act as a national point of reference for those seeking industry's views.

(c) To develop the contribution of British industry to the national economy.

(d) To encourage the efficiency and competitive power of British industry, and to provide advice, information and services to British industry to that end.

4. In furtherance of the principal objects set out in Article 3 of this Our Supplemental Charter the Confederation shall have the following ancillary objects and powers:

(a) To undertake the functions of the industrial organization most representative of employers in Our said United Kingdom under the constitution of the International Labour Organization.

(b) To purchase, take on lease or hire or in any other way acquire any real or personal property and any rights or privileges over or options of acquiring the same and to sell, lease, mortgage (by the issue of debentures, debenture stock or otherwise), exchange, partition and otherwise deal in every way with any real or personal property, rights or privileges of the Confederation.

(c) To construct, alter and maintain any buildings required for the purposes of the Confederation and to provide the same and any buildings and rooms in the occupation of the Confederation with all proper and necessary fixtures, fittings, furniture, apparatus, appliances and conveniences.

(d) To establish and support or aid in the establishment and support of associations, institutions, organizations, trusts and funds of all kinds in Great Britain and elsewhere.

(e) To do all such other lawful objects and things as may be incidental or conducive to the attainment of the principal objects of the Confederation.

5. Nothing in Articles 3 and 4 of this Our Supplemental Charter shall empower the Confederation to do anything in pursuance of its objects which would constitute an interference with any member of the Confederation in the conduct or management by that member of its own affairs or which is inconsistent with the retention by all members of the Confederation of their complete individual autonomy and independence of action.

6. No member of the Confederation shall have any personal claim on any property of the Confederation or make any profit out of his membership except in the case of and as a salaried officer of the Confederation but so that no member of the Council of the Confederation shall be appointed to any salaried office of the Confederation.

7. It shall be a cardinal principle of the Confederation:

(a) that all information furnished to the Confederation by a member and which relates to the affairs of that member shall be treated as strictly confidential and shall not be divulged except with that member's consent; and

(b) that in the furtherance of its objects the Confederation shall at all times have regard to the interests of all its members whether their businesses be large or small.

8. (a) Subject to the provisions of paragraphs (b) and (c) of this Article, the members of the Confederation shall consist of the persons who immediately prior to the date hereof were members of the Federation and the following:

(i) all persons who immediately prior to the date hereof were members of the Association or of the Employers' Confederation and who apply for and are admitted to membership of the Confederation within twelve months after the date hereof;

(ii) such other persons as may from time to time apply for and be admitted to membership in accordance with the bye-laws.

(b) An unincorporated body may not as such be or become a member of the Confederation.

(c) An unincorporated body which wishes to obtain the advantages of membership may appoint some individual or corporate body to apply for membership as its representative. Every representative so appointed who is admitted to membership shall be entitled to exercise all the same rights and privileges and be subject to all the same obligations in relation to the Confederation as those to which the Appointor would be entitled and subject if the Appointor were itself a member; and all the provisions of this Our Supplemental Charter and the bye-laws shall be construed and have effect accordingly. Such representative may from time to time be removed and replaced by the Appointor provided that every such representative shall *ipso facto* cease to be a member on the happening of any event on which his Appointor would, if it were itself a member, cease to be a member. Any such removal or replacement shall be made in writing in accordance with such regulations as may be prescribed from time to time by the General Purposes Committee referred to in Article 13 of this Our Supplemental Charter, and shall take effect on the date on which notice thereof is received by the Secretary of the Confederation.

9. (a) As from the date hereof and unless otherwise prescribed by or pursuant to the bye-laws, membership of the Confederation shall be divided into three classes, namely:

(i) Full Members,
(ii) Industrial Associates,
(iii) Commercial Associates . . .

Bye-Laws
ADMISSION OF MEMBERS

3. Subject to the provisions of the Supplemental Charter and these bye-laws:

(a) the General Purposes Committee may from time to time determine the terms and conditions upon which any persons shall be admitted to membership of the Confederation but shall not be bound to assign any reason for refusing to admit any person to membership.

(b) no person shall be admitted to membership unless and until there shall have been signed by or on behalf of such person in such manner as the General Purposes Committee may from time to time approve an application in writing on a form prescribed for that purpose.

(c) no person shall become a member of the Confederation unless and until the name of such person shall have been entered in the Confederation's Register of Members which shall be kept in such form as the General Purposes Committee shall direct.

(d) the rights of a member shall be personal to such member and shall not be capable of transfer or transmission.

QUALIFICATION OF MEMBERS

4. The following shall be eligible to be Industrial Members of the Confederation: any company or firm which is wholly or mainly engaged in productive or manufacturing industry in Great Britain (as opposed to trade of any type or services ancillary thereto), including producers of raw materials, manufacturers and converters, and companies and firms carrying out industrial processes or engaged in the construction industry or the transport industries.

5. The following shall be eligible to be employers and Trade Organization Members of the Confederation:

(a) any national employers' organization or national trade association which represents the interests of companies or firms referred to in bye-law 4;

(b) any other national employers' organization which is, or is represented on, or provides regular assistance to, a recognized negotiating body for the purpose of negotiations with Trade Unions.

6. The following shall be eligible to be Public Sector Members of the Confederation: any nationalized industry, public corporation or other public enterprise which would in other respects be eligible as an Industrial or Commercial Member and which in the opinion of the General Purposes Committee is properly admissible to membership as a Public Sector Member.

Public Sector Members, by virtue of their special relationship with the Government, shall be at all times dissociated from pronouncements on questions that might be the subject of political controversy.

7. The following shall be eligible to be Commercial Members of the Confederation: any company or firm which is wholly or mainly engaged in trade of any type, or in services ancillary thereto, in Great Britain.

8. The following shall be eligible to be Commercial Association Members of the Confederation:

(a) any national employers' organization or national trade association which represents the interests of companies or firms referred to in bye-law 7;

(b) any other employers' organization or trade association which, if it were a national organization or association would be eligible for membership under bye-law 5 or bye-law 8(a).

9. Notwithstanding anything in bye-laws 4, 5, 6, 7 and 8 but subject always to the provisions of Article 8(b) and (c) of the Supplemental Charter:

(a) unless the General Purposes Committee otherwise resolves either generally or in a particular case, no company which is a member of a Group of Companies shall be eligible for membership of the Confederation unless every other company in the Group which is eligible for membership of the Confederation either is or becomes a member thereof;

(b) an individual shall be eligible for membership of the Confederation if (but only if) he was a member at the time of the coming into effect of these bye-laws;

(c) the decision of the General Purposes Committee shall be final in determining, in cases of doubt, for which class of membership (if any) any person shall be eligible.

10. (a) Any person who immediately prior to the date upon which these bye-laws take effect was a Full Member or an Industrial Associate or a Commercial Associate shall (subject to the provisions of these bye-laws other than 4, 5, 6, 7 and 8) be deemed to continue in membership of the Confederation in whichever of the categories prescribed in bye-laws 4, 5, 6, 7 and 8 is most applicable to such person; and in the event of doubt such person shall be deemed to be eligible for such category or categories of membership as the General Purposes Committee considers appropriate.

(b) No member shall by reason of the amendment of the categories of membership effected by the adoption of these bye-laws or by any other reason be liable to pay more than one annual subscription in any one year.

(b)

Membership

In membership at 31 December 1970 were Companies

Industrial	11,436
Commercial Companies	193
Public Sector members	15
Employers' Organizations, Trade Associations and Commercial Associations	217

'The C.B.I. was particularly pleased to welcome an increasing number of Commercial Members, drawn chiefly from the City, who made a valuable contribution to policy-formulation in many fields of C.B.I. work.'

C.B.I.'S FINANCES DURING THE YEAR

Report by Sir Stephen Brown, Chairman of the Finance Committee

I am glad to report that during 1970 we earned a substantial surplus, amounting to £102,250 before taxation. This surplus more than wiped out the remaining deficit incurred in the first few years of the C.B.I.'s life. Corporation Tax for the year is estimated at £42,523 but, although this amount will be payable during 1971, it is likely that under the Trade Association agreement with the Inland Revenue we shall be able to reclaim a substantial amount if, for the reasons referred to below, significant deficits are incurred during the next few years.

Despite rapidly rising costs and the additional expenses likely to be incurred by our growing involvement in European affairs, we can be reasonably hopeful about the financial outturn for 1971. However, forecasts of expenditure during 1972 and 1973 indicate that we shall have carefully to examine our activities and financial arrangements to ensure that any expansion in our activities in Europe which may become necessary will not be hampered by lack of funds. Even if the U.K. does not join the Community we shall be faced with increased expenditure if we are to be able to respond to the calls on our services arising from the new situation. We shall be examining the extent to which our current activities are still matching the requirements of members, and whether there will be any scope for economies, but we cannot rule out the possibility of having to ask members to pay higher subscriptions if we are to avoid deficits which may arise after this year.

Details of the C.B.I.'s financial position for 1970 are contained

Income and Expenditure Account for the year ended 31 December 1970 (£)

Income

1969	1970	
1,036,862	1,122,441	Members' subscriptions
70,913	65,575	Rents receivable
29,052	40,423	Investment income (gross)
3,440	4,853	Participation in profits of Industrial and Trade Fairs International Limited (formerly British Overseas Fairs Limited)
2,019	1,540	Other income
1,142,286	1,234,832	

Expenditure

1969		1970	1970	
615,098			664,621	Salaries and wages
68,484			66,063	Staff contributory pension scheme and pensions
17,795			17,494	Overseas representation
46,214			43,733	Publications, printing and stationery, less revenue from sales
34,565			36,994	Postage, telephones and cables
58,495			64,960	Travelling and entertaining
				Expenses in connection with premises:
107,476		109,139		Rent and rates
19,255		20,247		Light, fuel and cleaning
4,403		17,392		Repairs and decorations
1,616		1,728		Insurance
5,400		3,240		Mortgage interest
3,262				Other expenses
			151,746	
28,536			29,460	General Expenses
4,091			4,115	Legal and professional expenses
1,200			1,350	Audit fee
30,929			28,495	Subscriptions to other organizations
968			5,803	Industrial surveys and other inquiries
4,999			—	Amount written off unquoted investment
15,259			17,748	Depreciation of office furniture, equipment and motor cars
1,066,045			1,132,582	
656			42,523	Corporation Tax payable for the year
75,585			59,727	Excess of income over expenditure for the year
1,142,286			1,234,832	

(c)

Balance Sheet at 31 December 1970 (£)

Assets

	1969	1969	1970	1970
Fixed Assets				
Freehold land and premises at cost	281,973		281,973	
Office furniture and equipment and motor cars at cost, less depreciation	89,827		100,117	
		371,800		382,090
Current Assets				
Debtors and payments in advance	98,479		80,193	
British Government Securities at cost (market value £5,600. 1969 £7,367)	7,294		5,584	
Local Authority and other loans	360,000		500,000	
Cash at bankers and in hand	24,297		62,766	
				648,543
		861,870		1,030,633

Accumulated Fund and Liabilities

	1969	1969	1970	1970
Accumulated Fund				
Balance at 31 December 1969		255,184		330,769
Add: Excess of Income over Expenditure for the year		75,585		59,727
		330,769		390,496
4 per cent Mortgage Loan Secured on freehold land and premises, repayable by annual instalments terminating in 1990		82,000		78,000
Current Liabilities				
Creditors and provisions		76,434	117,772	
Taxation		—	43,757	
Subscriptions received in advance		372,667	400,608	
				562,137
		861,870		1,030,633

Stephen Brown: *Chairman of the Finance Committee*

R. M. C. Nunneley: *Member of the Finance Committee*

J. Gough: *Secretary*

Report of the Auditors to the Members of the Confederation of British Industry.
We have examined the above balance sheet and annexed income and expenditure account. In our opinion they give respectively a true and fair view of the state of the Confederation's affairs at 31 December 1970, and of the excess of income over expenditure for the year to that date.

Peat, Marwick, Mitchell & Co. *Chartered Accountants* 11 Ironmonger Lane, London EC2P 2AR. 25 March 1971 in the Income and Expenditure Account and Balance Sheet set out overleaf.

Subscription income has risen due to the application to our scales of the percentage rise in the official index of salaries and wages, and I am pleased to report that there has again been a net increase in membership despite the continued difficult circumstances in which a number of firms have found themselves. Strenuous efforts will be needed to maintain a further net increase during 1971 in view of the general economic situation.

The surplus for the year was higher than I anticipated a year ago, due to the increase in membership subscriptions and the higher income obtained from investments in short and longer term loans. Income was again received from Industrial and Trade Fairs International Ltd.

Although underspending occurred on salaries and wages due to continuing difficulties in filling vacancies and delays in recruitment to senior staff posts, credit is due to the Director-General and the staff for their success in containing expenditure in face of rising costs.

During the year a policy of charging for some bulletins, required only by a proportion of members, has proved very successful and, although introduced only from 1 October 1970, the cost of publications, printing and stationery has been reduced by an extra credit of £11,000 during the year. It has also enabled us to produce more useful and better presented information.

Taking advantage of the cash available as a result of the surplus for 1970, it is intended during the current year to carry out a considerable programme of replacement of equipment, refurbishing of premises, etc., which has been delayed while the deficits of earlier years were being recouped. I am sure members will not grudge expenditure needed to provide the staff with a better working environment.

71
Industrial Policy Group, 1967
The Times Business News, 25 April 1968

Many of Britain's most influential industrialists gathered at a London club last night for a secret 'council of war' on the future aims and work of the much-publicized but as yet inactive Industrial Policy Group.

A long queue of chauffeur-driven cars waited outside the Canning Club in Hamilton Place, Mayfair, as Sir Paul Chambers

– recently retired chairman of I.C.I. – presided at a working dinner in a private room. Inside were some of the biggest names in British business, who are associated with a group once condemned by the ex-Chancellor, James Callaghan, as 'potentially sinister'.

I understand members had before them two memoranda prepared by the steering committee – it includes such names as Henry Lazell (Beecham), Lord Cole (Unilever), Lord Boyd (Guiness) and David Barran (Shell) – as guide-lines for the discussion.

The outcome of last night's meeting will be the early publication of a carefully drafted statement setting out the group's aims and motives to end once and for all the speculation about its continued existence.

In spite of the group's public silence since its formation in October, the members seem very keen to see that it stays in existence and makes an important contribution in the formation of public opinion about economic trends.

There has been a continuous sounding between group members – they have each contributed £1,000 – on the wisdom of making special statements on current issues. The fear has been that accusations that the group may be politically motivated against the Government would gain credence in spite of denials to the contrary.

It is now felt, it seems, that a clear firm statement on the group's future as a kind of top businessman's lobby working informally with the Confederation of British Industry is necessary.

The fact that last night members had before them a critical paper on Government spending suggests that the group is planning a lively future, involving itself in controversial issues as and when necessary.

The members include Lord Sieff (Marks and Spencer), Sir Harry Pilkington (Pilkingtons), Sir Maurice Laing (Laings), John Partridge (Imperial Tobacco), Sir George Bolton (Bank of London and South Africa), Mr A. F. McDonald (Distillers), Sir Joseph Lockwood (E.M.I.), Lord Netherthorpe (Fisons), Sir William McEwan Younger (Scottish and Newcastle Breweries), Sir Peter Runge (Tate and Lyle), Sir Cyril Harrison (English Sewing Cotton), Sir Reay Geddes (Dunlop), and Sir Stephen Brown (Stone-Platt Industries).

72
Association of British Chambers of Commerce:
Objects, 1970

The objects for which the Association is established are: . . .

3. (b) To discuss and consider questions concerning and affecting trade, commerce, manufactures and the shipping interests, at Meetings of Delegates from Chambers of Commerce; and to collect and disseminate information from time to time on matters affecting the common and separate interests of such Chambers, and the Commercial, Manufacturing and Maritime interests of the country.

(c) To communicate the opinions of the Chambers of Commerce, separately or unitedly, to the Government or to the various departments thereof, by letter, memorial, deputation or otherwise.

(d) To petition Parliament on any matter affecting trade, commerce, manufacture or shipping.

(e) To prepare and promote in Parliament, Bills in the interest of trade, commerce, manufactures and shipping of the country, and to oppose measures which in the opinion of the Association are likely to be injurious to those interests.

To take such action as may appear necessary or desirable to protect or promote the common and separate interests of Chambers of Commerce or the interests of trade, commerce, manufactures and shipping generally.

(f) To attain those advantages by united action which each Chamber would have more difficulty in accomplishing in its separate capacity . . .

73
The National Chamber of Trade: Objects, 1970

The objects of the National Chamber, as laid down in its Memorandum of Association, include, *inter alia*, the following:

To establish and support or to aid in the establishment and support of any Chambers or Associations formed for all or any of the objects of this Chamber and not for the profit of the members thereof; and to affiliate them to this Chamber.

To petition Parliament on any matter affecting traders or the interests of members of this Chamber.

To prepare, promote and support in Parliament, Bills affecting traders or the interests of members of the Chamber, and to oppose Bills or measures which in the opinion of the Chamber are likely to prove injurious to traders or those interests.

74
Trade Associations in the Distributive Trades, late 1960s
National Economic Development Office, 1969

General services

Most of the major associations include as part of their work a review of matters before Parliament.

About sixty associations run a legal advice service for their members. Rather less than twenty associations operate debt-collection services, and about the same number run clearing-houses for settlement of suppliers' accounts and give advice on accounting. Seven associations do stock sheet numeration for their members.

In addition several associations provide advice on insurance and on general trade information services . . .

General trade associations

There are several trade associations which have a general membership based on type of organization rather than type of trade.

The *Multiple Shops Federation* (M.S.F.) has about 470 members all of whom are retailers employing approximately 400,000 people in 45,000 shops. The following associations are affiliated to the Multiple Shops Federation and share the same offices and secretariat:

National Association of Multiple Grocers
Association of Multiple Retail Meat Traders
Multiple Wine Merchants' Association
Multiple Shoe Retailers' Association
Multiple Tailors' Association

Because of the very close connection between the parent organization and its affiliated associations, they have been given consecutive numbers in the analysis in Appendix 3 although they are mentioned by trade later on in this section. Where appropriate, member firms of the M.S.F. also belong to affiliated associations.

The M.S.F. and its affiliated associations provide a consultancy service for members on legal and taxation questions, and transport problems. They also give informal advice to members. All of these services are provided free of charge. The M.S.F. runs a Town Planning Reporting Service which is charged (at an economic rate) to members according to the number of their branches. The service provides information about schemes of redevelopment of towns and shopping centres, of schemes for the regulation of traffic, etc. In addition, meetings are arranged between members and central and local government authorities to examine and assess redevelopment schemes for town and shopping centres. Arising from these activities the Federation has published recommendations on 'The Planning of Shopping Centres'.

Surveys have been made by the M.S.F. of the practice of members in such matters as holiday arrangements, stock deficiencies, transport operations, methods of remuneration; the results being circulated among contributors. Transport surveys are based on an analysis of vehicles operated by members, their costs on the servicing and equipment of these vehicles, etc. Group visits are arranged to study warehouse layout and systems of members. Groups of members also meet regularly to consider matters relating to architecture, building controls and fire precautions. Meetings are arranged between surveyors acting for members to discuss rating problems. The Federation attempts to secure uniform hours of trading at special seasons of the year.

The associations also run an interfirm comparison scheme. The information collected is broken down by size of firm, analysed by the staff, and the whole operation for the M.S.F. and its affiliated associations costs between £1,500 and £2,000 per annum. The statistics are collected annually and the type of data varies slightly between the different associations.

The principal trade association for department stores is the *Retail Distributors Association* (R.D.A.) with over five hundred member stores. The *Independent Stores Association* (I.S.A.) is a smaller organization with seventeen members, many of whom also belong to the R.D.A. The qualification for membership of the I.S.A. is independent management control and a turnover of at least £1·3m per annum.

On training, the R.D.A. organizes specialist junior management courses and, for higher management, seminars on the 'business game' principle. In addition seminars are organized on particular subjects for all levels.

A consultancy service is provided on work study, accountancy, stock control and any aspect of store administration. A firm of professional consultants is retained by the R.D.A. to give advice on legal problems. All consultancy services are provided free of charge.

The R.D.A. runs a comprehensive interfirm comparison scheme. Most data is collected annually, but details of stock levels and turnover are collected monthly. In addition to the subjects listed in the questionnaire, the R.D.A. also collects data on transaction value. The data is averaged and broken down by merchandise groups, size of firm and geographical areas. The analysis is made partly by R.D.A. staff and patrly by outside firms and the results are made available annually to members. The estimated cost of this exercise is £1,500 excluding internal staff costs.

All developments bearing on the trade are under constant review by a series of specialist committees. Views and guidance are then communicated to members either through special publications or through meetings.

There are close links between the R.D.A. and the I.S.A. on a number of topics. The I.S.A. runs special conferences and seminars for junior executives, personnel controllers, staff trainers, buyers and departmental managers. It does not run a formal consultancy service but it informs members of latest developments. An interfirm comparison scheme is organized and a wide range of data is collected, mostly on an annual basis. It is presented in clear, broken down by merchandise groups. Provision of the data is a condition of membership.

The *Co-operative Union* is the policy-making body for the Co-operative Movement with membership from retail and wholesale co-operative societies, productive societies and other special types of societies. Within the Co-operative Union there are seven specialist trade associations: for bakery, grocery and provisions, dry goods, fuel, meat, milk, and laundry and allied trades. Each of these has a national executive which is serviced by Co-operative Union officials, the work of each association being dovetailed into the Co-operative Union trade advisory departments.

The Co-operative Union has an education department which provides for societies and individual students, courses, syllabuses, examinations and awards. It promotes local classes and groups, offers a wide range of correspondence courses, organizes short courses of education and training and runs the Co-operative College for more advanced residential courses.

The Co-operative Union runs a comprehensive consultancy service for its members and employs full time specialist advisers who visit members and produce reports and recommendations. A general advisory service is available on all trading, legal,

labour and constitutional questions. In addition to this consultancy service which is available on an individual basis, general
trade guides are produced, for example, for hair-dressing, jewel-
lery trades and motor trades. Many of the services provided by
the Co-operative Union are free but some, such as the specialist
trade advice, accountancy and taxation, are charged at an economic rate.

The Co-operative Union collects a great deal of comparative
data from its members for use in its interfirm comparison scheme,
which is published annually in 'Co-operative Statistics'. The
data is analysed by merchandise groups, size of societies and is
presented individually for nine geographical regions in the
U.K. The analysis is done by the staff of the Union and provision of data is voluntary although the great majority of societies
do partake. The whole operation costs an estimated £15,000 per
annum.

Currently, the Union is planning an efficiency audit service to
cover accounting, management accounting, trading and mer-
chandising efficiency.

The *National Chamber of Trade* (N.C.T.) is the national body
representing over 900 local Chambers of Trade and Commerce
throughout the U.K. In addition it has affiliated to it forty-three
national trade associations. Its overall membership is approximately 450,000 and it numbers among its members all kinds and
sizes of businesses and services. The questionnaire which was
sent out to trade associations was very largely inapplicable to the
N.C.T. which, because of its unique structure and organization,
deals more with general principles than with specific cases.

The N.C.T. however has a variety of committees, many of
them *ad hoc*, which consider problems and make recommendations to the Chamber's board of management.

The day-to-day work of the Chamber includes an administrative and technical advisory service on basic problems in the distributive trades, a general information and advisory service which
disseminates information through the N.C.T. Journal and other
informative booklets and leaflets.

Most of the members of the *National Alliance of Private Traders*
are private shopkeepers. The Alliance operates a service for
members where problems in connection with their businesses are
answered by the staff or honorary officers. It also operates, free
of charge, a debt collection service and has an arrangement with
an insurance company whereby policies specially designed to
meet the needs of shopkeepers and other private traders are
available to members at a 10 per cent rebate.

The *Federation of Wholesale Organizations* (F.W.O.) is a federation of the following wholesale organizations:

Electrical Wholesalers' Federation
Federation of Hardware Factors
Millinery Distributors' Association
Motor Factors' Association
Association of Engineering Distributors
Association of Musical Instrument Industries
The National Council of Coal Traders
Pottery and Glass Wholesalers' Association
Radio Wholesalers' Federation
British Stationery and Office Equipment Association
Wholesale Floorcovering Distributors' Association
Wholesale Footwear Distributors' Association
Textile Distributors' Association.

The F.W.O. therefore acts in a collective capacity for its constituent organizations on all matters concerning wholesale distribution, although it has no control over these individual constituent organizations. Membership is open to all distributors of consumer goods although, in fact, all members are non-food wholesalers.

The F.W.O. does not provide training facilities for members as this is undertaken individually by constituent organizations. It is however currently negotiating with the City and Guilds of London Institute for the introduction of a standard training course for wholesale operatives.

Similarly, the F.W.O. does not provide consultancy services or conduct interfirm comparisons as these again are provided by the individual constituent associations.

The *Mail Order Traders' Association of Great Britain* has a membership which represents over 60 per cent of the mail order trade. The Association does not undertake training, consultancy or interfirm comparison but it does provide a legal advice service for members.

The *National Market Traders' Federation* is a federation of retail market traders dealing in a variety of products. The Federation does offer individual services to members requiring help, but it is not possible for it to offer the sort of information normally given to such members by individual trade associations dealing with a specific trade. Here again many of the questions asked in the questionnaire were inapplicable.

The main function of the Federation is to represent members' interests collectively on market affairs such as rentals, development of markets, removal of markets due to town redevelopment and occasionally allocation of stalls. The Federation co-operates with market authorities and gives advice on the implementation of legislation affecting markets.

Grocers and provision dealers

In the grocery trades there are three principal retail trade associations, the *National Association of Multiple Grocers*, the *National Grocers' Federation* and the *Scottish Grocers' Federation*. In the wholesale trade there is the *National Federation of Wholesale Grocers* and the *Wholesale Grocers' Association of Scotland*. In addition the *Supermarket Association* represents retailers, wholesalers and manu·facturers.

In the grocery trade, training and educational facilities are provided through the Grocers' Institute. Some of the associations do not provide their own courses but co-operate with the Institute in framing programmes, others, such as the Supermarket Association, run comprehensive courses of their own in close consultation with the Institute.

The *National Association of Multiple Grocers* is affiliated to the M.S.F., and a number of the comments made about the services provided by the M.S.F. apply equally to the N.A.M.G. Members have access to the Town Planning Reporting Service, legal and taxation advice and the other services provided by the M.S.F. The N.A.M.G. runs its own interfirm comparison scheme collecting data annually on turnover, sales, labour force, and labour and occupancy costs. The data is processed by the Association's staff and is costed as part of the whole M.S.F. exercise.

The members of the *National Grocers' Federation* are both independent grocers and privately owned multiples. It operates through about 180 branches. Recently, associate membership of the N.G.F. has been open to manufacturers and national trading agencies of foreign and commonwealth countries.

The N.G.F. co-operates with the Grocers' Institute, the Retail Trades Education Council and the College for the Distributive Trades on education and training programmes. It also runs national and local seminars on general trade subjects. It is represented on the Retail Food Trade Wages Council, and operates an employment register for holiday relief management.

The N.G.F. operates consultancy services free of charge to its members partly through its own staff and partly by retaining professional consultants. It operates a personal trade information service which deals with all trade problems, and, through a special consultant, gives advice on compulsory purchase, redevelopment and rating. It also offers an advisory service on National Insurance and staff retirement and pension schemes and obtains special rates for members on insurance and purchases of equipment. A scheme is currently being considered for the formation of a Joint Consultative Committee embracing retailers, wholesalers and manufacturers to discuss common policy on commercial and legislative matters.

The *Metropolitan Grocers' Association* with its 340 members is the largest in the metropolitan area of London. It is affiliated to the National Grocers' Federation and also to the London District Council of Grocers' Associations. It has its own buying company, Metgro Buyers Limited, which is an integral part of the Association's services. M.G.A. delegates serve on all National Federation and London District Council Committees, thus assuring that its members are kept well informed and up-to-date with the trends in the trade.

The *Scottish Grocers' Federation* has a membership of some 3,600 retailers. Like the N.G.F., it co-operates with the Grocers' Institute in the provision of training facilities and is represented on the Retail Food Trade Wages Council.

The S.G.F. provides consultancy services for members through professional consultants and the association's staff on shop layout and design, accountancy, stock control, legal and insurance problems. They are mostly provided free, but the legal advice is usually on a fee-paying basis.

The Federation collects data on a number of topics for an annual interfirm comparison scheme. The data is coded and broken down by merchandise groups, size of firms, and cash or credit trade. The analysis is done by the Federation's staff and costs an estimated £200 per annum.

The Federation sponsors a 'Grocer of the Year' scheme whereby a prize of approximately £3,000 can be won by an 'ambitious and capable individual' to establish himself as a master grocer. The prize is given in the form of a £500 cash prize donated by the Federation and the balance in stock donated by manufacturers . . .

Greengrocers and fruiterers

There are three associations in this field; one, the *Retail Fruit Trade Federation* did not reply to the questionnaire. The other two, the *National Federation of Fruit and Potato Trades* and the *London Fruit and Vegetable Trades Federation* are both wholesale organizations.

The National Federation does not provide training facilities, but does provide an informal consultancy service for members given free of charge by the Federation staff. It also provides a legal advice service, a Board of Arbitration, handles insurance and status inquiries and negotiates shipping claims.

The London Fruit and Vegetable Trades Federation has several specialist standing committees which feed information to the main Federation. The Federation occasionally collects interfirm comparison data on turnover, labour force, margins, earnings and wage costs. The data is analysed by auditors and broken down by size of firm.

Bakers

The *National Association of Master Bakers, Confectioners and Caterers* has retailers, wholesalers and manufacturers as its members. It gives advice to members on training, but provides no educational or recruitment facilities. These are all available to members through the National Board for Bakery Education for which it provides the Secretariat.

The Association provides a consultancy service on shop layout and design, accountancy, rating and property, insurance, pensions and general trade legislation. This is provided by the Association's staff and professional consultants with collective guidance by panels of experts and through consultation with other associated trade organizations. These services are usually provided free of charge, unless they concern major projects.

The Association regularly collects interfirm comparison data on margins and profits, and occasionally on labour force and part-time working. The data is averaged and processed by the Association's staff. On group trading, the Association said that it encouraged the formation of central buying-groups within the trade.

The *Scottish Association of Master Bakers* has a membership of retailers, wholesalers and processors. Most of the services which it provides are geared towards the requirements of its members who actually produce bread.

Off-licences

Of the associations in the off-licence trade, three, the *Multiple Wine Merchants Association*, the *National Federation of Off-Licence Holders Association*, and the *National Federation of Licensed Victuallers*, have a solely retail membership. The *Wine and Spirit Association* has a membership of retailers, wholesalers and manufacturers, while members of the *Brewers Society* are mostly manufacturers.

The *Multiple Wine Merchants Association* is affiliated to the Multiple Shops Federation and its members are multiple retailers of wines, spirits, beer and other drinks. Like the other multiple associations, it does not undertake its own training but informs and advises members on available courses. Similarly association members use the consultancy facilities provided by the M.S.F. The M.W.M.A. conducts interfirm comparisons collecting data annually on the labour force and part-time working, and biennially on turnover, earnings and wage costs.

The *National Federation of Licensed Victuallers* is a federation of some 430 local licensed victuallers' associations and represents those associations and their individual members in national matters and negotiations. The provision of more intimate services to members is left in the hands of local associations. Members are mainly holders of on-licences.

Training facilities are not provided by the federation but it is affiliated to the National Trade Development Association which provides training for the trade. No formal consultancy service is provided but the Federation provides informal consultancy service free of charge.

The Federation pointed out that the relationships between licensees and brewers is unusual, because the latter are invariably the landlords of the properties, and the purchase and sale of goods is therefore controlled. As a result, there is frequent consultation between brewers and retailers at both national and local level.

The *National Federation of Off-Licence Holders* is an association of holders of retail liquor off-licences. The Federation does not at the moment provide training, but is giving this consideration.

The *Wine and Spirit Association* has retailers, wholesalers and manufacturers as members dealing in imported and home produced wines, spirits, liqueurs etc.

The main special services provided by the Association, in addition to trade defence, trade and consumer education, wine publicity etc. are official negotiations with British and foreign governments. In view of the nature of the trade, these can be complex.

The Association also provides a service for members in explaining complexities of Customs and Excise law, licensing law, food and labelling regulations and so on. It keeps closely in touch with developments in E.E.C., E.F.T.A., Council of Europe and other bodies, and its representatives attend many international meetings and conferences.

The *Brewers' Society* is basically a trade association of manufacturers supplying direct to retail premises, and members are closely involved in the catering industry, and only residually in the distributive trades. The questionnaire was therefore largely inappropriate.

Confectioners, tobacconists, newsagents

In this trade there are three associations with exclusively retail membership; the *National Union of Retail Confectioners*, *National Union of Retail Tobacconists* and the *National Federation of Retail Newsagents, Booksellers and Stationers*.

The *National Union of Retail Tobacconists* provides a full, general consultancy service for members including legal advice, a clearing-house and in some areas stock sheet numeration. It conducts annually an interfirm comparison exercise which is analysed by the associations staff. It is in close contact with manufacturers on a number of problems, including profit margins and trade terms.

The *National Federation of Retail Newsagents, Booksellers and Stationers* does not provide a consultancy service as such but has a research team that considers the many problems of the retailer and gives advice free of charge. It also provides a legal advice service and an insurance scheme.

The *Federation of London Wholesale Newspaper Distributors* is an example of a regional trade association. It occasionally collects data from members for use in an interfirm comparison, issues information on new merchandise, liaises with manufacturers on delivery, new products etc. and gives legal advice.

The *Scottish Tobacco Trade Federation* is a retailer–wholesaler organization and the *Wholesaler Confectioners Alliance* has a membership of wholesalers only.

Footwear

Within the footwear trade, there are three trade associations; the *Wholesaler Footwear Distributors' Association*, the *Multiple Shoes Retailers' Association* and the *National Shoe Retailers' Council*. These are united under one umbrella organization, the *Footwear Distributors' Federation*, which acts on behalf of the other three associations on problems common to all sections of shoe distribution.

The *Wholesale Footwear Distributors' Association* is the wholesale association; it collects interfirm comparison data on such matters as turnover, stock levels, and stock items monthly and annually, broken down by size of firms and geographical area . . .

The *Leathergoods Association of Buyers and Retailers Limited* is a newly formed association. Its main function is the promotion of sales of leather goods through the association's journal, seasonal catalogues, display materials and so on. The Association has a close relationship with the Leather Institute which provides courses for junior trainees and management, and, in addition, the association is about to launch its own management seminar. The Association emphasizes that it is developing its role at the moment and as yet has only a limited trade association function. In this trade there is a close relationship between manufacturers and retailers as evidenced by their joint advertising campaign and co-operation on a number of problems. A joint committee has been formed with the manufacturers to make a joint promotional effort for the industry.

The other trade association dealing in leather goods is the *Society of Master Saddlers Limited*. The Society organizes refresher training courses for members through technical colleges and provides consultancy on shop layout and design, work study, market research and accountancy through the Rural Industries Bureau. These consultancy services are provided free of charge to members.

The *Music Trades Association* is an association with a membership of retailers in the music instrument industry. Individual members generally initiate their own training although the Association operates an apprenticeship scheme for piano-repairing. The Association gives consultancy advice on shop layout and design, and stock control free of charge to members and is considering starting a scheme for the collection of interfirm comparison data.

Other non-food traders

The *National Federation of Sub-Postmasters* comes into this general category and is in fact not really a trade association but a registered trade union for sub-postmasters, many of whom have ancillary businesses. In this capacity the Federation provides an informal consultancy service, an interfirm comparison service on earnings, wage costs, margins and profits broken down by size of firms and analysed by the Association's staff.

The *Guild of British Dispensing Opticians* has a membership of retailers and manufacturers. Because of the nature of their members' business the questionnaire was largely inapplicable to this association. The Guild is very active in promoting training among its members and in providing for junior trainees' correspondence courses, and full and part-time courses at further education colleges. The Guild sponsors the publication of specialist technical material and runs a legal advice service for members and gives advice on insurance matters. Through membership of an international body, the Guild has contact with many overseas groups and gives advice based on their considerable educational experience.

Department stores

The two department store trade associations were dealt with under the heading 'general' . . .

Variety and other general

This is a miscellaneous category of trade associations and included in it are the *National Pawnbrokers' Association* and the *Retail Credit Federation*.

The *National Pawnbrokers' Association* is classified under the heading of the Distributive Trades although the business of members is the lending of money on security, therefore many sections of the questionnaire did not apply.

The *Retail Credit Federation* is an association of retailers dealing mostly in tailoring, drapery, footwear, fashions and some consumer durables. The membership of the Federation numbers about 2,400, covering around 150,000 employees. It has nine district councils and sixty-seven local associations.

The Federation provides training courses at all levels, mostly in the form of short residential courses. It also runs a general advisory service which gives advice to members on a variety of topics, including valuation and sales of business. These services are provided free, except for the latter, which is charged at an economic rate. Every two or three years, the Federation carries out a comparative statistical survey covering a number of items. The data is broken down by size of firms and the analysis made by an outside firm at a cost of approximately £350 per annum. The Federation undertakes a good deal of public relations work and provides lecturers in schools, training colleges, consumer groups etc. on the intelligent use of consumer credit.

The *Scottish Retail Credit Association* is directly affiliated to the Retail Credit Federation. The Association provides specialist training courses for salesmen–collectors and occasionally it collects interfirm comparison data on different subjects according to the objects of the exercise. The Association runs a specialized debt collection service in respect of removed accounts where customers have moved from one district to another. In addition the Association has organized through a professional debt-collector a scheme for collection of 'multiple debts' where an individual has become involved in credit debts beyond his ability to meet them. The Association also runs a clearing-house through the Scottish Retail Drapers' Association.

CONCLUSIONS

The results of this survey provide comprehensive information on the range of services provided by trade associations in the distributive trades. It also gives a clear indication of the large numbers of trade associations in distribution which, because of their overlapping coverage, comprise a complex structure. There is a wide variation in the size of their membership and in the range of services which they provide. At the same time there appears to be some duplication of membership between associations and of services in several trades.

Although this complex pattern of trade association representation may to a certain extent be inevitable in an industry in which over three million people are engaged and which covers over half a million establishments, it is arguable whether in this form many associations can provide the quality of service and level of representation which industry requires today.

Because the distributive trades employ such vast economic resources, it is in the interest of members to get advice which will help them to employ these resources more economically and profitably; and to be able to make the distributive trades' voice heard on national issues. These are functions which suitably organized trade associations can successfully fulfil.

It was most encouraging to note that many of the associations who replied to the inquiry indicated that they are considering extending the range of their services to members, particularly in the field of consultancy and interfirm comparisons. It is in these two fields that the E.D.C. believes that associations can do most to encourage the efficient development of their members.

Another notable feature arising from the inquiry was the number of associations who co-operate with each other in providing joint services for their members. In some trades, where there are associations with the same field of membership, there is great scope for extending this co-operation in joint ventures which individual associations may not be able to afford or where the membership is too small to warrant provision of the service by one association.

75
Aims of Industry Ltd: 'Say *No* to Nationalization', 1964
Observer, 23 February 1964

IF THE STATE TAKES OVER...

STATE CONTROL of free enterprise firms will cost millions. And it's people like you who will have to pay, faced with higher prices, and frustrating restrictions of all kinds. But *need* this happen? This decision is in *your* hands. You may well feel the price is too high. After all, with Free Enterprise you have found many more opportunities in your work – and your standard of living is higher. Remember, though the threat of State Control is real, it is still up to *you* to hold on to the freedom you've won.

SAY NO TO NATIONALIZATION

Issued by Aims of Industry in defence of free enterprise

76
The Economic League : General policy, 1964
This is the Economic League, Leaflet No. 14, 1964

The Economic League has been at work for forty-five years. It was in 1919 that a group of men met together with a common idea and a common aim. They believed that our standard of living depends upon the efficiency of British Industry, and all who work in it. They believed also that efficiency must spring from a common understanding so they set up an organization to work for that aim.

Understanding

The League believes that to be efficient industry must be free from discontent and all subversive influences. It believes also that the interests of employer and employee are not opposed. They depend upon one another. The more efficient and success-ful an industry, the better it is for everyone connected with it – workers, management, shareholders and consumers. On the other hand, if a firm or industry is undermined by subversive agitation everyone stands to lose, except those who planned the agitation to further their own ends.

The Economic League is convinced that the two main obstacles to efficient industry, and the whole national interest, are mis-understanding and planned agitation. Through its speakers and by means of its leaflets and other publications the League seeks to remove both obstacles. How? By creating a national under-standing of the problems of industry, commerce and finance. By directing the searchlight of truth and exposure upon Communists and others trying to damage Britain by upsetting her industry.

Non-party

The League knows that if it is to succeed in its work it must make a fair and honest approach to economic and social problems. That approach must be entirely free from party-political bias. The League is not connected, nor has it ever been connected, with any political party. Its money is provided by industrial federa-ions, by private firms, and by individuals who believe in its work. It does not accept money from any political party or organization. It does not support any form of party-political activity.

The unions

The Economic League believes that a strong trade union move-ment has a vital function to fulfil in Britain's economic and social progress.

It is constantly urging union members to attend branch meet-ings and to play their full part in discussions and union elections. On the other hand, the League is relentless in its opposition to those who seek to undermine the trade unions from within and who, by fomenting unofficial strikes, prevent the operation of the negotiating machinery. It seeks to secure goodwill among all engaged in industry. The Communists and other subversive forces such as the Trotskyists endeavour to use the unions as an instrument to further their struggle for power.

National interest

The League's approach to nationalization is from the economic and social, not the party-political, standpoint. It remains con-vinced that free enterprise is the most efficient method of conduct-ing the nation's vast competitive industries. The League wants to see the most efficient working of all British industry in the national interest.

THE ECONOMIC LEAGUE stands for STRAIGHT THINKING and RELENTLESS OPPOSITION TO SUBVERSION. IT IS ABSOLUTELY NON-PARTY.

77
The National Farmers' Union : Objects, Rules, etc., 1970

PART I . . .

3. Objects

The objects of the Union shall be:

(a) To promote the interests of farmers by any lawful ways and means which in the opinion of the Union may conduce to that end.

(b) To further or oppose legislation which, in the opinion of the Union, may be sound and beneficial or prejudicial to the interests of farmers or farming.

K

(c) To promote sympathetic understanding and good feeling between all persons interested in farming.

(d) To afford to all persons interested in farming, as well as to the community generally, facilities for discussion and the interchange of information and ideas concerning farming.

(e) To deal on a representative basis with all questions affecting the relations between landlords and tenants or between farmers and workers.

(f) To deal upon a representative basis with all questions and disputes of whatsoever nature affecting farming.

(g) To consider, discuss and advise on all questions affecting farmers or farming (including questions concerning wages and prices, restrictive conditions on the conduct of any trade or business, the terms and conditions of the employment of labour, tenure, compensation for improvements and disturbances, and the revision of Imperial and local taxation), and to circulate amongst the members of the Union and others, advice, information and statistics relating thereto.

(h) To prepare, recommend and supply equitable forms of contract between farmers, and also between farmers and those engaged in other trades or businesses.

(i) To furnish funds for the prosecution or defence of any actions or legal proceedings in cases deemed to affect farming. Provided that the law relating to champerty and maintenance be not thereby infringed.

(j) To establish branches in all parts of England and Wales with a view to obtaining information as to the special conditions prevailing in different localities, and to the protection and promotion of local interests and the discussion and ventilation of local questions.

(k) To take such steps as may be necessary or expedient to secure the adequate transport of the produce of farming and all materials used in or relating to farming at fair rates, facilities for attendance at markets by means of market tickets or otherwise and reasonable market tolls.

(l) To negotiate for and secure facilities and beneficial terms for the members of the Union in regard to insurance against fire, employers' liability and other risks.

(m) To arrange deputations and generally to ventilate the views of farmers, and to make better known to the Government and public all conditions and difficulties affecting farmers or farming.

(n) To subscribe to, assist, subsidize or co-operate with any association or institution whose objects are in whole or in part similar to those of the Union, and to subscribe to any funds or objects, charitable or otherwise, which may be deemed likely to promote the interests of farming or to benefit the members of the Union.

(o) To promote and facilitate co-operation amongst farmers and between farmers and other persons.

(p) (i) To grant pensions or gratuities to any officer or employee or ex-officer or ex-employee of the Union or to the relations, connections or dependants of any of them.

(ii) To effect group or other insurances or purchase, acquire or take out annuities, annuity bonds or other policies, whether immediate or deferred, for securing either unconditionally or subject to any terms and conditions, the payment of any such pensions or gratuities aforesaid and so that any such annuities, annuity bonds or policies may be taken either in the names of the said persons or of trustees for them or for the Union.

(iii) To establish, contribute to and support funds or trusts for the purpose hereinbefore mentioned in this sub-clause or any other funds, trusts, associations, clubs or institutions which may be considered calculated to benefit any of such persons.

(q) Subject to the provisions of the Trade Union Act, 1913, or any amendment thereof, to further the political objects mentioned in the Third Schedule hereto.

4. *General Organization*

The organization of the Union shall comprise a Council which shall be the executive of the Union and County Branches made up of Local or Specialist Branches.

4 (a). *Welsh Council of the N.F.U.*

(1) The Council of the Union may establish a Welsh Council of the N.F.U. (hereinafter called 'The Welsh Council') consisting of the members for the time being of the Welsh Committee of the Council of the Union and of additional representatives of each County Branch for an area which in the opinion of the Council of the Union comprises or includes part of Wales or Monmouth. Unless the Council of the Union shall otherwise determine, each such County Branch shall have three additional representatives.

(2) The Welsh Council shall be a consultative body for the interchange of views on matters within the objects of the Union of particular interest to members of the Union in Wales or Monmouth, for the co-ordination of the work of the Union's branches therein and for the improvement of communication between the Council of the Union and members in the Principality.

(3) The constitution, membership and functions of the Welsh Council shall (so far as the Council of the Union consider it appropriate to do so) be as further determined by the Council of the Union who may make regulations for the procedure of the Welsh Council and shall provide the secretarial and clerical assistance necessary for the conduct of its affairs.

(4) Members of the Welsh Council shall, when engaged on its work, be allowed travelling and out-of-pocket expenses upon such scale, and subject to such regulations, as the Council of the Union may from time to time prescribe.

(5) The President, Deputy President and Vice-President of the Union shall be entitled to attend, take part in and vote at the meetings of the Welsh Council.

(6) The Council of the Union may from time to time or at any time amend the constitution, functions or regulations of the Welsh Council or dissolve or reconstitute the same.

5. *Area Committees*

(1) The Council may with the consent of the County Branches concerned, group the County or Specialist Branches within any area and form an Area Committee consisting of representatives of the County or Specialist Branches within the Group.

(2) The constitution and functions of an Area Committee shall be determined by the Council and the Council shall make regulations for its procedure and may provide the secretarial and clerical assistance necessary for the conduct of its business.

(3) The expenses of the representatives of County or Specialist Branches attending or representing Area Committees shall not be defrayed from the funds of the Council.

(4) The President, Deputy President and Vice-President of the Union shall be entitled to attend, take part in and vote at the meetings of any Area Committee or Sub-Committee of an Area Committee.

6. *Affiliated Organizations*

(1) The Council may admit to affiliation with the Union any organization, institution, or other body of persons, whether incorporated or otherwise (hereinafter called an 'affiliated organization') which has objects, in whole or in part, similar to the objects of the Union and does not carry on any business for profit.

(2) Neither an affiliated organization, nor any of its members, shall, by virtue only of such affiliation, be deemed to be in membership of the Union and accordingly neither it nor they shall be

entitled as of right to attend or vote at meetings of the Council or Committees of the Council, or at any Committee of any Branch of the Union. Provided that representatives of an affiliated organization may with the previous consent of the Council, be admitted to meetings of the Council, or of any Committee of the Council, as visitors, or for the purpose of consultation.

(3) The services (if any) to be rendered by the Union to any affiliated organization shall be such as may from time to time be mutually arranged by the Council with that organization, and such services shall be rendered by the Union upon such financial and other terms as may from time to time be mutually agreed.

(4) The Council may at any time terminate such affiliation . . .

PART III
The Council

1. *Composition*

(1) The Council shall be the Executive of the Union and shall, subject as hereinafter mentioned, consist of the following persons, namely:

(a) The President, Deputy President, Vice-President and Honorary Treasurer for the time being of the Union.

(b) Such representatives of the County Branches as are hereinafter mentioned.

(c) The Chairman for the time being (if not a member of the Council in another capacity) of any of the following committees which are, for the time being, Standing Committees, namely:

(i) One committee concerned with the interests of Producer Retailers of Milk.

(ii) Not more than two committees concerned with Seed Growing.

(iii) Not more than five Committees concerned with the production of Fruit, Flowers, Shrubs, Young Plants or Trees, Glasshouse Produce and Vegetables.

(iv) One committee concerned with the policy and co-ordination of the work of the committees referred to under No. (iii) of this sub-clause.

(v) One committee concerned with Hill Farming.

(vi) One committee concerned with Agricultural Co-operation.

(d) The Vice-Chairman for the time being (if not a member of the Council in another capacity) of any of the following committees which are, for the time being, Standing Committees, namely:

(i) One committee concerned with the interests of Producer Retailers of Milk.

(ii) One committee concerned with the policy and co-ordination of the work of the committees referred to under No. (c) (iii) of this sub-clause.

(e) The following persons, unless members of the Council in another capacity, namely, the Chairman and not more than two Vice-Chairmen for the time being of one Standing Committee concerned with Poultry and Eggs together with not more than four other members of and elected by that Committee.

(f) Provided that in the event of any of the said Chairmen or Vice-Chairmen being unable to attend a particular meeting of the Council, the said committee or sub-committee may appoint from its members some other person to attend that meeting.

(g) Such past Presidents, past Deputy Presidents or past Vice-Presidents of the Union as may be elected by the Council as hereinafter mentioned.

(h) The Chairman and Vice-Chairman for the time being of the Welsh Council, unless members of the Council in another capacity.

(2) (a) No person other than a member of the Union may become or continue as a member of the Council or any Committee thereof.

(b) No paid official of any County, Local or Specialist Branch of the Union may become or continue as a member of the Council or any Committee thereof.

2. *County branch representation*

(1) The representation of the the County Branches upon the Council shall be calculated on the basis following, that is to say:

County Branch Paid-up Membership	Number of Representatives upon the Council
Not exceeding 1,500	1
Exceeding 1,500 but not exceeding 5,000	2
Exceeding 5,000 but not exceeding 7,500	3
Exceeding 7,500 but not exceeding 10,000	4
Exceeding 10,000	5

The paid-up membership of each County Branch shall be as stated upon the latest return made by the County Branch to the General Secretary of the Union specifying the number of members who, at the date of the making of the return, have paid in full their current year's subscription and are not in arrear with any previous year's subscription...

III. THE THIRD SCHEDULE
POLITICAL FUND AND OBJECTS

1. *Definition*

In this Schedule the expression 'political objects' means the objects to which Section 3 of the Trade Union Act, 1913, applies, that is to say the expenditure of money:

(a) on the payment of any expenses incurred either directly or indirectly by a candidate or prospective candidate for election to Parliament or to any public office, before, during, or after the election in connection with his candidature or election; or

(b) on the holding of any meeting or the distribution of any literature or documents in support of any such candidate or prospective candidate; or

(c) on the maintenance of any person who is a Member of Parliament or who holds a public office; or

(d) in connection with the registration of electors or the selection of a candidate for Parliament or any public office; or

(e) on the holding of political meetings of any kind, or on the distribution of political literature or political documents of any kind, unless the main purpose of the meetings or of the distribution of the literature or documents is the furtherance of statutory objects within the meaning of the Act, that is to say, the regulation of the relations between workmen and masters or between workmen and workmen or between masters and masters, or the imposing of restrictive conditions on the conduct of any trade or business and also the provision of benefits to members.

The expression 'public office' in this rule means the office of member of any county, county borough, district or parish council, or of any public body who have power to raise money either directly or indirectly by means of a rate.

2. *Political Fund*

(1) Any payments in the furtherance of such political objects shall be made out of a separate fund (hereinafter called the political fund of the Union).

(2) The Council shall have power to direct the transfer of any moneys or securities forming the political fund of the Union in excess of £20,000 to the general fund of the Council and to utilize such transferred moneys or securities for the general purposes of the Union.

(3) The Council shall cause a notice in the following form to be given to each member of the Union:

TRADE DISPUTES AND TRADE UNIONS ACT, 1946

Every member of the Union who does not object to contribute to the separate fund for payments in furtherance of political objects within the meaning of the Trade Union Act, 1913, will contribute to that fund. Every member of the Union has the right to be exempt from contributing to it. A form of exemption notice may be obtained by or on behalf of any member either by application at, or by post from, the general office or any branch office of the Union or from the Chief Registrar of Friendly Societies, 17 North Audley Street, London W.1. Such form, when filled in, should be handed or sent to the Secretary of the County Branch to which the member belongs. An exemption notice given within one month after the date of this notice will take effect as from the date on which it is given. Should a notice be given after one month from that date it will operate as from the following 1st January.

Such notice shall be published in such manner whether in the Union's Journal or report or otherwise, as notices are usually given by the Union or its branches to its members, and shall also be posted up and kept posted up for at least twelve months in a conspicuous place, accessible to members, at the office or meeting-place of each branch of the Union, and the Secretary of each branch shall take steps to secure that every member of the branch, so far as practicable, receives a copy of such notice, and shall supply a copy to any member at his request. The Council shall provide the Secretary of each Branch with a number of notices sufficient for this purpose.

(4) The form of exemption notice shall be as follows:

NATIONAL FARMERS' UNION POLITICAL FUND
(EXEMPTION NOTICE)

I hereby give notice that I object to contribute to the political fund of the National Farmers' Union, and am in consequence exempt, in manner provided by the Trade Union Act, 1913, from contributing to that fund.

Signature _____

Name of Branch_____

Address _____

Date_____ day of _____ 19____

The Council shall provide a sufficient number of such forms at the general office and at each Branch office of the Union for such members of the Union as require them; and a copy of such form shall be delivered either by the Council or by the Secretary of any branch to any member on his request, or on a request made on his behalf either personally or by post.

(5) Any member of the Union may at any time give notice on such form of exemption notice or on a form to the like effect that he objects to contribute to the political fund of the Union. Such notice shall be sent to the Secretary of the County Branch to which the member belongs and, on receiving it, the Secretary shall send an acknowledgement of its receipt to the member at the address appearing upon the notice, and shall inform the General Secretary of the name and address of the member.

(6) On giving such notice, a member of the Union shall be exempt, so long as his notice is not withdrawn, from contributing to the political fund of the Union as from the first day of January next after the notice is given or, in the case of a notice given within one month after the notice given to members under sub-clause (3) hereof or after the date on which a new member admitted to the Union is supplied with a copy of these rules under sub-clause (3) hereof, as from the date on which the member's notice is given.

(7) A member who is exempt from the obligation to contribute to the political fund of the Union shall not be excluded from any benefits of the Union, or placed in any respect either directly or indirectly under any disability or disadvantage as compared with other members of the Union (except in relation to the control or management of the Political Fund of the Union) by reason of his being so exempt.

(8) Any member may withdraw his notice of exemption on notifying his desire to that effect to the Secretary of his County Branch, who shall thereupon send such member an acknowledgement of receipt of the notification and inform the General Secretary of the name and address of the member so withdrawing.

(9) The Council shall give effect to the exemption of members to contribute to the Political Fund of the Union by making a separate levy of contributions to that fund from the members of the Union who are not exempt. No moneys of the Union other than the amount raised by such separate levy shall be carried to the Political Fund of the Union.

(10) If in respect of any subscription year the Council determine to raise a separate levy as aforesaid the same shall be due and payable on the first day of March in each year, and the amount thereof shall not exceed one third of the amount of the contribution which under the Rules of the Union he shall be

required to contribute to the general funds of such County Branch or of his local or specialist Branch or of the Union.

(11) The first levy shall not come into force until the expiration of one month from the publication of the notice to members under sub-clause (3) hereof, nor shall any levy come into force as respects a new member until the expiration of one month from his being supplied with a copy of these Rules under sub-clause (13) hereof on admission to the Union.

(12) Contribution to the Political Fund of the Union shall not be made a condition for admission to the Union.

(13) The Council shall cause to be printed a number of copies of these Rules for the Political Fund of the Union having at the end copies of the certificate of approval sufficient for the members of the Union, and a further number for new members, and shall send to the Secretary of each Branch a number of copies sufficient for the members of the Branch. The Secretary of each Branch shall take steps to secure that every member of the Branch, so far as practicable, receives a copy of these Rules, and shall supply a copy to any member at his request. A copy thereof shall also be supplied forthwith to every new member on his admission to the Union.

(14) A return in respect to the Political Fund of the Union shall be transmitted by the Union to the Chief Registrar of Friendly Societies before the first day of June in every year, prepared and made up to such date and in such form and comprising such particulars as the Chief Registrar may from time to time require, and every member of the Union shall be entitled to receive a copy of such return, on application to the treasurer or secretary of the Union, without making any payment for the same.

(15) If any member alleges that he is aggrieved by a breach of any of these Rules for the Political Fund of the Union, he may complain to the Chief Registrar of Friendly Societies and the Chief Registrar, after giving the complainant and any representative of the Union an opportunity of being heard, may, if he considers that such a breach has been committed, make such order for remedying the breach as he thinks just in the circumstances; and any such order of the Chief Registrar shall be binding and conclusive on all parties without appeal and shall not be removable into any court of law or restrainable by injunction, and on being recorded in the County Court, may be enforced as if it had been an Order of the County Court.

3. *Ballot*

The following rules apply to any ballot taken for the purposes of the Trade Union Act, 1913.

(1) The Council shall cause to be printed a number of ballot papers in the form hereinafter provided equal to the number of the members of the Union, and a similar number of envelopes, on which latter shall be printed: 'Ballot Paper, The Scrutineers, National Farmers' Union' followed by the address of the general office, and shall cause a number of such ballot papers and envelopes equal to the number of the members of the Branch to be sent in due time to the Secretary of each Branch. On receipt of such ballot papers the Secretary shall at once stamp every ballot paper with the stamp of the Branch, or, if there be no such stamp, shall sign them, and no ballot paper shall be used for voting which is not so stamped or signed.

The Council shall also cause to be printed and supply to every Branch a number of copies of these ballot rules, having at the end copies of the certificate of approval sufficient for the purposes provided in sub-clause (6) and sub-clause (15) hereof.

(2) Every ballot paper shall be in the following form:—

TRADE UNION ACT, 1913
THE NATIONAL FARMERS' UNION

Do you vote in favour of the resolution approving the furtherance of political objects within the meaning of the Trade Union Act, 1913 (as set out on the back hereof), as an object of the above Union?

Stamp of Branch or signature	YES
of Branch Secretary	NO

You must place a cross, thus 'x' in one, and only one, of the two spaces provided above; otherwise your vote will not be counted.

You must not sign or make any other mark on the paper; if you do, your vote will not be counted.

On the back of every ballot paper the following shall be printed:

The political objects referred to are as follows. The expenditure of money:

(a) on the payment of any expenses incurred, either directly or indirectly, by a candidate or prospective candidate for election to Parliament, or to any public office, before, during, or after the election in connection with his candidature or election; or

(b) on the holding of any meeting or the distribution of any literature or documents in support of any such candidate or prospective candidate; or

(c) on the maintenance of any person who is a Member of Parliament or who holds a public office; or

(d) in connection with the registration of electors or the selection of a candidate for Parliament, or any public office; or

(e) on the holding of political meetings of any kind or on the distribution of political literature or political documents of any kind, unless the main purpose of the meetings or of the distribution of the literature or documents is the furtherance of statutory objects within the meaning of the Act – that is to say, the regulation of the relations between workmen and masters, or between workmen and workmen, or between masters and masters, or the imposing of restrictive conditions on the conduct of any trade or business, and also the provision of benefits to members.

The expression 'public office' in the above means the office of member of any County, County Borough, District or Parish Council or of any public body who have power to raise money, either directly or indirectly, by means of a rate . . .

(17) The Council shall appoint three members of the Union, who are not members of the Council to be scrutineers, and at the date and time appointed for the counting of the votes the scrutineers shall destroy any ballot papers at the general office which have not been used for voting, and shall then open the envelopes and count the votes in the presence of the President of the Union, the General Secretary and as many members of the Council as desire to attend.

The scrutineers, or a majority of them, shall decide whether any ballot paper shall be rejected as being invalid under sub-clause (3) hereof, and shall forthwith separate any paper so rejected and mark it, 'Rejected'.

The scrutineers shall add up to the total number of votes given for and against, and the total number of votes rejected, and the result shall be certified on two forms of return supplied by the Chief Registrar of Friendly Societies, signed by the scrutineers, the President of the Council and the General Secretary. One of these returns shall be forthwith posted up, and kept posted up, in a conspicuous place accessible to members at the general office of the Union for at least one month, and the others shall be forthwith sent to the Chief Registrar of Friendly Societies.

A copy of such return shall be printed in the next available issue of the journal, report, or other periodical publication of the Union, if any, and a copy shall be sent forthwith to the Secretary of each Branch, and shall be handed by him for perusal to any member at his request.

(18) As soon as the result has been certified as aforesaid, the President of the Union shall secure the ballot papers which have been counted and those which have been rejected, respectively, in two sealed packets, and shall forthwith deposit them with the Union's trust securities, and keep them so deposited for six months. During that time they shall be open to inspection by the Chief Registrar of Friendly Societies or any person or persons authorized in writing by him, and shall, at his written request, be sent to his office. At the end of six months they shall be destroyed by or under the supervision of the President of the Union and the General Secretary.

FORM 12

TRADE UNION ACT, 1913

Certificate under Section 2 (3)

No. 18 C.T.

I HEREBY CERTIFY that the National Farmers' Union is a Trade Union within the meaning of the above Act.

Given this 19th day of January, 1921.

G. STUART ROBERTSON
Copy kept   *Chief Registrar*

FORM 14A

TRADE UNION ACT, 1913

Certificate of Approval of Political Fund Rules

NATIONAL FARMERS' UNION (Register No. 18C.T.)

I hereby approve the rules for the political fund of the above Union contained in the foregoing rules for the purposes of Section 3 (1) of the Trade Union Act, 1913.

Given this 19th day of August, 1959.

CECIL CRABBE
Copy kept   *Chief Registrar*

78
The National Farmers' Union: the leadership, 1965
Observer, 21 March 1965

Sir Harold Woolley's illness has set followers of agricultural politics wondering. Who could take over the N.F.U.?

The farmers' union is the best-organized and most successful lobby in the country. The Government treats it as sole interpreter of the farmers' wishes. All political parties cultivate it with care. Its links with Whitehall are very close – thanks to years of horse-trading over the Annual Price Review.

This great machine is a post-war development – and since the war it has in effect been driven by only four men. Three of them are still at the controls.

It began with a palace revolution in 1945. Until then, the N.F.U. had had annual presidents. That year the forty-two-year-old President, Ken Knowles, stepped down to become general secretary and the forceful Jim Turner became President. Turner stayed until 1960; Knowles is still there.

Two years later, the Agriculture Act set up the annual price-review system – a system so complicated, with its subsidies and grants and guarantees, that only a handful of people can possibly understand it.

One man who does is Asher Winegarten, an L.S.E. graduate (two Firsts in commerce and economics) and the union's chief economist since 1947.

Between them Turner the statesman, Knowles the tough administrator and Winegarten the expert and obdurate negotiator were a powerful force for no-change in agricultural policy – all the stronger because Turner determinedly kept out of party politics. Turner retired to quieter, better fertilized fields in 1960, as Lord Netherthorpe, the chairman of Fisons, and Harold Woolley took over.

And the union stayed very much a three-man show. People who have dealt with him have been heard to say: 'Woolley by name and woolly by . . .', but they quickly add: 'very formidable'. With the Government, he's been a long-winded and stubborn negotiator. Inside the union, he has made the decisions himself, using Winegarten's expertise and backed by the elder statesmen on the Council. He hasn't delegated a thing, not even, so they say, his great knowledge.

After fifteen years of Turner and five of Woolley, it is hard to see a successor. The fifty-one-year-old deputy president, Gwilym Tecwyn Williams – known as Bill – has been running things efficiently since Woolley's illness, and is a possible candidate. He is nice, calm, and experienced at the technicalities of the price review.

Or there are bright young men on their way up – notably thirty-nine-year-old Henry Plumb, a boyish-looking dairy farmer from Birmingham, who is on the important presidents' committee.

The decision can be put off – Woolley is expected back in charge at Agriculture House, the N.F.U.'s monstrosity in Knightsbridge, in a couple of months. But unless he trains up a successor, his eventual departure will leave the future structure of the rock-like N.F.U. interestingly uncertain.

79
The Country Landowners' Association: Objects and Rules 1970

TITLE

1. The title of the Association shall be *The Country Landowners' Association*.

OBJECTS

2. The objects and aims of the Association are:

(a) To be an Association of owners of agricultural and other rural land formed to promote and safeguard their legitimate interests so far as is consistent with the interests of the nation.

(b) To safeguard and develop the capital invested in the ownership of agricultural and other rural land (hereafter referred to as 'land') and to secure an appropriate return from these assets.

MEMBERSHIP

3. The following persons are eligible as Members of the Association:

(a) All owners of freehold land, not being urban land only, and their legal personal representatives

(b) A member of the family of an owner as defined in paragraph (a), where the owner is a Member

(c) The Trustees of settled land

(d) Corporate Bodies owning freehold land

(e) Partnerships in which one or more partners own land

(f) A tenant for Life of land who is not otherwise eligible

(g) A person (hereinafter called a Professional Member) whose professional or business activities are closely connected with agricultural or other rural land, and who is accepted by the Council for membership but does not otherwise qualify for membership under this Rule

(h) Trust Corporations, Banks, Insurance Companies and other bodies (who do not otherwise qualify for membership under this Rule) interested in the objects of the Association

(j) A Member who has divested himself of his land, but has elected to remain a Member, and

(k) Any other person whom the Council shall resolve to admit as a Member.

4. Any Members being Trustees, a Corporate Body or a Partnership shall respectively nominate one trustee, director or principal shareholder, or partner to have all the powers, duties and obligations of a Member.

5. Application for Membership shall be made in writing to the Secretary-General and shall be accompanied by such information as the Council may from time to time require to be furnished, such information to be verified in such manner as the Council may prescribe.

6. The election of Members shall be at the discretion of the Council and by any method they may decide to adopt.

Resignation

7. A Member may withdraw from the Association at any time by sending in his written resignation to the Secretary-General; the unexpired portion of a year's subscription shall not be repayable on resignation.

Expulsion

8. If it shall appear to the Council that any Member has been guilty of conduct rendering him unfit to remain a Member of the Association, the Council shall call upon him for an explanation or justification; and if no explanation or justification is given, or if the explanation is not, in their opinion, satisfactory, the Council may by resolution (passed by a two thirds majority of those present and voting) exclude him from the Association.

Subscriptions

9. (a) Every Member shall pay such minimum annual subscription as shall be in accordance with the scale of subscriptions from time to time approved and published by the Council after consultation with the Branches.

(b) A Member who is also an ordinary Member of the Timber Growers' Organization Limited shall, in determining the acreage of land on which his C.L.A. subscription is calculated, be entitled to leave out of account the woodland acreage in respect of which his current subscription to the Timber Growers' Organization Limited is paid. This concession shall apply to his C.L.A. subscription falling due on the same date as or next after the current T.G.O. subscription becomes due.

(c) A Member shall declare the total acreage of land he owns in England and Wales and, subject to his right to leave out of account the woodland acreage, to which paragraph (b) of this Rule refers, he shall pay the appropriate subscription therefor.

(d) The Council shall at their discretion have power to accept a rate of subscription lower than that published under paragraph (a) of this Rule.

10. A Member shall not be entitled to any of the privileges of Membership of the Association until he shall have paid his first annual subscription. If this is not paid within one month of his receiving notice of his election, the Council shall have power to declare the election void.

11. Annual subscriptions shall be due and payable in accordance with regulations to be promulgated from time to time by the Council. All subscriptions shall be paid to the Association in such manner as the Council shall from time to time direct.

12. In the event of any Member failing to pay his annual subscription when it has become due, his attention shall forthwith be drawn to the fact; and if he fails to pay it within three months of its becoming due, he shall be deemed to be in arrear, and shall be excluded from the Association at the discretion of the Council and in accordance with the procedure prescribed by them.

13. In the event of the Association incurring unusual expenditure in connection with a question affecting a limited number of Members only, such expenditure, or such portion of it as may be decided by the Council, may be met by an additional voluntary levy on the Members so affected.

The Council

14. The Association shall be managed by a Council comprising:

(a) The President, and the Deputy President, duly elected in accordance with Rule 15

(b) Representative Members elected by the Branches under the provisions of Rule 39 or nominated by the Council under Rule 20

(c) Not more than twelve Nominated Members appointed under Rule 18

(d) Not more than six individuals invited to represent the Institutional Members of the Association

(e) Past Presidents of the Association, and

(f) Trustees of the Association appointed under Rule 36.

15. A President and a Deputy President shall be elected from amongst the members of the Council at the relevant Annual

General Meeting to hold office for one year and shall only be eligible for re-election to the same office for one further year. They shall be ineligible for re-election to the same office for three years after ceasing to hold such office.

16. In the event of the death or resignation of the President during his term of office, the Deputy President shall thereupon become President for the remainder of his predecessor's term. Nevertheless he shall, at the conclusion of that term, be eligible for election and re-election under Rule 15.

17. The Council shall have power to fill any casual vacancy in the office of Deputy President.

Election of Council

18. At the meeting of the Council held before the Annual General Meeting of the Association in every year the Council may select by such method as they may decide, not more than twelve Members of the Association as Nominated Members of the Council for the next ensuing year. The names of the Nominated Members so selected shall be announced at the next following Annual General Meeting of the Association, and they shall thereupon become Members of the Council. They shall hold office for one year, and be eligible for renomination.

19. Representative Members (as provided in Rule 39) shall be elected at the Annual General Meeting of their respective Branches which shall have taken place not later than fourteen days before the date of the Association's Annual General Meeting. Their term of office shall commence immediately after election and they shall hold office for three years. They shall be eligible for re-election . . .

80
National Allotments and Gardens Society Ltd and Village Produce Associations

(a) Town and Country Planning Act, 1968
(*Bulletin*, October 1968)
(b) the Common Market (Annual Report, 1967–8)

(a)

AN ACT TO CONTROL PLANNING

A new Act, the Town and Country Planning Act, 1968, will shortly hit unsuspecting allotment-holders. It has some good points and at least one very bad one so far as we are concerned.

One good point: if planning permission is given and no action is taken within five years to use that permission the land reverts to its former notation on the Town Map. Such a clause could have helped many allotment societies who have seen their land go to education or housing only to lie derelict for many years against all efforts to bring it back into productive use. The planning permission would never have been sought, if education or housing committees had known that their inability to develop the land within a reasonable time was going to damn their arguments about the urgency of their claims.

Now a very bad point: planning decisions will be decentralized. County and County Borough planning officers will be in supreme control over planning applications in their own area. There are a few good planning officers who seek to weigh the merits of every case very fairly to ensure that a proper balance is maintained in the public interest, but there are far too many bad ones as Professor John Rex told them at their summer school. He said that the social implications of their actions were important and that they must try to get rid of their own naïve and partial view of life.

One of the last speeches of Mr Niall MacDermot, Minister of State at the Ministry of Housing and Local Government, to the Institute of Landscape Architects, emphasized that the modern developments having large areas of lawns, communal open space and garage forecourts stressed the need to consider who would pay for all the fancy planning.

What it amounts [to] is that we have not got a perfect planning system and the efforts of the many committees to get better planning and more public participation are useless unless there is some control from the top. We are sceptical of some of the much lauded ideas for telling the public what is happening by the use of expensive models and much high-class paper-work. The public could not care less. To put too much power in the hands of too many planners is, therefore, to deny to the more responsible citizen the right to the final arbitration of a govern- ment inspired inquiry. There was nothing wrong with the old idea of an independent inspector listening to the arguments of those affected by planning proposals. It did at least give the layman one of his very few opportunities of challenging erudite Counsel on level terms. The success of ordinary people in reversing deci- sions of planning authorities proves the point.

(b)

. . . The upsurge of interest in the Common Market moved Leicester A. & G.C. to ask for a campaign to offset the expected

14 per cent rise in the cost of food. By coincidence we learned from our continental friends what housewives were paying for the kind of vegetable crops normally grown on allotments and to our surprise we found that they were costing some 47½ per cent more than was being paid for similar crops by British housewives. We later had an opportunity to verify this figure with information provided by our delegates to the meeting of the International League of Allotment Societies in Luxembourg.

We seized on this to write to the Prime Minister and the Minister for Economic Affairs, who passed our letter on to the Minister of Agriculture, and to the press. The latter responded well, not so parliamentarians who agreed that prices would rise but that 'the 47½ per cent increase for vegetables which you envisage would be most unlikely to occur at all widely'. This suggests that there was some basis for agreement on our point that many vegetables that can be grown on gardens will cost a great deal more than the anticipated 14 per cent.

The Prime Minister's Secretary said that 'The more fundamental criticism is that the average British housewife buys much greater quantities of potatoes and of tomatoes than of spring cabbage, cauliflowers and lettuce. The suggested increase in her grocery bill could, therefore, be calculated only on a weighted basis.' Whether it was a weakness in the wording of the resolution or a misconstrued meaning attached to it by the Prime Minister the fact remains that the suggestion that 'all possible measures be taken by the Government and local authorities to make the maximum use of all our allotment land and supplement the gardeners' efforts to assist the National economy by achieving record home food production' was completely ignored . . .

81
Trades Union Congress

(a) Rules, 1970; (b) Structure and functions reviewed, 1970;
(c) Summary of statistical statement, 1970

(a)

RULES AND STANDING ORDERS

Part I: Constitution

Rule 1 Name, Office and Membership

(a) *Name and Office.* The name of the organization constituted by these Rules shall be the 'Trades Union Congress' (hereinafter called 'the Congress'), and its principal office shall be at Congress House, 23–8 Great Russell Street, London WC1B 3LS, or such other place as the General Council of the Congress (hereinafter called 'the General Council') shall from time to time decide.

(b) *Membership*: The Congress shall consist of such bona fide trade union organizations as shall be affiliated in the manner prescribed by these Rules.

Any such organization may make application to become affiliated to Congress and shall furnish copies of its Rules or Constitution together with such other particulars and information as shall be required by the General Council.

The General Council shall have full power to accept or reject any such application subject to the power of the next Annual Congress to overrule any such decision.

Rule 2 Objects

(a) The objects of the Congress shall be:

To do anything to promote the interests of all or any of its affiliated organizations or anything beneficial to the interests of past and present individual members of such organizations.

Generally to improve the economic or social conditions of workers in all parts of the world and to render them assistance whether or not such workers are employed or have ceased to be employed.

To affiliate to or subscribe to or to assist any other organization having objects similar to those of the Congress.

To assist in the complete organization of all workers eligible for membership of its affiliated organizations and subject as hereinafter set forth in these Rules to settle disputes between the members of such organizations and their employers or between such organizations and their members or between the organizations themselves.

In pursuance of such objects the Congress may do or authorize to be done all such acts and things as it considers necessary for the furtherance of those objects and in particular shall endeavour to establish the following measures and such others as any Annual Congress may approve:

Public Ownership and control of natural resources and of services—

Nationalization of land, mines and minerals.

Nationalization of railways . . .

Rule 5 *Qualification for General Council*

(a) No candidate shall be eligible for election on the General Council unless he is a delegate (as per Rules 17 and 18) and the organization so represented shall have paid the fees provided by Rule 3 during the year previous to his or her election.

(b) No candidate shall be eligible for election on the General Council who has privately assisted, during the year preceding the Annual Congress, in the production of anything made by non-union labour, or by such firms as may be declared unfair by the interested trade society, or who has continued to assist privately in the production of anything made by non-union labour, or by such firms as may be declared unfair by the interested trade society, after such matters have been pointed out to him or her.

Rule 6 *Nomination of General Council*

(a) Each affiliated organization shall have the right to nominate candidates to represent it in its Group on the General Council.

(b) Organizations which include women members shall, in addition, have the right to nominate one woman member for the General Council, subject to the provisions of Rule 5.

(c) All nominations for the General Council shall be sent to the General Secretary at least seven weeks prior to each Annual Congress, and the list of names shall be published on the agenda paper containing the propositions that are to be discussed at the Annual Congress. If, however, a candidate dies before the election takes place, the General Council shall have power to authorize the acceptance of fresh nominations from the unions in the Group to which the affiliated organization which nominated such candidate belongs, anything in these Rules and Standing Orders notwithstanding. Ballot papers containing the names of such candidates shall be supplied to delegates on the day of election.

(d) Where, due to the withdrawal of a candidate before election or to any other cause, there is an insufficiency of candidates to fill the number of seats in the Group concerned, the General Council shall have power to call for fresh nominations from the unions in such Group, anything in these Rules and Standing Orders notwithstanding.

Rule 7 *Election of General Council*

(a) The General Council shall be elected by ballot vote at each Annual Congress, the nominees in each Group securing the

highest number of votes to be declared elected. Delegates shall
not be permitted to cast votes on any ballot paper for a number of
candidates in excess of the number of persons required to be
elected.

(b) Canvassing or the bartering of votes for any position or
purpose shall be strictly forbidden. Any candidate on whose
behalf such means are employed shall be disqualified for election
to any position at that Congress and at any subsequent Congress
for a period of three years unless it can be proved to the satisfaction of the General Council that he or she was in no way responsible for the infringement of this Rule.

(c) The ballot papers shall be issued by the Scrutineers, and
after being filled up shall then be immediately placed in the box
without inspection by the delegates other than those of the
organization voting.

(d) Any delegates found guilty of violating this Rule shall at
once be reported to Congress, named by the President and expelled. Such delegate or delegates shall not be eligible to attend
Congress again for three years.

(e) A notification of the penalties likely to be involved in the
infringement of this Rule shall be included in the instructions
printed on each ballot paper.

Rule 8 *Duties of General Council*

(a) The General Council shall transact the business in the
periods between each Annual Congress, shall keep a watch on all
industrial movements, and shall, where possible, co-ordinate
industrial action.

(b) They shall watch all legislation affecting labour, and shall
initiate such legislation as Congress may direct.

(c) They shall endeavour to adjust disputes and differences
between affiliated organizations.

(d) They shall promote common action by the Trade Union
Movement on general questions, such as wages and hours of
labour, and any matter of general concern that may arise between
trade unions and trade unions, or between employers and trade
unions, or between the Trade Union Movement and the Government, and shall have power to assist any union which is attacked
on any vital question of trade union principle.

(e) They shall assist trade unions in the work of organization,
and shall carry on propaganda with a view to strengthening the
Trade Union Movement, and for the attainment of any or all of
the above objects.

(f) They shall also enter into relations with the Trade Union and Labour Movements in other countries with a view to securing united action.

(g) They shall have authority to invest and administer the funds of the Congress and to make grants to any organization or person, whether in Great Britain or abroad, for such purpose as it seems desirable, but in so doing they shall have regard to the directions, if any, from time to time given by Congress. They shall also have authority to raise funds for any special purpose and to invest and administer such funds and to make grants therefrom.

(h) For the purpose of carrying out the objects of the Congress, of conducting its affairs and in relation to the matters specifically referred to in this Rule the General Council shall have power to utilize the funds and property of the Congress, to enter into any transaction and by any one or more of their members to execute in the name and on behalf of the Congress any deeds or documents that may be necessary.

(i) The General Council shall have power whenever they deem necessary to convene a Special Congress or Conference to deal with any contingency that may arise, and to arrange the agenda and procedure whereby the business of such meetings shall be conducted.

(j) In the event of a legal point arising which in the opinion of the General Council (after consultation with Counsel) should be tested in the House of Lords in the general interests of trade unionism, the Council shall be empowered to levy the affiliated societies *pro rata* to provide the necessary expenses. Any society failing to pay the levy shall be reported to Congress.

(k) In order that the Trade Union Movement may do everything which lies in its power to prevent future wars, the General Council shall, in the event of there being a danger of an outbreak of war, call a Special Congress to decide on industrial action, such Congress to be called, if possible, before war is declared.

(l) The General Council shall prepare a Report of their work for submission to the Annual Meeting of Congress. The Report shall contain a list of the General Council meetings with dates, and also names of those members who were present at such meetings. The Standing Orders of Congress, and the General Council shall be published with each Annual Report of the proceedings of Congress.

Rule 9 *Appointment of Committees*

Special Committees shall be appointed by the General Council to deal with any questions which may arise from time to time.

Rule 10 *General Secretary*

(a) The General Secretary shall be elected by Congress, and shall be *ex officio* a member of the Congress and the General Council. His salary and conditions of service shall be determined by the General Council. He shall remain in office so long as his work and conduct give satisfaction to the General Council and to the representatives attending Congress, and shall be provided with all necessary clerical assistance, office accommodation and facilities for conducting the business of the Congress and the General Council.

(b) Should a vacancy occur between the annual meetings of the Congress the General Council shall have power to fill such a vacancy temporarily.

Rule 11 *Industrial Disputes*

(a) It shall be an obligation upon the affiliated organizations to keep the General Council informed with regard to matters arising as between them and employers, and/or between one organization and another, including unauthorized and unconstitutional stoppages of work, in particular where such matters may involve directly or indirectly large bodies of workers. The General Council shall, if they deem necessary, disseminate the information as soon as possible to all organizations which are affiliated to the Congress, and which may be either directly or indirectly affected.

(b) The general policy of the General Council shall be that unless requested to do so by the affiliated organization or organizations concerned, the Council shall not intervene so long as there is a prospect of whatever difference may exist on the matters in question being amicably settled by means of the machinery of negotiation existing in the trades affected.

(c) If, however, a situation has arisen, or is likely to arise, in which other bodies of workpeople affiliated to Congress might be involved in a stoppage of work or their wages, hours and conditions of employment imperilled the General Council may take the initiative by calling representatives of the organization into consultation, and use their influence to effect a just settlement of the difference. In this connection the Council, having ascertained all the facts relating to the difference, may tender their considered opinion and advice thereon to the organization or organizations concerned. Should the organization or organizations refuse the assistance or advice of the Council, the General Council shall duly report to Congress or deal with the organization under Clauses (b), (c), (d) and (h) of Rule 13.

(d) Where the Council intervenes, as herein provided, and the organization or organizations concerned accept the assistance and advice of the Council, and where despite the efforts of the Council, the policy of the employers enforces a stoppage of work by strike or lock-out, the Council shall forthwith take steps to organize on behalf of the organization or organizations concerned all such moral and material support as the circumstances of the dispute may appear to justify.

Rule 12 *Disputes between Affiliated Organizations*

(a) Where disputes arise, or threaten to arise, between affiliated organizations, the General Council shall use their influence to promote a settlement.

(b) It shall be an obligation on the affiliated organization or organizations concerned to notify the General Council when an official stoppage of work is contemplated in any dispute between affiliated organizations whether relating to trade union recognition, trade union membership, demarcation of work or any other difficulty.

(c) No affiliated organization shall authorize such a stoppage of work until the dispute has been considered by the General Council, as provided by Clause (f) of this Rule.

(d) Where a dispute between unions has led to an unauthorized stoppage of work, it shall be an obligation on the affiliated organization or organizations concerned to take immediate and energetic steps to obtain a resumption of work.

(e) The affiliated organization or organizations concerned shall notify the General Council as soon as possible of any stoppage of work which involves directly or indirectly large bodies of workers, or which if protracted may have serious consequences. In addition to such notification, the affiliated organization or organizations concerned shall inform the General Council of the causes and circumstances of the dispute and of the steps they have taken, or are taking, to secure a resumption of work.

(f) Upon notification from an affiliated organization, as required by Clauses (b) and (e) of this Rule, or upon the application of an affiliated organization, or when they deem necessary, the General Council shall have the power to investigate cases of dispute or disagreement between affiliated organizations and to refer such cases to the Disputes Committee.

(g) If the parties to a dispute fail to submit the case to the Disputes Committee of the General Council as provided by this Rule, it shall not be permissible for such dispute to be raised at any Annual Congress.

(h) The General Council shall have power to summon the contending affiliated organizations to appear before the Disputes Committee of the General Council, and to require such organizations to submit all evidence and information that the Disputes Committee may deem essential to enable it to adjudicate upon the case.

(i) If the result of such an inquiry be that the complaining organization fails to prove the charge, it shall bear the whole cost of the investigation including the expenses incurred by the defending organization.

(b)

STRUCTURE AND DEVELOPMENT
Interim Report to Congress

1. The basic reason for engaging in a re-examination of the T.U.C.'s functions and structure is that the environment in which unions operate is changing, and that these changes also require changes on the part of unions.

2. In the last twenty years there has been no significant increase in the number of workpeople, or in the proportion of the workforce, organized in trade unions. There have however been significant changes in trade union membership in different industries – marked declines in mining, railways, textiles and steel for example, and marked increases in trade union membership in the public services and among professional, technical, scientific, supervisory and clerical workers. Relatively high levels of employment and a marked increase in the rate of technological change have had a significant impact on industrial relations including collective bargaining. There has been a shift towards plant and office-level bargaining which has to some extent reinforced, but has often developed as an alternative to, industry-wide bargaining. The increasing diversity of members' needs and the changes in bargaining-patterns and levels have necessitated changes in the structure of unions, in the services they provide and in their administrative methods.

3. It emerged clearly from the discussion at the 1969 Congress and from the comments by unions that trade unions currently attach high priority to making themselves more representative, to improving and rationalizing collective bargaining, and to making such structural changes as are needed to achieve these ends. The instruction by Congress to the T.U.C. to review its own structure and establish a new pattern for future development reflected the growing attention that unions are giving to

finding solutions for their own problems. This report examines how this is to be done and, in particular, what help the T.U.C. can give. It takes as its theme that the best way in which progress can be made is to build on the best of what has been achieved, rather than by making radical and abrupt changes for their own sake.

The role of the T.U.C.

4. Congress itself is responsible for laying down broad lines of policy, and for exercising such authority over the constituent unions as they have delegated to it. The General Council, guided by their functional Committees and advisory bodies and Conferences, apply and interpret that policy between Congresses. Congress is and must always be the ultimate policy-making body, but as the formulation and administration of policy have become more closely interwoven the ability of Congress to initiate and to innovate has declined. This has been accompanied by a corresponding growth in the responsibility of the General Council. Even so the General Council must command the confidence of Congress: the policies they propose and pursue must be seen clearly by Congress to be well-conceived and thus to be worthy of endorsement and support.

5. The T.U.C. is primarily concerned with developing policy rather than with acting as an executive body. It provides a means through which unions can collectively achieve objectives which they cannot achieve, or which it would be difficult for them to achieve, separately. It identifies things which unions should be doing, but which for one reason or another they are not doing, and stimulates them to take the necessary action. It reminds individual unions or groups of unions of their duty to take into account the interests of other unions, and the broader interests of trade unionists as a whole. It thus establishes standards of good trade union practice. These are its internal functions. Externally, it represents the movement to the Government and other outside organizations, asserting the independence of the trade union movement and the right of trade unionists to a share in decisions which affect them, accepting the corresponding obligations and reminding unions of those obligations, and when necessary defending particular unions against external bodies.

6. The basic fact that the Executive Committees of unions are accountable to their members means that for most practical purposes unions must be autonomous. This is however compatible with leadership of their members by Executives and with leader-

ship of the movement by the T.U.C., and it is consistent with unions taking a broader view of the interests of working people than might be dictated by unqualified concern with the immediate interests of their own membership. But it means that the authority of the T.U.C. must, with clearly specified and justified exceptions, be defined in terms of influence, not of power. The T.U.C.'s authority derives from a willingness by unions, and by their members, to abide by decisions to which they are parties. The role of the T.U.C. is to facilitate the reaching of agreed decisions by democratic processes. Where it has the right to compel unions to adhere to decisions it is because unions themselves have collectively given it that right.

7. The T.U.C. is inevitably distant from the branch room and from the shop and office. That can be a weakness but it can also be a strength. It is a weakness if it leads to an inadequate understanding of the reality of the industrial situation as it appears to the men and women in the factory and the office. It is a strength in so far as the T.U.C. – and especially the General Council – can take a more objective view based on a wide range of considerations and can make a longer-term assessment of prospective developments. The T.U.C. has the perennial problem of reconciling the special interests of particular unions, or groups of members, with the general interests of the trade union movement, and of deciding when which set of interests should prevail. This has on occasion led the T.U.C. to make general statements which, because they are capable of different interpretations, offend none and are minimally acceptable to all. A propensity not to offend and not to appear to be interfering with union autonomy has historically often led the T.U.C. to eschew taking initiatives.

8. Recent years however have seen marked changes in all these respects. More emphasis has been put on the T.U.C.'s job of drawing conclusions for action from the experiences of unions (e.g. in *Programme for Action*); on becoming involved in particular industrial and economic situations (e.g. in relation to the steel industry and the industries with Economic Development Committees, and in wages developments); and on stimulating action by unions (e.g. in amalgamations, trade union training, and spheres of influence). The T.U.C. has been extending the range of its services to unions, has been establishing standards of good trade union practice over a wide area, has been intervening in more specific ways for defined purposes, and has been exercising more initiative in the field of industrial relations. It is in these directions that progress can best be made. This report examines

how the T.U.C. can help unions to become more representative, to improve their effectiveness in collective bargaining, and to use their resources more efficiently; and what changes this would require in the structure and functions of the T.U.C. itself.

Increasing the representative capacity of unions

9. Becoming more representative involves unions both in recruiting and holding more members and also in ensuring that their policies reflect the needs and the views of their members.

10. For the purpose of identifying target areas for recruitment it would be helpful if unions knew more accurately than at present the proportions of their members who are working in different industries, and the proportion of the organizable workers that they have in membership in each industry. Unions should examine the pattern of distribution of their membership in order, as a minimum, to identify situations where with relatively little effort a high existing degree of membership can be built up to and held at 100 per cent.

11. More unions are now adopting the check-off as a means of ensuring maintenance of membership. The General Council intend to examine the extent and the nature of existing check-off systems and to make the information available to unions. Unions might also study the cost to them of recruiting new members, and also the cost of short-term membership, particularly in the light of the fact that more frequent changing of occupations has implications for the turnover of trade union membership.

12. The 1969 Congress resolution called for co-ordination through the T.U.C. of trade union activity in extending membership recruitment in unorganized areas.

13. The General Council have already initiated through their Organization Committee a study of what help the T.U.C. might give in this field. As the next step they have decided to conduct a pilot scheme with the unions involved in a particular area of weak organization. The scheme will entail a detailed examination of the potential membership in the area in question; the resources of the union; and possible methods of conducting a recruitment campaign. The unions in conjunction with the T.U.C. will draw up the physical plans for the campaign. If the proposed experiment is successful similar exercises can be carried out elsewhere, but in any case much should be learned which can be of value in pointing the way ahead.

Recognition

14. Establishment of an adequate degree of organization is itself the best guarantee of securing recognition. Even so, in some situations evidence that the union has recognition or will be able to win it if it can secure enough members may well be a necessary basis for organizing. The power of the Commission on Industrial Relations to examine complaints by unions that they are unreasonably being refused recognition should be of assistance to unions both in specific cases and in changing the attitudes of other employers. Nevertheless, this will not give an 'open sesame' to recognition, and unions will still need to combat the reactionary attitudes of some employers. In doing so they have the right to look to the T.U.C. for assistance. The T.U.C. might be able to help by approaching the Confederation of British Industry to put pressure on a firm if it is in membership of the C.B.I. Where the C.B.I. is unwilling or unable to help, the T.U.C. may, if it is satisfied that the union has established its claim and that recognition would not lead to inter-union difficulties, consider giving assistance more directly to the union. This might take the form of a direct approach to the employer, or of asking other unions concerned for their assistance. As a last resort the T.U.C. has the right in exceptional circumstances of sponsoring an appeal by a union for financial assistance from other unions. Obviously assistance cannot be given unconditionally by the T.U.C. Intervention by the T.U.C. is only warranted if in its judgement an important principle is at stake, and that it is not possible for the union to secure recognition by other means.

Inter-union relations and closer working between unions

15. In their replies to the T.U.C. circular, unions laid emphasis on the need to avoid the haphazard growth of multi-unionism and 'catch-as-catch-can' organizing. It is unlikely that inter-union rivalry is a serious impediment to recruitment – indeed it can stimulate recruitment – though it may have an effect on some trade unions' finances by holding down the level of contributions. Although inter-union rivalry is sometimes advanced by employers as an excuse for refusing recognition it is doubtful whether it has much significance in this connection. It is, however, desirable to eliminate such competition in order to avoid the waste of trade union organizing resources and to prevent friction between unions.

16. The Bridlington Principles already provide a code of conduct for unions, and in approving the changes to Rule 12 the

special and ordinary Congresses held in 1969 endorsed the General Council's view that failure by unions to reconcile their disputes peacefully was a matter of concern to the movement as a whole. The General Council intend to examine, in the light of their experience, whether the Bridlington Principles or the powers or practices of Disputes Committees, need to be changed.

17. However useful these arrangements may be as methods of settling disputes between unions, they are at best ways of solving problems that should never have arisen. One proposal that has been made for avoiding conflicts between unions is that where a new opportunity for organization appears, the T.U.C. should be empowered to determine, after consulting unions which have a prima facie interest, which unions should have the right to recruit. The General Council do not doubt that in the vast majority of cases agreement could be reached between unions, and their role would consist of bringing unions together and providing such services as might be needed, as they have recently done in connection with the organization of university non-academic staffs and of staffs of training boards. There may be cases in future where it is impossible to achieve a mutually agreed settlement, but the General Council believe that, rather than propose a change of rule forthwith to empower them to make a determination in such instances, it would be better to proceed on the assumption that this will not be necessary, and to report to Congress if they consider that the need for such a change has arisen.

18. A growing number of unions have set up bilateral or in some cases multilateral machinery for resolving disputes between themselves. This is a wholly desirable development in which the General Council are taking an active interest and, following a survey of existing inter-union procedures and spheres of influence agreements, they have written to affiliated unions recommending them to review their arrangements with other unions with whom they are in frequent contact. The circular reminded unions of the advantages of developing procedures for resolving particular issues and also specific arrangements concerning spheres of influence, transfers of members and benefit rights, recognition of cards, and demarcation of work. The General Council will be reviewing the progress made by unions in reaching agreements, particularly in areas of special difficulty.

19. The main stimulus to closer working is the need to agree on bargaining objectives in forthcoming wage negotiations. This is

discussed in more detail in the following section, but a related aspect is the desirability of unions meeting regularly to determine, in the light of prospective changes in their industries, longer-term strategy for recruitment, organizational development and the provision of services to members. In some industries, Federations and the trade union sides of National Joint Councils provide basic machinery which could be developed more systematically in this direction, but it is clear from the replies of many unions that they consider that the functions and activities of these bodies need to be reviewed. In some cases these reviews might extend to examining whether there is unnecessary duplication in cognate N.J.C.s and whether they might be combined to provide more effective bargaining units.

20. One subject which was broached in Resolution 22 of the 1969 Congress is whether unions should adopt standard practices in relation to benefits and protection of membership rights on the transfer of members. This issue is not confined to transfers of members within the same industry, and it can be argued that the need for such protection is more likely to arise in the case of trade unionists who move from one industry to another, but broadly the same considerations apply in both situations. Two proposals for achieving this have been put to the General Council. The first is that the transferring union should continue to treat the member as a full member until the receiving union can accept him into full benefit, and the second is that the receiving union should accept as a full member an applicant who has been in membership of another affiliated union for a reasonable period. There is a prima facie case for saying that, if a member who has to transfer through no fault of his own is to have accelerated entry into full membership, whatever special obligations are involved should lie on the receiving rather than on the transferring union, as he represents an addition to the strength of the receiving union. The member should however have been in compliance for a stipulated period, and the transfer should, of course, be in accordance with the Bridlington Principles. As was mentioned earlier the General Council have recommended unions to develop arrangements for the transfer of members and benefit rights and they have asked their Organization Committee to examine the implications of these specific proposals.

21. Apart from the possibility of establishing Industrial Committees, examined later in this report, the General Council are, through the medium of the Collective Bargaining Committee, in

the process of defining cognate groupings of unions which might be brought together to discuss common problems in the negotiating field. It might be possible to use the same machinery to promote discussion of closer working generally.

(c)

SUMMARY OF STATISTICAL STATEMENT

Trade group	No. of unions	No. of delegates	Membership	Affiliation fees £ s. d.
1. Mining and Quarrying	3	65	321,940	24,145 10 0
2. Railways	3	40	290,111	21,758 6 6
3. Transport (other than Railways)	9	97	1,656,804	124,260 6 0
4. Shipbuilding	3	13	124,153	9,311 9 6
5. Engineering, Founding and Vehicle-Building	13	96	1,465,691	109,926 16 6
6. Technical Engineering and Scientific	5	38	242,640	18,198 0 0
7. Electricity	1	34	392,401	29,430 1 6
8. Iron and Steel and Minor Metal Trades	12	35	151,786	11,383 19 0
9. Building, Woodworking and Furnishing	9	58	380,536	28,540 4 0
10. Printing and Paper	6	64	391,765	29,382 7 6
11. Textiles	25	44	148,470	11,135 5 0
12. Clothing, Leather and Boot and Shoe	10	51	260,662	19,549 13 0
13. Glass, Pottery, Chemicals, Food, Drink, Tobacco, Brush-Making and Distribution	11	67	455,532	34,164 18 0
14. Agriculture	1	19	115,000	8,625 0 0
15. Public Employees	11	126	1,200,740	68,272 10 0
16. Civil Servants	14	97	657,808	49,138 19 0
17. Professional, Clerical and Entertainment	12	54	338,278	25,370 17 0
18. General Workers	2	62	807,853	60,588 19 6
	150	1,060	9,402,170	*£683,183 2 0

*Fees payable in respect of the Financial Year ended 31 December 1969.
Total membership includes 7,233,902 men and 2,168,268 women members.

82
British Medical Association: Objects and Membership

Memorandum of Association
of the
BRITISH MEDICAL ASSOCIATION

1. The name of the Association is the 'British Medical Association'.

2. The registered office of the Association is to be in England.

3. The objects for which the Association is established are:

(1) To promote the medical and allied sciences, and to maintain the honour and interests of the medical profession.

(2) To hold or arrange for the holding of periodical meetings of the Members of the Association and of the medical profession generally.

(3) To circulate such information as may be thought desirable by means of a periodical journal, which shall be the journal of the Association, and by the occasional publication of transactions or other papers.

(4) To grant sums of money out of the funds of the Association for the promotion of the medical and allied sciences in such manner as may from time to time be determined on.

(5) Subject to the provisions of Section 19 of the Companies (Consolidation) Act, 1908, to purchase take on lease exchange hire or otherwise acquire any real and personal property and any rights or privileges necessary or convenient for the purposes of the Association.

(6) To sell improve manage develop lease mortgage dispose of turn to account or otherwise deal with all or any part of the property of the Association.

(7) To borrow any moneys required for the purposes of the Association upon such terms and upon such securities as may be determined.

(8) To do all such other lawful things as may be incidental or conducive to the promotion or carrying out of the foregoing objects or any of them.

Provided that the Association shall not become or seek to become a trade union within the meaning of the Industrial Relations Act 1971 but shall be registered only in the Special Register provided for by the said Act.

4. The income and property of the Association, from whatever source derived, shall be applied solely towards the promotion of the objects of the Association as set forth in this Memorandum of

Association, and no portion thereof shall be paid or transferred directly or indirectly by way of dividend or bonus or otherwise, by way of profit to the persons who at any time are or have been Members of the Association, or to any person claiming through any of them, provided that nothing herein shall prevent the payment in good faith of remuneration to any officers or servants of the Association, or to any Member of the Association or other person in return for any services actually rendered to the Association.

5. The fourth paragraph of this Memorandum is a condition on which the licence is granted by the Board of Trade to the Association in pursuance of Section 23 of The Companies Act, 1867. For the purpose of preventing any evasion of the terms of the said fourth paragraph, the Board of Trade may from time to time, on the application of any Member of the Association, impose further conditions which shall be duly observed by the Association.

6. If the Association act in contravention of the fourth paragraph of this Memorandum, or of any further conditions, the liability of every Director hereinafter called Member of Committee of Council shall be unlimited, and the liability of every Member who has received any such dividend, bonus, or other profit aforesaid, shall likewise be unlimited.

7. Every Member of the Association undertakes to contribute to the assets of the Association in the event of the same being wound up, during the time that he is a Member, or within one year afterwards, for payment of the debts and liabilities of the Association contracted before the time at which he ceases to be a Member, and the costs, charges and expenses of winding up the same, and for the adjustment of the rights of the contributories amongst themselves such amount as may be required, not exceeding the sum of one guinea, or in case of his liability becoming unlimited, such other amount as may be required in pursuance of the last preceding paragraph of this Memorandum.

The following Articles are the Regulations of the Association adopted in pursuance of a Special Resolution passed 29 June 1910, and confirmed 22 July 1910, except in so far as such Articles have been since duly added to or otherwise altered . . .

II. MEMBERSHIP,
TEMPORARY MEMBERSHIP AND ASSOCIATESHIP
Eligibility for Membership

3. Any Medical Practitioner registered or provisionally registered in Great Britain or Ireland under the Medical Acts or

the Medical Practitioners' Act, 1927 (No. 25 of 1927), of the Republic of Ireland or any other legislation for the time being in force in the Republic of Ireland relating to registration or provisional registration of Medical Practitioners and any Medical Practitioner who, though not so registered or provisionally registered, is possessed of any medical qualification the holding of which is a condition precedent to his being eligible to be so registered or provisionally registered and any Medical Practitioner residing within the area of any Branch of the Association not in Great Britain or Ireland who possesses such medical qualification as shall, subject to the Bye-laws, be prescribed by the Rules of the said Branch, shall be eligible as an ordinary Member of the Association. Provided always that no person shall be eligible for membership of the Association without the previous sanction of the Council if (had he previously been a member) his membership would automatically have terminated under Article 12(c). Subject as aforesaid, the mode and conditions of election to membership shall from time to time be determined by or in accordance with the Bye-laws.

Eligibility for Temporary Membership

4. The Association shall have power to elect as temporary members persons whose names are entered in the Register of Temporarily Registered Medical Practitioners maintained by the General Medical Council or persons resident in the United Kingdom who though not so temporarily registered are possessed of any medical qualification the holding of which is a condition precedent to their being eligible to be so temporarily registered. Temporary Members shall have such privileges as may from time to time be conferred on them by or under the Bye-laws.

Honorary and Extraordinary Members

5. (1) The Association shall have power to elect as Honorary Members such persons and in such manner as the Bye-laws may provide. Honorary Members shall be eligible for election as President of the Association and may hold the office of President, President Elect, Immediate Past President, Past President or Vice-President, but an Honorary Member shall not be eligible for election to or eligible to hold any other office in the Association. The Association may admit Honorary Members to such privileges (other than that of receiving notices of General Meetings or of voting as Members of the Association) as may from time to time be conferred on them by or under the Bye-laws.

(2) Each Division or Branch shall have power to admit to certain of the privileges of membership of such Division or Branch, other than that of voting: (*a*) Members of the Association who are not entitled to be Ordinary Members of such Division or Branch; and (*b*) members of the medical profession, or persons distinguished in other sciences, who are not eligible as Ordinary Members of the Association. The Bye-laws may prescribe the designation under which persons shall be admitted to such privileges, the nature of the privileges to be conferred upon them, and the conditions of admission thereto.

Associates

6. Each Branch of the Association not in Great Britain or Ireland shall have power to elect as Associates such persons and in such manner as the Bye-laws may provide and to admit Associates so elected to such privileges (not being inconsistent with the provisions of the Regulations and of the Bye-laws) as may from time to time be conferred on them by or under the Bye-laws.

An Associate shall not be a member of the Association or of any Division or Branch thereof for any purpose, and no Associate shall act as a Member of the Council, representative or officer of the Association or of any Branch or Division, or be entitled to receive notice of or to be present or to vote at any General Meeting of the Association.

Subscriptions

7. Save as otherwise provided by the Regulations or Bye-laws every Member Temporary Member and Associate shall pay to the Association a subscription of such amount as may for the time being be prescribed by the Bye-laws. In the case of Members or Associates the said subscription shall be considered due in advance on 1 January of each year, or in the case of Members or Associates elected during the year, at the time of election. In the case of Temporary Members, the said subscription shall be considered due in advance at the time of application for election as a Temporary Member and shall cover a period of twelve months from the time of such application. Provided always that in the case of any person who shall have been a Member of the Association for a period of fifty years no further annual subscription shall be payable as from 1 January next succeeding the expiration of such period. Provided further that the Regulations and Bye-laws may provide that any Member admitted to membership

before 31 December next occurring after the expiration of one year from the date of the grant to him of a qualifying diploma within the meaning of the Medical Acts may compound his subscriptions for such period as may be prescribed by the payment of a lump sum but so that each of the foregoing provisos shall be without prejudice in the case of a Member who is a Member of a Corporate Branch or of a Corporate Group to his obligations as such Member of the Corporate Branch or of the Corporate Group.

8. Each year's subscription shall entitle the Member to all privileges of membership of the Association, including that of receiving the Journal for the current year, and to the ordinary privileges of membership of that Division and of that Branch of which he is an ordinary Member. Each year's subscription shall entitle the Temporary Member to the privileges which may for the time being be conferred on Temporary Members by or under the Bye-laws.

Each year's subscription shall entitle the Associate to the privileges (not being inconsistent with the provisions of the Regulations and of the Bye-laws) which may for the time being be conferred by or under the Bye-laws on Associates of that Division and of that Branch of which he is an Associate . . .

83
National Union of Teachers:
Objects and Constitution, 1970

OBJECTS

2. The objects of the Union shall be:

(a) To associate and unite the teachers of England and Wales.

(b) To provide means for the co-operation of teachers and the expression of their collective opinion upon matters affecting the interests of education and the teaching profession.

(c) To improve the condition of education in the country, and to obtain the establishment of a national system of education, co-ordinated and complete.

(d) To secure for all State-aided Schools adequate financial aid from public sources, accompanied by suitable conditions.

(e) To afford to Her Majesty's Government, the Department of Education and Science, the Local Authorities for education, and other organizations – public or private – which have relation to educational affairs, the advice and experience of the associated teachers.

(f) To secure the effective representation of educational interests in Parliament.

(g) To secure the solidarity and extend the influence of the teaching profession.

(h) To aid and/or join with other Societies or Bodies having objects altogether or in part similar to the objects of one or some of the objects of the Union and to contribute to subsidize or otherwise assist or take part in the working, management or control thereof. To negotiate and enter into arrangements for amalgamation or federation in such manner as may be prescribed by law and upon such terms as may be agreed with other Societies or Bodies of Teachers.

(i) To secure the recognition of the teaching profession as a diploma-granting authority.

(j) To watch the administration and working of the various Education Acts and other Acts of Parliament connected with Education, the Regulations made thereunder and the Memoranda and Circulars issued by the Ministers concerned; to endeavour to amend their terms and administration when educationally desirable; and to endeavour to secure the removal of difficulties, abuses and obsolete regulations detrimental to progress.

(k) To maintain a high standard of qualification, to raise the status of the teaching profession, and to ensure that all the posts in the Educational Service of the country are open to members.

(l) To afford advice and assistance to individual members in educational and professional matters, and in legal cases of a professional nature.

(m) To extend protection to teachers whenever necessary.

(n) To watch the administration of the Superannuation Acts and Pension Regulations, and to endeavour to secure their amendment where necessary.

(o) To promote the welfare of the Teachers' Assurance and the Teachers' Benevolent Fund.

(p) To promote, establish, acquire or carry on or assist in so doing an undertaking or Company providing or about to provide Life Assurance and/or Fire Insurance for the benefit of members, their widows, children and dependants, and such other persons as are eligible to join the Teachers' Assurance, and for this purpose to subsidize or otherwise assist and take, or otherwise acquire and hold any interest in such undertaking or Company.

(q) To purchase, lease, exchange or otherwise acquire any real and personal property, and to construct, alter and maintain any buildings required for the purpose of the Union, and to sell, improve, develop, lease, mortgage or otherwise deal with all or any part of the property of the Union.

(r) To establish or aid or join with other Societies or Bodies in establishing charitable trusts of an educational nature and to subscribe to charitable trusts of such nature as are already in existence.

CONSTITUTION

3. *Conference Authority.* Conference is the supreme authority of the Union.

4. *Executive.* (a) The affairs of the Union shall be managed by a Central Executive Body (hereinafter called 'the Executive').

(b) All decisions of the Executive involving the salary policy of the Union as approved by Conference must be in accord with that policy except that if at least three fourths of the Executive present decide that circumstances are such that Conference decisions in this category must be disregarded, such decisions must be reported to a Special Conference for ratification at the earliest opportunity.

5. *Constituent Associations.* (a) The Union shall consist of such Local and Central Associations of Teachers (hereinafter referred to collectively as 'Constituent Associations') as may be affiliated by the Executive.

(b) Every Local Association shall appoint a President, Secretary, Treasurer and Committee.

(c) Subject to the provisions of Rule 30 (a) a Constituent Association shall admit to membership teachers recognized by the Department of Education and Science as qualified teachers, or possessing such alternative qualifications as may be accepted by the Executive: and also teachers recognized by the Department of Education and Science as Temporary Teachers provided that any such Temporary Teacher shall cease to be eligible for membership immediately his recognition as a Temporary Teacher expires (see Appendix I).

(d) All Constituent Associations shall forward a copy of their rules to the General Secretary of the Union by 31 December of each year.

(e) No alteration of, or addition to, the rules of a Constituent Association may be made, nor may any change be made in the title of a Constituent Association, without the sanction of the Executive.

(f) The Executive shall exclude from the National Union of Teachers any affiliated Constituent Association which declines to bring its rules into accord with the general rules of the Union.

6. *County Associations.* (a) A group of Local Associations and sub-associations within the area of either an administrative county or of an *ad hoc* Education Authority may be recognized by the Executive as a County Association, but not more than one group shall be so recognized in the area of one administrative county or *ad hoc* Education Authority.

(b) The Executive may remove from the list of County Associations any County Association which holds no meeting or makes no report to the Executive for the space of twelve months.

(c) All County Associations shall forward a copy of their rules to the General Secretary of the Union by 31 December of each year.

(d) No alteration of, or addition to, the rules of a County Association may be made, nor may any change be made in the title of a County Association, without the sanction of the Executive.

(e) The Executive shall exclude from the National Union of Teachers any County Association which declines to bring its rules into accord with the general rules of the Union.

OFFICERS AND EXECUTIVE

7. The election of the Officers of the Union (except the President) and other members of the Executive as hereinafter mentioned, shall take place biennially after the election held in the year 1960. In that year and subsequently in the year of an election the Officers shall consist of the President, the Senior Vice-President and Junior Vice-President, the Ex-President and the Treasurer of the Union elected in accordance with these Rules. In the year commencing at the Annual Conference next following an election, the Officers shall consist of the President, the Senior Vice-President, two Ex-Presidents and the Treasurer of the Union elected in accordance with these Rules. In both years there shall be, in addition, thirty-three other members of the Executive elected in accordance with Rule 14 together with such other co-opted members as may be nominated under the provisions of Rule 15 (n), and such other members nominated under the terms of the Joint Partnership Schemes as laid down in Appendix IIIA and IIIB.

8. Subject to the provisions of Rule 10 (c):

(a) The Senior Vice-President elected in accordance with Rule 12 shall be the President in the year following his or her election and shall hold office as Ex-President during the two years next following provided membership of the Union be retained.

(b) The Junior Vice-President elected in accordance with Rule

12 shall be the Senior Vice-President in the year following his or her election and shall hold office as President and Ex-President respectively during the two succeeding years provided membership of the Union be retained.

9. All members of the Executive except the President and the Senior Vice-President shall retire biennially but shall be eligible for re-election.

10. (a) No paid official of the Union may be a member of the Executive.

(b) In the event of a Member of the Executive applying for a paid post to which the appointment is made by the Executive, such member shall be suspended from membership of the Executive with effect from the date of the submission of his application until the confirmation by the Executive of the aforesaid appointment. In the event of a member of the Executive being appointed to such a paid post as aforesaid, he shall be deemed to have resigned his membership of the Executive with effect from the date of the said appointment.

(c) Teachers who are not in full-time teaching service or who have retired or have otherwise left the profession shall be disqualified for nomination for or election to the Executive. Any member of the Executive who retires from full-time teaching service shall relinquish his or her membership of the Executive on the last day of the Annual Conference next following such retirement except the Senior Vice-President who shall relinquish his or her membership of the Executive on the last day of the Annual Conference at which he or she relinquishes the office of President.

11. *Nominations and Elections (General).* (a) The Secretary of each Constituent Association shall give to the members (other than Associate Members as defined in Rule 30 (d)), at least seven days' notice of the time and place of meeting to make nominations for the biennial elections of Senior and Junior Vice-Presidents, Treasurer and members of the Executive, but such nominations shall not be invalidated by the failure on the part of any member to receive such notice or by the failure on the part of any Constituent Association to hold a nomination meeting provided that in each Electoral District one or more Constituent Associations have made a valid nomination.

(b) The nominations must be made on a form provided for the purpose, and must reach the General Secretary not later than 15 December in the year preceding the election.

(c) The consent of any candidate to seek election may be withdrawn on or before 15 January of the year of election.

12. *Nomination and Election of Vice-Presidents.* (a) Every Constituent Association may nominate two members of the Union for the offices of Junior and Senior Vice-President whose election shall be conducted in accordance with the procedure laid down in Rule 14 (f) and shall be made at the same time as the biennial election of members of the Executive. The votes shall be recorded on the same voting paper.

(b) The member so nominated must have been a full member of the Union for the seven years immediately preceding the election.

13. *Nomination and Election of Treasurer.* (a) Every Constituent Association may nominate one member of the Union for the Office of Treasurer.

(b) The member so nominated must have been a full member of the Union for the seven years immediately preceding the election.

(c) Teachers who have retired or who have left the profession shall be disqualified for election.

(d) The election of the Treasurer shall be made at the same time as the biennial election of members of the Executive, and the votes shall be recorded on the same voting paper.

14. *Nomination and Election of Executive.* (a) Every Local Association may nominate as Candidates for the Executive as many members of the Union as there are members to be elected for the district.

(b) Members so nominated must have been full members of the Union for the three years immediately preceding the election.

(c) A candidate for the Executive must be nominated by a Local Association within the district he seeks to represent and such district shall include the Local Association through which his annual subscription to the Union is paid.

(d) No candidate may accept nomination in more than one district.

(e) Central Associations may nominate candidates for the Executive of the Union subject to the limitation imposed on Local Associations in Rule 14 (a). Each such candidate must be nominated in accordance with Rule 14 (b) and 14 (d), for a district in which he or she is in service as a teacher.

(f) The election of the Officers of the Union, the other members of the Executive and the Examiners of Accounts shall be conducted under the system of proportional representation with the single transferable vote. The results of the elections shall be declared as provided by Rule 15 (h).

15. The biennial election of the Executive shall be made in the following manner:

(a) England and Wales shall be divided into twelve Electoral Districts and the members of the Constituent Associations affiliated to the Union shall be apportioned amongst these districts in such a manner as the Executive may from time to time determine.

(b) The Executive shall have power to readjust from time to time the boundaries of contiguous Electoral Districts, due regard being had to the wishes of the Constituent Associations.

(c) No Electoral District shall have less than two members of the Executive. Subject thereto the unit qualifying any Electoral District to have a member of the Executive shall be obtained by dividing the total membership (other than Associate membership) of the Union by thirty-seven. Each Electoral District shall have as many members as it has complete units. Those Electoral Districts having the largest number in excess of the completed units shall be entitled to an extra member until the full number of thirty-seven members is reached. The total membership used in obtaining the unit shall be that published in the last Annual Report prior to the date of the election.

(d) The officers of the Union, with the exception of the Treasurer, shall be members of the Executive for their respective Electoral Districts and the number to be elected in such Electoral Districts shall be reduced accordingly. The respective Electoral Districts for which the President, Junior Vice-President (when holding that office), Senior Vice-President and Ex-Presidents are members of the Executive shall be those Districts which include the Local Association through which their respective annual subscriptions to the Union were paid for the year immediately preceding their election as Junior Vice-President.

(e) Every member of the Union for the year preceding an election (other than Associate Members) shall be entitled to one vote in elections under this Rule and under Rules 12, 13 and 45 and the voting-paper for each such member shall be sent to the Secretary at least four weeks before Easter.

(f) The voting-papers shall be supplied to such members by the Secretary of his or her Association not less than seven days before the latest date for their return to the office. The voting-papers must reach the office of the Union not later than midday on Monday, fourteen days before Easter Monday.

(g) The votes shall be counted in London, and the counting shall commence after midday on Monday, fourteen days before Easter Monday by members resident in the Metropolitan or Extra-Metropolitan Districts: and the results shall be declared at the first session of Conference. A representative of the Electoral Reform Society shall act as Returning Officer. A recount shall take place if demanded by any candidate. Such demand must be received at the office of the Union not later than the first post on the Tuesday before Easter.

(h) A representative of the Electoral Reform Society, in his capacity of Returning Officer, shall declare elected the candidates having at the conclusion of the election the largest number of votes. The result of the election shall be certified by him, and his certificate shall include a record of any transfer of votes and of the total number of votes credited to each candidate after any such transfer. A copy of the certificate of the election shall be kept by the General Secretary, and shall be available at the offices of the Union for inspection by any member of the Union upon request.

(i) In the event of a scrutiny being demanded by any candidate, such demand shall be made before the close of the Conference or in the case of a by-election within one week of the declaration of the result. A representative of the Electoral Reform Society shall have power to order a scrutiny and to make all necessary arrangements.

(j) Subject to the provisions of Rule 10 (c) members of the Executive shall hold office from the day following the close of the Conference at which their election is reported until the last day of the Annual Conference immediately following the holding of the next biennial election.

(k) In the event of the Treasurer being also elected a member of the Executive for any District, the number of members to be elected for that District shall be calculated without reference to his election as a member of the Executive.

(l) The election shall not be invalidated by any omission on the part of the Local Secretary to issue the voting-papers to the members.

(m) If before the latest time for delivery of nomination papers and before the latest date upon which voting-papers are to be supplied to members (other than Associate Members) by the Secretary of a Constituent Association a candidate who remains validly nominated dies, or becomes disqualified for election under the Rules of the Union, the Returning Officer shall countermand the election for the Electoral District affected and all the proceedings with reference to the election for that Electoral District shall be commenced afresh provided that no fresh nomination shall be necessary in the case of a candidate who stood nominated at the time of the countermand of the election. On the election being countermanded the Returning Officer shall order the election to be held on such day as he may appoint. Any fresh nominations from the Local Associations in the District or from a Central Association shall be received by the General Secretary within fifteen days from the date such election is countermanded.

16. *Meetings of Executive.* (a) the Executive shall meet:

(i) Monthly, except in August;

(ii) At such other times as the President and Secretary may deem fit;

(iii) When a requisition signed by twelve members stating in writing the object of the meeting has been received by the General Secretary.

(b) The meetings shall be held in London or such other place as may be agreed upon by the Executive.

(c) In any meeting of the Executive duly summoned, twenty members shall form a quorum.

(d) The travelling expenses of the members of the Executive in attending meetings of the Executive and of Conference shall be defrayed out of the funds of the Union.

17. *Vacancies.* (a) Any vacancy arising between elections in the office of President, Senior Vice-President or Ex-President may be filled by the Executive from its own body until the next biennial election. Any vacancy in the office of Treasurer arising through the operation of Rule 10 (c) at the Annual Conference next following a biennial election shall be filled by an election held in accordance with the procedure laid down in these Rules for an ordinary election of Treasurer. Any vacancy in the office of Treasurer arising otherwise than by reason of the operation of Rule 10 (c) shall be filled by the Executive from its own body until the next biennial election. Any vacancy arising at any time in the office of Junior Vice-President shall be filled by a special election held in accordance with the general procedure laid down in Rule 17 (b).

(b) In the event of any vacancy being declared in the Executive between 31 December of the year preceding the year of the biennial election and the Annual Conference of that year, such vacancy shall not be filled until the holding of the biennial election. In the event of a vacancy being declared between the Annual Conference of the year of an election and 31 December of the year following, the procedure and time-table set out in this rule shall be observed:

(i) The Secretary of each Constituent Association whose members have been allotted to the Electoral District in which the vacancy occurs shall give to the members (other than Associate members) at least seven days' notice of the time and place of the meeting to make a nomination.

(ii) The nominations must be made on a form provided for the purpose and must reach the General Secretary within three weeks from the date of the vacancy being declared as aforesaid.

(iii) A further week shall be allowed during which period any candidate shall be permitted to withdraw.

(iv) The special election shall take place as soon as possible thereafter on such a day as may be appointed by the Executive, who shall have power to make all other arrangements for the conduct of the election.

(v) Every member of the Union, through the Constituent Associations in the Electoral Districts concerned, for the year preceding the election (other than Associate members) shall be entitled to one vote in a special election.

(c) Any nomination made pursuant to this rule shall not be invalidated either by the failure on the part of any member to receive a notice calling a nomination meeting or by failure on the part of any Constituent Association to hold a nomination meeting, provided that in any Electoral District one or more Constituent Associations have made a valid nomination.

(d) If any member of the Executive shall be absent from the meetings of the Executive and its committees for three successive months without reasons which are considered sufficient by the Executive, such person shall cease to be a member and shall not be eligible for re-election until the next biennial election.

OFFICIALS

18. (a) The officials of the Union shall be the General Secretary and all other officials whose offices have been sanctioned by the Annual Conference.

(b) The power to appoint or dismiss any official of the Union shall be vested in the Executive.

(c) No paid official of the Union may be a member of the Executive, a representative of an Association at Conference, or a Trustee of the Union . . .

84
National Association of Schoolmasters:
Objects, Composition of the Teaching Profession, 1970

(i) To regulate relations between schoolmasters and their employers; to regulate the professional relations between schoolmasters; to regulate professional relations between schoolmasters and other teachers and other employees in the education service.

(ii) To protect and promote the interests of its members generally, and in particular to ensure that the salaries of school-masters are determined in the light of the special factors (e.g. family and career responsibilities) influencing the recruitment of men to, and their retention in, the teaching profession.

(iii) To protect and promote the interests of the education service generally, and in particular to ensure that schoolboys over Infant School age come predominantly under the influence of schoolmasters.

(iv) To secure the representation of schoolmasters' interests on public and private bodies concerned with education or related matters.

(v) To afford the Secretary of State for Education and Science, the local education authorities and other bodies with an interest in the education service the advice and experience of the Association and its members.

(vi) To render legal advice and assistance in professional matters to members of the Association, in accordance with the Rules of the Association.

(vii) To render financial and other assistance to members or their dependants in distress.

Teaching is unique in that it is the only occupation employing well-educated men and women in which men form the minority. The reason for this is partly educational and partly historical. It was generally conceded that children of Infant School age should be taught by women because, perhaps, women teachers more easily take the place of the child's mother at this stage.

The N.A.S. has always asserted that after leaving the Infant School boys and girls need the influence of a teacher of their own sex. This view is supported by the vast majority of parents. It does not mean that boys and girls should be taught exclusively by teachers of their own sex: it means that the balance of staffing must ensure a sufficient number of well-qualified men and women.

This sensible approach to the question of staffing stands in stark contrast to the official policy of the large mixed teachers' union, which is that 'men and women teachers are readily interchangeable'. The logic of this is, of course, that all teachers could be men or all teachers could be women.

It is because men form a permanent minority of teachers that their special interests have to be safeguarded. The N.A.S. exists to do just this. It believes that these special interests can be defended without harm to the general interests of the profession as a whole.

'UNITY'?

'Professional unity' is a slogan frequently used by those who advocate that the solution to the problems which confront the teaching profession lies in the formation of an 'all-in' union invested with the power of a professional registration and disciplinary body. Teachers, they argue, have common interests and should, therefore, belong to a common organization. The fallacy behind this argument is readily apparent, for it is clear that while all teachers share *some* common interests there are other important matters on which their interests diverge and sometimes conflict.

It was this very fact which caused a group of schoolmasters within the large mixed union to leave it and found the N.A.S. in 1919. Certain of their interests were being sacrificed in the interests of the permanent majority of members, the women, and only by this means could they ensure that they were fully safeguarded.

85
Howard League for Penal Reform: activities, 1970
An Appeal, n.d.

HOWARD LEAGUE ACTIVITIES

The League's main effort is at present concentrated on the following activities:

1. *Information* is the key to reform. It may concern either malfunctions within the existing system, or ways in which the system itself should be changed; or on the other hand promising innovations in this country or abroad which ought to be more widely known and developed. Information is collected by the staff, Council and members of the League, to build up as accurate as possible a picture of the present situation. It is obtained in several ways, especially through personal contacts and visits to Government departments, penal institutions, offenders and others concerned; from books, journals and unpublished reports; and in correspondence. Local groups of Howard League members will be developed to extend this work throughout the country.

2. *Policy.* The information collected is used by the Council of the League and its working parties as the basis for policy recommendations. The League investigates areas of concern and issues

reports; in addition it is frequently invited to give evidence to Royal Commissions and official committees of inquiry.

3. *Reform*. The Howard League puts forward its views by all appropriate means. It publishes its reports, Journal, newsletters and occasional pamphlets. It makes representations to government departments. It holds meetings and conferences, both for the general public and as a forum for the exchange of ideas among the different professions concerned with offenders, including the judiciary.

4. *Educational activities*. The Howard League works to spread information and understanding among the general public, so as to promote a climate in which improved methods will flourish. In addition to the methods already mentioned, it supplies information to members of both Houses of Parliament, journalists, teachers, students and other members of the public. It provides speakers for meetings. A library and information service is being built up for the use of staff and members; booklists have been prepared on several subjects, and it is hoped to produce information leaflets.

5. *Howard Centre of Penology*. The Centre was set up by the Howard League in 1967. At present it is holding courses in group treatment methods for those concerned with offenders; other courses are being planned. Its other function, which will be developed when resources are available, is to promote and advise upon research projects in fields where information is needed.

86
The English Party, 1957: Manifesto, 1961
Leaflet, Monmouth, November 1961

We oppose the entry of our country into the Common Market. Our complete independence must be maintained.

We propose an immediate pact of non-aggression with the Soviet Union.

We agree with Russia that Germany must remain divided.

We do not believe in N.A.T.O. nor in the re-arming of Western Germany. Foreign troops must be removed from our land.

We support nuclear disarmament. Failing success we consider England must maintain reasonable atomic weapons for her own protection.

We consider that a nuclear war must be the ultimate war and our only responsibility would be to our native land.

We desire a national wage structure for all workers.

We propose graduated old age pensions with freedom to retain all earnings. (Under this scheme, pensions would rise with age.)

We do not support an official colour bar. But individuals have a right to associate with whom they like and forced integration of any kind could not be tolerated by us. The English race is primarily a white one.

We aim at ties with the Commonwealth with every help and assistance given to members; citizens of the Commonwealth being received here as visitors, students, or occasionally workers, with all possible courtesy.

We consider that in handing over sections of our former Empire, protection for our financial interests must be made covering a period of at least twenty-five years or compensation to be paid to us.

Self-government to be offered on conditions and with safeguards.

We do not support the construction of a channel tunnel or bridge.

Financial

We believe that a capital gains tax on large financial transactions should be made.

We are of the opinion that the near monopoly control of any section of our business life is undesirable and laws to protect us in this direction are needed.

Education

We suggest that a child should only come under State control between the ages of six and fifteen. The compulsory teaching of older children is not in accordance with our Charter (aim No. 2). Higher pay for fewer and better-qualified teachers would result.

Agriculture

We advocate a system of differential subsidies which would benefit the small farmer while costing the large producer relatively little.

Parliament

According to our charter (aim No. 7) we support separate parliaments for England, Scotland and Wales. England would be ruled by the English in an English parliament.

Defence

We believe in the maintenance of a reasonable amount of protective forces. We consider that an enlarged Navy is essential to our prestige. We would maintain a highly modernized National Home Guard as an important part of our defence.

Immigration

To reserve England primarily as a home for the English, immigration would be strictly limited to very desirable persons essential to our country. Many immigrants who have arrived in England during the last twenty-five years would be invited to return to their native lands. Some would be deported.

87
Campaign for Nuclear Disarmament, 1960s

B.B.C. radio documentary feature, May–June 1966, in the *Listener*, 23 March 1967*

In the months which followed the 1959 General Election and a third consecutive Conservative victory, many political commentators speculated about the likelihood of another Labour Government in their lifetimes. Today, with like exaggeration and at any rate until the recent by-elections, the question has been reversed: how many consecutive victories at the polls by the Labour Party will there be before the Conservatives return to power?

A key moment in the revival of Labour fortunes and the party's dominance today was the 1960 Scarborough conference; and the catalyst was the Campaign for Nuclear Disarmament. Chemists would probably dispute the term catalyst because if the defeat of the Labour Party leadership at the Scarborough conference was the real moment of the swing of the political pendulum, since then C.N.D. has declined; or, as Christopher Driver, author of *The Disarmers*, put it: 'By September and October 1960 I think the movement had begun to go to seed and everything that's happened since suggests that this was in fact so'. (I am of course aware that the C.N.D. issues discussed in this article are not the total political conflict present at Scarborough 1960.)

When Ivan Yates of the *Observer* began the Third Programme inquiry, we were impressed by the findings of a B.B.C. reporter

*This article was based on a documentary feature produced by Anthony Moncrieff, which was first broadcast in May and June, 1966 and repeated in March, 1967 in a revised version.

in Trafalgar Square last Easter Monday. He recorded typical slogans: 'Hands off Vietnam', 'Polaris, out, out, out', 'Get your Anarchists' badges, Easter badges', 'Yanks out', 'Against racialism', 'Votes at eighteen', 'You name it, we've got it' – the original, purer slogan 'Ban the bomb' appeared to have been mislaid. Yates and I were seeking opinions in answer to four questions. 'What has been the political significance of the Campaign for Nuclear Disarmament? Did the movement influence Labour Party policies? Were the strategic arguments significant? Does the Campaign have a future?'

Readers can assess the future of C.N.D. for themselves this weekend. I accept the evidence of Alastair Buchan, Director of the Institute for Strategic Studies, who argued that the Campaign for Nuclear Disarmament has had no influence on defence policy: it merely 'raised the threshold of interest in [defence issues] even though the debate it produced was rather a muddled one'. In this article, which is only about a quarter the length of the broadcast, I want to concentrate on the political questions.

Canon Collins, first chairman of C.N.D., explained the political tactics and policies: 'It was a moral campaign, but it was also a political campaign – because I personally and I think lots of other people with me do not believe you can separate morals from politics, any more than you can separate religion from politics. So it was primarily a moral campaign directed to political ends. I felt the most realistic thing we could do was to stir up public opinion, to let political people realize that there was a feeling in the country about it. That the Conservative Party would be unlikely to change policy in the direction we wanted. We hoped that the Labour Party would be stirred through the trade unions and general supporters to realize that they must base defence and foreign policies in future on Britain without the bomb . . . Right from the very beginning of the campaign there were inevitable divisions of thought and feeling, very much feeling. There were those who wanted a general protest against everything they didn't like. There were those who wanted an organization which would in effect become a political party. There were those who wanted just a pacifist demonstration, a development of non-violent techniques. Whereas I always felt that the campaign should concentrate itself upon changing the Labour Party opinion and all the floating voters who would vote to make a Labour Party effective as a political power.'

Perhaps the most divisive element of all, commented Ivan Yates, stemmed from C.N.D.'s President, Bertrand Russell. He and the Reverend Michael Scott gathered together a group –

which they called the Committee of 100 – to express opposition to British nuclear policy by non-violent civil disobedience. Except, again to quote Christopher Driver, who takes the view that the split between Collins and Russell 'which came into the open just before the Scarborough Conference [and] could hardly have been more unfortunately timed' – support for the Campaign fell away after Scarborough 'because it split organizationally' – I do not propose to delve into the differences between C.N.D. and the Committee of 100, differences which will occupy some brave contemporary historian for a large slice of time and effort.

Stuart Hall, former editor of *New Left Review*, who now teaches at Birmingham University and is widely regarded as one of the leading thinkers of the movement, qualified the views of Canon Collins. Hall said: 'I don't think there is ever a single policy. I think in the beginning the notion that the movement had first of all to try to persuade one of the major political parties, and therefore inevitably the Labour Party, to its point of view, was taken as the central strategy.'

He went on to argue that the early Aldermaston marches would themselves 'have been somewhat split as between a Labour Party tactic, and trying to build up a movement outside the Labour Party. And I think that would have been true really consistently right throughout. There was always an attempt to bring pressure to bear on governments and parties. Always at the same time a sense that unless the movement could call up its troops outside of the political parties it wouldn't really have much effect.'

On Wednesday afternoon, 5 October 1960, at Scarborough, the Labour Party Conference defeated the platform on the issue of unilateralism. Had there been a successful takeover bid by C.N.D.? The issue was more complex, even if the result was foregone – as Ivan Yates explained: 'The unions were already committed one way or the other. The previous month the T.U.C. had done a two-way split, voting both for the official party statement and at the same time for a unilateralist motion put forward by Frank Cousins: the first renounced the policy of Britain's remaining an independent nuclear power but supported the western alliance, based on nuclear weapons, and the second opposed any defence policy which was based on nuclear weapons. At Scarborough the miners, the railwaymen, the engineers, the shopworkers, the transport workers were all lined up against Mr Gaitskell and the party leadership . . . When Hugh Gaitskell came to wind up the dramatic debate on defence at Scarborough, he knew he was going to be defeated in the vote. So did his audience. But he knew too that he was not going to accept defeat –

neither he nor, he was sure, the majority of the Parliamentary Labour Party. His audience were not aware of this and the process of their enlightenment took up a long passage in his peroration. Hugh Gaitskell said:

"Frank Cousins has said this is not the end of the problem. I agree with him. It is not the end of the problem because Labour M.P.s will have to consider what they do in the House of Commons. What do you expect of them? You know how they voted in June – overwhelmingly for the policy statement. It is not in dispute that the vast majority of Labour M.P.s are utterly opposed to unilateralism and neutralism. What did you expect them to do? To change their minds overnight, to betray, to go back on the pledges they gave to the people who elected them from their constituencies? And supposing, supposing they did do that, supposing all of us, like well behaved sheep, were to follow the policies suddenly of unilateralism and neutralism, what kind of an impression will this make on the British people? Well, you do not seem to be clear in your minds about it, but I can tell you this. I do not believe that the Labour Members of Parliament are prepared to act as time-servers. I do not believe they will do this, and I will tell you why. Because they are men of conscience and honour. Because people of the right, so-called right and so-called centre, have every bit as much justification for having a conscience as well as people of the so-called left. I do not think they will do this because they are honest men, loyal men, steadfast men, experienced men, with a lifetime of service to the Labour movement. There are other people too, not in Parliament, in the party, who share our convictions. What sort of people do you think they are? What sort of people do you think we are? Do you think we can simply accept a decision of this kind? Do you think we can become overnight the pacifists, unilateralists, and fellow-travellers that other people are? . . . We may lose the vote today and the result may deal this party a grave blow. It may not be possible to prevent this, but there are some of us, I think many of us, who will not accept that this blow need be mortal, who will not believe that such an end is inevitable. There are some of us, Mr Chairman, who will fight and fight and fight again to save the party we love."'

Some observers only saw the defeat of the Labour Party leadership. Others wondered where C.N.D. would stop. But the nuclear disarmament campaign was already past its peak. Christopher Driver explained (in answer to questions from Ivan Yates): 'I would put the climax in the spring of the same year, for several reasons. The most scientific reason is the Gallup Poll figures. In April 1960 there were 33 per cent of the population who were prepared to say 'give up nuclear weapons entirely' and another 27 per cent who would say 'pool them all with Nato'. This coincided with the votes cast at various union conferences in favour of unilateral disarmament and these votes, of course, projected forward into the Scarborough Conference decision. And both these things, I suspect, were immediately caused by the independent military event of the failure of Blue Streak and its cancellation by the Conservative Government, which clearly brought home not only to several politicians – the defence experts in the Labour Party and so on – but also to the public at large that really Britain could now no longer hope to go it alone in this matter . . .'

'That was the moment when George Brown and Harold Wilson appeared to be altering the Labour Party's defence policy.'

'Yes, indeed. They seemed to alter it very dramatically in the course of a parliamentary debate while Mr Gaitskell was away, rather ironically, addressing the Socialist International at Haifa. He came back and they had to meet him at London Airport and tell him what they had done. So that there was all this stir going on at this time . . .'

'But aren't you really then giving the reason for public awareness and for changes in policy to purely military matters and not to the success of C.N.D. itself?'

'I think it needs a military, a factual precipitant event to enable a protest movement to capitalize on what has happened. If there hadn't been C.N.D. and if there hadn't been all this argument going on in the papers and in the Labour Party's constitutional machinery, no doubt the event itself would have passed comparatively unnoticed, but I think the event was necessary.'

Of course C.N.D. had a more basic argument: it was not *just* saying that after the cancellation of Blue Streak Britain did not have an independent nuclear deterrent and would find producing one too expensive in the future. Christopher Mayhew (a former Navy Minister), Labour M.P. and staunch supporter of Mr Gaitskell at the Scarborough Conference, summed up the issue at the Party Conference as C.N.D. neutralism *versus* the Nato alliance: 'Really fundamentally the [C.N.D.] argument was that Britain should contract out. Not that it was wrong for the Americans to have it or the Russians to have it if the other had it, but that Britain herself could somehow contract out, which meant become neutral – come out of Nato.'

Ivan Yates asked Mr Mayhew if it was strictly on defence

grounds that he wanted the Scarborough decision reversed. 'Defence mainly, yes; but of course, everything was tied up in it. The leadership: I believed in Hugh Gaitskell, his leadership. Then there was the issue of the Parliamentary Labour Party. Actually I spoke in Scarborough on that issue, on whether the Parliamentary Labour Party should be subordinate to the Conference. I remember an argument I had with Hugh Gaitskell at the time. He wanted me to speak in the debate on the main issue of the nuclear weapons. I argued that what really mattered was that the Conference should not be allowed to dictate to the Parliamentary Labour Party because I felt – quite rightly, I'm sure looking back – first that the Parliamentary Labour Party would always remain loyal to Hugh Gaitskell and to his ideas. Second that constitutionally it would be monstrous to have M.P.s dictated to by an outside body; and third because the Parliamentary Labour Party reflected public opinion far more accurately than the Conference.'

'What do you think played the largest part in securing the reversal of the Scarborough decision?'

'It was the making of the new Labour Party, frankly. It meant that all the moderate, or right-wing people in the party suddenly stood up; they stood up at the party meetings. They stood up at the trade union branches, where they had never had the guts to stand up before. It was then, and to some extent still is, a weakness of our movement that if we are attacked from the Right, we stand up and hit back like lions; but if we are attacked from the Left there is an awful tendency to sit down like a lot of hypnotized rabbits, even though you don't really go with this loudmouthed fellow who says he believes in the true socialism. After Scarborough that changed, and the moderate men and the rightwing men said, "We're not going to be pushed around any more". They stood up in the local constituency parties. They organized themselves in C.D.S., and in the thing I help to run – the Multilateral Disarmament Campaign. As soon as they once stood up they found a great majority on their side, as is always the case.'

The Campaign for Democratic Socialism (C.D.S.), a grass roots movement, was launched shortly after the Conference. Ivan Yates commented: 'The ground had been very well prepared. Nearly six months before, a group of Labour Party members, all of them supporters of Mr Gaitskell, had come together after the failure of the attempt to amend Clause 4 of the party's constitution to see if they could not stiffen the party behind moderate policies. All through that summer they were meeting, drafting a manifesto for their movement. They decided to wait for the Party Conference before launching out. In the aftermath of defeat, they were ready. Their immediate aim was to work within the party and the unions to get the Scarborough decision reversed. As things turned out, they were successful . . . So we have this curious paradox: the party leadership and their supporters were well prepared to fight back after their defeat at Scarborough. It was the victors – the Campaign for Nuclear Disarmament – who were taken by surprise.'

Canon Collins gave his opinion of why this was so: 'Partly because we were a Campaign and not a political organization. There was no what you might call inherent discipline in the movement. So one saw already the a-political people, and some of the anti-political people, and the anarchists, and Trotskyists, and so on – and the people who were frightfully keen on non-violence as a practical way of life politically; all these were in that meeting at Scarborough we held after the Conference business was over that day. And one saw there the beginnings – or one should have seen there the beginnings – of why we lost.'

Stuart Hall made a different point. He thought C.N.D. failed to carry the Scarborough resolution into any kind of action: 'Exactly how to make that decision effective in terms of an impact on the whole performance of the party in Parliament on defence and foreign policy matters, nobody really knew. Gaitskell was defeated on defence and foreign policy questions but he was still the leader, he still commanded the machine and so on. I think that was really the crucial factor. I think C.N.D. could have pressed its case in a much harder way in that year, but I don't think they would have won.'

The Campaign for Nuclear Disarmament was not equipped, or even prepared, to translate its ideas into political power. Other policies have prevailed in the Labour Party, and last month the wife of Defence Secretary Healey launched Britain's latest Polaris submarine at Birkenhead, where some 2,000 C.N.D. supporters had gone to demonstrate. Later in 1960 the *Parliamentary* Labour Party strongly supported Mr Gaitskell, rejected unilateralism, and asserted its authority over Conference, perhaps for all time. In any case, at Conference a year later the Scarborough decision was reversed. Right or wrong about the issue of Britain's nuclear weapons, Mr Gaitskell fought for what he believed in. The majority of party members, perhaps other voters too, admired his stand. The political pendulum began to swing.

88
Campaign for Democratic Socialism, 1960s
(a) *The Times*, 12 June 1961; (b) *Daily Herald*, 14 June 1961

(a)

Mr Gaitskell has won. He has not only beaten the unilateralists but, for the purposes of this autumn's Labour Party conference, has put them to rout. This is the Damascene revelation that broke upon the Labour movement last week as more trade unions switched back from their unilateralist commitments of a year ago and contributed their quota to the votes that are massing for a return to multilateralist policies at Blackpool.

To show the transformation that is taking place we need to do no more than rescore the voting at Scarborough last year. A majority of 407,000 against Mr Gaitskell was then the unilateralists' most glittering prize. But if that card vote were to be called again today, taking account of the swing by the engineers, shopworkers, builders, foundrymen, locomotive men and vehicle-builders, Mr Gaitskell's majority against unilateralism would be more than two million at least.

We may well ask what has happened, how it happened, and, what significance it may have for Labour. Significant it must prove to be in more than one way. It is important enough, for instance, that the unilateralist campaigners and their variously motivated supporters on the Left should now be suffering their first big strategic *political* defeat. But we are witnessing more than that: Mr Gaitskell and his loyalist majority in the Parliamentary Party have surely exploded the theory that the party conference is the policy-making body which issues orders to the M.P.s and their chosen leader. None of last year's exaggerated claims for the powers of conference can be seriously made for years to come – until, in fact, the Labour rank and file have a total lapse of memory.

There is a sense in which Mr Gaitskell, single-handed, turned the tide within the movement he leads. By a display of courage and integrity that we have not the pleasure of seeing every day in politics he gave the Parliamentary Labour Party a chance to consolidate for 'sanity' (to use his own word) when the line had broken everywhere else: and at some personal cost he gained the time for the national executive committee to redraft defence policy and stop the party's rush towards disintegration.

Mr Gaitskell, and none other, is the hero of the story. But at any rate one of the most fascinating chapters tells of the part played by the Campaign for Democratic Socialism in organizing the strength of the rank and file at grass-roots level; and we shall not understand the Labour movement until we know what they have achieved and how they achieved it.

C.D.S., with Mr W. T. Rodgers, the former Fabian secretary, and Mr Denis Howell, the victor in the Small Heath by-election, among its leading spirits, came into being after last year's disastrous conference. Its article of faith was simply this: that the heart of Labour was still sound and multilateralist and that if only the ordinary rank and file could make themselves truly heard and effective they would reject the unilateralist commitments foisted upon them by comparatively small but well-briefed factions. Its leaders set about creating what could be called a counter-revolution within the constituency parties and trade union branches.

The constituency parties came first. Key men, long in Labour service and with much local experience at ground level, were recruited as supporters. About 250 of them were made 'whips', to whom full plans for the overthrow of unilateralists and Left-wingers could be confided without fear of betrayal. They made sure that the multilateralist case and vote never went by default, and they challenged the unilateralists at every point, with an organized vote to back them.

From C.D.S. headquarters in London skilful tactical guidance went out, expertly drafted speeches were issued, model motions and amendments were supplied at need. The counter-revolution got into full swing, and today there are 3,000 supporters in small and large 'cells'. What at various times the *Tribune* Socialists, the unilateralists and the Communist Party had done, C.D.S. began to do; and in some centres, like Birmingham and Leeds, the C.D.S. men are probably gaining the upper hand at every turn. At the last party conference it was reckoned that 60 per cent of the constituency vote went to Mr Gaitskell, often against the delegates' mandate. This year, C.D.S. believe that they can hand over 80 per cent of the constituency vote.

At first C.D.S. were timid about the unions, but in January they decided to infiltrate some of the smaller ones, at least to the point of learning the multilateralist strength. They were pleasantly surprised. One small union, the Metal Mechanics, were easily and almost casually converted in a pub one Sunday when Mr Howell met the standing order committee, and put the simple question whether they believed in defending Britain. Today C.D.S. is believed to have made sure of forty of the seventy-seven votes that will decide the N.U.R. for multilateralism or unilateralism at Edinburgh on 3 July, and they are working (not quite so hopefully) on the Tailors and Garment Workers, another unilateralist union, in readiness for Scarborough on 19 June.

Both the locomotive men and the foundry workers, who have recoiled from unilateralism already, had several C.D.S. well counselled supporters in at the kill; and it ought not to surprise anyone if something is heard from supporters working inside the T. and G.W.U. when it meets in Brighton from 10 to 14 July. (Nobody thinks Mr Cousins can be defeated on his home ground, but every multilateralist in the Parliamentary Party and C.D.S. is determined to give him a close race.)

The leaders of C.D.S. would not extravagantly claim that they are mainly responsible for the Labour transformation now in process, but they are sure that at last they are creating the conditions in which the true democratic voice of the movement can find an effective sounding-board. They have seen that the unilateralists should be challenged in all the cloak-and-dagger aspects of Labour politics, and we should not be wrong to conclude that C.D.S. will stay in business so long as there is work to do. That could be for ever.

(b)

Quiet men who hate getting up to make a speech, men who had their doubts about the way the Labour Party was going but said nothing or stayed away – these are the men who have won the bitter struggle for control of the Party.

For the struggle *is* won. The takeover bid for the Labour Party by the neutralists and the extreme Left, under the moral cloak of unilateral disarmament, has been utterly defeated.

The final blow was yesterday's decision by the Union of Shop, Distributive and Allied Workers to vote for the Gaitskell policy and drop the Padley–Crossman compromise plan.

Hugh Gaitskell, and two thirds of the Labour M.P.s who backed him, guaranteed that the Labour Party would never be surrendered without a fight to a finish.

As long as they were ready to fight for the future of the Party, the takeover bid begun at the Scarborough Conference last October could never be completed.

But to defeat the bid, and to rout it as it has been routed, needed something more.

It required that the voice of the ordinary rank-and-file Labour and trade union voter be heard in the local Labour Parties, in trade union branches and district committees.

Three men decided that it could be done. They believed that the silent men could be induced to speak, and to vote.

They were W. T. Rodgers, former Secretary of the Fabian Society; Frank Pickstock, a former stationmaster at Wigan who had won an Oxford scholarship, and Dennis Howell, the young Football League referee, then an ex-M.P.

With twenty-three other Labour candidates, councillors and trade union leaders they issued a manifesto opposing neutralism and proclaiming their belief that the voice of the majority of the Party had been drowned by an active and articulate minority.

They got the blessing of Lords Attlee and Dalton, and of that great Socialist, Professor R. H. Tawney.

That was fine as far as it went, but it would be forgotten in a week. So the twenty-six men contributed £200 between them and with that they began the Campaign for Democratic Socialism.

Support flooded in. More than 3,000 people wrote to offer help. Without asking for money, postal orders and cheques were sent by Labour Party members from all over the country.

Rodgers, Pickstock and Howell, who had been doing most of the work in their spare time, knew then that they were right, and that the quiet men and women who form the majority of the Party could be roused to assert themselves.

They set up an office, published a monthly called *Campaign*, issued leaflets, wrote thousands of letters, spoke at meetings and drew up resolutions.

Within weeks the unilateralists, and the people who said that if you didn't believe in the nationalization of everything at once you weren't a Socialist, met unexpected opposition.

Men who had never spoken at a Party meeting rose to put the Gaitskell case. Often, to their surprise, they found a dozen other quiet men who had never said much supporting them.

Men and women who had given up going to party or branch meetings because they were sick of listening to attacks on the Party leader decided to go back and fight. Many stood for election to the key management committees, and were elected.

The Campaign for Democratic Socialism had tapped the solid, sensible core of the Party who wanted a Labour Government, not a political sect.

In the last six months more than ten thousand letters have been received and answered by the Campaign. The organization is growing, and will go on, after the next Party Conference in October, to mobilize the members for the election victory they now believe possible.

Today at least 70 per cent of the local Labour Parties back

Hugh Gaitskell, and it may turn out to be nearly 80 per cent at the next conference.

It is just a year ago since Rodgers and Pickstock first met and they will celebrate that meeting this month. Both have given up a lot to conduct the Campaign.

Rodgers, who was working for the Consumers' Association, was told he had to give up his political activities or his job. He gave up his job, but got a part-time job working for a publisher.

Pickstock, the solid anchor-man of the team, gave up his leisure and saw his home transformed into a committee room.

Dennis Howell, too, gave up all his free time to work for the Campaign, and had his faith confirmed when he won Labour's biggest by-election victory at Small Heath last March.

But the real winners are the ordinary rank-and-file Labour supporters. Impressed by Gaitskell, disgusted with personal attacks and spurred by the Campaigners, they went to their meetings – *and voted.*

89
The Peace Movement: through the eyes of the Multilateral Disarmament Information Centre, London

Reprinted from *New Daily*, November 1963

. . . With the end of the war in 1945 there was in the United Kingdom great admiration for Russia's war-time achievements, and great hope that the allied effort in war might be continued in peace. The public were not then aware of the difficulties we had had during the war with the Russians. However, disillusionment came quickly and with the late Mr Ernest Bevin at the Foreign Office the facts of the post-war international climate were soon accepted.

There were, however, always on the Left of the Labour Party and in the lunatic fringe of politics, groups of people who were critical of Bevin, who tended to apologize for Stalinism and to blame the West for Russia's intransigent attitudes.

Nevertheless, throughout the decade of 1945 to 1955 the Communist Party of Great Britain (C.P.G.B.) had only limited successes in exploiting the discontented Left and the lunatic fringes – apart from the World Peace Movement.

The Peace Movement, launched at the first World Peace Congress in Paris in April 1949, produced the Communist-controlled British Peace Committee (B.P.C.) and its various subsidiaries; they had a fairly limited amount of early success but soon began to lose their public appeal because they were so obviously Communist-inspired; but they nonetheless managed to exploit students and to secure publicity for B.P.C. international conferences.

They also secured unfavourable publicity about the implementation in the U.K. of N.A.T.O. resolutions on sporting and cultural exchanges with East Germany. However, by the late 1950s the British Peace Committee had become fairly ineffective except as an irritant to the authorities.

Meanwhile, in the late 1950s various largely non-Communist movements against nuclear weapons came into existence and greatly increased in size and influence. These were the Campaign for Nuclear Disarmament (C.N.D.), formed in 1957, and the Direct Action Committee against nuclear war (D.A.C.).

The initial aim of the C.N.D. was to persuade the Labour Party to adopt its unilateral, anti-nuclear policy. The intention was to create a mass movement of passive 'Christian' protest – hence the Easter Aldermaston protest marches. To apply this pressure of public opinion the Labour Party and trade unions were to be infiltrated at all levels from National Executives to local ward parties, youth organizations and union branches.

The D.A.C. differed from the C.N.D. in that it specifically encouraged demonstrators to break the law and to give no cooperation to the police when they were arrested.

At first the C.P.G.B., hoping for a revival in the popularity of the British Peace Committee, opposed both the C.N.D. and D.A.C.; these two organizations preached unilateralism and the C.P.G.B. adhered to the Soviet view on nuclear disarmament, i.e., nuclear weapons should only be banned on a multilateral basis and as part of a general agreement on disarmament. In fact Mr John Gollan, the General-Secretary of the C.P.G.B., called for a revival of the B.P.C. in the course of the twenty-sixth Annual Congress of the C.P.G.B.

Shortly afterwards, however, the C.P.G.B. made a complete *volte face* in its attitude towards the C.N.D. and the D.A.C. and henceforth Communists in Britain supported C.N.D. and D.A.C. demonstrations and policies, and infiltrated the C.N.D. and D.A.C. organizations wherever they could.

C.N.D. and the Labour Party

Differences between C.N.D. and the Labour Party arose because C.N.D. tried to [secure], and virtually succeeded in securing, the

M

adoption as official Labour Party policies of the unilateralist programme.

It is fairly true to say that a good number of members of the Labour Party were not concerned at C.N.D. activities and could, in fact, see certain values in them, so long as C.N.D. only amounted to a passive protest movement in the street. Once, however, C.N.D. and their supporters became a force to be reckoned with inside the Labour movement, moderate and right-wing Labour politicians and trade unionists reacted with vigour.

The fight within the Labour Party and the trade union movement was only taken up effectively and with the necessary intensity at the moment when C.N.D. had victory within their grasp and the 1960 Annual Conference of the Labour Party at Scarborough had voted in favour of an anti-nuclear policy.

Fortunately, however, at that very moment, when C.N.D. might have concentrated on consolidating their position legally within the Labour Party, extremist elements in C.N.D., led by Bertrand Russell, and anxious to follow a more militant policy, formed the Committee of 100 at Scarborough in October 1960.

The original Committee of 100 was formed with 107 members with Bertrand Russell as President. Whilst the immediate formation of the Committee was to some extent due to the personal differences within C.N.D. about which Russell felt most strongly the basic reason for the creation of a new organization was that the founders of the Committee of 100 believed that mass civil disobedience would strengthen the anti-nuclear movement.

Their supporters were dissatisfied with the political tactics of C.N.D. which they regarded as slow and inadequate. Opposed to them were the less militant elements of C.N.D. who believed that more progress could be made by avoiding a quarrel with the Labour Party and consolidating their position as an internal pressure group within the Labour Party.

The original Committee of 100 were almost all of the upper and middle classes with no trade union leaders and indeed no member with an industrial background. It was not until the Committee was re-constituted in September 1961, after many of the original Committee members had been imprisoned, that the Committee came to have members with industrial backgrounds. The 1960 Committee differed considerably from the 1961 Committee, which included Communists, ex-Communists, ex-Trotskyists, anarchists or syndicatists and trade unionists.

Observation of Committee of 100 demonstrations and an analysis of the occupations of those arrested at them show that the support for the Committee is almost entirely from middle-class elements, that it contains a high percentage of young people with a good standard of education, including university students and in contrast very few industrial and manual workers.

The exception was in the case of the anti-Polaris demonstrations at Holy Loch when the Scottish Communists, many of whom were factory workers, took an overt and active part on the instructions of their district committee.

The numbers of those arrested and fined after various uni-lateral demonstrations has included a noticeable proportion of clergymen, but not Roman Catholic priests. There has been a substantial participation in demonstrations by coloured students; 'student', 'actress', 'doctor of medicine', 'playwright', 'singer', 'school attendance officer', 'clerk', 'lecturer in physics' and 'consultant in neurology' are among the professions given by those arrested at demonstrations.

These Committee of 100 supporters are on a rough analysis frustrated younger members of the Labour Party who first supported C.N.D. and then were attracted by the call for more action. A second group are thought to be largely non-political people – in terms of membership and active participation in normal political activities but people who are genuinely appalled at the thought of nuclear war.

This group is potentially dangerous in that they might be deceived by any well-conceived propaganda gimmick.

A third group are avowedly anarchists who basically believe all politics to be futile and corrupt; they are mainly interested in denigrating existing democratic institutions.

Lastly there are a small number of Communists.

Thus in the autumn of 1960 the situation in Britain was of a peace movement which had had hitherto unprecedented success both in the Labour movement generally, and in the streets and in particular at the 1960 Labour Party Conference but was at the moment of its success already a divided force.

Within the Labour Party and the trade union movement there was, amongst the leadership, a very deep sense of crisis and a determination to resist the C.N.D. attempt to take over the Labour Party. In Liberal and Conservative political circles and within H.M. Government, there was also deep concern about the successes of C.N.D.; there was particular concern that British C.N.D. and Peace Movement activities might lead allies and friends abroad, and for that matter potential aggressors abroad, to doubt the determination of Britain to stand by international obligations undertaken by successive governments since 1945.

The gradual decline 1961–3

These years saw the decline of C.N.D. from the heights it reached at the Labour Party Conference at Scarborough in October 1960. Under the late Mr Gaitskell's leadership moderate and informed opinion was rallied in the Labour movement generally to counter C.N.D.

The Campaign for Democratic Socialism and a few other small organizations were created especially to counter C.N.D. but generally the fight was carried out within the normal Labour Party and trade union organizations. There was no confrontation on the streets but there were some hard exchanges in the normal course of decision-making.

The outcome was that the C.N.D. anti-nuclear policy was rejected by the Labour Party and at the time of his death earlier this year Mr Gaitskell was the leader of a united Labour Party, but with an embittered Peace Movement with its various elements still very active to his political left.

The fact that the Peace Movement in its various forms was active on the streets, much publicized to the Press, radio and television should not obscure the important fact that they were being defeated where it mattered politically in the Labour Party.

The Easter march of 1963 was perhaps the greatest propaganda success of C.N.D. – and also probably its last great fling. The extremist elements in the Committee of 100 organized the 'Spies for Peace' campaign – disclosing details of a Regional Seat of Government – R.S.G.6 in Berkshire – which they raided. The publicity achieved was of international proportions – and the resulting public and editorial condemnation was such as to make many people wonder whether there would ever be another Aldermaston march.

Even before the 1963 march began the differences within the Peace Movement were already substantial and publicly known. In addition to the differences between the Committee of 100 and C.N.D. there were open differences within the Committee of 100 arising from the multitude of views ranging from Pacifist Christian to Communist.

Furthermore some of the more militant activities of the Committee of 100 had failed to evoke the required response. In trying to maintain picket lines outside the U.S. Embassy in London in 1962 the Committee of 100 had eventually to resort to small daily payments to the pickets; and in September 1962 a planned demonstration outside the Air Ministry was called off for lack of sufficient volunteers. The Cuban crisis in itself produced a crisis with the Peace Movement since some supporters used this as a pretext for renewed anti-American demonstration, and were apparently in favour of Castro possessing those nuclear weapons they were supposed to abominate everywhere.

Nevertheless Easter 1963 saw the largest aggregation of people for the annual march from Aldermaston to London. The march has acquired a certain pattern over the years. Though as a spectacle it looks untidy, dirty and unrepresentative the fact is that over the years the standard of conduct has steadily improved as have the number of participants. The number of marchers walking the whole way has steadily increased and unruliness has decreased.

Nonetheless, there is still a good deal to criticize about the march, such as the behaviour of those taking part in creating noise and litter, and the popular Press have not failed to play up the fact, that to many of the large proportion of young people involved, it is all something of a lark with prospects of promiscuity, sharing sleeping bags and a general breaking out of normal bonds.

A feature of the marches in 1962 and 1963 has been the way the C.P.G.B. advertised its presence. Previously the C.P.G.B. had formed a policy of merging itself into the background but in the last two years Communist participation has been openly advertised as such with the carrying of banners, the provision of loudspeaker vans and a special daily supply and sale of copies of the *Daily Worker*.

The show-stealing 'Spies for Peace' gimmick in the 1963 march probably sealed the fate of future marches. Considerable publicity has always been given to the Aldermaston march – but there was a growing realization before the march began in 1963 that publicity was not in itself enough; the newspaper editorial and public reaction to the 'Spies for Peace' campaign brought home the lesson that massive publicity can be massively damaging.

C.N.D. propaganda tactics

The C.N.D. propaganda antics have been very successful in securing a wide hearing for their protesting voice. In this they have been aided by the following factors:

Professional advice: C.N.D. have throughout had professional publicity advice on a paid basis from Messrs Mountain & Molehill Ltd, an avowedly left-wing organization.

C.N.D. have secured a great deal of voluntary help from individuals employed in mass media activities.

In an atmosphere of left-wing political frustration C.N.D. have in particular received a sympathetic hearing from many 'Left-minded' news editors in all media throughout the country.

The whole of the C.N.D. approach has been angled at the youthful protestations against 'the follies of the Establishment'.

C.N.D. have successfully applied the following well-tried publicity tactics:

Symbolism: the C.N.D. symbol is very effective in impact, whether on walls or produced in a neat lapel pin. It is, in fact, probably the most successful symbol since the swastika. It is easy to reproduce.

Press relations: C.N.D. have ensured that their every activity, from the national to the tiniest little demonstration at a country village war memorial receives Press coverage. By efficiently carrying out their Press Relations, and exploiting the sympathy of news editors, C.N.D. have come automatically to be regarded as news.

Names: they have followed the well-known tactic of attracting to their cause the names, and in many cases the participation, of people prominent in non-political walks of life, such as the theatre, the arts, science, etc.

Finally, C.N.D. with their symbol, their youthfulness, their beards and their bedraggled appearance when demonstrating have provided the political cartoonists with ready-made material which they could scarcely be expected to resist; admittedly, some of the better cartoonists have, in recent months, produced material which is anti-C.N.D. – such as Osbert Lancaster's 'Pocket Cartoon' of the aristocratic mother of a C.N.D. daughter exclaiming, 'But the Greeks haven't got a bomb!' when her daughter went out to demonstrate against Queen Frederika with a C.N.D. banner.

C.N.D. have of course, been helped in all this by the particular awareness in young people in Britain today of publicity. It is true to say that virtually all sections of society, particularly the younger elements, now rejoice in personal publicity.

The fact is that there is a publicity-seeking trend of behaviour at all levels of the British public today.

The financial basis of C.N.D. remains a well-kept secret. Various of the usual money-raising devices are in regular use; collections, sales of literature, leaflets, posters, badges; fees for participating in rallies, summer schools, profits from organizing international travel – including visits behind the Iron Curtain – and so on.

C.N.D. however, have salaried organizational staff in London and salaried regional secretaries throughout the country. The impression is given of a substantial annual budget to pay the basic organizational costs.

A figure of £40,000 per annum as a basic budget has been mentioned but no details of the sources and size of C.N.D. finances are known. The C.P.G.B. does not, of course, disclose its finances to party members, or to any public body, but repeatedly appeals for funds for various purposes.

The success of the unilateralist peace movement within the Labour Party has to be viewed against the background of substantial political frustration which increasingly beset the Labour Party in the 1950s. They lost the General Elections of 1951, 1955 and 1959. The older leadership retired and was replaced by a younger group of men, whose leader, the late Hugh Gaitskell, seemed out of touch with the rebellious mood of his younger followers.

In an overall political situation where there was scant prospect of a Labour electoral victory there were inevitable searches for some method of breaking out of the normal pattern of slow movements of national opinion and only occasional changes of Government.

Looking at Government expenditure and examining the regular demands for more expenditure on the social services, housing, education, etc., many intelligent members of the Labour Party came to believe that the only way out of their current impasse was to pursue a unilateralist disarmament policy which would be morally justifiable and which would release resources to meet these domestic demands.

Much of this reaction was not thought out to its logical conclusion and the unilateralist disarmament policy served as an umbrella to cover a great deal of emotional feeling. This trend of thought was sustained by an urge to break with the past, helped in some quarters by anti-Americanism and reinforced by an anti-war feeling. This widespread emotionalism about nuclear matters was also helped by the ostrich-like attitudes of people, many of them individually influential in their own non-political fields, who did not like the 'Cold War' and 'massive deterrent' situation but, whilst unable to offer any practicable alternative, confidently advocated for Britain a complete break on a unilateralist basis – with an implied invitation to proceed from that point to build a 'brave new world'.

These sentiments had a great appeal to a substantial number of Labour Party and trade union members. The unilateralist umbrella could cover many genuine hopes for social betterment.

Moreover, the unilateralist cause was carried forward by dedicated and hard-working proponents who operated on every level in both the trade unions and in the Labour Party.

The unilateralists were the militants of 'the movement'; they almost ran away with it!

Why the unilateralists failed

The unilateralists failed because they could not convince the experienced leaders of the Labour Party and the trades unions that their cause was politically practicable.

The late Mr Gaitskell and his colleagues who opposed the unilateralists did so for the following hard reasons:

Though holding the United States in high regard they were not uncritical of the Americans, and were not, and are not, willing to regard world peace as a Moscow–Washington problem.

They recognized, and still do recognize in 1963, that the Labour Party could not win a General Election on a unilateralist defence policy.

Finally, the British trades unions are basically conservative and anti-Communist in attitude. The Communist penetration of the Electrical Trades Union reminded those who needed reminding that the Communists never give up, and the older trades unionists became wary of Communist influence in the unilateralist movements.

Most of the influential trade union leaders believe from experience that trades unions in Britain are primarily concerned with industrial problems and political issues involving defence and foreign policy can never long hold the centre of the trade union stage.

The elder statesmen of the trades union movement knew, therefore, that if they held on they would probably win fairly quickly. Their judgement has been proven correct by subsequent events.

90
Royal Society for the Prevention of Cruelty to Animals : policy, 1965
Guardian, 23 January 1965

The Royal Society for the Prevention of Cruelty to Animals called yesterday for a ban on the battery system of egg-production, the de-beaking of poultry, the 'sweat box' system of rearing pigs and the rearing of rabbits in battery cages.

The recommendations are in a memorandum submitted to the technical committee appointed last year by the Ministry of Agriculture to examine the conditions in which livestock are reared. The society claims that much of the criticism of intensive systems comes from farmers, biologists, veterinary surgeons and others well qualified to judge.

The society demands that the law should be strengthened and extended to cover intensive systems of livestock husbandry. It believes that the prolonged and close confinement of any living and active creature is morally wrong and should be made an offence in law. It urgently demands the framing and enforcing of suitable regulations to govern and standardize conditions under which animals are reared and kept in buildings for food-production and for slaughter.

In all systems of intensive egg-production where large numbers of birds are housed together, the buildings used should be licensed by the local authority and regularly inspected to ensure observance of certain minimum standards of construction, furnishing, lighting, heating, feeding and watering facilities, density of stocking and general hygiene.

Regulations should be framed and enforced on the use of artificial lighting in poultry houses, when employed to stimulate laying. All 'intensive' produce should be suitably marked when retailed.

The R.S.P.C.A. states that the use of drugs, growth stimulants, and other additives to the food of livestock reared intensively should be made the subject of a separate inquiry, with a view to controls being introduced. Premises where poultry are slaughtered on any wholesale scale should be licensed and supervised, and electrical pre-stunning (by means of an approved apparatus) should be made compulsory.

Buildings in which veal calves are reared by intensive systems should also be licensed and regularly inspected. The use of multiple pens should be made compulsory. The close and solitary confinement of calves in darkness should be prohibited. Calves and other cloven-hoofed animals should not be housed on slats.

91
Shelter, National Campaign for the Homeless, 1966: assessment of housing situation, late 1960s–1971
Facts about Shelter, n.d.

BRITAIN'S HOMELESS FAMILIES
Who are they?

During 1969, 22,804 people were admitted to reception centres, hostels and other temporary accommodation for the homeless in England and Wales. These people are 'officially homeless'.

But Shelter believes any family is homeless if it is living in housing conditions so unfit or overcrowded that it cannot lead a normal family life. These are our 'hidden homeless'.

The families who suffer most are: those with incomes at or below supplementary-benefit level (estimated to be 2 million households September 1968); those with more than four children, as there is very little accommodation large enough for them; those young families that have to move to the larger cities in search of work; the elderly and the disabled; the fatherless families.

They are caught in a trap. They pay high rents for substandard accommodation and lose their chance of saving for something better. They are often unable to move out of the city because their only security is the husband's job. They are on long waiting lists for council houses and often have little motivation or savings for buying their own homes.

The housing problem can be summed up as the shortage of homes at the right price in the right place, of the right size and the right standards.

For the most part, the homeless are ordinary working people who do not need 'welfare support' – at least not if we can help them in time with a home. This is why Shelter must finance an 'emergency rescue operation'.

THE COST OF HOMELESSNESS AND BAD HOUSING

The cost of homelessness and bad housing in financial terms: in one London borough in 1970 the cost of maintaining one family in a reception centre was estimated to be £26 a week. It costs about £14 a week to keep one child 'in care' as a result of homelessness.

More important, is the unseen human cost: children whose education is ruined before it starts because overcrowding makes play and homework impossible.

Physical, mental and emotional ill-health are other factors of human cost. Damp, dismal, insanitary conditions and over-crowding impose an intolerable strain on families, particularly the mother.

Cost in terms of productivity must also be counted. A family man living in such conditions does not stand an equal chance of succeeding in our highly competitive society.

The cost of homelessness is high and is rising higher as the cost of living goes up and society makes more demands on people's personal resources.

This is why Shelter campaigns in the press, on television and at public meetings to urge the government of the day to divert more national resources to solving the housing problem.

THE HIDDEN HOMELESS
Where are they?

The Government White Paper – 'The Housing Programme 1965–1970'–states:'In Great Britain some three million families still live either in slums, near slums or in grossly overcrowded conditions.'

The Ministry of Housing and Local Government Survey February 1967 says that there are 1.8 million dwellings in England and Wales unfit for human habitation. In addition a further 4.7 million homes are unsatisfactory, requiring either expenditure on repairs or the addition of basic amenities such as a bath, a hot water system and an internal W.C. The last census shows that the number of people in Great Britain living at a density of more than 1.5 persons per room was nearly 1,700,000.

The housing problem is at its worst in our major cities.

London where 190,000 applicants were on the waiting list for a home in 1969 (most recent figure available).

Glasgow where 46,500 applicants were on the waiting list in 1970 and where one-fifth of the housing stock is estimated to be unfit. The city has twenty-five of Britain's forty most overcrowded districts.

Birmingham where 10,000 families are living in overcrowded conditions and 22,000 applicants are on the waiting list.

Liverpool where there were 11,500 applicants on the waiting list in 1970. Four thousand families are in overcrowded conditions.

Manchester where 9,500 applicants are on the waiting list in 1971. Four thousand families live in overcrowded conditions.

HOW SHELTER HELPS

Shelter is a registered charity. But it is more than that – it is a campaign for Britain's homeless and badly housed. It is a movement of people all over the country who are facing up to the reality of a housing emergency situation.

Shelter raises vital funds to enable non-profit-making housing associations to buy older property, convert it and turn it into several good, simple, self-contained flats to let at reasonable rents to families in housing need. Sixty per cent of Shelter's money is allocated by a representative committee who decide on the amount of money and to which areas it should be sent.

Housing associations, themselves registered charities, can borrow between six and ten times the Shelter gift money from public sources. The Shelter money is vital, however, to keep the rents at the level which needy families can afford.

£325 of Shelter gift money is all that is required to rehouse a family for life.

In addition to rescuing families through housing associations Shelter is carrying out three major projects: two in Liverpool and Bradford into urban renewal through community participation and one in London into housing aid and advice.

The Shelter Neighbourhood Action Project (*S.N.A.P.*) is involving the residents and the local authority in the total improvement of a twilight area of Liverpool 8. *The Bradford Shelter Housing and Renewal Experiment* (*S.H.A.R.E.*) is an experiment in linking housing advice and improvement with community and race relations.

The Shelter (Family) Housing Aid Centre (*S.H.A.C.*) provides a focal point for inquiries from London families on all aspects of housing: the greatest emphasis, however, is placed on helping people to buy their own homes and, through the Out-of-London Scheme, to move out of the city to towns where there are jobs and homes. Rented accommodation is also found where possible through housing associations.

Shelter believes that these projects are a vital method of bringing about reform in the housing field. But, because for every family Shelter rehouses there are at least 100 it cannot help, Shelter must campaign on a broader front to bring the housing problem to the notice of the public and to try to bring pressure to bear on the authorities to make housing a higher priority for national resources.

Shelter is getting results. It has raised nearly £3,000,000 in its first four years. On the completion of the 1970 housing programme Shelter is rehousing at the rate of nearly 5,000 families a year – 100 families every single week.

Shelter's publicity and reports such as 'Face the Facts' and 'Happy Christmas' have received national coverage on television, in the press and have aroused considerable public interest.

Shelter cannot work without your help in rescuing families and helping to bring about the long-term solution to the housing problem.

92
Child Poverty Action Group : recruiting letter, July 1967
Circular letter, 7 July 1967

I am writing to ask whether you would be willing to become a member of the Child Poverty Action Group. We are a non-political body with charitable status. Our aim is to promote action to relieve poverty among families with children. Our proposals are explained in the enclosed leaflet. I am also sending you a copy of our journal, *Poverty*, which is sent free to all members.

It is now officially agreed that in June 1966 there were about half a million children below the official poverty line – most of them in families with a full-time bread-winner. They cannot receive help under the present law from the Supplementary Benefits Committee.

Though there is now no disagreement about the facts, the government has not yet decided what action should be taken. This is, therefore, a crucial time for our campaign. To make the maximum impact, we need more money. This is why we are making our first major drive for membership.

Although we hope this will be a short campaign, we ask you to subscribe by seven-year covenant, which enables us to supplement your financial sacrifice with a contribution from the Inland Revenue. In the event of the Group winding itself up within the seven years, your covenant would automatically lapse.

Membership costs £1 a year. If you are in a position to give us more it would be greatly appreciated. The future of over half a million children depends upon this campaign. Please give us your support.

93
Abortion Law Reform
(a) Association Appeal to write to M.P.s (*New Statesman*, 26 May 1967)
(b) Inquiry demanded by 250 M.P.s (*The Times*, 24 July 1970)

(a)

ABORTION LAW REFORM

Final stage in the Commons

FRIDAY 2 JUNE

Last year was important. This year is vital . . .

WRITE NOW TO YOUR M.P.

at the House of Commons, London S.W.1

Reform has majority support in the country. For this Bill to become law it is vital that ALL supporting M.P.s attend and vote. Urge your M.P. to be present on Friday 2 June to support David Steel's Bill on the occasion of its Third Reading.

(b)

More than 250 M.P.s of all parties and beliefs have signed a motion calling for an immediate independent inquiry into the Abortion Act.

Mr St John-Stevas, Conservative member for Chelmsford, sponsor of the motion, said he hoped this massive number of signatures would help Sir Keith Joseph to come to a positive decision and set up an inquiry under an eminent doctor such as Sir John Peel or Lord Brock.

The move comes in a week when statistics show that legal abortions are approaching 100,000 a year. The latest figures for March, April, May and June are: March, 6,162; April, 6,141; May, 7,876; June, 7,065.

Of the June operations 3,973 were in National Health Service hospitals and more than 3,000 in private nursing homes.

The motion says that an inquiry should assess the effects of the Act on the health of the nation, as well as on its legal, social and moral life, and should recommend any changes in the law that would be in the public interest.

Mr St John-Stevas said the motion reflected deep anxiety in the country about the working of the Act. He welcomed Sir Keith Joseph's recent statement that he was studying the situation. It was right that he should have time to reflect on the issues, but it was also fair to ask for a reasonably quick decision.

Not only Parliament but the official representatives of the medical and nursing professions wanted an inquiry. He had the support of the British Medical Association, the Royal College of Obstetricians and Gynaecologists, the Medical Defence Union,

The Royal College of Nursing, the Royal College of Midwives and the National Association of Theatre Nurses.

The inquiry should investigate, among other things, the operation racket in the private sector, fringe activities and the means of taking disciplinary or legal action against those who abused the Act.

The Act's effect on the N.H.S. in putting strain on normal gynaecological services should be considered. He was also concerned about the lack of any system of after-care in the private sector, and what this might mean in terms of illness and death.

A matter for anxiety was the position of those opposed to abortion on conscientious grounds. A situation was fast approaching in which many in the nursing service might well refuse to carry out abortions. The events at Stobhill and Stepping Hill hospitals had shown that nurses, in particular, were under increasing strain.

Mr St John-Stevas said that his campaign was not directed to the repeal of the Act but to amending it and removing abuses. The Act was the only piece of major social legislation that had been passed in modern times without a preceding up-to-date inquiry. This was the root of the trouble, and it should be put right.

94
The Anti-Concorde Project 1967

(a) *New Statesman* 21 July 1967; (b) *Guardian*, 10 February 1969

(a)

The Anti-Concord Project

STOP THE CONCORD

The Anti-Concord Project has been founded by a group of some hundreds of people including scientists, artists, businessmen, civil servants, housewives, farmers, doctors, teachers, professors, M.P.s, etc., who are concerned and alarmed at the efforts being made to develop supersonic transport aircraft.

We shall inform the public of the facts about the expected effects of the use of such aircraft (S.S.T.s) and shall oppose their construction and use. We see this as a clear case of a choice having to be made – is technology to be sanely controlled or is it to be allowed increasingly to degrade and destroy our environment?

We regard the development of S.S.T.s as a disaster for the general public and for aviation. It is evident that this development was undertaken without sufficient consideration, that it is enormously costly, and that if they are used S.S.T.s will, as a result of the 'sonic boom' (produced throughout the entire flight at supersonic speeds), cause intolerable disturbance and damage.

We believe that these effects will not be tolerated, and that S.S.T.s will have to be banned. Our immediate aims are both to help create in Britain a climate of public opinion in which it will be possible for the Government to terminate work upon the Concord, and also to press the Government to make this decision.

Our further aim (in co-operation with similar movements in other countries) is to help to bring about the banning of S.S.T.s internationally.

To these ends we intend to commence large-scale advertising, and for this purpose we need money. The names of all contributors and sponsors will be published except where anonymity is desired.

Contributions and requests for further information, to:

The Anti-Concord Project
Convener, Richard Wiggs,
70 Lytton Avenue,
Letchworth, Hertfordshire...

Sponsors of the Project at present include

Professor Cedric A. B. Smith, University College, London
Dr William A. Shurcliff, Harvard University
Dr Ronald V. Sampson, Bristol University
Sir Geoffrey and Lady Keynes
Canon W. R. F. Browning, Oxford
J. R. Ravetz, Senior Lecturer, Leeds University
Dr Paul Mestitz, Victoria, Australia
David Holbrook, author and educationalist, sometime Fellow of King's College, Cambridge
Dr R. M. S. Perrin, M.A., B.SC., PH.D., University of Cambridge
Michael Foot, M.P.
Dora Russell
Arthur Darlington (farmer)
Revd C. G. Sykes, M.A., B.D., M.TH.
Professor and Mrs Victor Ehrenburg
Professor Bernard Groom, formerly of McMaster and Montevideo Universities
Malcolm Muggeridge
Hugh Jenkins, M.P.

(b)

Supersonic airliners would cause widespread serious disturbance and much damage. Their development is not 'progress'. Their introduction is not inevitable.

It has yet to be proved that the Concorde is a viable airliner. But its manufacturers and the Government assume that if trials show that it can carry full loads between Europe and the U.S.A., and if sufficient orders are obtained, it will go into quantity production. This is not an adequate basis for decision. Indeed, at every stage, decisions to begin and to continue with the Concorde project have been based upon inadequate grounds.

We wish to encourage public discussion of these questions: *Is there any good reason at all for building supersonic airliners? Should the attempt be stopped now?*

At present increasing attention is being given to problems of damage to the environment resulting from the side-effects of rapidly developing technology. These effects have been largely unforeseen. They are still largely discounted and ignored. When a new development is *certain* to produce seriously harmful effects we must not be committed to it for trivial reasons and without adequate evaluation of the consequences.

Supersonic aviation will undeniably have very disturbing and inescapable effects upon people on the ground and on ships. Some effects are predictable and can be balanced against the benefits that are claimed. Others – for example the effects of extensive pollution of the upper atmosphere – would be insidious, long-term and possibly irreversible.

When the present Government took office four years ago it tried to withdraw from the Concorde project. This was prevented by the French – who have now themselves cut expenditure on the Concorde. We urge both Governments now to cancel it.

All public spending must be subject to considerations of priority. In the context of world poverty and of the economic difficulties of the nations involved, projects such as the supersonic airliners should be very low in order of priority, even if they were not fraught with problems, and even if they were not extremely antisocial.

In this context the 'benefit' to a small minority of travellers of crossing the Atlantic in three and a half hours instead of six and a half is trivial. Large reductions in door-to-door travelling-time can be achieved by improved transport between airports and city centres, with customs procedures carried out en route. This would benefit far more people. Whereas if supersonic airliners are introduced, they might have to be given priority for landing – greatly delaying other aircraft.

The Governments supporting these projects have, by the commitment of vast sums of public money, gained a vested interest in their continuation which directly conflicts with the Governments' responsibilities to the people. Each of these projects is an

M*

enormous 'brain drain' in the country concerned, diverting great endeavours, and valuable resources, into antisocial purposes. *The processes by which such projects are initiated and supported should be investigated.*

Initially, as an Anglo-French co-operative effort, it was regarded as preparing the way for Britain to enter the Common Market. As this has failed, it has been continued in order to compensate for reduction in 'defence' work and to support an ailing and unprofitable section of the aircraft industry.

The original estimate (November 1962) for the cost of research and development was £150 to £170 millions. £310 million has already been spent. This fact is sometimes given as a reason for continuing – but the latest (unofficial) estimate for research and development is £600 millions. With three years still to go, 'Concorde may yet cost £1,000 million' (*Management Today*, August 1968). As has been admitted in the House of Commons, little of this money (entirely provided by the British and French Governments – the manufacturers are risking none of their own) will ever be recouped.

Already the Concorde is a year behind schedule. Current costs are £2 million per week . . .

95
'Women's Lib.', 1969-71
The Times, 11 January 1971

The cause of the liberation of women from the subjugation of man and society, which has aroused deep passions in the United States in the past year, will publicly make its first major appearance in Britain on 6 March, when the movement is to hold its first full-scale demonstration in London.

The four main themes of the British movement, agreed between groups throughout the country, will be stridently stated. They are equal pay, free abortion and contraception on demand, equal educational opportunity for men and women, and adequate day care and nursery education. They are all of equal importance, according to the movement.

During the weekend the National Women's Coordinating Committee, which includes representatives of liberation groups throughout Britain as well as of other women's groups, met in Oxford to settle the plans for the demonstration.

The committee decided that floats would be used, but did not determine the route through London. Plans for a picket of the

Playboy Club in Park Lane were also discussed, but no decision was taken.

The waitresses (bunnies) employed in the club have been criticized by the movement since its foundation. Members feel that they symbolize the subjugation and degradation of women.

The meeting also considered plans for a major demonstration on 6 March in the North to coincide with the London march. It would be designed to emphasize the support the movement has. A decision on whether it should be held was postponed until the next meeting.

Before the main demonstration there will be smaller statements of the cause. On St Valentine's Day several south London groups of the Women's Liberation Workshop will hold a demonstration. Another is likely on 12 February when the adjourned case of alleged demonstrators arrested during the Miss World competition is resumed at Bow Street Magistrates' Court.

There is strong feeling among the Women's Liberation Workshop that women demonstrators should not be judged by a male court, or indeed by a male jury. As they explained: 'Men can sympathize, but they cannot fully understand a woman's position.'

But who are the Women's Liberation Workshop, and who makes up the liberation movement in Britain? In the workshop, which is based in London, there are fourteen area groups and between 150 and 200 active members. More than 1,000 women have expressed interest in the group. There is now an office in central London and when I paid a visit they were dealing with forty new applications, all of which had come in during the past few days.

The liberation movement first appeared in Britain in February 1969, with the embryo of the workshop and other sympathizers. In September 1969 the loose federation of London area groups, which makes up the workshop, was formed, and in February 1970 the National Women's Coordinating Committee came into existence. This includes groups such as branches of the National Joint Action Committee for Women's Equal Rights, Mothers in Action and Socialist Woman Members, as well as such women's groups as the workshop and the Women's Liberation Front.

The membership of the workshop is primarily middle-class, according to a group of its organizers. There is a high proportion of university graduates, and most members are in their twenties or thirties. There are students, principally postgraduates, and many members have small children.

The workshop is a diffuse federation of groups because its

members believe that this form of democratic organization encourages women to come to their own decisions about their role in society. 'We want to encourage a movement from the grassroots' was how one Battersea organizer put it.

The workshop is firmly against the idea of leadership. 'We do not want the ideas just to come from above and others to follow.' This is one reason why they have not had many public acts, and have forsworn the publicity sought by other pressure groups.

'We believe in converting people's opinions from within and not pushing them into changing them' was how another organizer put it. They admit this may mean that the revolution they see as necessary in British society may take fifty years to achieve, but that does not weaken their dedication.

In the words of its manifesto, the workshop 'seeks to bring women to a full awareness of the meaning of their inferior status and to devise methods to change it. In society women and girls relate primarily to men; any organization duplicates this pattern: the men lead and dominate, the women submit.

'We close our meeting to men to break through this pattern, to establish our own groups and to meet each other over our common experience as women. We want eventually to be, and to help other women to be, in charge of our own lives.'

In the latest edition of the workshop's magazine, *Shrew*, there is an attack on one institution in society which the women's liberation groups feel strongly about – the family. 'Sexism sets women aside (on a pedestal) as passive servants of society in general and men in particular . . . Economically she reduces the cost of maintaining the labour force, since housework and childcare constitute a huge amount of essential but unpaid production.'

As the manifesto says: 'We are economically oppressed in jobs we do full work for half pay, in the home we do unpaid work full time. We are commercially exploited by advertisements, television and the press. Legally women are discriminated against. We are brought up to feel inadequate; educated to narrower horizons than men. This is our specific oppression as women. It is as women therefore we are organizing.'

96
The Westway Motorway: tenants' protest, 1970
The Times, 29 July 1970

Banners out for yesterday's ceremonial opening of Westway, the 'three-minute motorway' from White City to Paddington

and Britain's longest elevated road, were in protest, not cele-
bration.

Before the traffic began the people of North Kensington made
their demonstration against this giant of the motor age with
protests shouted from top-floor windows as the ministerial
opening procession passed by.

'It was all very English; the courtesies were observed,' Mr
George Clark, chairman of the Golborne Social Rights Committee, said as a copy of his protest was carried away from the
speech-making at Lord's Tavern by Mr Peyton, Minister of
Transport. A Cabinet meeting prevented Mr Peyton from opening the motorway.

Mr Heseltine, Parliamentary Secretary, cut the tape at
Paddington separating the official party from a two-lane jam of
local people bearing banners. 'Don't fly over people's lives',
'Shut the ramps' and 'Rehouse us now' they ran, and there was
a cry of 'We'll be on your back, Minister.' The ceremony over,
police cleared the lanes without trouble and the large official
party in cars and coaches poured along the skyway.

Beyond Westbourne Park Road the parallel line of Acklam
Road top-storey windows about twenty yards from the east-
bound carriageway came into view. From the parapet of four
houses men and women held in place a long legend: 'Let us
out of this hell: rehouse us now.' And near the new junction with
the future West Cross Route more banners demanded: 'Rehouse
Bramley Street and Walmer Road now, or else . . .'

Mr Desmond Plummer, Leader of the Greater London
Council, devoted as much of his speech at Lord's to deploring
disruption of the environment as to the building of the road.

Keeping people informed had meant 100,000 letters, an
inquiry hot line, and the resident engineer always available to
the public, he said.

Mr Peyton thought millions who enjoyed it would contrast it
with the old and tangled scene below and would spare a thought
for those to whom it was not a blessing. The frigid phrase of the
planners – 'injurious affection' – did not convey anything of
what it would mean to those who lived in its shadow and within
range of its unceasing din. He could not offer any instant remedy
to this grave and growing problem. How to compensate such
people was, in that classic phrase, 'under review'.

Mr Clark was allowed to make his speech of protest on the
spending of £30m., more than enough to rebuild that part of
North Kensington and give every family a good modern home at
rents they could afford.

The road is about two and a half miles long and cost over £33m. It links the main road from Oxford at White City with the new Marylebone fly-over, and is expected to carry 45,000 vehicles a day.

97
National Federation of Pakistani Associations, 1969
The Times, 2 January 1969

The leading Pakistani organization in Britain – the National Federation of Pakistani Associations – is in the throes of a fierce struggle for control between militant and moderate groups. The moderates narrowly unseated the chairman and acting secretary, Mr Tozammil Huq and Mr Zakaria Choudhuri, who committed the federation to the Black Peoples' Alliance last year, in twice-postponed elections at Birmingham on Sunday. Predictably, six local associations from London and Birmingham have now challenged the election results.

The new chairman and secretary, Mr Asif Jahangir, of Rochdale, and Mr Abdur Raquib, of London, were elected by eight and fourteen votes respectively out of nearly 600 votes after a confused and bitterly contested six and a half-hour-long count. Six votes were officially declared missing, but a recount was refused.

The challenging associations are demanding fresh elections. They allege blatant irregularities in the collection of the proxy votes – which made up some 520 of votes cast – and claim that the elections should have been decided on the votes of delegates present (who gave Huq and Choudhuri comfortable majorities).

The issue is not whether the federation, which represents over 30,000 Pakistanis in Britain, should adopt Black Power policies or violent protests. Both groups believe (for now) in a multi-racial solution here. They differ over tactics – and personalities.

Mr Tasadduq Ahmed, the founding president and a moderate, says that the federation is a 'broad-based united front organization' and as such should avoid controversy. He claims that there has been a breakdown of previously cordial relations between the federation and the Pakistan High Commission and British Government under Huq and Choudhuri. 'We have pledged ourselves to restore stable relations.'

Mr Choudhuri says: 'We do not fight for the sake of fighting. We are not antagonistic to the High Commission or the Government here. Our point is that issues should be discussed, and publicized, and then stands should be taken. We don't believe that we should cultivate officials and go to them with a begging bowl. When we take up an issue we should fight it with whatever authority is concerned – be it a local authority or the Pakistan Government.'

98
Black Power, 1970
Sunday Telegraph, 2 August 1970

The crowd of 100 coloured people chanting Black Power slogans who tried to enter Caledonian Road police station, Islington, and snatch back a prisoner last Monday has given police all over the country a new problem.

It is feared such attacks will be repeated. Undermanned police stations have only their ticker-tapes and telephones to call up rescuing commandos.

Underlining the threat was a meeting of leaders of all the black militant movements in London on Wednesday to consider forming a joint command and placing themselves on a war footing. The meeting was called by Michael Abdul-Malik, 39, leader of the Black Muslims and president of the Racial Adjustment Action Society.

Also present were the Black Eagles, centred on London's Portobello Road market area, and Black Panthers. The Eagles number about 150 young people, wear all black, and although militant at times adopt the slogan 'get a brick and build' rather than 'get a gun'. The Panthers have chapters all over the country, with strong followings in Brixton and Notting Hill, and are potentially more violent.

The meeting was held in the Black House, the complex of adjoining terrace houses, shops and empty factories in Holloway Road, which is being converted by voluntary labour into a social commune. This enterprise has been financially helped by churchmen, pop singers, actors and industrialists.

It was from the commune that the crowd, including many teenagers, poured out on Monday to besiege the police station. Three policemen and some of the invaders were hurt.

M.I.5 and the Special Branch are now re-assessing the threat of the militant movements. A change has been seen in their tactics.

Until now they have been regarded as small, imitative of the

United States movements, centred round a handful of personalities and untypical of immigrants as a whole. Their supporters have been estimated at a few hundred.

Now many coloured teenagers are discontented and ready to close a Black Power fist or shout a slogan.

The two sides of Black Power – menacing or conciliatory – are found in its leader Abdul-Malik, also known as Michael X. A teenage immigrant who worked in Cardiff's Tiger Bay dock area, he is a self-taught intellectual, former rent collector and self-avowed minister of religion.

Inside Black House, Michael X made no secret of the movement's menace. 'Black people are going to take matters into their own hands because we have been unable to get justice anywhere,' he said to me. 'Any time law and order does not take justice into account, then law and order is a useless phrase.

'If we decided to enter a police station to take anyone out at any given time there's no way of stopping it. We know that under the buttons of the uniform is a man: he's not as strong as we are. But we would like to find a method of stopping these things from happening. It's obvious someone is going to be hurt. We're not eager to place ourselves on a war footing. As warriors it's obvious if you want to pull down a town at any time we can do it. All one needs is petrol and matches. But we would much rather find ways of working to establish harmony between peoples.'

He believed his movement, R.A.A.S., had won supremacy over the others because it was 'bigger, stronger, more numerous, richer'.

The R.A.A.S. has twenty-seven chapters in various parts of the country, always tied to an enterprise that will bring in some money to carry on the activity. In Reading it has a barber's shop and the rooms above it.

Michael X believed that Black Power should not cause offence to anybody. A black minority that has been powerless and which suddenly gets very strong was useful to the country. Its members rose early and worked hard.

He said Peregrine Worsthorne had rightly pointed out in the *Sunday Telegraph* last week that European nations were gathering together in their own interests – 'older heads are polarising themselves, but the people of the Third World are moving in another direction.'

He went on: 'If we as people who are sitting in the heart of a white industrial complex recognize that people of pale skins are moving together and getting richer, people of dark skins then have to pull themselves together. Something must be done to redress the imbalance.'

He explained: 'If our language is strong, arrogant, violent, we simply articulate what people feel. I hate violence. There's nothing we want more than to live in peace.'

The Black Muslims have increased their influence by their good work. The Black House has rehoused thirty-four homeless families, rescued drug addicts, taught self-help and repatriated the old who wanted to return to their homelands.

Temporarily out of funds, the commune has not yet completed a restaurant and supermarket which, it is hoped, will finance the remainder of the enterprise. At the lowest ebb, when the hard core of workers were eating only one meal a day, Canon Collins, Precentor of St Paul's and founder of Christian Action, gave them £100 to buy food from a personally administered gift fund.

Canon Collins said: 'I was impressed by what I saw. They've done an amazing job with nothing much behind them. There's a sense of community and fellowship and self-help. I was particularly interested in the work they were doing with people they had more or less picked off the streets.'

Among others who have given money for social work are the Beatles and Mr Nigel Samuel, 23, son of the late Mr Howard Samuel, the property director. Sean Kenny, the stage-designer and director, helped to plan the lay-out of the restaurant. He said: 'I try to break fences by friendship, help and encouragement.'

Dr Huddleston, Bishop of Stepney, said: 'Black House is in my episcopal area. If it's to get off on the right foot it needs a good deal of care, guidance and help.

'You're not going to wish Black Power away. It's there. So few people are really prepared to take any trouble to understand it. They have a Muslim chapel and are planning a Christian chapel, and I have promised to do all I can to help them to get established.'

Scotland Yard, which also has the Black House in its 'parish', fears that a fringe of extremists who support Black Power might operate protection racket strong-arm tactics among the black community to raise funds for the movement on a regular basis. It is also known that there are supporters, not any of the leaders, who have been convicted for drugs trafficking.

There are signs of a break between the most militant elements and the *comparatively* conciliatory Michael X. Detectives fear that if this happened a Kray gang-type tyranny could bestraddle the coloured world.

99
Universities' Committee for Soviet Jewry, 1970

The Times, 28 December 1970

Several hundred people yesterday protested at the Soviet Embassy in London against 'the show trials of Jews in the Soviet Union'. The protest was organized by the Universities' Committee for Soviet Jewry.

Mr S. Clinton Davis, Labour M.P. for Hackney Central, and two members of the committee, Mr Phil Marcus, chairman, and Mr Michael Steel, took an appeal into the embassy. The appeal, addressed jointly to Mr Kosygin, the Soviet Prime Minister, and the Soviet Ambassador in London, Mr Smirnovsky, demanded that the Leningrad sentences be commuted and that other Jews awaiting trial in Russia be released.

Mr Marcus said later that the Soviet Consul told them that the appeal process in the Leningrad case might take up to two months.

The Board of Deputies of British Jews yesterday sent a telegram to Mr Smirnovsky calling for a repeal of the Leningrad sentences. On Boxing Day Cardinal Heenan, Archbishop of Westminster, sent a telegram to the head of the Russian Orthodox Church, appealing to him to intercede with the Soviet Government 'to show clemency to our Jewish brothers'.

Tel Aviv: As a wave of rage swept through Israel at the Leningrad sentences Mrs Golda Meir, the Prime Minister, said in speeches at mass meetings that Israel was not pleading for mercy on behalf of the prisoners but demanding justice. The main focal point of public demonstrations has been the Wailing Wall in Jerusalem where more than 100,000 Israelis made pilgrimages to manifest their solidarity with Soviet Jews.

The Knesset (Parliament), meeting in special session in Jerusalem on Friday, described the Leningrad prisoners as 'innocent victims' and called on enlightened public opinion to prevent 'judicial murder'.

Jerusalem: Silent prayer for the Leningrad trial Jews was offered at the site of Calvary in the Church of the Holy Sepulchre by Christians living in Israel.

Geneva: The International Commission of Jurists, in a telegram to the Supreme Soviet in Moscow, called for clemency 'in view of the tragic events suffered by Jewish people in our time', and expressed its regret that the Soviet authorities were still regarding as traitors people exercising their right to emigrate.

The Swiss writer Friedrich Dürrenmatt and other Swiss

intellectuals in an appeal to the Soviet Embassy in Bern called for a retrial which would be open to international observers.

Rome: The Italian Communist Party has called on the Russians not to carry out the death sentences, and the party newspaper *L'Unita* yesterday urged clemency at the appeal stage.

The Italian Government has instructed its Ambassador in Moscow to convey to the Russians Italian public feeling on the trial sentences.

Brussels: The Belgian Government has appealed to the Soviet Government to commute the death sentences, intervening 'as the interpreter of public opinion in Belgium'.

Copenhagen: Mr Hilmar Baunsgaard, the Danish Prime Minister, condemned the death sentences and urged that they be commuted on appeal.

Oslo: Mr Per Borten, the Norwegian Prime Minister, expressed deep shock at the death sentences.

Canberra: In an appeal to the United Nations Secretary-General, the Australian Prime Minister, Mr John Gorton, said that there was a clear need for all the facts of the case to be established for the world to see.

Ottawa: Jews demonstrated outside the Soviet Embassy in protest against the 'barbaric savagery' of the sentences.

100
Council for the Advancement of
Arab-British Understanding: Statement, 1970

Advertisement, *The Times*, 5 June 1970

PEACE DEPENDS ON ISRAEL

Three years ago today war broke out again in the Middle East – for the third time since the dismemberment of Palestine began in 1947. In these three years there has been no progress towards the establishment of a lasting peace between Israel and her Arab neighbours. On the contrary, the Middle East now seems to be sliding rapidly towards a new conflict. And this time who can say where it may end?

The key to peace in the Middle East lies in Israel's hands. It is Israel which holds the position of strength and which has benefited beyond measure from the events of the past twenty-two years. And thus it is with Israel that the onus rests of reversing the present trend towards new and worse conflict and of making a fresh start towards peace.

Israel can and should make the initial concessions which will open the door to conciliation. Tragically, Israel missed a unique opportunity after the June war to show magnanimity in victory. Having won the war, Israel has ever since been losing the peace.

But it is still not too late if only Israel will have the courage and wisdom to try what concessions and conciliation may achieve in place of threats, reprisals and reliance on military strength.

Israel says she has accepted the settlement outlined in the Security Council Resolution of November, 1967. But so far her actions speak differently. What are now needed are not words, but some positive acts of conciliation.

Here are four steps which Israel could take at once and which would, we believe, open the way to peace:

First, renounce the illegal annexation of East Jerusalem.

Second, remove the Israeli settlements planted on the West Bank since June, 1967.

Third, allow back the Arabs uprooted from Gaza and the West Bank during and after the June war.

Fourth, undertake to withdraw from the occupied territories in return for an undertaking by Israel's Arab neighbours to observe the ceasefire and to renounce belligerency, backed up by effective international peace-keeping action.

We believe that, even at this late hour, such action on Israel's part could turn the key in the Middle East deadlock.

101
The Common Market: the battle for public opinion, 1970
The Times, 13 November 1970

A massive campaign to win the hearts and minds of the British people for or against going into Europe is under way. It is likely to be the biggest exercise in public persuasion of its kind ever undertaken in Britain. At present it is a straight fight between those in favour and those against entry, but all shades of political opinion are involved, because the issue cuts across party lines.

Both sides recognize that public opinion has a crucial role to play in the final decision, for the real battle to join the Common Market will not be fought in Brussels. It will be fought in the House of Commons, which is directly influenced in various ways by popular feeling.

Of course, the negotiations now taking place in Brussels are of crucial importance. From them will emerge 'the terms' on which according to present expectations, the Commons will make up its mind and vote.

But the immediate target in the battle to win support one way or the other is the party conferences next year. The position they take on Europe will be extremely influential on M.P.s especially the uncommitted centre.

Opinion in diplomatic circles in Brussels, and among the civil servants whose task it is to pore over the fine print, is that the negotiations, as such, will be successful. Yet this optimistic assumption, which the British side shares, could be proved wrong.

But assuming the negotiations continue as they have started, in a reasonably constructive spirit, and that the Six prove willing to allow some give and take, Mr Rippon's timetable – to have the essential terms clear by next summer – may well be achieved.

The party conferences would then have plenty to bite on. If the Government's intention was to see what terms it could negotiate, this would be the answer, or most of it, for the whole negotiation would not be completed until the end of 1971.

Accordingly, an intense and concerted campaign in favour of entry is being staged by the European Movement in Britain. This is the organization, headed by Lord Harlech, which unites a variety of pro-European groups. It includes the Conservative Group for Europe, the Labour Committee for Europe and a revived Trades Union Committee for Europe.

The various groups seeking to keep Britain out of Europe were consolidated last February under the banner of the Common Market Safeguards Campaign, which is also conducting a vigorous campaign in the country.

The objective of the European Movement, in this first phase up to the party conferences, is to tell the public what entry into Europe really means. Its aim is not directly to 'win over' public opinion, though of course that is the underlying goal.

It is rather, in the words of Mr Ernest Wistrich, director of the movement, to try to present the issue, not as the black-and-white affair it is now regarded as, but as a policy which, on balance, can be seen to have – even if you disagree with it – advantages for Britain. More concisely, 'to replace ignorance and hostility by facts'.

The campaign to achieve this appears to be extremely thorough. It is based on sending out speakers, distributing pamphlets and so forth, but with an intensity which only a passionate conviction of the rightness of its cause could sustain.

The Safeguards Campaign is no less convinced of its rightness. But its basic objective is to keep public opinion in its present mind which, according to the polls, is solidly 'anti'.

Mr Ron Leighton, secretary of the campaign (who shares with Mr Wistrich the distinction of having stood as a Labour candidate for Parliament), also organizes speakers and publications. 'While public opinion is against British entry,' he says, 'we think it will be impossible and impractical for the Government to force this thing through.'

The European Movement sends out about eighty speakers a month and this will increase to about 400 a month next year. It is making a special effort to present the case for Europe to the housewife, with a series of regional conferences.

The campaign may also advertise in newspapers. It is already planning a special effort among trade unions, and the advertisement shown on this page, for example, will appear in the Christmas issues of the journals of the Transport and General Workers' Union, the Electrical Trades Union and several others.

Where does the money come from? Each side depends on subscriptions from supporters, but here the European Movement is in a far stronger position. It raised more than £450,000 from donations after the Lord Mayor of London's banquet last year, at which the leaders of the three political parties spoke in favour of British entry. This money, however, was for educational purposes, not propaganda.

New funds are needed for the coming publicity campaign, and the response is said to be good. Firms contribute from £100 a year and individuals from £3. The aim is to raise a six-figure sum.

The Safeguards people have received virtually no help from firms (a comment, no doubt, on where industry stands on the issue), and depends entirely on donations from well-wishers. After the opening of their campaign they got 10,000 individual members, all of whom contributed at least a pound or two. Speakers are being arranged at the rate of two or three a day.

No one can predict how public opinion will move on the European issue. It has been strongly in favour before, notably during 1967 when the attempt by Mr Wilson and Mr Brown to start negotiations ran into the sand of General de Gaulle's obduracy.

Now it is against, according to the National Opinion Poll published in the *Daily Mail* last month. This showed 24 per cent in favour of joining compared with 61 per cent against and 15 per cent 'don't knows'.

But what was interesting about this poll was that, although the total figures were about the same as six months previously, it showed that the Conservatives were becoming more sympathetic, and Labour supporters more unsympathetic.

£7 MORE IN YOUR
CHRISTMAS PAYPACKET
INSIDE THE COMMON MARKET

*When the Common Market started in 1957 weekly incomes in Britain averaged £2 more than in the six common market countries.

*13 years later, weekly incomes in Britain are £5 less.

We are losing £7 a week outside the Common Market. Incomes in the Market are growing nearly twice as fast as Britain. The anti-marketeers want to keep us out.

DON'T LET THEM! YOUR EARNINGS
WILL GROW FASTER WITH BRITAIN
IN THE COMMON MARKET

I would like the *straight* facts

Name _____

Address _____

_____

Send to: Alan Lee Williams
Trade Union Committee for Europe
78 Chandos Hse, Buckingham Gate, London SW1

This trend bears out the conviction among those involved in the present campaign that the essential battle will be fought at the Labour Party conference next year. The Labour platform won by only a whisker this year. If next year the conference votes against accepting the terms, Mr Wilson might find his freedom of manoeuvre inhibited, and face a serious split in his party.

A contest has begun for the body and souls of the 1922 Committee, which speaks for backbench Tory M.P.s. Sir Tufton Beamish, the Member for Lewes, is recruiting Members for his Conservative Group for Europe, and at a pound a time. Sir Derek Walker-Smith, the M.P. for East Herts, is doing likewise for his 25 Club men who take their doubts to dinner on Britain in Europe. New diners are turned over to Mr Neil Marten, the Member for Banbury, who is the vice-chairman of the all-party Common Market Safeguards Campaign and the 'Ludendorf' of the Tory anti-marketeers. As recruiting becomes more fevered, the whips keep their eye upon the rivals, totting up their own figures in what must be the most important calculation of this Parliament.

At present, Sir Tufton's 'army' is the larger of the two. The Conservative Group for Europe has ninety-eight M.P.s on its books, and has set a target of 150. Of the ninety-eight, sixty-nine are back-benchers, of whom twenty-three are newly elected to the House. Its President is the Prime Minister, its Patron, Sir Alec Douglas-Home. Apart from Mr Rippon, Cabinet Ministers who have joined include Mr Barber, Sir Keith Joseph, Mr Peter Walker, Mr John Davies, Mr William Whitelaw and Mr Peter Thomas. Ministers include Michael Heseltine, Christopher Chataway, Eldon Griffiths, David Howell, Peter Kirk and Nicholas Ridley. The Group, to which many well-known Conservatives outside Parliament also belong, has a secretariat and an office.

The 'antis' arrange themselves differently. The 25 Club (which has in the past entertained Mr Heath to dinner) meets some three times a year. But it has been recently decided to build up its numbers, and Mr Toby Jessel, the newly elected Member for Twickenham, is to be seen pacing the corridors, accosting colleague and Clerk in search of new blood. And perhaps not before time, for a glance at the better-known 'antis' would reveal such veterans as Mr Ronald Russell, Mr Robert Turton, Sir Stephen MacAdden and Mr Ronald Bell. Mr Burden has joined the colours, and so, too, has Sir Gerald Nabarro, while if one Wimbledon Member has been lost through the retirement of Sir Cyril Black, another has been gained in the person of Mr Michael Havers. In all, there are twenty-one Tory patrons of the Common Market Safeguards Committee (all M.P.s are patrons), the majority of whom are members of Derek's Diner.

But Sir Derek Walker-Smith is too busy at the bar to provide the day-to-day leadership that is necessary in the Commons. Mr Neil Marten is the more active, skirmishing at question time and speaking up and down the country. He has been reinforced as a consequence of the election. Colin Mitchell is against Europe, and so too are David Mudd, Marcus Fox, Carol Mather and Roger Moate; Mrs Fenner, Mrs Oppenheim and Miss Elaine Kellett disapprove; altogether eighteen of the newly-elected signed a precautionary early-day motion in July. It is now being claimed that there is a hard core of forty determined enough to flout a three-line whip and a second group of thirty-five who have little enthusiasm for entry into Europe. Then there are Mr Powell and Mr Biffen, who, while perhaps the most sophisticated opponents of all, have kept themselves aloof, and there are hints that several Conservative ex-ministers are about to change their minds. The strength of the anti-marketeers has never been greater.

Activity is not limited to Westminster. Neil Marten and others have addressed on behalf of the Common Market Safeguards Campaign 'several hundred' meetings already this year.

Outside Westminster public opinion seems to be against entry into Europe in the ratio 63; 22; 15. The two polls conducted by N.O.P. this year on this issue have shown virtually no change. Inside the Conservative Party in Parliament, the situation is still unclear. Sir Tufton can claim sixty-nine back-benchers; the anti-Common Marketeers will talk of eighty, but it is possible only to identify positively some thirty-two of them. The Europeans have thus a two-to-one advantage of the committed. But when the sixty-eight members of the Government are accounted for, there are still some 160 M.P.s who have not yet paid a subscription to anyone. In the meantime recruiting goes on apace, the evidence of such activity being the cluster of questioners who rise behind Mr Rippon in the House, throwing their nets in an attempt to ensnare him whenever he reports progress, and a similar group of friends who by use of prepared questions put their case to party, House and country.